LITERACY ASSESSMENT

Helping Teachers Plan Instruction

Fourth Edition

LITERACY ASSESSMENT

Helping Teachers Plan Instruction

J. David Cooper

Ball State University, Retired

Nancy D. Kiger

University of Central Florida, Retired

WADSWORTH
CENGAGE Learning

Australia • Brazil • Japan • Korea • Mexico • Singapore • Spain • United Kingdom • United States

Literacy Assessment: Helping Teachers Plan Instruction, Fourth Edition
J. David Cooper and Nancy D. Kiger

Publisher/Executive Editor: Linda Schreiber-Ganster

Acquisitions Editor: Christopher Shortt

Senior Development Editor: Lisa Kalner Williams

Editorial Assistant: Linda Stewart

Associate Media Editor: Ashley Cronin

Marketing Manager: Kara Kindstrom Parsons

Marketing Assistant: Dimitri Hagnere

Marketing Communications Manager: Martha Pfeiffer

Content Project Management: Pre-Press PMG

Creative Director: Rob Hugel

Art Director: Maria Epes

Print Buyer: Paula Vang

Rights Acquisitions Account Manager, Text: Roberta Broyer

Rights Acquisitions Account Manager, Image: Leitha Etheridge-Sims

Production Service: Pre-Press PMG

Text Designer: Marsha Cohen

Photo Researcher: Pre-Press PMG

Copy Editor: Pre-Press PMG

Cover Designer: Irene Morris

Cover Image: Influx Productions/Getty Images New growth sprouting from book

Compositor: Pre-Press PMG

For product information and technology assistance, contact us at **Cengage Learning Customer & Sales Support, 1-800-354-9706.**
For permission to use material from this text or product, submit all requests online at **www.cengage.com/permissions.** Further permissions questions can be e-mailed to **permissionrequest@cengage.com.**

Library of Congress Control Number: 2009939794

ISBN-13: 978-0-495-81386-6

ISBN-10: 0-495-81386-9

Wadsworth
20 Davis Drive
Belmont, CA 94002-3098
USA

Cengage Learning is a leading provider of customized learning solutions with office locations around the globe, including Singapore, the United Kingdom, Australia, Mexico, Brazil, and Japan. Locate your local office at: **www.cengage.com/global.**

Cengage Learning products are represented in Canada by Nelson Education, Ltd.

To learn more about Wadsworth, visit **www.cengage.com/wadsworth**

Purchase any of our products at your local college store or at our preferred online store **www.ichapters.com.**

Printed in the United States of America
1 2 3 4 5 6 7 13 12 11 10 09

BRIEF CONTENTS

CONTENTS

Chapter 3

Specific Literacy Assessment   49

PART TWO
Literacy Stages: Assessment and Instruction   217

Chapter 8
Early Emergent Literacy   219

Contents

PREFACE

Literacy Assessment: Helping Teachers Plan Instruction has always been a text that has helped preservice and in-service teachers do the most effective job possible in planning and carrying out quality literacy instruction. The Fourth Edition has been developed to continue this standard and to give teachers the tools to help every student achieve success in reading and writing. We started this Fourth Edition by talking and listening to these teachers to determine what they needed to do a more effective job. We asked them to tell us how this book is helpful and what it needed improvement upon. Additionally, college and university instructors from around the country gave us feedback about what they liked about this text and what needed to be improved. With this information in hand, we planned a revision designed to support teachers in today's classroom.

Major Goals of this Revision

We had three major goals in mind as we planned and executed this revision:

1. Create a teacher-friendly text that will help preservice teachers learn what they need to know and do to be effective teachers of literacy.

2. Provide in-service teachers a reference book that they will continuously refer to as they increase their skills in teaching literacy.

3. Make *Literacy Assessment: Helping Teachers Plan Instruction*, Fourth Edition a teacher-friendly, reader-friendly text that makes readers say "WOW! This is really helpful to me in my classroom teaching."

From the front cover to the internal reorganization of this text, *Literacy Assessment: Helping Teachers Plan Instruction*, Fourth Edition will help teachers see what they can do to help their beginning readers and writers mature and flourish.

Major Organizational Features

This text is divided into two primary sections:

- **Part One—Tools and Techniques for Assessment-Based Literacy Instruction**—This section helps teachers understand the tools, techniques, and procedures they can use before instruction, during instruction, and after instruction to assess students' needs, monitor progress, and plan the type of instruction each student needs to grow into a successful reader and writer. Throughout this section, teachers will see how every classroom activity helps identify students' needs and monitor their progress. Teachers will develop a beginning understanding of the Response to Intervention (RTI) concept and see that continuously delivering good instruction to all students is what this is really all about. The seven chapters in this section can be taken in order or may be used to fit the customized needs of a class.

- **Part Two—Literacy Stages: Assessment and Instruction**—This section of the text helps teachers develop an understanding and an appreciation for the way students grow into reading and writing by progressing through a series of overlapping stages from Early Emergent Literacy to Fluent Reading and Writing. Each stage is broken down into a series of benchmarks or standards with suggestions provided for assessment and instruction. Chapters may be read in order or may be used out of sequence to fit the needs of a specialized class or learning situation.

Throughout this text, the focus is on planning effective literacy instruction tailored to students' needs.

Updated Features of the Fourth Edition

Literacy Assessment: Helping Teachers Plan Instruction, Fourth Edition, has been reorganized to make the overall text more useful to teachers. The two main sections, as described above, make the text more reader-friendly and allow instructors and in-service leaders to customize the way they use the text.

Each chapter has revised features that include the following:

- **Standards Focus**—The International Reading Association Standards for Reading Professionals are identified at the beginning of each chapter. Students will know from the outset what they will be learning to help them become effective literacy teachers.

- **Graphic Organizers**—A new one-page graphic organizer gives the reader a clear preview of the chapter. This feature can be used before the chapter is read to build background and can be used as discussion starter after reading to help students summarize what they learned.

- **New Terms**—New terms are identified to help the reader preview the chapter content. All terms are defined in the chapter and are included in the glossary at the end of the book.

- **Opening Scenarios**—The revised opening scenarios set the tone for each chapter with realistic classroom scenes. The opening scenarios serve as a jumping off point for chapter content.

- **New Summaries**—A new bulleted summary helps the reader review content and identify the key points covered in each chapter.

- **Video Cases**—Where appropriate, TeachSource Video Cases are referenced throughout the chapters to link the text to a real classroom.

All of these features work together to make a very student-friendly text that new teachers will want to retain as a valuable classroom reference throughout their teaching career.

Content Changes in the Fourth Edition

The content of the fourth edition of *Literacy Assessment: Helping Teachers Plan Instruction* has been revised and updated throughout.

Reconceptualized Chapter One—Chapter one has been rewritten to help pre-service and in-service teachers develop a beginning understanding of the Response to Intervention (RTI) concept and how it fits with Assessment Based Literacy instruction.

RTI References throughout the Text—Throughout the text appropriate references are made to help teachers develop a beginning understanding of RTI.

Emphasis on Diversity—More examples that depict the diversity of all classrooms has been included.

Refined Definitions—All definitions were reviewed and revised to enhance clarity.

Updated Research References—Research references were updated as required.

Increased Emphasis on the Connection between Assessment and Instruction—Greater emphasis was given to the connection between assessment and instruction.

New Children's Literature Titles—New children's literature has been woven into the text where appropriate.

New Photos—Additional new photos have been included to enhance various concepts throughout the text.

Ancillaries for this Text

The ancillaries that accompany this text include video cases and an enhanced website.

Learning Resources for the Student

The premium website offers access to the TeachSource Video Cases, 4–6 minute video modules presenting actual classroom scenarios, supported by viewing questions, teacher interviews, artifacts, and bonus videos. The Video Cases let students experience the complex and multiple dimensions of true classroom dilemmas that teachers face every day. Other study tools and resources include links to related sites for each chapter of the text, tutorial quizzes, glossary/flashcards, downloadable resources and checklists, and more. Go to www.cengage.com/login to register for these resources using your access code. If your text does not include an access code card, go to www.ichapters.com to obtain an access code.

Teaching Resources for the Instructor

The instructor area of the premium website offers access to password-protected resources such as an electronic version of the instructor's manual and PowerPoint® slides. Go to www.cengage.com/login to access these resources.

Electronic Instructor's Manual

The Instructor's Manual includes chapter summaries including key terms, blackline masters, classroom activities/discussion suggestions, and assessment ideas. We understand that there are as many ways to organize and teach a text as there are instructors to teach it. However, instructors should find some useful ideas here that may save some time in developing a syllabus and in conducting the class.

Acknowledgments

This text is a reflection of the ideas and thoughts of many individuals. We wish to give special thanks to each of the following:

- The preservice and in-service teachers who gave us many ideas for improving this text and making it more practical and teacher friendly.
- Michael D. Robinson, Curriculum Support Specialist in the Miami-Dade County Public Schools for his comments and feedback on each chapter.
- To our outside reviewers for their ideas for this edition:

  Deborah Ellermeyer
  Clarion University

  Joyce Jeewek
  Benedictine University

  Melinda Miller
  Sam Houston State University

  Jackie Osborne
  Bowling Green State University

  Deanna Stoube
  St. Ambrose University

  Josephine Wilson
  Bowie State University

- Lisa Kalner Williams, Senior Development Editor, who gave us valuable guidance in improving this text.
- For the designer, Marsha Cohen, and design director, Robert Hugel, who came up with a fresh new look for the fourth edition of this text.
- Carrie Wagner and Jan Turner for their excellent and efficient way of putting together the final text.
- Linda Stewart and Ashley Cronin for their great ideas in creating the new website for this text.

  To all of these individuals, we say THANK YOU!

J. D. C.
N. D. K.

PART I

Tools and Techniques for Assessment-Based Literacy Instruction

Tim Hall/Cultura/Jupiter Images

Standards Focus (See inside back cover)

Standards for Reading Professionals: 1, 2, 3, 4, 5

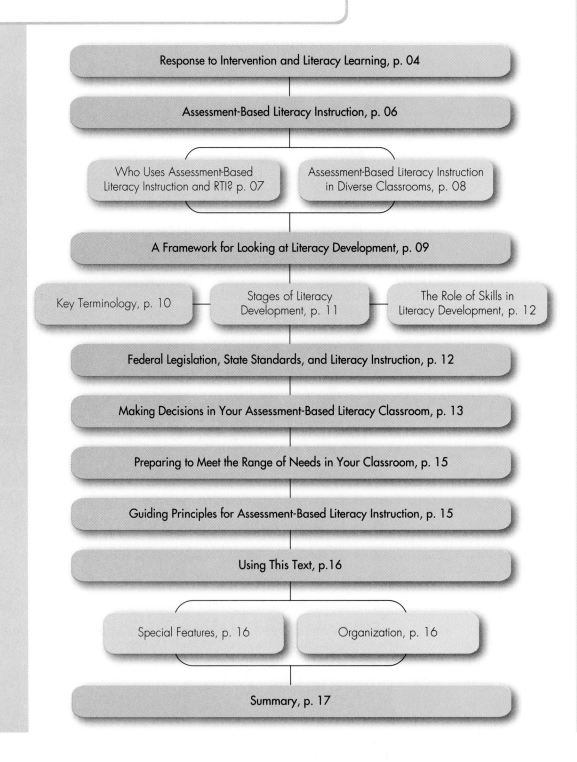

1

A Framework for Effective Literacy Instruction

It is early in the school year. Dolores Alvarez, a third grade teacher at Jefferson School, is listening to Sara read aloud a portion of the book *Ain't Nobody a Stranger to Me* (Grifalconi & Pinkey, 2007). As Sara reads, Ms. Alvarez takes a running record (you will learn more about this later). After the reading, Ms. Alvarez asks Sara to retell what she has read. Ms. Alvarez notes that Sara read 100 percent of the words correctly, but she could retell only part of what she read.

Later Ms. Alvarez makes notes on a 5″ × 8″ note card devoted to Sara's reading. Mrs. Alvarez writes:

> Sara Brown, 3rd Grade
> Reading
>
> - Excellent fluency—100%
> - Has developed many of the skills of a fluent reader
> - Needs instruction at the beginning stage of fluent reading with heavy emphasis on comprehension; was unable to retell story events

At the beginning of the year, Ms. Alvarez listens to each of her students read aloud as part of determining their instructional strengths and needs and their stage of literacy development. Within the first few weeks of school, she will have heard every student.

While Ms. Alvarez has been listening to Sara, the other twenty-seven students in her classroom have been writing. Ms. Alvarez asked them to write at least two paragraphs about themselves and encouraged them to include some of the items she has listed on the chalkboard:

- Favorite subject and why it's your favorite
- Best thing about school last year
- Activity you like best

NEW TERMS

- Response to Intervention (RTI)
- scaffolding
- second-language learners
- standard

- Types of books you like to read
- Most important thing about you
- Anything else you want to tell about yourself

This writing forms another part of Ms. Alvarez's approach for determining each student's instructional strengths and needs and stage of literacy development. Besides looking at writing fluency, she pays attention to the students' interests, self-concepts, and attitudes. For each student, she records notes on a 5" × 8" card. All teachers at Jefferson School are going through this same process. This is the first step in Jefferson School's Response to Intervention (RTI), a plan designed to prevent students from having problems in literacy learning. The RTI process will be discussed later in this chapter.

Ms. Alvarez and other teachers in the school are operating assessment-based literacy classrooms. They start the year by gathering information about each student's reading, writing, and other language skills. This information is needed to make a tentative determination of each student's stage of literacy development and determine which students need intervention to ensure that they have continued successful growth in literacy. Based on this initial determination, teachers plan the types of instructional activities and literacy experiences to help students continue to progress in their literacy development. Notice some of the key features of Ms. Alvarez's approach to literacy instruction:

- She uses **authentic assessment** activities; activities that involve real reading and real writing. Students read books and write about themselves.
- Her assessment activities look just like good instructional activities. In a well-designed, well-managed, assessment-based classroom, you cannot tell instructional activities from assessment activities.

This text is written for both preservice and inservice teachers. We assume you have some background in literacy development and instruction. Perhaps you have taken a course in literacy, reading, or language arts; perhaps you have done some independent reading in the area or have experience in teaching literacy.

Supplement this book by reading some of the resources listed on this text's website under "For Additional Reading"

Another useful resource is the section that lists terms new to each chapter, which appear in **boldface**, and the glossary at the back of the book that defines the terms.

In this chapter, we develop the concept of an assessment-based literacy classroom and focus on what it is and how it operates. We discuss how this fits with the RTI concept and how RTI relates to classroom instruction. Further, we look at a framework for thinking about literacy learning as a series of stages along a continuum of one's educational path.

RTI and Literacy Learning

RTI is a multi-tiered approach to the early identification and support of students with learning and behavior needs. The RTI process begins with high-quality instruction and universal screening of all children in the general education classroom.

Struggling learners are provided with interventions at increasing levels of intensity to accelerate their rate of learning. These services may be provided by a variety of personnel, including general education or classroom teachers, special educators, and specialists. Progress is closely monitored to assess both the learning rate and level of performance of individual students. Educational decisions about the intensity and duration of interventions are based on individual student response to instruction. RTI is designed for making decisions in both general education and special education, creating a well-integrated system of instruction and intervention guided by student outcome data (www.rtinetwork.org/learn/what/ar/whatisrti; Allington, 2009; Mesmer & Mesmer, 2009).

RTI is the process of looking at how each student is performing in relation to a given set of standards or goals for literacy learning. Based on the assessment, which includes the monitoring and evaluation of each student's performance, scientifically supported instructions and interventions are given to help a student achieve a given goal. This concept has developed throughout the United States based on the Individuals with Disabilities Act (IDEA), Public Law 108-446 (U. S. Department of Education, 2006). Nearly every state education department now requires schools to develop a plan for RTI.

Many models and frameworks have been presented to define and explain RTI. The pyramid presented in Figure 1.1 shows our interpretation of the RTI concept and the Tiers (or Levels) of Intervention as they relate to classroom instruction. The International Reading Association (IRA) has adopted six key principles to guide the thinking of teachers and administrators in relation to RTI (*Reading Today,* 2009). Everything in this text is an excellent fit with RTI—and the principles suggested by IRA. To view these principles and to link to more information about them, visit the website for this text. There are several key points that you should keep in mind when thinking about RTI:

- Classroom instruction is the foundation of all three Tiers or Levels of Intervention. The first Tier or Level of Intervention begins in the classroom. This text is focused heavily on what classroom teachers should do to provide effective literacy instruction.

- There is still much confusion and discussion in schools about how the RTI plan or model should work. In this text, we do not attempt to resolve the issues or answer all the questions related to RTI. This text provides classroom teachers the support and skills needed to provide all students the literacy instruction required to be effective learners.

- This text will help all teachers provide appropriate literacy instruction within the RTI framework no matter how their school defines and develops its RTI plan.

- It is also our strong belief that all teachers within a school, ***not just those in special education***, must be involved in developing and carrying out the RTI plan to make it work effectively.

You will see that most of what should be done in effective classroom instruction and Tier I intervention is what good **literacy** teachers have always done or should have always done.

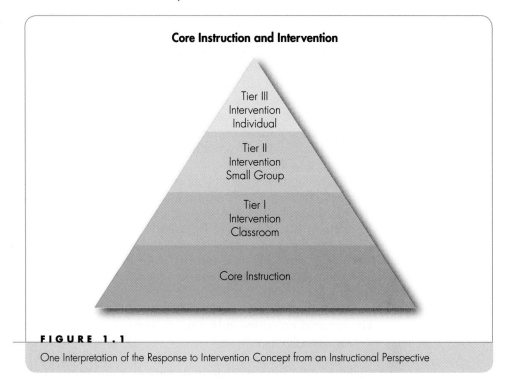

Core Instruction and Intervention

Tier III
Intervention
Individual

Tier II
Intervention
Small Group

Tier I
Intervention
Classroom

Core Instruction

FIGURE 1.1

One Interpretation of the Response to Intervention Concept from an Instructional Perspective

Assessment-Based Literacy Instruction

Assessment-based literacy instruction fits right in with RTI and focuses on assessment, continuous monitoring of student progress, and evaluation. In assessment-based literacy instruction, you continually gather information and monitor student progress to make decisions about what instruction and interventions will support students' literacy growth (McKenna & Walpole, 2005; McTighe & O'Connor, 2005).

- **Assessment** is the process of gathering information about what students can and cannot do.
- **Monitoring—Progress Monitoring** is the process of looking at each student's performance in daily learning experiences and tests, noting how he or she is progressing in relation to what has been taught and what the student is expected to learn.
- **Evaluation** is making judgments about students' literacy development based on information you have gathered and changing instruction and intervention as needed.

For example, when Ms. Alvarez had Sara read from *Ain't Nobody a Stranger to Me* she was assessing Sara's reading. When she wrote comments on Sara's information card, she was evaluating Sara's fluency and comprehension. As Ms. Alvarez provides instruction for Sara and other students, she will see if they are learning and determine whether they are making progress in their literacy growth. If the students are not making progress, their instruction and/or interventions will be changed immediately.

You may have heard the expression "assessment informs instruction and instruction informs assessment." In other words, instructional activities and experiences yield information about student performance; information about student literacy performance affects decisions about literacy instruction and experiences. Each nourishes the other; they blend seamlessly back and forth. Every teaching event is an assessment because you learn something about your students while in the act of teaching. Everything you learn affects how you teach.

Imagine two people batting a balloon back and forth. One person represents assessment, while the other represents instruction. The balloon stands for literacy development. The only way to keep that balloon in the air is for the two sides to work together. Literacy development takes place when assessment and instruction work together.

As a teacher who uses assessment-based literacy instruction, you know and use many different tools and techniques for assessment. (We will survey these in Chapters 2 to 4.) The assessment process involves much more than just testing. It uses all teaching and learning experiences, as well as tests, in determining where students are and what they need to support their growth in literacy. You also use a variety of instructional routines (described in Chapter 6) to provide the instruction needed to help each student gain power in literacy.

Who Uses Assessment-Based Literacy Instruction and RTI?

The process of assessment-based literacy instruction and RTI must be sufficiently manageable to make it possible for all teachers to use it. Even though the process of literacy development is quite complex (Flood, Jensen, Lapp, & Squire, 1991), this text is about making the assessment-based process teacher-friendly and usable by any classroom teacher.

Some teachers have classes of twenty-five to thirty-five students or more, while others work with small groups or individuals. The assessment-based literacy process can and should be used in all these settings; by classroom teachers as well as by all others responsible for literacy development. Title I teachers, resource room teachers, special education teachers, teachers of students acquiring English, and any others who take part in this process will select the procedures most appropriate for their particular students. For example, teachers of students acquiring English will select procedures based on what they know about the students' first-language literacy and second-language acquisition.

Assessment-based literacy instruction will help you create a **Comprehensive Balanced Literacy Program**, which combines the essential elements for effective literacy learning. It is the most effective type of program to use, and it helps all students achieve success in literacy development (Snow, Burns, & Griffin, 1998). **Intervention** is the part of this program that offers additional instruction for students who experience difficulty in learning to read and write. This concept will be fully developed in Chapter 6.

The key to making the assessment-based literacy model and RTI work in a school is accepting the idea that each teacher works with colleagues as a team for each student's good. Regardless of where instructional programs are located—in the regular classroom, in a resource room, or elsewhere—*every teacher* should work from the same concept of literacy development. Learning to use the assessment-based literacy model helps you achieve consistency in all literacy programs within your school. This consistency leads to better learning for students (Allington & Walmsley, 2008). There will be more about working with colleagues in Chapter 7.

Assessment-Based Literacy Instruction in Diverse Classrooms

The term *diverse classrooms* refers to the typically wide variety of individuals who make up a class. Think about classrooms with which you are familiar. Even if you have seen only a few, you probably realize that most classrooms today have students from many cultures and many language backgrounds. Some students speak languages other than English. Some come from cultural backgrounds quite different from the community in which the school is located. Some students are dealing with conditions that make learning especially challenging. Teachers need to recognize and accommodate diverse students, whatever the nature of that diversity.

As we work with teachers in all parts of the country, we find that they have children who speak Chinese, Spanish, and English all in the same classroom. Some classrooms have students representing as many as thirty or more languages and cultures, including those who speak nonmainstream varieties of English. Projections indicate that not long after this book is published, 50 percent of all public school students will be "minority" students. Most of these students will be **second-language learners**—acquiring English as a second language (Jones, 1997)—also known as **English-language learners**, or *ELL students*. In this book we use these terms interchangeably.

Fifth-grade students work cooperatively, learning from and supporting each other.

© Ellen Senisi/
The Image Works

We believe there are some constants in working with second-language learners:

* You will most likely have at least some students in your classroom whose first language is something other than standard English.

* Depending on their age and their stage of literacy, these students may or may not already be literate in another language, and this will influence how you help them become literate in English.

* Despite such potential differences, most of the assessment questions you ask will remain the same for all students. That is, you will need to find out the same things about second-language learners that you need to learn about any other students: Where are they now in terms of oral language, reading, and writing in English? What are they ready to do next? How do they feel about themselves? How can you arrange instruction, materials, and the environment to help them?

Generalizations are risky for any group of children. For ELL students, lack of ability in English may be their only commonality. They may vary as to whether they are ready to speak in English or are still in the silent period where they may understand the new language but be reluctant to attempt to speak it. Some may already be writing in the new language, some not. Further, ELL students may vary in terms of the educational background and literacy of their parents (in any language), whether English is being learned in the home, whether the family wants to maintain its language of origin, and more. The areas in which these children differ from one another may be more important than the single area that unites them: lack of proficiency in English (Krashen, 1982).

Another type of diversity in today's classrooms involves students who are "exceptional" in some way. As a result of **inclusion programs,** most students with disabilities are now placed in regular classrooms whenever possible. Typical classes may include, for example, students with **learning disabilities, attention-deficit disorder (ADD)**, or **attention-deficit–hyperactivity disorder (ADHD)** (Lerner, 2006). Other students may be exceptional by being classified as **gifted and talented**. Again, this wide range of variation need not change your basic approach to literacy.

A basic premise of this text is that assessment-based literacy instruction is for *all* students, not a select few. As you develop an understanding of the process, you will learn how to assess your students regardless of their differences. As you study the classroom scenarios and the instructional suggestions in this book, pay close attention to the ways of meeting the needs of every student in your classroom.

A diverse classroom is a strong classroom. The greater the diversity, the greater the opportunity to help all students develop literacy in a real-world environment and develop an appreciation for diverse languages and cultures.

A Framework for Looking at Literacy Development

Literacy development, formally defined, is the process of learning to read, write, speak, and listen, with thinking being an integral part of each (Holdaway, 1979). Literacy may also include viewing—the process of looking at graphic and visual media in a critical, evaluative way. While we believe viewing is a vital component of literacy, we do not deal with it separately, as it involves the same thinking skills used for listening and reading.

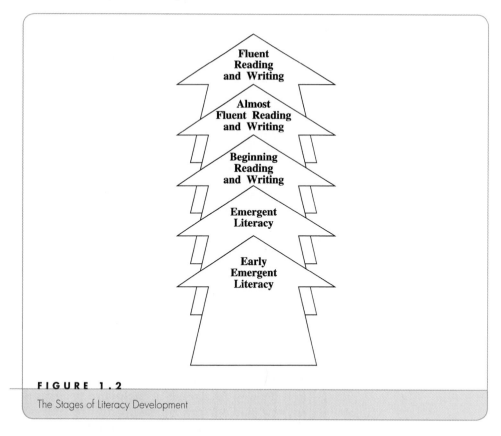

FIGURE 1.2

The Stages of Literacy Development

In the process of learning or developing literacy, students go through a series of stages. This series is best viewed as a continuum, with the stages blending into one another. But progression does not occur as smoothly as you might think it does (Adams, 1990). In any given classroom, there are likely to be students at several different stages. In fact, any given child may be doing some work that is typical of one stage while also doing some things that are typical of another stage.

We view literacy development in five stages that overlap and flow into one another. Figure 1.2 depicts the flow of these stages. A student might still be developing the characteristics, strategies, and skills of one stage while moving into and beginning development in another stage.

Key Terminology

As you begin to think about stages of literacy development, two terms will come up frequently:

- **Standard** refers to a degree or level of performance that is expected for students at a certain time.
- **Benchmarks,** as we use the term in this book, are behaviors exhibited by students that serve as evidence of a certain stage of literacy development. In education, the term *benchmark* has come to mean a reference point in relation to an individual's development, and our usage draws on that general meaning.

The terms *standard* and *benchmark* are often used interchangeably. In more precise usage, however, standards tend to be broad and general, whereas benchmarks indicate specific tasks that students might perform to show they have met a standard or one part of a standard.

In this book, we use the term *stage* to refer to groups of benchmark behaviors that typically occur together as children move along the literacy continuum. These may correspond roughly to certain grades for some students. However, children move along the continuum at various rates, and development isn't smooth; that is, children may exhibit behaviors typical of more than one stage. For the most part, though, each stage grows out of and is dependent on the previous one. Observation of certain behaviors helps a teacher infer where a child is on the continuum. For example, familiarity with various genres is one benchmark of the Early Emergent Literacy stage; knowing and being able to repeat several nursery rhymes is an observable behavior associated with that benchmark.

Research supports the division of literacy development into stages (Rupley, Wilson, & Nichols, 1998). Further, dealing with literacy development in terms of stages along a continuum avoids some of the problems associated with the concept of reading levels (see a detailed discussion of reading levels in Chapter 4).

Now let's look more closely at the five stages of literacy development.

Stages of Literacy Development

The five stages of literacy presented in this text were developed by examining research sources spanning more than thirty years: (Adams, 1990; Anderson, Hiebert, Scott, & Wilkinson, 1985; Armbruster & Osborn, 2001; Chall, 1967; Hiebert, Pearson, Taylor, Richardson, & Paris, 1998; Juel, 1988; Learning First Alliance, 1998; National Reading Panel, 2000; Snow, Burns, & Griffin, 1998). In addition, we examined purported research-based curriculum guides from state and county departments of education and local school districts too numerous to list. We also studied the standards adopted by various states. We identified benchmarks, common characteristics, and components for each stage and used our combined wisdom and the wisdom of other colleagues in the field to guide our decisions.

Each stage is discussed in detail in Chapters 8 through 12. A complete list of the benchmarks for all stages can be found in the Resource File at the end of the book.

These, in brief, are the five stages:

1. **Early Emergent Literacy:** At this stage, children develop the foundations of literacy. It usually occurs before the student enters kindergarten, and it includes such aspects of literacy as developing oral language and being curious about print. Second-language learners usually have reached or surpassed this stage in their first language.

2. **Emergent Literacy:** During this stage, the child becomes more interested in literacy. He or she exhibits such behaviors as using more standard oral language patterns and forming and naming letters. Concepts about print, such as recognizing a word, also develop during this stage. Most children move through this stage by the end of kindergarten or at the beginning of grade 1.

3. **Beginning Reading and Writing:** In this stage, oral language expands and the student begins to actually read and write in conventional ways. Word analysis

skills develop, and students begin to develop fluency in reading. Understanding of the meanings of many words increases. This stage continues through first grade for some students and into second or third grade for others.

4. **Almost Fluent Reading and Writing:** During this stage, the child is growing more sophisticated in all aspects of literacy. He or she reads silently more than in the previous stage, does more writing, and has an oral language that shows increasing vocabulary. For most students, this stage may begin toward the end of second grade and continue into the beginning of fourth or fifth grade, although some students reach it by the end of first grade and others not until later than fifth grade.

5. **Fluent Reading and Writing:** By this stage, the student is using reading, writing, and oral language for a variety of purposes. She or he has attained most of the skills of reading and writing. This stage may begin in fourth grade (or even earlier) for some students, and it continues to develop through the upper elementary grades and into middle school and high school. In fact, fluent reading and writing development continues throughout one's life.

As you can tell from Figure 1.2 and from this brief description of the stages, there is much overlap among them. Students seldom finish one stage before moving into another. Moreover, some students reach a plateau and remain at a particular stage for a period of time. Thus, literacy development can be described as a "jerky continuum."

The Role of Skills in Literacy Development

Years ago, when educators realized that literacy is much more than a set of discrete skills that an individual must master, some teachers assumed that skills were unimportant in literacy development and were not to be taught at all. *This simply is not true.*

All literate individuals possess and use many different skills. Readers and writers develop literacy and learn to use skills by having many successful reading and writing experiences and by being given instruction with strategies and skills that will help them move forward in their literacy development. The process is much like learning to play the piano. You learn your first little piece. You play it over and over, and in the process you develop "fluency." You are then taught a new chord, key signature, or rhythmic pattern (one that you lack or are unable to use). Once you learn the new "skill," you can learn new pieces.

Similarly, as students move through the various stages of literacy, they learn various skills and strategies. As they become fluent with these, they move into the next stage. As we describe each stage in later chapters, we will have a good deal to say about these matters.

Federal Legislation, State Standards, and Literacy Instruction

Teachers face many issues in using assessment-based literacy instruction. Two critical ones are government legislation and the standards adopted by their state.

• **Government legislation.** The No Child Left Behind (NCLB 2001) was designed to help schools create reading programs that will ensure that all students make **adequate yearly progress,** which is a term that is defined by each individual state. The RTI concept that we discussed earlier in this chapter is based on the Individuals with Disabilities Act (IDEA), Public Law 108-446 (U. S. Department of Education, 2006). Various aspects of federal legislation are constantly being updated. To stay abreast of these changes and learn more about NCLB and IDEA, use the websites found on the website for this text.

- **State standards.** Most states have standards that schools are supposed to follow in developing their reading/literacy curriculum. To find out more about your state's standards or the standards of any other state, do an Internet search using the parameter "(fill in the state)'s educational standards"; you will find thousands of articles and websites with the most current information.

The question is, however, how do federal legislation and state standards fit with assessment-based literacy instruction? The answer is "very well." Assessment-based literacy instruction is a framework that helps you accomplish the goals of all federal legislation focused on helping children learn to read and write. As you examine the standards of your state, you will see that they are similar to (if not the same as) the benchmarks that we present for each stage of literacy development. Therefore, what you are learning from this text will assist you in making the decisions required to help students achieve your state standards and make adequate yearly progress.

Making Decisions in Your Assessment-Based Literacy Classroom

The decision-making process in your assessment-based literacy classroom involves three steps, which are circular in nature (see Figure 1.3):

1. Take samples of each student's literacy (listening, speaking, reading, or writing).
2. Compare each student's performance to the stages of literacy development.
3. On the basis of what you learn from these first two steps, plan instruction and carry it out.

This decision-making process will help you plan instruction and determine each student's progress in literacy development. By continually comparing each student's performance to the stages of literacy development, you will be able to evaluate how each student is progressing and determine what is needed to help him or her further develop literacy skills. Further, this process will assist you in comparing each student's performance to local, state, and national standards and monitor progress as required for your school's RTI program.

We assume that when you provide instructional support, you will do so by **scaffolding;** that is, you will offer a great deal of support in the beginning and then gradually withdraw support as the student becomes more proficient. In most cases, you will move gradually from teacher **modeling** (demonstrating) to guided practice and then to the achievement of student independence through practice and application (Pearson, 1985).

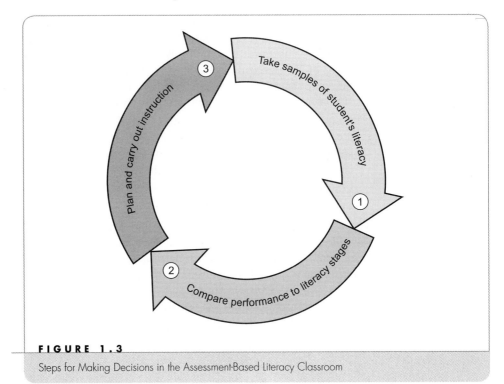

FIGURE 1.3

Steps for Making Decisions in the Assessment-Based Literacy Classroom

Instruction, including one-on-one time with a teacher, will enable this student to develop her literacy skills.

© Ted Foxx/Alamy

Preparing to Meet the Range of Needs in Your Classroom

Students bring to the classroom many characteristics and circumstances that can influence learning. These include home conditions, health and diet issues, language background, and existence of disabilities or special gifts. While these various elements influence learning, they rarely are the direct or sole cause of learning problems.

We will illustrate throughout this text how a teacher should consider these factors in planning instruction. It is our belief that appropriate instruction will keep students progressing in their literacy development regardless of outside factors.

What students must accomplish to become literate is the same regardless of any special needs they may have; therefore, all students should be viewed in relation to the same stages of literacy development. It is important to know how to provide quality instruction appropriate to the students' level of literacy development.

Within schools, there are many types of instruction that can support the needs of students. For example, these include

- the regular classroom instruction provided by a single teacher.
- interventions provided at different tiers or levels as students need them.
- inclusionary instruction in which special-needs students remain in the regular classroom with the aid of support personnel such as special teachers or teaching assistants.
- **pullout programs** in which individual students or small groups leave the classroom for a period of time for special instruction.
- **extended-day programs** in which special instruction is provided before or after school.

The value of any of these programs depends on how consistent or congruent they are with the classroom program. Pullout programs in particular have long been criticized as counterproductive (Allington & Walmsley, 2008). But whatever the arrangement in your school, we believe that using the decision-making process for the assessment-based literacy classroom and RTI will help you meet the needs of *all* students. The remainder of this text will illustrate how you can do this.

Guiding Principles for Assessment-Based Literacy Instruction

Three important principles should guide you as you develop an assessment-based literacy classroom. These principles have been inherent throughout this chapter, but we would like to make them as explicit as possible.

1. *Every teacher responsible for literacy in the school uses the same stages of literacy development and the same RTI guidelines as the core for planning each student's literacy instruction.* By focusing on the stages of literacy development, teachers work with a common framework. This helps bring about consistency in literacy development for all students.

2. *Assessment of literacy development focuses on students' strengths and needs in relation to the stages of literacy development.* Evidence from a variety of sources shows that students learn most effectively by focusing first on what they can do.

Then teachers provide new teaching activities and learning experiences to help students progress to the next stage of literacy development.

3. *Assessment should be an ongoing process based primarily on the results of instructional activities used to promote literacy development.* Your assessment may sometimes be supported by other formal and informal assessment procedures, such as tests, but your daily instructional activities with students yield the most useful information. In the assessment-based literacy classroom, all teaching activities and experiences provide an opportunity to assess and evaluate students in relation to the stages of literacy development as well as monitor progress to meet your RTI plan.

Using This Text

Literacy Assessment: Helping Teachers Plan Instruction, fourth edition, is designed to be both a textbook and a handbook for preservice and inservice teachers. It offers many guidelines about how to look at students at the various stages of literacy and plan the types of instruction each student needs. After you have read the book, it will remain handy as a reference.

Special Features

Several features in each chapter will assist you as you read the book or use it as a reference tool:

* *Standards Focus:* At the beginning of each chapter, we indicate which standard from the *Standards for Reading Professionals—Revised 2003* (International Reading Association, 2004) is addressed in the chapter. The standards are listed inside the back cover. Use this feature to see what standards are covered in the chapter.

* *Graphic Organizer:* Each chapter begins with a Graphic Organizer that shows the main sections and subsections of the chapter with page numbers. Use this feature to preview the chapter, to locate specific sections, or to review after reading.

* *New Terms:* Following each chapter's Graphic Organizer is a list of terms you need to know that are new to the chapter. These terms appear throughout the chapter in boldface and are defined in the glossary at the back of the book. (Important terms that have been introduced previously are not listed again.) Use this feature to review important terms and concepts.

* *Summary:* Following the text of each chapter, a summary presents key points in an easy-to-follow bulleted format. Use this feature to check your own knowledge of what you have learned.

* *Website:* The website accompanying this text provides resources to help you extend your learning. These include *For Additional Reading, TeachSource Video Cases,* and *Websites.* Use these features to learn more about an area of interest.

Organization

The text is divided into two parts, each with a different focus.

Part One: Tools and Techniques for Assessment-Based Literacy Instruction. This section contains Chapters 1 through 7, which will help you develop a framework for assessment-based literacy instruction and learn the assessment tools, techniques, and instructional procedures that you can draw on in your classroom. Chapter 7 offers guidance in working with families, with your teaching peers, and with other professionals on the school staff, as well as suggestions for maintaining and extending your own professional growth.

Part Two: Literacy Stages: Assessment and Instruction. Chapters 8 through 12 present each of the five stages of literacy development (one stage per chapter). The benchmarks for each stage are discussed in detail, along with assessment ideas and suggestions to help you plan instruction and apply the assessment-based literacy concept in whatever instructional role you play. Each chapter has an opening section that makes useful connections to other chapters.

The Resource File provides directions for accessing and using the website that supports this book. You can view the sample forms, checklists, and charts shown in this book as well as additional forms and checklists. Many of these can be downloaded.

The Resource File also provides the benchmarks and associated behaviors for all five stages of literacy development, a readability graph, and several word lists. Following these pages you will find a glossary, a list of children's literature cited in the book, references, credits, and an index.

Summary

- Response to Intervention (RTI) is a framework for looking at each student's strengths and needs in literacy learning and continually monitoring progress to determine a student's success and growth.
- RTI involves core instruction and three tiers or levels of intervention.
- Core instruction is the foundation for each tier of intervention.
- Assessment-based Literacy Instruction focuses on assessment, continuous monitoring of student progress, and evaluation.
- All teachers within a school use Assessment-based Literacy Instruction and RTI. Assessment-based Literacy Instruction and RTI work effectively in diverse classrooms.
- The terms standards and benchmarks are critical to understanding assessment-based literacy instruction and RTI.
- Literacy learning can be looked at as a series of overlapping stages ranging from Early Emergent Literacy to Fluent Reading and Writing.
- Teachers must stay abreast of government legislation and their state standards.
- Assessment-based Literacy Instruction requires a continuous process of decision making on the part of the teacher.

 Please visit the premium website for *Literacy Assessment*, Fourth Edition to access the TeachSource Video Cases, chapter web links, For Additional Reading, tutorial quizzes, glossary flashcards, online checklists, downloads, and much more! Go to www.cengage.com/login to register your access code.

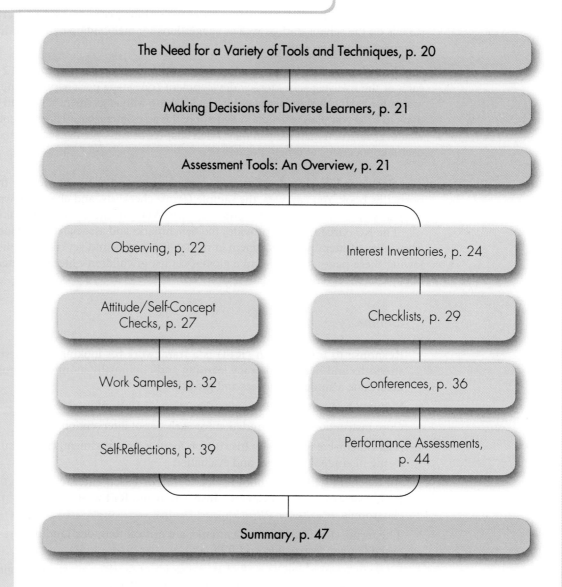

2

Tools for Gathering Information in the Classroom

NEW TERMS

- anchor papers
- anecdote
- attitude/self-concept check
- checklist
- conference
- formative
- interest inventories
- K-W-L chart
- metacognition
- observing
- performance assessment
- risk taking
- rubrics
- self-reflection
- summative
- think-aloud
- work samples

P olly Logan's third-grade classroom hums with activity. Some children are reading with a partner. Some are talking with a buddy about a piece of writing. Some are reading independently. As the children work, Mrs. Logan circulates with her clipboard and checklists. From time to time she stops to talk with a child. Then she records the child's name, the date, and a brief note. She moves on. The child continues working. Afterward, Mrs. Logan will transfer the notes she has made into her notebook.

Later in the day, Mrs. Logan sits at a table for a brief individual conference with a child. She has several such conferences scheduled for today. By the end of the week, she will have spent some time alone with each child in her class. During this particular conference, she asks the child to share a reading log and talk about his reading. Then she gives him an unfamiliar book to read aloud while she keeps track of his accuracy on a yellow pad. Later she inspects her records of the child's oral reading to help her decide whether he and a couple of others need a minilesson about a particular strategy. During conferences with other children, she may follow various other procedures.

On the same day, during their Writing Block, the children work from their writing folders. These contain prewriting clusters, rough drafts, and revisions. Not all children are at the same point in the writing process. Mrs. Logan refers to the folders when she plans instruction.

Today is Monday, so the children compile their individual spelling lists for the week. Some words they choose themselves—words they want to learn how to spell. Two children are working with the learning disability teacher to develop lists that combine student and teacher choice. Some words are drawn, with Mrs. Logan's help, from consistent misspellings in daily writing. Many children are confused about when to double the final consonant before adding inflected endings. Therefore, Mrs. Logan puts on the list several words that follow this pattern. She plans a whole-class minilesson on this useful generalization.

Today the children are also completing a unit on endangered animals. Each child has chosen one animal to study and has used several sources to complete a **K-W-L chart** (Ogle, 1989). The **K** section shows what the child already knows. The **W** section lists the child's questions—"What I want to learn." The **L** section, which the children complete today, explains "What I learned." Each child now shares what he or she has learned. Mrs. Logan notes which children are unable to synthesize and summarize. She plans a series of minilessons on these skills before they embark on the next unit.

Also, as the oral reports are given, Mrs. Logan pays close attention to the speaking and listening abilities of her students. Noting that Kathy is still painfully uncomfortable standing in front of the class, she decides to help her in two ways: (1) with techniques to overcome her shyness and (2) with alternative ways to share information. Mrs. Logan also notes that Sara is quite attentive, and that she asks a question. Sara's facility with English is growing rapidly; a month ago, she would not have volunteered to speak aloud in class.

Finally, some children seem to have forgotten about how an audience should behave. It's time for a review of the listening guidelines that the class drew up at the beginning of the year. The students need to rededicate themselves to these guidelines or draw up new ones.

From the classroom described, you can see that Mrs. Logan assesses her students' literacy daily in many ways. She constantly monitors their growth and progress. Every time she interacts with or observes the children in her classroom, she learns something that helps her to meet their needs. She knows that no one's memory is perfect, so she keeps careful notes and organizes her information in such a way that she can refer to it when she plans individual, group, and whole-class instruction. She also uses the information during family conferences.

Teachers ask themselves many questions about each child: Who is this child? What is he doing during the day? During reading? During listening? What does this child think about himself? What is he interested in? How does he approach tasks? Where does he fit into the broad stages of literacy development? How do I gather, organize, and use data about all these things? In this chapter, you will begin learning about tools and techniques for answering such questions.

The Need for a Variety of Tools and Techniques

This chapter introduces tools that can be used for assessment in any learning area. Chapter 3 introduces some specific informal tools for assessing literacy. Chapter 4 covers assessing reading levels and readability; Chapter 5 introduces standardized tests. In Chapters 8 through 12, we will refer to these tools again and again as we focus on each stage in depth. Often we will elaborate and expand on procedures.

Every teacher needs an assortment of tools and techniques that allows literacy assessment to be ongoing, nonintrusive, nonthreatening, and productive. As you read, it may seem there are far too many tools and techniques for any teacher to need or have time for. We provide many so that you can make choices on the basis of your students, your setting, your materials, and your purpose for assessing.

Literacy can't be measured like a piece of string or weighed like a chicken. You can't use a ruler or a scale. Language goes on inside a child's head, where you can't see it. Your job is to find ways to look at what a child does and says and make inferences about what goes on in the child's head. These inferences help you plan instruction and a learning environment in which further literacy growth will flourish.

You need to look at children as they are actually engaged in listening, speaking, reading, and writing. Each of these language modes has many variations. The child reading a Harry Potter book may use different strategies than when reading a book about sperm whales. The child who writes fluently when making up stories about ghosts and goblins may bog down when trying to write a report about President Lincoln.

We reaffirm that *you* are the decision maker. We can give you information about tools and techniques and how to use them. We can also help you determine how to think about decisions you need to make. But we cannot make the decisions for you.

Making Decisions for Diverse Learners

We believe that the same generalization holds true for assessment as for instruction: make the assessment fit the student. Therefore, in our discussion of each assessment tool, we also will address how that tool or technique might be modified for diverse learners.

All classrooms are diverse in at least some ways. For example, in any classroom you are likely to have students at more than one literacy stage. And even those who seem to be at the same stage may exhibit differences in such traits as personality, interests, attitudes, and work habits.

Further, you may have students for whom English is a second (or even a third) language, students whose culture or family background differs significantly from that of the rest of the community, and students whose learning is affected in some way by a learning disability or a physical, mental, or emotional condition. These are just a few of the many individual differences that make up a diverse classroom.

To accommodate some differences, you may need to make adjustments as you assess. A few possible accommodations are a translator for those who are not yet fluent in English, a microphone adaptation or interpreter for those with a hearing impairment, special writing implements for those who have trouble holding a traditional pencil, and extra reassurance for those who lack confidence.

Ideas to help you make decisions for assessing and teaching diverse learners are provided where they will be most useful, with each tool and technique in Chapters 2 and 3. You will continue to find such ideas throughout each of the remaining chapters in this book. It's worth noting that in any class you will find as many ways children differ from one another as ways they are alike. We believe these differences enrich both your life and the lives of the students in your classroom.

Assessment Tools: An Overview

Following are eight assessment tools: observing, interest inventories, attitude/self-concept checks, checklists, work samples, conferences, self-reflections, and performance assessments. For each tool, we follow a consistent format. We

- define the tool and state its purposes.
- offer a description.

- present a discussion of procedures and samples of how those procedures are used.
- suggest adjustments or adaptations you might make or ideas to keep in mind for students with diverse needs.
- end with more general comments about the tool or technique.

While you will not use all of these tools at one time, you do need to know about each so that you can decide which to use to achieve your assessment purposes.

Observing

Observing involves close watching of a student's behavior while he or she is engaged in a particular activity or task. It serves four purposes:

- To look at students as they perform normal, authentic literacy tasks
- To look at the products or results of those tasks
- To plan instruction
- Sometimes to determine students' progress

DESCRIPTION

Observing is perhaps the teacher's most powerful tool, but only if it stems from a thorough knowledge of literacy development. With such knowledge, you will know which responses and behaviors indicate typical growth and which indicate a need for special help, a change in support or materials, or a more detailed assessment. Bear in mind that no judgment about a child's literacy (or anything else) should ever be based on only one observation.

Later in this chapter you will find a discussion of checklists, which rely on observation: you observe whether or not a behavior is present and indicate this on the checklist. However, in this section we are dealing with observation that is not tied to a checklist. Rather than checking certain behaviors, you write a note about what you see—an **anecdote**. It is as though you are telling a very brief story about a moment in a child's day.

PROCEDURES AND SAMPLES

Most teachers have a favorite way to record and organize observational notes, but one thing is true for everyone: if you don't write it down, you *will* forget it.

Observation notes need to be specific or they will be of no use to you later. Mostly you will write what a child does or says, not what he or she doesn't say or do, unless the child typically exhibits a particular behavior and the absence of this behavior is important. For example, a note that says, "Tuesday: Johnny didn't ask for any help today" is not useful. You don't know which Tuesday or even perhaps which Johnny. Further, you don't know what activity Johnny was engaged in that did not require help. Valid inferences are not possible. Should you rejoice because he didn't ask for help, seeing it as a sign that he is using strategies independently? Or should you be concerned because he doesn't seem to be aware of when he needs help, is still reluctant to ask, or may not be actually working at all but only daydreaming at his desk?

Fifth-grade students are working independently on various projects while their teacher observes unobtrusively.

© Bob Daemmrich/The Image Works

A more useful note might read:

10/7 Johnny M.

During paired reading, helped partner use context on unfamiliar word. Johnny seems to be using what was taught in yesterday's lesson.

You may decide to take observation notes (anecdotal records) on five or six children every day of the week so that you have at least one note per child per week. However, if a certain child is puzzling you, you may want to record several observations of that one child during a week, maybe even several each day. As you examine your notes over time, a picture may emerge that will help you make wise decisions.

There are many ways to record observation notes:

- *Sticky notes:* These can be identified with the child's name, the date, and a brief statement (see Figure 2.1 for examples). The notes are transferred to a notebook or file folder where you are accumulating assessment information.

- *Gummed address labels:* These can be used in the same way as sticky notes. After writing on them, the teacher peels them from the sheet and transfers them to the permanent file.

- *Index cards:* Cards can be taped to a clipboard, one for each child. When a card is full, file it and replace with a new one.

- *Computer:* Some teachers keyboard notes as they observe. Another option is to scan handwritten notes into individual electronic files for each child.

- *Your own method:* You can devise your own method. You need a method that is fast and easy to use; otherwise, you may be tempted to neglect this valuable tool.

> **2/6 Mei**
>
> During buddy reading with kindergartner who is still not speaking English. Did picture walk first and asked for predictions. Is using strategies we use in class. Taking more risks with her own English during buddy reading than she does in our class.

> **2/6 Richie M.**
>
> During DEAR (Drop Everything and Read). Book about frogs. Was clearly puzzled about something on one page, a word or concept. Held place with finger and flipped back through earlier part. AHA! Went back to place that had him stumped and read on.

FIGURE 2.1

Observation Notes from Mrs. Lacy's Second Grade

DIVERSE LEARNERS

Students may behave differently with their special teacher from the way they behave in your classroom. Therefore, you may want to ask a student's special teacher to observe the child in your classroom and share observations with you. For example, a second-language learner may be quite at ease in the bilingual or ESL class but timid in the regular classroom. Everyone who teaches the child should share in both assessment and evaluation.

COMMENTS

No one makes good observations right away. The best way to learn is simply to begin. Observe a child, write a note, and draw a conclusion. Look at your note a week later. Is it still helpful?

You may want an experienced observer to help you. Compare the specificity of what you have noted with that of the "expert." Compare your conclusions.

Don't abandon this tool just because you feel it is cumbersome and unhelpful at first. It is probably the most powerful tool a teacher has.

Interest Inventories

Interest inventories reveal a student's interests, not only in school subjects but also in outside activities. Children who read and write about things that interest them are more highly motivated and are better able to access their existing prior knowledge. These inventories have two major purposes:

- To determine each child's interests
- To plan instruction

DESCRIPTION

Several types of interest inventories have been published over the years. Often these are meant also to assess attitudes. For emergent readers and writers, the teacher may read items aloud and have the children mark pictures that indicate a scale from "I love it" to "I hate it." More competent readers and writers can read the items themselves and respond on a scale or in writing. You can also devise your own interest inventories. (See Figures 2.2 and 2.3 for partial examples.) Using what you learn from interest inventories, you can begin to build your classroom library and also help steer children to appropriate sections in the media center or on the Internet.

Teacher-Read Items
1. On the weekend I like to read comics.
2. My favorite books are about animals.
3. I like true stories best.
4. I like scary stories best.
5. . . . .
6. . . . .

Child's Page

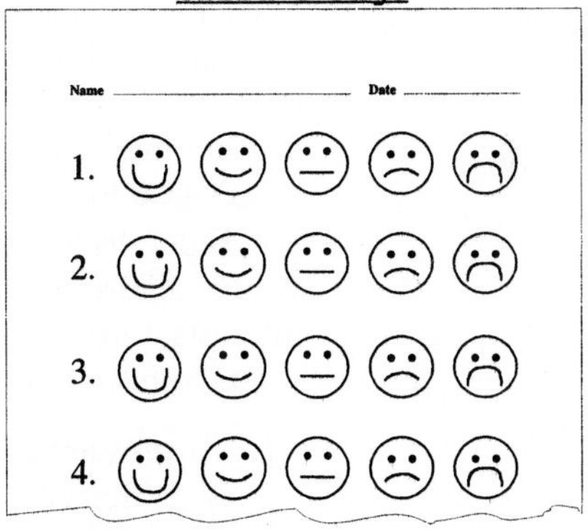

Name _____ Date _____

FIGURE 2.2

Partial Sample of Interest Inventory for Younger Children

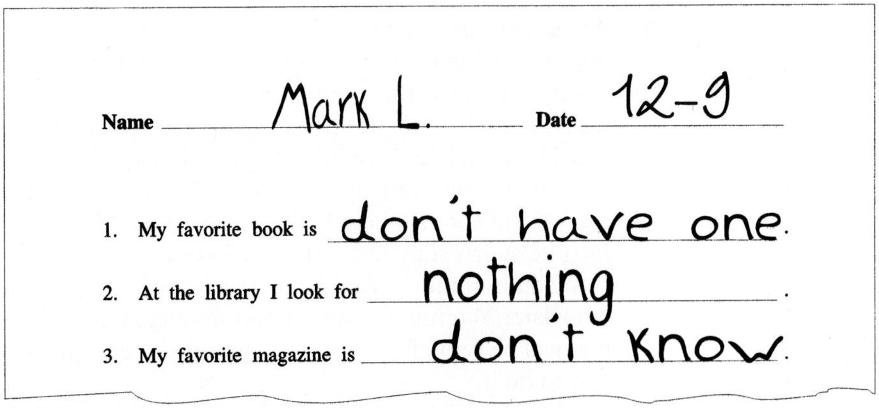

Name ___Mark L.___ Date __12-9__

1. My favorite book is ___don't have one___.
2. At the library I look for ___nothing___.
3. My favorite magazine is ___don't know___.

FIGURE 2.3

Partial Sample of Interest Inventory for Older Children

PROCEDURES AND SAMPLES

If children are to respond on paper by marking pictures or symbols after you read to them, first describe the purpose and procedure briefly. Explain that the activity will help you find out what each child is interested in. Tell students that their interests may be things they already know about or things they have always wanted to learn about. Ask them to be completely honest, as there are no right or wrong answers. Explain that you will read each item to them twice and give them time to decide on a response.

If children are to respond to open-ended items in writing, reassure them that they are free to use any word that is in their heads, spelling it as best they can. The variety of responses you receive can help you make significant discoveries about your students, even when the responses show an obvious reluctance. Look, for example, at the partial responses of an older child shown in Figure 2.3. It seems clear that this student is unwilling to share his interests (though he might be more forthcoming in an interview or a group discussion). He may feel that his interests would not be acceptable to you. He may be revealing a negative attitude or self-concept. Look for signs of interest in anything. Then gather books to share with him. Note his response when you read aloud from a variety of books about a variety of topics. He may want to read for himself the book you have just read, especially if his negative responses are masking his feelings of inadequacy.

What about children who are too young for a written interest inventory? With very young children, responses on published interest inventories may not reflect their true interests. Little children like to please adults and may say what they think their teacher wants to hear. Following are three procedures that are useful for such children:

1. **Interview:** Spend a few minutes alone with each child chatting about his or her interests. Chat as you leaf through picture books or magazines. Questions about how the child spends free time are helpful. Be sure to take notes.

2. **Collage:** Show the children a collage you have made about yourself. Ask the children to look at your collage closely and draw conclusions. They will probably be right on target. Then allow them to make their own collages on construction paper or in file folders. Collages are helpful to show during a family conference.

3. **All-about-me books:** Children construct books with pictures or any other appropriate items, to help others know who they are and what they are interested in. Discuss the purpose of the books with the children, and brainstorm ideas for each page. Besides a page for personal information (appearance, age, and so on) and family items ("Who lives at your house?"), you may have pages such as the following: my favorite thing to do by myself after school, what I'd like to read about, where I'd like to go most in the world, my favorite game, my favorite sports star, or my favorite books.

   Children may create some pages early in the school year and add to the book later. You might scan art and writing attempts into an electronic portfolio that will be kept all year. This technique is very open-ended. There is no wrong way to do it.

4. **My Bag:** Invite students to put items in a bag to represent interests outside of school. These will be clues to help you choose books for the student and plan instruction. (*Reading Today,* Vol. 26, No. 3, December 2008/January 2009, p. 8.)

DIVERSE LEARNERS

Students who are fluent in another language but not yet fluent in English may be unable to reveal the extent of their interests through some of the inventories suggested here. To help them express their interests, look for someone who speaks their language to interpret for them. This might be a bilingual child in your school who is already fluent in English, a family member, or a community member who is fluent in English and willing to spend some time in your classroom.

Pictures can also help you learn about the interests of a student who is not yet fluent in English. For example, gather a group of pictures of different sports and sit with the child. Pick up one picture and indicate through facial expression whether or not you like the sport. Then do another picture, then another. Finally, move the pictures toward the child, and with raised eyebrows, invite the student to choose his or her own favorites. The same simple strategy can be used to learn about such things as favorite foods, games, and leisure activities. This procedure can also be used with other types of diverse learners.

COMMENTS

Don't generalize about children's interests. Model a wide range of interests that are not gender specific. All topics are valid. Whatever a child's interest, there are always things to read and write about it.

Help children become interested in new things by sharing your own interests, reading aloud about a wide range of topics, and inviting children with unique interests to share. You must, however, avoid telling children that they "should" be interested in something.

Attitude/Self-Concept Checks

Attitude/self-concept checks are instruments used for three principal purposes:

- To learn about a child's attitude toward himself or herself (the self-concept)
- To learn a child's attitudes toward school, learning, and literacy
- To plan instruction

DESCRIPTION

Attitude/self-concept checks include those that you administer as well as students' self-evaluations. In addition to observation, you can use checklists, response scales, open-ended interviews, self-reporting, personal journals, and other instruments to gather information.

You can also devise ways to help children assess themselves in terms of their attitude toward a given task and their self-concept related to that task. Sometimes these are worksheets with specific items to be completed. Sometimes this is best done in an open-ended manner, such as in a journal.

```
        Teacher-Read Items
    1.  I am a good writer.
    2.  I make up good stories.
    3.  I am good at helping others
        read.
    4.  . . . . . . . . . . . .
    5.  . . . . . . . . . . . .
```

FIGURE 2.4

Partially Completed Attitude Survey for Children Who Cannot Read Items for Themselves

PROCEDURES AND SAMPLES

Use caution with a scale, checklist, or other instrument on which either you or your students will be responding with writing or some other kind of mark. Be sure children understand the purpose of the assessment. They must know there are no right or wrong answers; you are simply trying to find out how they feel about things. Our examples focus on literacy, but others can easily be devised for any subject.

Sometimes, as you read items aloud, children are either to mark a picture (perhaps from a series of happy to sad faces) or to check the response closest to the way they feel (see Figure 2.4). With such a procedure, be sure there are clear ways for children to keep their places, perhaps with a marker. Remember, some children may not read well, and they may need arrows or symbols so that they don't lose their place on the page.

Tell children not to mark until you have read each item twice. Then state how they are to respond. For example, "If this is exactly how you feel, put an X on the happiest face. If you never feel this way, put an X on the saddest face. If you feel somewhere in between, put an X on the face that is closest to the way you feel most of the time."

Read each item without inflection, expression, or any verbal or facial clue as to which response might please you. Children are very skillful at judging such nonverbal clues.

Children who can read the items themselves may respond by marking a scale of some kind or by writing an open-ended response (see Figure 2.5). In either case, be sure they understand the directions. Allow them to ask for help decoding words, constructing meaning, and framing responses. Spelling is not important here.

In an interview or journal situation or in a self-evaluation, similar principles apply. It is vital that children feel free to respond honestly about their feelings. When students are self-evaluating, you must be sure they understand what they are to evaluate and how to think about it. They must understand that the only self-evaluation worth anything is the honest one. Perhaps most important, they must understand the purpose of such self-evaluation. It may be helpful for you to model how you evaluate yourself in terms of your attitude toward a task.

Figures 2.4 and 2.5 offer two partial samples of instruments you may find helpful. Complete forms of these types can be downloaded from the website. See the Resource File following the last chapter for directions.

Find forms in some of the "For Additional Reading" books on the premium website for this text.

Name ___Tommy_____   Date __2-10_____

1. When I go to the library, I ____am excited_____ .

2. At DEAR time, I ____am bothered by noise___ .

3. When we work in groups, I____feel stupid_____ .

FIGURE 2.5

Partially Completed Attitude Survey on Which Child Reads Stems and Writes Answers

DIVERSE LEARNERS

Cultures vary widely in the ways they define acceptable behavior, and some children may have been taught that modesty and humility are more important traits than overt self-confidence. Some children may be uncomfortable when asked to talk about what they are "good at." If you see a discrepancy between responses on a form such as we've shown and a child's actual performance, you may probe further during a one-on-one conference. Your job is to try to understand the cultures from which the students come and to help all students begin to feel at home in the culture in which they find themselves.

COMMENTS

Attitude/self-concept checks are only samples of how the child felt on a particular day. Some assessments are needed only at the beginning of the year or with a new student.

Be careful not to deny children their feelings. Teachers sometimes respond to a child's comment, such as "I hate reading," by denying it: "Of course you don't hate reading, Susie. Reading is wonderful." Instead, find a way to accept the feeling honestly: " Perhaps you'll change your mind soon." Allowing children to save face is an important boost for their self-concept.

Checklists

A **checklist** is exactly what it seems to be—a list of items with a place to check whether or not each behavior is present at a given time and perhaps to what degree. In literacy assessment, checklists serve three purposes:

- To help you organize your observations or other information you collect about students' performance on given characteristics or items

- To plan instruction
- To compare evidence of behavior over time and thus help you determine students' progress

DESCRIPTION

Checklists generally use symbols of one type or another (for instance, ✔, +, and 0) to note whether a behavior is present or absent. Sometimes the symbols indicate whether or not a trait is present consistently, occasionally, or not at all. At other times the symbols may indicate degree, such as "very effective," "somewhat effective," "not effective," and "not observed."

A checklist may focus on a single area, such as "using the writing process" or even "editing." It may list grade-level-appropriate decoding skills, such as these:

Reads unfamiliar words syllable by syllable

Reads on to use context

Refers to earlier part of book where word first appeared

Uses pictures

Substitutes a syntactically and semantically acceptable word for one he or she can't decode

Find sources for checklists in some of the "For Additional Reading" books on the premium website for this text.

Many published reading/language arts programs provide numerous checklists to help teachers track student performance. Some schools develop checklists based on schoolwide, districtwide, or statewide benchmarks. Some teachers prefer to make up their own checklists so that they exactly match what they want to observe. Benchmark checklists for each of the literacy stages are in Chapters 8 through 12.

Base your choice of which checklist to use on curricular decisions. You might ask yourself:

- What needs to be observed systematically?
- How can it be broken down into items that I can check as the children work independently or in groups?
- How can I word such a checklist so that it provides me with useful information for any one of a variety of purposes: for planning instruction, for sharing with the child, for sharing with families, for grade cards, for comparing my class and each child against my school's (school system's, county's, state's, or nation's) standards?

PROCEDURES AND SAMPLES

Checklists can be used unobtrusively to note whether or not a certain behavior, skill, or ability is present on that day at that time. Tell children that from time to time you may be marking things on a list, and reassure them that this will help you do a better job as their teacher.

Keep the list(s) handy, perhaps on a clipboard. Have a place to file such lists when complete so that you can use them for whatever purpose they were meant to serve.

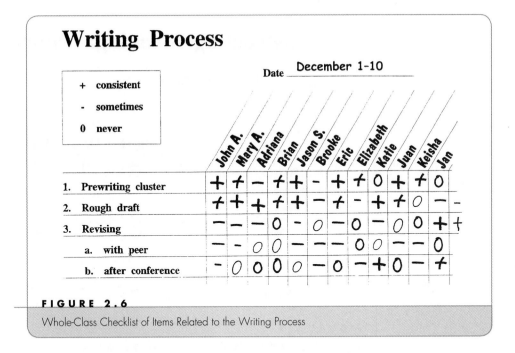

FIGURE 2.6

Whole-Class Checklist of Items Related to the Writing Process

Checklists with items down the side and children's names across the top allow you to check the whole class on a single page (see Figure 2.6). The advantage of this format is that you can see at a glance which areas need attention for the whole class, for a group of children, or for individuals. Look again at Figure 2.6. Revising is a weak area for most of the children listed here. A whole-class lesson should be planned.

Some checklists, in contrast, are intended to track performance of one child on the same task over a period of time, such as a semester or school year (see Figure 2.7). This format allows you to see growth (or lack of growth). This kind of checklist is good to share with families. The checklist in Figure 2.7 shows that Donald was unable to retell a story successfully at the beginning of the year beyond the topic and main character's name. By February, however, he was recalling and retelling most of the significant elements in the story.

DIVERSE LEARNERS

You may want to code class lists in some way to remind yourself about behaviors that may relate to the diversity of the students. For example, if you check participation in a discussion group, note which children may not be participating because they are not confident in their oral language use yet. In such a case, failure to participate may have little to do with the child's understanding of the subject under discussion. You may want to have a private conversation about the topic with the child to allow him or her to speak without the whole class listening.

Constructing Meaning: Story

Name ___Donald___

	Dates				
	9/9	**10/12**	**11/16**	**1/13**	**2/3**
1. Topic	+	+	+	+	+
2. Setting					
Place	–	0	–	+	+
Time	0	0	–	-	+
3. Characters					
Major	+	+	+	+	+
Minor	0	–	–	+	+

FIGURE 2.7

Individual Checklist of Items Related to Constructing Meaning

COMMENTS

Be careful not to attempt so many checklists that you lose sight of their purpose or are unable to use the information to promote literacy growth in your children.

A beginning teacher may want to use checklists that have been found useful by colleagues. With experience, you may devise and revise your own checklists to meet your own purposes.

Items must be specific to be useful. "Retells stories successfully" is not helpful. If any items in the student's retelling are missing or weak, you need to be able to indicate this, so it is probably best to break down the story elements on your list: for instance, Topic or Problem (conflict), Character(s), Setting(s), Significant Events, and Resolution.

Work Samples

Work samples provide evidence of a child's actual work in the classroom and serve three important purposes:

- To look at students' work that results from learning
- To plan instruction
- To compare the level or quality of work over time and thus help you determine students' progress

DESCRIPTION

Samples of authentic work by a student yield direct evidence of performance. These may include everything from spelling tests to projects to published writing.

Such samples are particularly good to share with families. Samples of work collected over a period of time can show a child's growth and allow you, the child, and the family to see clear proof of the child's progress. Work samples may form part of a child's portfolio (to be discussed in Chapter 3) or other file into which you put periodic samples of each child's work.

PROCEDURES AND SAMPLES

Decide what kinds of samples you will collect. This decision will depend on your purpose. For example, if you want to show the child's growth in reading, you might keep a cumulative list of books the child has read, along with written responses to some of them. Figure 2.8 presents such a sample of a student's responses to independent

Name Sam   Date April 20

Book	Date	Comments
1. All About Snakes	9/3	I liked it.
2. Alligators All Around	10/15	It was good.
3. Who Lives in the Forest?	11/29	I learned new stuff.
20. Joe Goes to Work: He Sits Down to Draw	3/6	It was interesting to learn about a cartoonist. I think I'd be good at this, too.

FIGURE 2.8

Samples of a Child's Written Responses to His Independent Reading

Name _Susie_____   Date _10-18___

1. Homework returned: Ⓜ Ⓣ W Th Ⓕ⒭

2. Books returned: (On time)   Late

3. Next week: ____Neighborhoods_____

4. Papers in packet:

    a. _Spelling_____
    b. _Math_____
    c. _Social Studies Test_____

Teacher Comments: _Susie had a good week.___

Parent Comments: _____

FIGURE 2.9

Cover Page for a First-Grade Packet Containing Work Samples

reading. Each of Sam's responses is dated. The growth both in the child's ability to respond to literature and in his interest in reading is clear.

Many teachers collect work samples for each child during the week and send them all home in a large envelope on Friday, along with a letter explaining what's been going on during the week. (Work can be scanned into an electronic file first.) You and the student may decide together which work samples to save to show his or her family how much he or she is growing in literacy. The cover page may also outline future events and activities. It addresses all caregivers and has a place for you to jot a personal note for each family. A checklist of some kind is often included, perhaps tallying how many times homework was completed, how often books were returned on time, or any other information you wish to convey.

If you send a packet home weekly, ensure that the envelope is returned by creating a place for responses and questions. This then becomes a two-way communication between home and school—the beginning of a dialogue. Figure 2.9 presents a sample cover page for a work packet to be sent home.

DIVERSE LEARNERS

It does little good to send home a packet of work with a cover letter in English if the child's family cannot read English. Find out whether anyone in the family knows English or whether there is a friend who can translate. If no one in the family knows English, try to find a community member or other professional who can translate the communications that go home from your class. Such an effort will go a long way toward making a child feel part of your community.

COMMENTS

We believe children should have some say about which samples of work are saved as "evidence." In our classrooms, we have often selected three types of work samples:

Yours: This sample was selected by the student.

Mine: This was a sample we (the teachers) wanted to include.

Ours: This was a sample we and the student agreed together to include.

Selecting samples to save in this way helps students feel more involved in the process.

All work samples should be dated when collected. Even if the products show little improvement over time, you can usually reassure the family (and show evidence) that the child is becoming more comfortable with the process and you expect to see improved products soon.

Look for ways to emphasize progress. For example, a child's spelling scores may still be low, but the nature of the misspellings may show growth. Perhaps Rene's wrong spellings at first reflected random letters, whereas now (though she still makes mistakes) there is clear evidence of her growing ability to connect phonemic segments with letters representing those segments.

These students are speaking informally with their teacher about a book they are reading in a small group.

© Catherine Yeulet/ istockphoto.com

Conferences

The term **conference** in the context of literacy assessment refers to a meeting between the teacher and an individual student to discuss some aspect of the student's work. For the teacher, a conference of this type has five main purposes:

- To provide a time to have direct interaction with one student
- To zero in on specific items or points
- To clarify some particular point
- To plan instruction
- To determine students' progress

DESCRIPTION

When used with a clear purpose in mind, conferences are an essential part of a literacy environment (Calkins, 1994). This section deals with conferences designed specifically for assessment purposes. You might hold only a few conferences on any given day.

The literacy assessment conference is short, about five to ten minutes, and focused on gathering information about the child's literacy status. It may focus on construction of meaning, oral fluency, mechanical skills in writing, attitudes, or any other aspect of literacy. A conference may have several purposes. For example, while assessing oral fluency during a conference, you may also assess the child's attitude toward **risk taking,** or willingness to attempt to read even when not sure of accuracy.

PROCEDURES AND SAMPLES

The following steps apply to any kind of conference:

1. *Explain the purpose and procedure to students.* Role-play to establish behavior during the conference for those who are conferring and for the rest of the class. A chart can remind the class what to do while the teacher is having a conference. Figure 2.10 shows one such chart.

2. *Use a timer.* Conferences should be short—no more than five to ten minutes. Don't have a conference unless you have a valid purpose. The child's (and your) time could be better spent engaged in reading and writing.

3. *Have a chart of reminders for students.* To help children remember what to bring to a conference, post a chart with reminders like this:

   HAVING A CONFERENCE TODAY?

   Bring the following:
   —Your book
   —Your reading journal
   —Your writing folder

TEACHER HAVING CONFERENCES? HERE'S WHAT YOU CAN DO

1. Read to yourself.

2. Read with a partner.

3. Write.

4. Use the computer (check schedule).

5. Go to the library (check schedule).

6. Work on research project.

7. Do any other quiet activity.

DO NOT INTERRUPT EXCEPT FOR EMERGENCIES!

YOU KNOW WHAT THEY ARE!

FIGURE 2.10

Chart Showing Activities Children May Do While the Teacher Is Having a Conference with an Individual

4. *Post a schedule each day.* To help students keep track of who has a conference at what time and where, you can post a schedule:

    LITERACY CONFERENCES TODAY:

WHO	WHEN	WHERE
Jamal	11:15	Round table
Chandra	11:40	Round table
Pete	1:30	Writing corner

    Keep a master chart for yourself so that you don't overlook anyone.

5. *Have a record sheet for each child.* Include a place for the date; the child's name, age, and grade; and notes. You may want to record notes about different areas, such as reading and writing. You may also want to record conclusions about the child's needs. (See Figure 2.11.) A half-sheet may be sufficient for your purpose.

INDIVIDUAL CONFERENCE RECORD SHEET

Name _____ Date _____

Age _____ Grade _____

Purpose of today's conference:

Observations:

Conclusions/Instructional needs:

Goals for future:

FIGURE 2.11

Sample of a Form for Use in Conference

6. *Monitor yourself as you conduct assessment conferences.* You job is to get a notion of what is going on in the child's head, so don't plant ideas, nudge, or give hints. The child must feel free to respond honestly and openly.

7. *End each conference on a positive note.* Ask the child to tell you what he or she feels good about. When you use praise, focus on the work, not the child. Say, "This story was exciting to read," rather than, "You are a good writer."

You will undoubtedly think of other ways to facilitate conferences.

Find forms in some of the "For Additional Reading" books on the premium website for this text.

DIVERSE LEARNERS

You should have individual conferences with every child, even one who does not yet speak English. You might spend the time teaching each other the words for objects in the room or in pictures. Talk informally and naturally, accepting that only a little of what you say may be understood. The student will respond to the attention and your obvious caring attitude.

Students may exhibit cultural differences that puzzle you. For example, you may assume that children should look at adults when they speak, but in some cultures looking an adult in the eye is disrespectful, whereas looking down is a sign of respect. You may be used to patting a child's shoulder, but some children do not accept the touch of others. Some children may not understand when you are laughing *with* them and think you are laughing *at* them. Some children may never want to remove their coats because they have lived in an environment where personal belongings may be stolen if one lets go of them.

You'll need to accept and understand whatever cultural differences a child brings to your class. You and your students need to earn each other's trust.

Children are skilled at drawing teachers off task. Tell the child who does so that you'd love to hear about the new puppy (or whatever the child's enthusiasm may be) at another time, or suggest that the student write about it. Then get back on task.

During assessment conferences, resist the effort to coach the child to the "right answer." Instead, suggest that the child pretend to be alone and talk out loud about what is going on inside his or her head. For some children, you may need to model thinking out loud several times.

Remember that many personal things may impinge on a child's behavior at any given moment. A single assessment conference is only a tiny piece of the whole picture.

Self-Reflections

Self-reflection means thinking about oneself. In literacy assessment, student self-reflection serves these purposes:

- To help you find out how students perceive their own work and how they have performed
- To give you insight into why a particular student feels he or she is having difficulty in a certain area
- To plan instruction

DESCRIPTION

As applied to literacy assessment, self-reflection includes thinking about broad ideas such and "How do I feel about myself as a reader and writer?" For our purposes, self-reflection includes both self-assessment and self-evaluation:

- *Self-assessment* asks questions about process and product, such as
  "What is giving me trouble?"
  "Did I do my part in a group project?"
  "What is my biggest problem in writing a report?"

- *Self-evaluation* seems to put a value on things, asking questions like these:
  "Am I getting better at (a certain task or skill)?"
  "What am I good at?"
  "What still needs work?"

Later in this section, we show you some sample forms you might give students for self-reflection. Many others are possible, of course.

Students may bring written self-reflections with them to conferences, though it is not always necessary. The greatest value of reflection comes during the act itself as students think about their work. Self-reflection should lead students to set their own goals and become more self-directed and independent learners.

MY PERSONAL CHECKLIST FOR STUDYING FOR A TEST

✚ = Done   ✓ = Close, but not quite   0 = Not done

Study Steps	Teacher Think-Aloud
✓ 1. Read chapter when first assigned.	*I used to wait to read the chapter until after the teacher had discussed it. I couldn't participate in the class discussion and I was always behind. This time I began reading on time but didn't finish.*
✓ 2. Make a K-W-L chart.	*For the last chapter I just began reading. This time, I tried to use a K-W-L chart to give me a purpose for reading. It helped, but I didn't think up "What I Want to Know" questions that fit the chapter. I need to get better at this or use a different strategy.*
✓ 3. Use sticky notes to mark major ideas.	*I can't mark in the book, so I used to try to remember the important parts or write them all down as I went along. Now I use sticky notes. Sometimes I find that an idea I put a note beside as I read is better stated later in the chapter and I can simply remove the note. I don't get so bogged down this way. I still need to work on using too many notes. Sometimes I can't tell an important idea that might be tested from one I just find interesting.*
✚ 4. Write vocabulary/ concepts on cards.	*Last time I tried to study by flipping back and forth from the page to the glossary. Putting important terms on cards with definitions on the back made it easier to review them for the test.*
✚ 5. Summarize sections in my head as I read.	*Last time I thought that if I understood each section as I read, that would be enough to do well on the test. That was not bad for multiple-choice questions, but not good enough for essay questions.*
✓ 6. Summarize in writing.	*I never used to write as I studied. This time I tried to take the time to write my summarizations when I reread. Writing forced me to organize my thoughts and use the vocabulary. I didn't start this soon enough, though, and didn't get all the way through the chapter.*
✓ 7. Feel prepared for test.	*On the day of the last test I felt worried even though I had studied. At least I had read the chapter and understood it. This time I was much more confident.*
✓ 8. Get a B or higher on test.	*I got a C last time! This time I got a B+!* *I have improved in my ability to prepare for a test. And it feels good not to be scared on the day of the test. I found out I liked the subject more than before. I guess when you really work to understand something, you like it more. Next time I'll try to have a plus on every item in my list, and maybe I can get an A. Also, I need to revise my checklist. I forgot to read the end-of-chapter summary first, and I forgot to use subheadings to help me predict.*

FIGURE 2.12

Modeling of One Teacher's Self-Reflection Process for the Fifth Grade

PROCEDURES AND SAMPLES

The following steps will help you get started with the process of having children reflect honestly about their own literacy:

1. *Model the process.* For example, you might share your own strategies when studying for a test and how you have evaluated yourself in terms of using those strategies. Imagine, for instance, that you are currently taking a science course to bolster your teaching in that area. You might compare your self-evaluation from an earlier study session with a recent one. You could explain what you learned about yourself from the process and how it will direct your literacy in the future.

    Figure 2.12 presents an example of a teacher's own study checklist, along with a **think-aloud** commentary used to model self-reflection for fifth graders. You can adapt this process as necessary to allow you to use your personal self-reflections as a model for your students.

2. *Begin with just one simple form* (see Figures 2.13 and 2.14). For example, ask children to rate themselves in two or three areas and respond in writing to some questions. When you think children are comfortable with the process, you may

Self-Reflection — Literature Group

Name _____ Date _____

Title of Book _____

Author _____

Illustrator _____

Use the scale for each of the following:

(Scale: 5 = Wonderful, 4 = Pretty good, 3 = Okay, 2 = Not so good, 1 = Ooops)

How I felt about the book   _____

How well I read the book   _____

My part in discussion circles   _____

My journal response during the reading of the book   _____

Write about your literature discussion group. What is the best part? What is the worst? How would you change it? How would you change the way you participate?

_____

_____

_____

FIGURE 2.13

Form for Children to Use After Reading a Book and Participating in a Literature Discussion Circle

Self-Reflection — Independent Reading

Name _____ Date _____

Title and Author _____

Mark the scales:

1. How I felt about the book:

             Loved it   Okay   Didn't like it

    Explain your marking _____

    _____

    _____

2. I understood the ideas:

             Mostly   Some   Not much

    Explain your marking _____

    _____

    _____

What else would you like to say about reading this book?

_____

_____

FIGURE 2.14

Form for Children to Use After Independent Reading

want to introduce a more complicated form or additional forms for other areas (see Figure 2.15). Obviously, with very young children the process will be much less complicated. You are building a habit of self-reflection, something that does not come easily to many people.

3. *Encourage oral self-reflection as part of literature discussions and conferences.* Model such thinking yourself. For example, you might comment during a discussion that Linda gave you a whole new way of thinking about a story you thought you knew very well.

4. *Ask children to file self-evaluations in their folders and bring them to conferences.* At the conferences, discuss these self-evaluations with the students, asking questions to help them think more about their own literacy.

The form shown in Figure 2.15 can be adapted in many ways. For example, for nonfiction you might want to specify prereading behaviors related to whatever you have been teaching, such as examining graphics or making a K-W-L chart. Among the strategies to use during reading, you might want to specify summarizing at the

THINKING ABOUT MY READING

Name _____   Date _____

Title and Author of Book _____

_____

	All the time	Sometimes	Hardly ever
Before reading, did I			
* Preview the book			
* Predict			
During reading, did I			
* Stop and think			
* Change predictions			
After reading, did I			
* Retell to myself			
* Respond			

What do I need to do better? _____

_____

FIGURE 2.15

Student Self-Monitoring Checklist

end of each subsection, jotting down unfamiliar terms. Strategies for use after reading could include returning to the K-W-L chart.

Complete versions of the forms shown in Figures 2.13 to 2.15 can be found on line at the website for this text.

DIVERSE LEARNERS

Students from some cultures (but certainly not all) may find it difficult to admit they perceive themselves as good at anything. Try to find ways to allow them to express honest self-evaluations. For example, very young children might choose a badge that shows how they feel about themselves that day.

Encourage appraisal that focuses on the work. Begin with simple statements, for example, "I wrote a good sentence today" or "I finished ten math problems." Help students begin to feel comfortable telling at least one positive thing about their school experience each day.

Help students focus on something specific they can do to help themselves improve the quality of their work. For example, instead of "I need to work harder," which is too general, say, "I need to learn how to narrow my topic to something I can handle in depth."

If a second-language learner is not yet comfortable writing in English, encourage the student to write in whatever language she or he chooses—the value is in the writing, not in whether or not you can read it. Gradually, English words will appear.

C O M M E N T S

Self-evaluation involves **metacognition**—knowledge and control of one's own thinking and learning—and is not easy for any of us, especially for young children. However, this is an important part of the learning process, especially the process of learning to read, write, and become literate (Brown, 1980).

Be sure children understand the purpose of self-reflection. While your goal is to promote this kind of reflection independent of assigning it, overuse can have exactly the opposite effect.

Children will feel free to be honest only if you have established an environment based on trust and risk-taking. Once students feel comfortable with the thinking process and with responding openly both orally and in writing, consider involving them in devising appropriate self-reflection forms. For example, at the beginning of a collaborative project, children can work with you to decide how to evaluate the project, the group, and themselves as members of the group.

Performance Assessments

A **performance assessment** is based on a particular task performed by the student and serves three basic purposes:

- To see how well students apply what they are learning in real-world situations
- To determine students' progress
- To plan instruction

DESCRIPTION

Performance assessments involve authentic, real-world tasks that demonstrate a student's literacy knowledge and skill. Often they are part of ongoing instructional activities. Examples include posters, plays, oral or written reports, construction projects, and graphic support of scientific experiments.

PROCEDURES AND SAMPLES

Each performance assessment will be different and will depend on the specific items to be assessed. Here are some general criteria to follow in using any performance assessment:

1. *Identify the strategies, skills, and knowledge the task will demand.* Some of these may have been previously taught and are presumed to have been mastered. Others may be items you plan to teach prior to students' actually performing the task.

2. *Devise a task that requires the use of these strategies, skills, and knowledge.* You may devise the task yourself, or you may work in collaboration with your students.

3. *Develop a rubric to evaluate the performance task.* **Rubrics** are sets of guidelines or scoring guides and criteria for determining that a student has learned or accomplished something. Rubrics often include examples of acceptable responses or give

several sample responses that show the degree to which an individual has attained something. For example, rubrics for writing often present three or four sample papers to show the varying degrees to which an individual has learned to do some type of writing. These sample papers are called **anchor papers,** because they give a point of reference to "anchor" the decision about the student's degree of success.

You may elicit the help of your students in developing your rubric. Each objective identified should be judged as having been met or not met and, perhaps, to what degree. If you enter "rubrics" in a search engine such as Google, you will find links to numerous websites.

4. *Share the rubric with all students as the task begins.* Be sure students understand each part of the rubric. Encourage them to refer to it as they complete the task. Examples of writing rubrics appear in Chapter 11.

5. *Invite students to use the rubric to evaluate themselves independently.* Compare their results with your own. Collaboratively, decide which unachieved items were the result of a need for further instruction or reteaching (something for you to do). Alternatively, help students decide which items might have been achieved with more effort, better organization, and willingness to ask for help when needed (something for them to do).

The partial rubric shown in Figure 2.16 was used for assessing Ms. Leonard's culminating activity for a fourth-grade social studies unit that grew from the state social studies curriculum framework. The overarching concept was that prejudice affects behavior and has far-reaching consequences.

To begin, Ms. Leonard identified some of the literacy strategies the children needed to research and prepare a culminating presentation. These included doing research in the media center, using the Internet, posing questions and framing tentative answers, synthesizing information, identifying significant information, distinguishing fact from opinion, presenting data in logical form both in writing and orally, and using visual aids. If other curricular areas, such as math and music, were also included in this unit, each area might have items on the rubric.

Ms. Leonard had taught lessons on the appropriate skills and strategies before launching this unit, and she continued the lessons as the unit progressed over three weeks. The children were allowed to choose among several projects as possible culminating performances. Together with the children, Ms. Leonard developed a rubric for assessing each type of project that described each level of performance achievement. The children had copies of the rubric available as they prepared their projects so that they could assess themselves as they worked. Ms. Leonard also encouraged them to log their actions as they worked. Students can use the rubric to assess their projects, and Ms. Leonard can compare their assessments with her own.

DIVERSE LEARNERS

You may find it difficult to impose the same rubrics on the work of every student. Group projects are useful because they allow you to mix students of varying abilities and competence. The students can work on a common goal, with each individual contributing whatever he or she can best do to the whole. For example, students who are not yet fluent in English might contribute graphics or music to a report. Each student might then be assessed twice. One assessment, of the whole product, would

PROJECT RUBRIC: SOCIAL STUDIES UNIT

Name _____ Date _____

Unit _____ Project _____

Other Members of the Group _____

_____

Scale: O = Outstanding, P = Pretty good, B = Beginning, N = Not yet

Task		Achievement
1. Gather information	O	Several print sources, Internet; synthesized, analyzed
	P	Several sources, information not synthesized, no conclusions
	B	Only one or two sources
	N	Only one source

FIGURE 2.16

Partial Rubric for a Fourth-Grade Culminating Activity

be the same for every student in the group. A second assessment might be based on your (and the student's) perception of individual participation. This second assessment would allow for the diversity in the group.

C O M M E N T S

Performance assessments can be **summative;** that is, they can be used to derive a grade for a project. For example, each level of skill used to complete a project may be associated with a letter grade: the most competent performance might earn an A, a slightly lesser performance a B, and so on to the lowest possible grade.

Performance assessments can also be **formative,** yielding information you can use to meet the needs both of individual students and of your class as a whole. If you find that students score low on certain items on your rubric, it may be because you need to reteach, or teach differently, some of the strategies and skills.

Not every project needs to be assessed with the specificity of a rubric. Sometimes a project may be assessed with a simple pass/fail standard. You don't want students working hard on projects only because of the payoff. You want them to discover the pleasure of pursuing an interest and sharing it with others.

Summary

- A variety of tools can be used as part of literacy assessment. In observing, you watch students closely while they are engaged in a particular task and you record anecdotal notes—as specific as possible—about what you see.

- Interest inventories help you identify materials and plan instructional activities that keep students involved and motivated. These inventories range from published pencil-and-paper measures to collages and all-about-me books.

- Attitude/self-concept checks are similarly varied. Sometimes they take the form of a student's own reflections in a journal. Often, however, they involve a form on which the student marks a choice or writes responses. Whatever the format, these checks can help you determine a child's attitudes toward school, toward learning, and toward himself or herself.

- Checklists are lists of items that allow you to mark whether a behavior is present or absent and (often) to what degree. With such a device, you can make a quick record of what you observe during a particular activity. Checklists may be designed for use with an entire class or with a single student.

- Work samples are collections of a particular student's work. You can use them to gauge the child's progress over time and to serve as a basis for discussion with the student and his or her family. Often you will want to involve students in the process of deciding which work samples to save.

- Conferences, as discussed in this chapter, are short conversations between a teacher and an individual student to discuss some aspect of the student's work. Though they last only five to ten minutes, they provide invaluable information about a child's literacy status.

- Self-reflections consist of a student's own thoughts about his or her progress. They may involve either self-assessment (thoughts about process and product, such as "What is giving me trouble?") or self-evaluation (value judgments, such as "Am I getting better?"). Even with young children, you can encourage the process of self-reflection by beginning with simple questions and modeling the process yourself.

- Finally, performance assessments involve authentic tasks that demonstrate a student's literacy knowledge and skill. These assessments can be summative (used to derive a grade) or formative (used to judge student progress and guide your further teaching). To assess each type of performance, you use a specific rubric designed for that purpose.

- These tools will be helpful in assessing all students, no matter how diverse. Each is likely to be part of your literacy assessment at one time or another. Every teacher needs to command a variety of assessment options.

- Chapters 8 through 12 will help you decide which tools to use and when. You will also learn how to use assessment to plan and carry out instruction. We can give you tools and techniques, but you must make informed choices.

 Please visit the premium website for *Literacy Assessment*, Fourth Edition to access the TeachSource Video Cases, chapter web links, For Additional Reading, tutorial quizzes, glossary flashcards, online checklists, downloads, and much more! Go to www.cengage.com/login to register your access code.

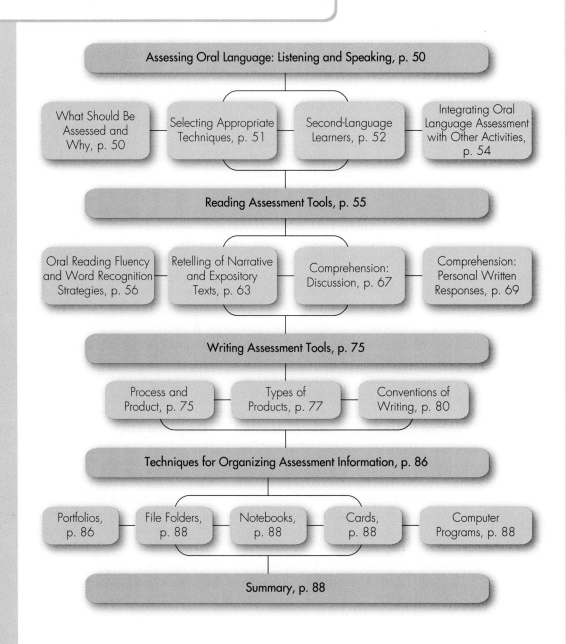

3

Specific Literacy Assessment

NEW TERMS

- aesthetic listening
- alphabetic principle
- conventional stage
- critical listening
- efferent listening
- expository text
- fluency
- functions of language
- grade-level
- graphophonic cues
- holistic scoring
- inter-rater reliability
- learning logs
- miscue
- morphology
- narrative text
- phonemic awareness
- phonetic stage
- phonics
- portfolio
- precommunicative stage
- retelling
- running record
- self-correction
- semantic
- semiphonetic stage
- story maps
- summarizing
- syntactic
- transitional stage

It is first thing in the morning, and Jim Edwards's fourth graders are just arriving. The desks are arranged in groups of six. The children settle into their places and take out their journals. A suggested journal topic is on the board, but many children have chosen their own topic.

As the children finish journaling, they put their journals into a milk crate near Mr. Edwards's desk. Then they take out their writing folders, which are in containers on each group of desks. While the children are writing, Mr. Edwards responds to a few journals, commenting only on content, not mechanics. His written comments are almost a dialogue with each child.

(If we followed Mr. Edwards over the course of a week, we would see him respond in writing to every child's journal at least once. Usually, he reads two or three journal entries as students move into the next activity. Some he reads outside of school hours.)

Mr. Edwards then circulates among his students as they work on the writing in their individual folders. A bilingual volunteer has arrived; he confers with Mr. Edwards and then pulls up a chair beside one student. The children are at various stages of the writing process. Some are doing prewriting activities such as making semantic webs about their topics or brainstorming a list of ideas for topics. Some are writing first drafts. Some are conferencing with a peer, who suggests revisions to make the writing clearer and initials the draft when the conference is over. Some students are revising. Some are doing final editing, checking spelling with hand-held spell checkers and looking at capitalization and punctuation. A couple of students are at the computers to input final drafts from their final edited revisions. The child who is being assisted by the bilingual volunteer is doing his first draft in Spanish; then, together, they will rewrite in English at the computer.

When writing time is over, the children break into literature groups. One group is reading *Spiders* (Bishop, 2007). Mr. Edwards sits in on this discussion. Several times during the discussion, he marks a checklist on a clipboard. He participates in the discussion occasionally, but only as another reader, not as the leader.

In the afternoon, Alison gives an oral report on penguins. She has used a variety of research sources, including a CD-ROM and DVD. She speaks from notes and uses a chart on an easel. (She is also working on a PowerPoint presentation, she tells us, but it isn't finished yet. She and Mr. Edwards are both learning how to do this.) The rest of the class listens attentively and asks questions when she is finished. The questions are relevant, and Alison is able to answer some, but not all, of them. Those she can't answer she makes a note about. She tells the questioner she will try to find the answer later and suggests they search the Internet together.

Mr. Edwards is assessing his students and monitoring their progress all day long, and he knows how what he learned today will affect his instructional plans for the future.

In Chapter 2, you learned about some tools that are useful in assessing most curricular areas, as well as affective factors such as interests and attitudes. In this chapter, we introduce assessment tools specific to literacy: listening and speaking, reading, and writing, as well as some ways to organize information. In Chapter 4, we present ways to assess the reading levels of students and the difficulty level of materials, and in Chapters 8 through 12, we link assessment to instruction.

Assessing Oral Language: Listening and Speaking

We believe that you, the classroom teacher, should closely observe each child's natural, everyday use of listening and speaking (Resnick & Snow, 2009). Your first job is to decide what you need to know and why. Then you must devise ways to assess each child in terms of what you need to know.

If you use school-developed standards and sample indicators, what you learn in this chapter will help you. If your school does not have adequate indicators and checklists, you can use what you read here and in Part Two to make up your own assessment instruments.

We do not discuss hearing or articulation problems per se. If you have a child with such a problem in your class, you must document the difficulty and refer the child for possible special help. Listening comprehension is discussed in Chapter 4 in connection with informal reading inventories.

What Should Be Assessed and Why

For purposes of discussion, we look at listening and speaking separately, though they are closely interrelated. You will often assess both as you assess reading and writing.

LISTENING

Each aspect of listening also applies to reading. Children who cannot do these things while listening will undoubtedly have difficulty when trying to do them while reading—or writing. There are three main kinds of listening:

1. **Aesthetic listening** refers to listening for pleasure, as we do when we listen to a story, a play, or a television sitcom. Aesthetic listening can be divided into subcategories: listening to relate to a personal experience, to retell, to predict, to enjoy the sounds of language, to detect nuance, or to recognize literary style.

2. **Efferent listening** refers to listening for the purpose of learning. Some subcategories are: ability to note sequence, to compare and contrast, and to summarize material one has listened to.

3. **Critical listening** involves making judgments. Some subcategories are: to detect bias, to recognize persuasive techniques, to synthesize with prior knowledge, and to recognize the validity of a source.

Listening is not the same as "paying attention." A child can listen well without looking at you. Conversely, a child can look at you with seemingly rapt attention and be daydreaming rather than listening. A child may listen to you explain something and immediately ask you to repeat it just for him or her. Usually, this is not because the child didn't listen, or didn't understand; more likely, it is due to a lack of self-confidence. If you feel a child isn't listening, it may be that something else is going on: a need for attention, a negative attitude, or distractions on the child's desk, in the classroom, or outside.

On the other hand, a child may pay close attention but not understand what is being said. Such a child might have auditory memory problems. Or perhaps the child gets distracted as you talk. For example, in the first chapter of *Anastasia Krupnik* (Lowry, 1979), when Anastasia's teacher begins to explain an assignment on poetry, Anastasia stops listening to the teacher and begins listening to the words in her own head about a poem she wants to write. So, be careful about drawing hasty conclusions based on flimsy evidence.

SPEAKING

Speaking includes all the kinds of talk in which children may engage, such as conversations, show-and-tell, oral reports, debates, discussions, storytelling, questioning, interviews, role playing, readers' theater, and video.

Another way to look at speaking is in terms of how successfully a child uses the language. You may know these as the seven **functions of language** (Halliday, 1975), and they apply to written as well as oral language:

1. *Instrumental:* conversations, satisfying a need
2. *Regulatory:* directions, rules, gestures
3. *Interactional:* conversations, discussions, sharing
4. *Personal:* show-and-tell, debates, discussions
5. *Imaginative:* dramatic play, storytelling
6. *Heuristic:* interviews, seeking of information
7. *Informative:* reporting, telling, discussing, conveying information

Children begin learning all of these functions very early in life. The functions are not a prescription for what should be taught; rather, they are descriptive—how children (and adults) use language. If you have children who seem to struggle with one or more of the functions of language, you may provide activities to help them become more comfortable.

Selecting Appropriate Techniques

Almost everything you do in the normal course of a day in the classroom affords opportunity for assessment of oral language. A number of the tools mentioned in Chapter 2 are especially useful; here are a few suggestions for applying them.

Observation. Watch and listen to your students. Note growth, but also observe any problems in usage, nonstandard English, failure to express ideas, and inability to follow directions. Your anecdotal records about reading and writing should also include what you observe about each child's speaking and listening skills.

Checklists. Checklists can be made for almost anything you want to assess. List what you expect to see, and check whether it is present when you observe. For example, if you have read a book aloud to your class, you can use a checklist to note whether students were able to listen aesthetically. During a story retelling or a book talk, you might use a checklist to be sure the child followed the agreed-on format: giving an introduction, naming the book and author, telling the story elements, using story language, using gestures, and so forth. During a discussion, you might use a checklist to assess whether children are listening to one another (you know they are if they respond to the content of one another's comments), sharing, taking turns, being courteous to each other, and exhibiting other aspects of talking and listening appropriate to a discussion.

Conferences. Whatever the primary purpose of a conference, this is a perfect time to note listening and speaking behaviors. You and the child are talking one on one.

Second-Language Learners

In our diverse society, an increasing number of children come to school not yet speaking English or not yet fluent in English (Opitz & Harding-DeKam, 2007). These children have a wide range of possible histories, of which the following are only a few:

1. The child may have been born in the United States but into a household where no English is spoken.

2. The child may have been born in another country. The family may have come to this country for a variety of reasons: refuge from war or other extreme hardship, a desire to pursue a better life, or a desire to live here temporarily with the goal of returning home within a few years.

3. The child may already be a reader and writer in another language or in several other languages.

4. The child may not yet be a reader or writer in any language.

5. The child may live in a family that wants to promote bilingualism at home, or the child may need to switch from learning in English at school to speaking his or her native language at home.

Despite some commonalities about students who are acquiring English, each is unique. Any time we give a name to a group of kids, we are in danger of failing to see them as individuals.

At one time, these students were labeled LEP, which stood for "limited English proficiency." Current terms are more positive: "students acquiring English" or "English-language learners" (ELLs). Labels for programs have included ESL (English as a Second Language) and ESOL (English for Speakers of Other Languages).

We will give you only some basic information about assessing ELLs or students acquiring English; you should also read periodicals and consult specialists in your school. The issue of how best to meet the needs of these students is far from settled, nor is this book a forum for a discussion of this topic.

LEVELS OF LANGUAGE PRODUCTION

The following are widely accepted stages of language production that students go through as they acquire English (Krashen & Terrell, 1983). *Production* in this sense refers to speaking, whereas *reception* means listening.

1. *Preproduction:* As students begin to acquire English, they may not speak much. This stage is often referred to as the *silent period.* This is a natural stage; the child's lack of spoken response is not laziness or stubbornness but quite normal. In a supportive environment, the child will eventually begin to speak. You may elicit a response by asking students to point to a picture, draw a picture, or hold up a yes/no card. From the beginning, children should be encouraged to use one another's names when responding.

2. *Early production:* When the child begins to respond orally, it is often with one- or two-word answers. The child's receptive (listening) ability is usually ahead of his or her productive (speaking) ability. First responses may include only the key words, omitting articles, verb endings, inflections, adjectives, and adverbs. The wise teacher accepts these efforts with pleasure, perhaps elaborating on what the child has said. Either/or questions can be helpful because they give the child the words necessary to answer appropriately and demonstrate comprehension.

3. *Speech emergence:* At this stage, the child uses phrases or short sentences, though these are still incomplete and often nonstandard. We never know what is happening inside a child's head. Some talk may sound quite natural, as though the child is thinking in English. At other times, the child may still be thinking in his or her first language and attempting to translate into English. If you have ever learned a second language yourself, you'll recognize these attempts.

4. *Intermediate fluency:* After some time (a few months or a year), a student may be close in functioning to others of the same age or grade, though still building receptive vocabulary. True fluency may take several years (Cummins, 1996). Actually, we all continue to build receptive vocabularies throughout our lives. That is, we hear (or read) words we have never heard or read before—or at least we aren't aware that we have. As we continue to hear or see the word, it acquires meaning for us. Eventually we feel secure enough to try using the word in conversation and in writing. If others understand us, we continue to use it. The word has become a part of our vocabulary.

USING A CHECKLIST TO MEASURE LEVELS OF LANGUAGE PRODUCTION

Your school system may have checklists designed for measuring a child's stage in language production. When a child is first registered for school, staff members often determine whether English is spoken in the home as a first language and, if not, what language is spoken. On the basis of that information, a specialist does an assessment to determine what level of help the child might need and how the school might best provide it. The child may be placed with special teachers for some or even most of the day but may participate in your classroom for the opening of the day, for special classes, for lunch, and for recess.

You may devise your own checklist for the levels of language production. You may also devise a checklist to use informally during discussions so that you can sample the child's language use at regular intervals over time. You, the child, and the family will be able to see how the child is growing in English usage. Most reading programs address the needs of students acquiring English and will provide many specific ways to include these children in your classroom language and reading activities.

Integrating Oral Language Assessment with Other Activities

The listening and speaking that children do in the classroom (aside from social use) should be related to curriculum; you do not need to devise special tasks for assessment. Children will use both listening and speaking all day long as they engage in activities related to their regular subjects. Many teachers and students cooperatively draw up guidelines that can be posted in the classroom and revised as the year goes on. Here is one set of guidelines suggested by third graders:

HOW TO HAVE A GOOD DISCUSSION

- Don't interrupt.
- Stick to the topic.
- Talk loud enough.
- Call people by name.
- Listen to other ideas.
- Don't argue.
- Don't hurt anyone's feelings.
- If one person hasn't said anything, ask what he or she thinks.

You can assess many things during classroom instructional activities. For example, in Mr. Edwards's class described at the beginning of this chapter, Alison was giving an oral report on penguins. The following areas of literacy could be assessed; undoubtedly there are more.

LISTENING

- Efferent listening by Alison (in preparing her report, she listened to the audio portion of a CD-ROM and a DVD)
- Efferent listening by the class (to the report)

SPEAKING

- Alison's use of the informative function of speech
- Her presentation skills
- Her ability to synthesize

Alison gives an oral report to her class.

© Elizabeth Crews/ The Image Works

- Her ability to engage her audience
- The class's questioning after the presentation

READING

- Alison's efferent reading (she read many sources to learn information)
- Her ability to synthesize those sources
- Her ability to read information on websites

WRITING

- Alison's prewriting: generating ideas, selecting a topic
- Her note taking (from the many sources)
- Her outlining of the presentation

Reading Assessment Tools

In this section, we discuss reading assessment that is directly tied to making instructional decisions and yielding information that can be shared with the student and his or her family. Other kinds of assessment, such as determining student reading levels with an informal reading inventory, readability, and assessments tied to published reading programs or to local or state standards, will be discussed in Chapters 4 and 5.

We address four areas of reading assessment: 1) oral reading fluency and word recognition strategies, 2) retelling of narrative and expository texts, 3) comprehension as shown by discussion, and 4) comprehension evidenced in personal written responses. Further information is threaded throughout Chapters 8 through 12.

Oral Reading Fluency and Word Recognition Strategies

Fluency in oral reading means the ability to read aloud words of connected text smoothly and accurately (National Reading Panel, 2000). Often fluency is described as rate of reading and accuracy. Along with fluency itself, a useful assessment considers the strategies the child is using to recognize words. Overall, the techniques described in this section serve eight main purposes:

- To infer the child's fluency when he or she is reading either unfamiliar or familiar text
- To infer the child's use of strategies to figure out unfamiliar words
- To assess the quality of oral reading (for instance, good inflection versus word-by-word reading)
- To judge whether a child reads fluently in **grade-level** materials (for instance, whether a second-grade child reads a second-grade book)
- To judge whether a child reads with similar fluency regardless of genre
- To note the child's attitude, self-concept, and risk-taking behaviors
- To use individual results to plan instruction
- To determine student progress and share this information with the child and family

For a more complete discussion of fluency, see *The Struggling Reader,* Chapter 6 (Cooper, Chard, & Kiger, 2006).

DESCRIPTION

The first step in assessing a child's oral reading fluency and use of strategies involves having the child read a book or selection to you. As the student reads, you keep a record on a piece of paper indicating both the words read correctly and the **miscues** (mismatches or errors). Several recording systems are available. Each system is somewhat different, though all provide a way to know what the child said while reading. Figure 3.1 shows one useful coding system; see Goodman and Watson (1987) for another.

Later you can examine your record of the child's miscues to determine their acceptability in both **semantic** (meaning) and **syntactic** (word order) respects. You can also look at how similar a miscue is to the text in terms of letters or sounds. This helps you infer which strategies a child is or is not using.

Clay (2000) calls this kind of fluency assessment a **running record.** As a part of the Reading Recovery Program (which requires special training), running records may be taken for a book introduced on the previous day (and so is somewhat familiar), or with new material. However, the concept of "taking a record" of oral reading may be applied in many other situations with different kinds of text and different purposes.

- **Substitution:** Write what the child said instead of the correct word; if what is said is not a real word, write the best phonetic representation you can.

penny ←(what child said)

pony ←(word in text)

- **Omission:** Write the word and circle it.

daylight

- **Self-correction:** Put **SC** next to the substitution or omission.

SC ←(indicates child corrected self)

penny ←(what child said)

pony ←(word in text)

- **Teacher-pronounced:** Write the word and put **T** above it.

happiness T

FIGURE 3.1

One Possible Coding System for Oral Reading

Some teachers regularly take a fluency record of whatever book a child is currently reading independently and use the results to plan minilessons for individuals, small groups, or the whole class. Other teachers take running records from whatever book the class (or group) is currently reading to judge whether the difficulty level seems appropriate for each child.

Some teachers use passages from unfamiliar books or from published informal reading inventories. They assess each child with the passage designated at his or her current grade level and judge whether the child is below, on, or above grade level—a practice that implies an acceptance of the concept of a text's "readability," discussed in some detail in Chapter 4. Some teachers use an assessment that bases the running records on a collection of small books of various difficulty levels; for example, the *Developmental Reading Assessment* (Beaver, 2002), which acknowledges the prior work of Clay, has been widely field-tested. We will discuss these concepts and instruments further in Chapter 5.

Some teachers like to take two running records: one on material with which the child is familiar and another on unfamiliar material. Another choice also involves two running records: one on **narrative** material (a story) and one on **expository text** (information). The procedures for taking the running record are the same regardless of your purpose or choice of material.

PROCEDURES AND SAMPLES

The procedure that follows incorporates ideas from many sources; there is no one right way to code oral reading. The point is to code in such a way that it will be clear later. Although it takes practice, anybody can learn to do it, including aides and volunteers. However, conclusions and inferences should be left to the teacher.

Besides actual reading, certain aspects such as fluency, attitude, self-concept, and style of reading (with good inflection or word by word and labored) may be noted while taking a running record. If others take the running records, teach them to note behaviors and attitudes. A tape recording of the child's reading may also be helpful.

A Suggested Procedure. Here is the procedure we suggest for assessing oral reading fluency and word recognition strategies:

1. Choose a book or selection (or have the child choose). The sample should have about one hundred words.

2. Sit where you will not be disturbed for a few minutes. You will need a piece of paper. A form such as the one shown in Figure 3.2 helps, but any lined paper will do. Record the child's name, the date, and the selection title and pages. Sit beside the child so that you can see the text as she or he reads, or make a copy of the text for yourself.

3. Until children are accustomed to the procedure, reassure them about its purpose. You want a sample of how the child reads when there is no one to coach him or her, so resist your natural inclination to teach as you take a running record. If the child simply balks at an unknown word and refuses to go on, tell him or her the word and mark it *T (teacher-pronounced)*.

4. As the child reads, keep track of accuracy line-by-line and write a check mark for each word read correctly. Record the starting and stopping times for the reading.

5. At the same time, if a child miscues (makes an error) or leaves out a word, record the type of error using the coding system presented in Figure 3.1 (or whatever other system you are comfortable with). Figure 3.2 shows an example of a coded record sheet for a book with one line of text per page.

6. Calculate the correct percentage of words by dividing the total number of words read correctly by the number of words in the sample and multiplying by 100:

$$\frac{\text{Total Words Read Correctly}}{\text{Number of Words in Sample}} \times 100 = \underline{\hspace{2em}}\% \text{ Accuracy}$$

For example, the record sheet in Figure 3.2 shows 81 correct words out of a possible 85, which works out to 95 percent:

$$\frac{81}{85} \times 100 = 95\% \text{ Accuracy}$$

Note that in this system, a **self-correction**—a child's spontaneous recognition and correction of a miscue—is counted as correct.

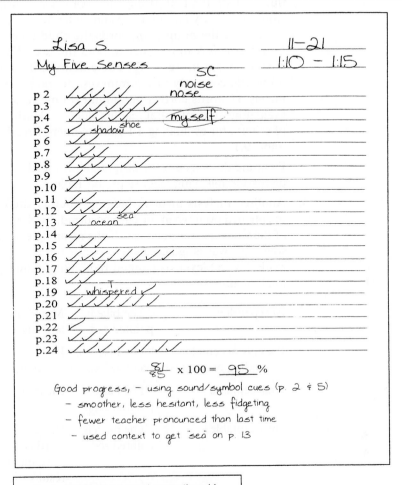

FIGURE 3.2

Partial Marked Form of a Running Record

A score above 90 percent is usually considered acceptable. A score below 90 percent indicates that the material is probably too difficult for the child to read without strong teacher support. If the child scores above 94 percent, you probably won't have learned much about the child's use of strategies and may want to choose a more challenging passage.

7. The time it took the child to read the text is important in determining the rate aspect of fluency. If the child read smoothly and quickly, he or she shows

fluency with the text. If the child read very slowly, he or she may be calling words accurately but not be reading fluently.

Divide the number of words the child read correctly by the number of minutes it took him or her to read the text. This will give you the words-correct-per-minute score. For example, if Mark, a second grader, read 93 words correctly in 2½ minutes, his rate of reading would be approximately 37 words correct per minute. Some educators recommend norms for evaluating students' oral reading fluency (Hasbrouck & Tindal, 2006). A set of criteria for evaluating a 1-minute fluency read can be found in Chapter 9, Table 9.1.

8. Examine the miscues for insight about the child's use of strategies. (See the discussion following these steps and Table 3.1.)

9. Another analysis involves judging whether the meaning of a sentence was maintained even when miscues occurred. Look at each sentence in the context of the whole passage and ask, Is the meaning essentially the same? Does it still sound the way language should sound? For example, assume the text sentence reads, "The bicycle is painted red." The following are some judgments you might make:

Acceptable	"The bike is painted red."	Maintains meaning and sounds like language.
Possibly acceptable, depending on context	"The bike was painted red."	Past tense may or may not change meaning significantly.
Unacceptable	"The bark is painted red."	Meaning is lost.
Unacceptable	"The bicycle painted red."	Bicycles do not paint; omission of the word is changes both language and meaning. However, if the omission results from a dialectic or second-language usage difference, you might judge it acceptable and plan instruction based on verb forms.
Possibly acceptable or unacceptable	"The bicycle is painted blue."	Acceptability depends on how critical the color is to the passage.

When you have judged each sentence in terms of acceptability, you can calculate a percentage score for this aspect of the child's reading:

$$\frac{\text{Total Sentences Read Correctly}}{\text{Number of Sentences in Sample}} \times 100 = \underline{\hspace{1cm}}\% \text{ Acceptability}$$

For example, if the reading sample had 20 sentences total and you judged that 18 of them were read acceptably, the student's score would be:

$$\frac{18}{20} \times 100 = 90\% \text{ Accuracy}$$

Analyzing Miscues. Analysis of the miscues from running records allows you to make some inferences about the strategies, skills, and information a child is using. Let's look at Lisa's miscues as recorded in Figure 3.2. In practice, we would never draw conclusions from single examples, but this exercise will help you understand the possible inferences.

First, does the child base her choice of a word on what would make sense in the story (semantics)? Lisa said "sea" for "ocean" on page 13. She clearly thought about meaning as she read this word. She hardly needed to note the letters on the page; she said the word that made sense. This is a strength.

Second, does she base her choice on what kind of word belongs in a certain slot in the sentence (syntax)? If so, when she substitutes a word for one she doesn't recognize, the substitution will yield a sentence that sounds like English even if it doesn't make any sense. For example, Lisa said "shoe" for "shadow." Both are (or can be) nouns, but the meaning is lost. If this kind of miscue occurs frequently, Lisa needs to be taught to monitor her own reading, asking herself, Does this make sense?

Third, does the child say a word that matches what she sees, whether or not it results in a sentence that sounds like language and makes sense? A child who does this might say "horse" instead of "house." These two words are quite similar visually, and they are similar phonetically at the beginning and end. The child who pays attention primarily to such **graphophonic cues** (symbol and sound—the letter on the page and the sound that it stands for) may read right on, undisturbed by the lack of semantic or syntactic fit. Lisa's substitution of "noise" for "nose" may fit this explanation. An abundance of this kind of miscue may indicate an overreliance on **phonics,** using sound/symbol knowledge to figure out the probable pronunciations of words. Lisa needs to balance her phonics strength with self-awareness and learn that what she reads must sound like language and make sense.

Fourth, how does a child treat her miscues? Self-correction indicates competence. If a child has substituted "home" for "house," she will probably feel no need to self-correct, since meaning was not interrupted. The competent reader, however, will self-correct if she says "horse" rather than "house." Such a child often giggles at herself, recognizing that she made a "silly mistake." Lisa self-corrected the miscue "noise" on page 2 in Figure 3.2.

Some children will not attempt any word they think they do not recognize. They feel that they cannot make an attempt unless they are absolutely sure they are correct. This kind of child may need support for risk-taking as a part of reading instruction.

As you can tell, a great deal can be learned from taking a record of a child's fluency. In order to open a little window into the child's thought processes, you must be sure the child is reading material that challenges but does not overwhelm her. If it is too easy, she will not miscue often enough for you to tell what is going on. If it is too hard, she will stumble so often and get so discouraged that she will miscue on words that normally give her no trouble. Table 3.1 presents some possible miscues and examples of what they might indicate for instruction.

DIVERSE LEARNERS

Inability to use word recognition strategies is only one explanation for less-than-fluent oral reading. Sometimes the student's oral reading deviates in ways that simply reflect his or her oral language. (See the fourth and fifth patterns in Table 3.1.)

TABLE 3.1

Examples of Miscue Patterns and What They Might Mean for Instruction

MISCUE PATTERN	INSTRUCTIONAL MEANING	COMMENTS
1. High ratio of self-correction of miscues that changed meaning	A strength. Child knows when meaning is lost and looks again and corrects. If child is reading fast, you might suggest more attention to visual cues.	Self-correction (which requires repeating a word or more) used to not be considered a strength. Now we welcome self-correction as a sign of attention to meaning.
2. Miscues show a high percentage of graphophonic similarity (that is, miscues have many of the same sounds and letters as the target words) with few self-corrections	Child needs to be taught more strategies to use when meeting an unfamiliar word. Focus should be on meaning of text first, then confirming with letters on the page.	If the child's miscues are similar to the target words but result in nonsense, either nonwords or words that make no sense, *and* if the child reads right on, this may indicate an overreliance on phonics to the exclusion of other strategies. Phonics is an important part of decoding, but only if it is combined with attention to meaning.
3. High number of teacher-pronounced words	Not enough information to make an instructional decision. Try to figure out why the child will not try to say the words independently: Fear of failure? Lack of knowledge of other strategies? Knows other strategies but does not use them unless prompted? Past experience with expectations of absolute accuracy? More observation in other settings is necessary.	There is a danger in drawing too many conclusions from too few data. Patterns of miscues occurring only during running records aren't enough. Sometimes the best instructional decision is to gather more information. For example, you might take another fluency record with different material.
4. Syntactic substitutions such as "he be going" for "he is going"	The child is, in effect, translating written text into his or her own language patterns—a pretty sophisticated thing to do and one that works only if the child does, in fact, understand the words on the page. You might make plans to deal with the need for school language (that of teachers and books) as well as everyday language.	When children restate text in their own dialect, it is not a reading problem. One of your goals will be to help them be comfortable with book language, but do not mistake this for a reading difficulty.
5. Phonological substitutions such as "tree" for "three," common among speakers of Hawaii Creole English	If it is clear from the context that the child means the number (the correct word) and not the plant (the incorrect word), this is not a miscue.	Continue to model standard pronunciation of words. Do not stop a child's oral reading to "correct" nonstandard pronunciations that arise from dialect or any other cause.

(continued)

TABLE 3.1

Examples of Miscue Patterns and What They Might Mean for Instruction (*continued*)

MISCUE PATTERN	INSTRUCTIONAL MEANING	COMMENTS
6. Large number of miscues that show little or no graphophonic similarity to target word, do not retain meaning, and do not make syntactic sense	More information is needed. Child appears not to use any strategies and not to be bothered by lack of sense. Text may simply be too difficult. It is also possible that something else is going on in the child's life that keeps him or her from focusing on text. You need to explore further.	If the child makes this kind of miscue frequently and the total percentage of words correct is less than 90, you need to try an easier passage. But if the percentage correct is above 90, and all miscues are of this kind, it appears that the child can deal only with words already "memorized" and has no idea how to approach an unfamiliar word.

Such deviations may not indicate reading difficulty; they may indicate a high degree of comprehension in that the student has read the material, understood it, and rephrased it in his or her own vernacular.

Other conditions may also inhibit a student's performance on this task. Second-language learners may still be shy about their pronunciation of words in English even though they may read fluently to themselves. Further, students may have low self-esteem, speech articulation difficulty, distractibility, lack of interest in the subject matter, lack of background for the subject matter, vision problems, hunger, family concerns—the list is almost endless.

COMMENTS

A running record or a fluency record (the two terms may be used interchangeably) is simply a sample of a child's reading on a given day with a given piece of text. Conclusions should always be tentative. Take the running record for what it is worth—an authentic piece of evidence about the child's reading that day. Use it to plan ways to help the child grow.

You want your students to participate in this assessment willingly and confidently. Therefore, keep the experience focused, businesslike, and pleasant. Greet each child warmly; thank him or her when you are finished. At first, children may feel intimidated, fearful, or unsure about what is expected of them. Reassure them. In time, the procedure will be routine for both you and the children.

Retelling of Narrative and Expository Texts

Retelling involves having a student read material silently or orally, and then the student tells about it out loud using his or her own words. Sometimes the term **summarizing** is used for this process. Retelling has four key purposes:

- To assess comprehension of narrative and expository material
- To assess the ability to tell specific story elements of narrative material
- To assess the ability to tell important ideas and significant details of expository text, as well as factors related to text structure such as sequence, comparison and contrast of ideas, and fact and opinion
- To make instructional decisions and plans

DESCRIPTION

Retelling of narrative material often involves presenting all the elements of the story—characters, setting, problem, events, and resolution—in basically the same sequence in which they occurred in the story. Children may use story language as they retell, sometimes repeating whole phrases verbatim, though they use mostly their own words. Here is a partial retelling of *The Little Red Hen:*

> *A little red hen found some grains of wheat. She asked, "Who will help me sow the wheat?" The duck said no. The pig said no. Everybody said no. So she did it herself. Then she asked who would help her…*

A student may also retell in a summary form by stating the main problem and resolution or the theme:

> *This story is about a hen who finds some wheat. She keeps trying to get other animals to help her plant it and cut it and make bread from it. No one will help. She does it all herself…*

Retelling of expository material (nonfiction or informational material) differs from retelling of narrative material. Such retelling should not include every detail but should make clear that the reader understood the topic, the main idea(s), and the significant details. Expository retelling should also indicate that the reader grasped how the ideas were organized and how they related to one another.

PROCEDURES AND SAMPLES

The following procedures have evolved from Morrow's (1989) guidelines for the use of retelling diagnostically as well as from our own experiences with students and teachers:

1. Either you or the student may select the text to be read. If you are using retelling at intervals to show growth, the texts should be conceptually comparable.

2. Before the retelling begins, read the text yourself. (It is possible to listen to a retelling of a story you don't know and assess whether or not all the elements are present in the retelling, but this is not usually recommended.)

3. If you have chosen the text to be read, identify the story elements or ideas that you expect the reader to include to demonstrate understanding. You might use a retelling form such as those shown in Figures 3.3 and 3.4.

4. Have the student read silently and immediately retell. Give only generic prompts such as "Keep going; you're doing fine." Check off items if you are using a form. Make notes if you are not using a form.

RETELLING: NARRATIVE

Name __Jamal__   Date __10-9__

Title of Story and Source __The Doorbell Rang (reader)__

✓ = indicates whether student told about element unaided or after prompting by teacher
— = indicates student could not tell even with prompting

Elements Included	Unaided	Prompted
1. Setting (time, place, weather)	✓	
2. Character		
Major(s)	✓	
Others		✓ (some)
3. Problem	✓	
4. Story Events		
Includes all major events		NO ✓
Tells mostly in sequence		—
5. Solution		
Tells how the problem was solved	✓	
Tells how the story ended		—

Comments/Analysis: __Needed much prompting Reluctant to speak unless he was sure he was right.__

Future support needed: __Model and encourage risk taking. Minilesson sequence (small group). Reinforce "how authors end stories" during discussions and analyze and compare.__

FIGURE 3.3

Marked Retelling Record: Narrative Text

5. If anything important was omitted, probe a bit to determine whether the student can tell about what was omitted. Indicate on your record which parts of the retelling emerged only with prompting.

6. Make notes regarding other aspects of the retelling, such as whether the student adopted story language, recalled story-specific words, injected personal comments, was precise in recalling details, or attempted total recall or verbatim retelling.

RETELLING: EXPOSITORY TEXT

Student Name Brenda   Date 2/6

Selection/Author Scaly Babies. G. Johnston & J. Cutchins
Ch. 1 Baby Snakes – intro. pp. 4-5

Parts Included	Unaided	Prompted
Topic	✓	
Main idea(s)		✓
Supporting details	✓ (3) but could not elaborate	
Explanation/relating ideas/conclusion	—	—

Comments/Analysis: After prompting elicited the main idea, asked Brenda why she thought the author wrote the book. She couldn't think of any reason. Prompting failed to elicit any details about how the information was presented or ideas about why an author might have chosen to organize it that way.

Future support needed: Plan minilessons on text structure. Be sure to explore how authors might decide about organization.
Plan lessons on identifying main idea(s) — first when stated literally, then when implied — whenever it occurs in a paragraph — then in a longer selection

FIGURE 3.4

Marked Retelling Record: Expository Text

In the narrative retelling form shown in Figure 3.3, Jamal's strengths are apparent from the checks in the "Unaided" column. The comments have to do with Jamal's needs and with ideas for instructional support. During a family conference, you would naturally comment first about Jamal's strengths.

Figure 3.4 shows a form you might use to assess a child's ability to retell, or summarize, expository text. Depending on the text read (and perhaps only with older students), some teachers also ask readers about the author's purpose: to entertain the reader, inform the reader, or persuade the reader to think or behave in a certain way. Brenda, whose retelling is recorded in Figure 3.4, shows strength in her ability to tell the topic and some details. She needed prompting to tell the main idea and was unable, even with prompting, to discuss any ideas further, show how the ideas related to one another, or draw any conclusions. The form allows the teacher to comment on Brenda's performance and note future instructional needs.

DIVERSE LEARNERS

Students whose oral language is inhibited by some factor such as lack of fluency in English or a learning disability may find retelling particularly difficult. Although such students may be able to demonstrate understanding of what they have read when asked direct questions, generating the language necessary for retelling may present challenges they cannot meet. We suggest that at first you give students options, such as drawing pictures of parts of a story or responding to either/or questions. Then you can ease these students into retelling through prompting.

For example, you might say, "Who was this story about? Who were the main characters? Who else was there? Tell me about the setting… Where did it happen? When? Tell me about the problem [the main character] had. Now let's talk about the events… What happened first?" As you continue in this vein, you are putting the language of retelling as well as the language of the story into the students' heads. Gradually diminish your prompts as students' confidence grows. Don't confuse inability to generate the words during retelling with inability to comprehend.

COMMENTS

Be cautious about judging a student to be inadequate at retelling narrative or expository text. You need to determine if retelling of both kinds of text has in fact been taught. Retelling of expository material in particular may be neglected in the elementary grades, yet it is essential in higher grades. We urge you to make retelling of expository text just as much a part of your daily activities as retelling of stories.

Retelling should be selective. Your students may need to be taught how to identify and retell just the key parts. On the other hand, if they tend to leave out key elements, they may need to be taught why those elements are important. Ideas about such instruction are woven through later chapters.

Comprehension: Discussion

The meaning a reader finds in a text arises not merely from the printed page but also from the reader's process of interacting with the text to create or "construct" meaning (Cooper, 2006). Classroom discussions of literature can be particularly useful in this process. The three main purposes for literacy assessments based on discussion are:

- To assess construction of meaning or other aspects of reading, such as retelling, summarizing, locating of text to support a point, fluency in oral rereading, understanding of idiomatic and other figurative language, and appreciation of authors' craft

- To assess use of appropriate discussion behaviors such as participation, listening to others, and acceptance of ideas without censure

- To help plan instructional decisions

DESCRIPTION

While there may be a structure or set of guidelines that children follow during a discussion, the actual event is unpredictable and may veer off in unplanned directions. Whatever happens, you can glean valuable insights.

You can focus on one child or a group in a discussion. Indicators can be listed on a grid vertically, with children's names across the top, as shown in Figure 3.5. We believe the best discussion assessment is devised by each individual teacher to meet individual needs. You might, for instance, want to observe behaviors related to participation, listening to others, accepting ideas without ridiculing, and so forth. Another time, you might want to observe the ability to retell certain portions, the ability to predict, knowledge of idiomatic language, fluency in oral rereading, and so forth. You make up the list based on what you want to know.

PROCEDURES AND SAMPLES

Using a grid like the one in Figure 3.5, devise a code for marking behaviors. A simple one is shown there.

Inform the children that you will observe during their discussion and make notes. Sit where you can observe without interrupting the flow of a natural discussion. Some teachers are able to record observations as they participate. In such cases, it is almost impossible to separate assessment from instruction, nor is there any reason to do so. *Assessment should be a natural part of instruction.*

Discussion Check

Book/Story _____

Date _____

```
+   = often
S   = sometimes
-   = hardly ever
N/O = not observed
```

	John	Mary A.	Allen	David	Brian	Kathryn	Tomas	Rosalyn
Listens to others								
Participates								
Takes turns								
Accepts all ideas								
Sticks to story								

FIGURE 3.5

Discussion Observation Grid

Use what you have observed to plan instruction. After instruction, use the same form to assess both your success in instructing and the children's growth as a result of the instruction.

DIVERSE LEARNERS

Children who are not yet fluent in English may feel lost in a group discussion. Imagine how you might feel in a crowd of people tossing ideas back and forth in a language you are only just beginning to learn. Keep the discussion group very small at first so that the student can follow the conversation more easily, and keep in mind that lack of fluency in English may inhibit full participation.

Fluent class members probably will use informal language, idioms, and sentence fragments, which also make it hard to follow a conversation. The English-language learner may still be translating into his or her own language to understand. The reverse may be true in responding: thinking of the words in his or her first language and then translating into English. Oral rereading may be halting, and pronunciation may be heavily accented. Discussion group members need to be patient and give the second-language learner a chance to feel part of the group.

Help all your students accommodate and include the not-yet-fluent English speakers. Talk with the class about the need to clarify idioms for all listeners, not just second-language speakers. Model how a good listener in a discussion may paraphrase the speaker's words to ensure that the meaning was understood before responding. Model using mispronounced words correctly in a discussion but not "correcting" mispronunciation. Everyone should follow the same good rules: each person should be allowed whatever time is needed to gather his or her thoughts and formulate a comment.

COMMENTS

It takes time for children (and adults) to learn to have good discussions. At the beginning of the school year, you may want to assess your students' ability to conduct a discussion and to show construction of meaning as they do so. This will provide baseline data on which to build instructional plans.

You might first assess only discussion behaviors; children first need to learn how to treat one another and how to participate in a successful discussion. When these behaviors are established, you might then assess evidence of construction of meaning during discussions.

Comprehension: Personal Written Responses

Teachers have always asked children to write in response to what they have read. For the teacher, these personal written responses serve four main purposes:

- To assess cognitive aspects of literacy such as prior knowledge, construction of meaning, and understanding of story elements and text structure
- To assess knowledge of subject matter and concepts

- To assess affective aspects of literacy such as interests, self-concept, and attitudes
- To help plan instruction

DESCRIPTION

A variety of written responses can yield useful information about a child's literacy. Among these are **story maps** (graphic representations that visually show the story elements), journals, individual K-W-L or other charts, **learning logs** (students' own daily records of their learning activities and the concepts they have learned), and variations of these devices. These responses can be used to help you learn about a child's interests, self-concept, attitudes, prior knowledge, ability to construct meaning in general, and knowledge about literary elements and text structure.

The use of written responses for assessment purposes is perhaps the most open-ended of all. There are no set guidelines, specific checklists, or forms to fill out. *In fact, every time you read something a child has written about a piece he or she has read, you will learn valuable information about that child.*

PROCEDURES AND SAMPLES

As you get started, you may structure the children's written responses part of the time. Until you are comfortable with the notion of using everything that happens in the classroom as assessment, structure will help to keep you on track.

Here is one idea. List items to which you want children to respond in writing after they read a story independently. Post the list on a chart or make photocopies. The items will depend on what you want to know and on the age of the children. They might include things such as these:

- Write about your favorite character.
- Write about something that puzzled you.
- Tell why you would (or would not) like to read another story by the same author.
- In two sentences, say something about the story to make others want to read it.

After the children have read an informational book, your items will differ somewhat. They might include questions such as these:

- What was the most important new thing you learned?
- What else do you want to know about the subject?
- Tell why you would (or would not) recommend this book to a friend.

In a typical *response journal,* in which students write about what they are reading, there are no specific questions. As you read children's journals, note which students have little to say, responding with only one or two words. You'll want to help them learn to respond more fully or find books that engage them more.

Written retelling of a story, in a journal or elsewhere, can reveal both the strengths and weaknesses in a student's comprehension. Figure 3.6 and Figure 3.7 are two sample written retellings of *Chicken Little.* Note that Lee has included all the essential elements in his retelling, whereas Sheryl has omitted key elements. You would investigate further to decide what kind of instructional help Sheryl needs.

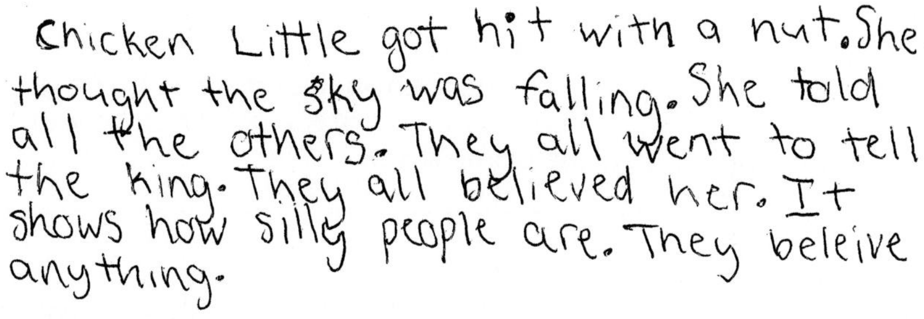

Chicken Little got hit with a nut. She thought the sky was falling. She told all the others. They all went to tell the king. They all believed her. It shows how silly people are. They beleive anything.

FIGURE 3.6

Lee's Retelling of *Chicken Little*

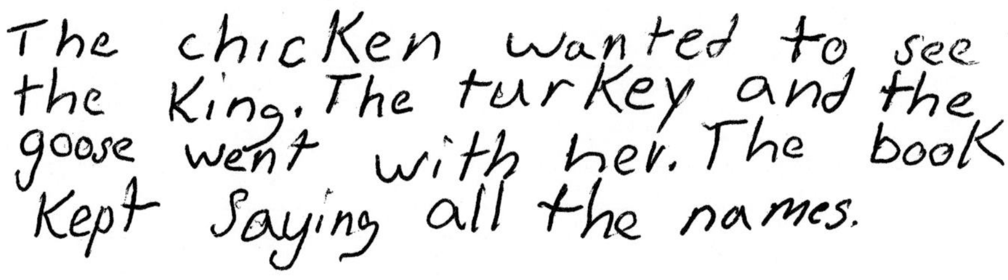

The chicken wanted to see the King. The turkey and the goose went with her. The book kept saying all the names.

FIGURE 3.7

Sheryl's Retelling of *Chicken Little*

In a *dialogue journal,* the teacher provides ongoing written responses to the student's comments. Figure 3.8 shows such an exchange. Jamal is retelling every detail. The teacher models retelling only important parts and giving a personal response. The teacher also tries to motivate Jamal to explore some other kinds of books.

Figure 3.9 shows a double-entry journal with separate columns for the student's predictions and later responses. Liz's entries show that she reacted strongly to this book, *Blubber* (Blume, 1974). She may be more sensitive to her own weight problem than anyone realized. Her prediction that the children who were so mean would be punished reflects an idealized view. Her teacher might consider having a class discussion about why life isn't always fair or perhaps one about group mentality.

Figure 3.10 shows a reading log with Erika's personal response to the book *Song and Dance Man* (Ackerman, 1988). Erika didn't seem to see any point to the story. She would benefit from being in a literature discussion group with children who dig a little deeper.

9-10 (Jamal)
  First he went in the house. Then he got scared by a noise. Then a cat ran out. Then he went home. Then he came back.

_____

9-11 (Teacher)
  You really remembered everything, didn't you? I just read a mystery about horses that were being given drugs to make them run faster. It was very bad for them. In the end, of course, they caught the bad guys. I'm glad, because I love horses.
  See me if you'd like a mystery to read next.

FIGURE 3.8

Dialogue Journal with Teacher as Child Is Reading a Book from a "Horror" Series

September 9
Blubber by J. Blume

Predictions	What happened
Jill will be nice to Linda because Jill is telling the story.	Jill laughed at Linda with everyone else. I think they are mean.
A teacher's job is to make them stop being mean.	The teacher didn't find out why they were laughing.

FIGURE 3.9

Liz's Double-Entry Journal Entry, Written While She Was Reading Judy Blume's *Blubber* (1974)

FIGURE 3.10

Erika's Reading Log Response to *Song and Dance Man*

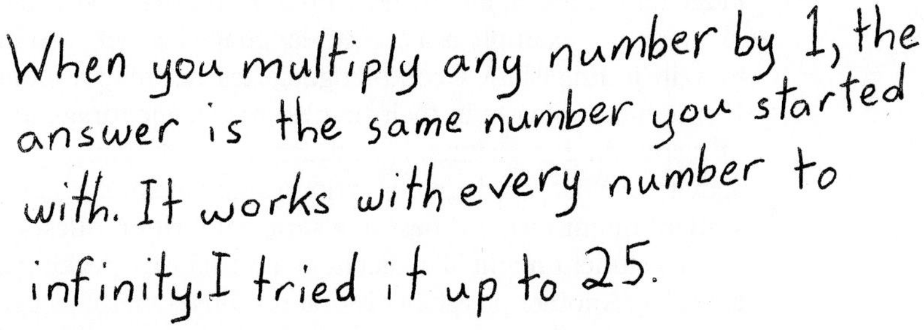

october 12

Song and Dance Man
by Karen Ackerman
This was a dumb book.
Who wants to
read about an old man?
I didn't like the pictures.

FIGURE 3.11

Paul's Learning Log: Multiplying by 1

When you multiply any number by 1, the answer is the same number you started with. It works with every number to infinity. I tried it up to 25.

Learning logs can be similarly revealing. Your children may keep learning logs for math or science, for instance. When you read what the children record, you can note which children understood the concepts and which children need more work. Figure 3.11 is a sample learning log written by Paul, a third grader, after an introductory lesson on the concept of multiplying by 1. Figure 3.12 was written by Sammy after the same lesson. Which boy clearly grasps the concept, and which boy needs further teaching?

First you put the number.
then you put X
Then you put =
Then you put the answer.
The answer is the number

FIGURE 3.12

Sammy's Learning Log: Multiplying by 1

DIVERSE LEARNERS

Written responses to reading can provide insights only if students can write with enough skill to truly express themselves. Some students will find it difficult, if not impossible, to demonstrate anything about their reading ability through writing.

For example, a student with a learning disability that makes written expression difficult may read widely and deeply with admirable comprehension but may be able to produce very little when trying to express a response on paper. One of our own children read and understood content far beyond his years, but his handwriting was labored and his spelling such that it was virtually impossible to know what he intended to write. To judge his reading ability by his written responses would have been a huge mistake.

Another example is a second-language learner who may not yet be fluent enough to write in English. A second-language learner may respond only with drawings at first. If students can write in their first language, encourage it; the idea is to build the habit of responding in writing. If a student is just beginning to write in English, adapt the activity to whatever degree of written ability he or she currently exhibits. The nonfluent student might respond best to a series of written questions with a choice of answers. Such a student might also dictate to an English-speaking buddy or volunteer who acts as scribe. Another possibility is oral responses, perhaps using a cassette recorder.

Some students may write more fully on a computer. Find the method that works best with an individual student's needs.

COMMENTS

Be wary of turning all writing into assessment. You don't want to kill children's joy in writing. With overuse, the response journal could become as deadly as the old-fashioned book reports many of us remember.

As you analyze a child's written response to reading, keep your purpose in mind. If your purpose is assessment of the child's ability to construct meaning, only content is relevant. The conventions of writing—such as spelling, usage, and punctuation—are not part of assessing construction of meaning. While you may note these, do not let poor mechanics cloud your judgment.

Writing Assessment Tools

We have discussed using written responses to text as a way to learn about a child's reading. In this section, we discuss using writing of many kinds, including response to text, as a way to assess writing. Throughout the chapters devoted to the stages of literacy development, you will find references to what is discussed here, with elaborations and modifications appropriate to each stage.

This section is divided into three main parts: (1) process and product: assessing a student's use of the writing process as well as the final product; (2) types of products: reports and other kinds of writing suitable for assessment evidence; and (3) conventions of writing: grammar/usage, mechanics, and spelling.

Process and Product

Children do a great deal of writing in today's classrooms. Some of it involves what is called the *writing process:* prewriting, drafting, revising, editing, and publishing. This process is appropriate when children write stories, reports, essays, and other kinds of writing that lead to a final, finished product. We will discuss other kinds of writing, such as journals, in the section on types of products. Here we limit our discussion to those that involve process as well as product.

PROCESS

Each student should have a writing folder to store works-in-progress. Each piece of work should have the child's name and date. The folder should contain "evidence" of all stages of the process, beginning with whatever prewriting techniques the child used to generate ideas and organizational plans. These include, but are not limited to, drawings, lists, semantic webs (a variation of semantic maps, illustrated in Chapter 6), and free-writing.

All drafts should be kept and labeled "First Draft," "Second Draft," and so forth. After a conference with you or with a peer, the person who conferred should initial the draft and date it. After revising, the last draft should show editing and proofreading marks to be followed when creating the final version for publication.

As you review writing folders, you will be able to note who is having trouble with which steps of the process and determine how you might group students for further instruction. You'll need to determine what might cause a problem. For example, if evidence of prewriting is missing, is it because the student didn't do any, doesn't know how, knows how and thinks it's a waste of time, or lost it? Instructional decisions depend on answers to these kinds of questions.

Perhaps the most common explanation for a child's failure to make good use of the writing process is the simplest: he or she was never taught how to use it or given adequate guided practice. Ask yourself if you have actually taught—that is, modeled, presented, collaborated, practiced, and so forth—each step of the process. No matter what grade you teach or whether you believe this process was thoroughly taught in a lower grade, you need to reteach and reteach and reteach. Good, clear writing is seldom "mastered."

Every writer knows that revision is a crucial part of writing. Still, we see classrooms in which children go directly from first draft to editing. We want children to understand and accept that writing well involves a process.

When you assign writing that does not allow for revision, such as an essay question, we urge you not to require best thinking, best handwriting, correct spelling and mechanics, and correct usage, all on what may essentially be considered a first draft. You probably have experienced how difficult it is to think clearly and at the same time pay attention to careful handwriting, let alone remember your own personal spelling/usage demons.

If your students are writing directly with a word processing program, you will need to adapt your assessment procedures. Most writers revise continually as they write on a computer. It is almost impossible, therefore, to see a clear succession of revisions. Until you are sure a child is indeed revising, you may ask that each draft be printed before revisions are made. All children need to feel comfortable writing in this way, and you need to feel comfortable letting them, even though you may not have pieces of paper showing each step in the process.

PRODUCT

You may assess a final product to help make instructional decisions and share the results with a child's family. Yet a single mark, such as an 87 or a C+, is of little use to you, the child, or the family. The criteria must be clear. What counted: Spelling? Grammar? Content?

Holistic scoring of writing, a widely used technique, involves assigning a single score to a piece of writing based on the overall quality of both content and mechanics using clearly stated criteria. Often rubrics are prepared or drawn from previously written papers. The rubrics may be accompanied by sample responses—sometimes called *anchor papers*—for each of the possible number scores. Numbers usually run from a

This student revises his written work electronically in the school's computer room.

© Matt Antonino, 2009/ Used under license from Shutterstock.com high of 6 to a low of 1, but other ranges, such as 4 to 1, are possible. Student papers are compared to the anchor papers and are given the number score of the closest match.

If you are going to assess your students' writing holistically for a state-, district-, or school-wide program, you will be given directions and rubrics. You may not score the papers yourself. Special readers are trained in applying the rubrics to ensure a high degree of **inter-rater reliability;** that is, a given paper will be assigned the same score no matter who reads it. However, you should understand the rubrics and apply them to the writing your students do in preparation for the assessment, so you will be successful in coaching them to do their best. When such assessment is carried out on a school-wide basis, it assesses how well we are teaching writing just as much as it assesses each child's writing.

Holistic scoring may be useful in illuminating areas that need more instruction. Perhaps many of your students lack the ability to organize their thoughts logically. Analyze your teaching. Have you ever really taught your students how to organize their thoughts as they write? *The simplest, and perhaps likeliest, explanation of why a child is unable to do something is that no one has taught it sufficiently.*

To apply holistic scoring to classroom assignments, decide first how many levels you want. (An even number will force you not to score everyone in the middle.) Next, prepare descriptors for each level. A descriptor can be something that should be present in the paper or something that should not be there. There should be clear differences between levels. The descriptors may include elements related to the following: content, conceptual level, thoroughness, organization, use of language, conventions (spelling, punctuation, grammar), interest, freshness, and any other items you have established.

In many cases, you and your students together can establish what makes a paper a 6 or a 5, an A or a B. Be sure students understand the descriptors used for making judgments, and why these are considered elements of a good paper. Then the students can apply such rubrics to their own writing by rereading their work and checking the descriptor statements that apply. They can assign themselves a score based on which level had the most checks. Figure 3.13 presents a partial generic rubric. As you can see, each step down from a 6 would retain some of the same standards, but to a lesser degree.

Figure 3.14 is part of a rubric developed for a specific culminating project in grade 4 following a unit of study on state history. The students worked with the teacher to develop the rubric and used it to guide them as they wrote their final reports. Then each student evaluated his or her own report. The teacher also evaluated each report. Both scores were recorded and shared with the students' families.

Types of Products

We have talked about using pieces of work produced through the writing process to learn about the child's understanding and application of that process. In this section, we discuss reports and other types of writing products you can use to assess writing progress.

REPORTS

Written reports are usually the culminating product of some process or activity. They can take many forms: research reports, book reports, science experiment reports,

Score	Descriptors
6	Name and date on paper
	Title
	States main idea in opening paragraph
	Supports main idea
	New paragraph if giving second main idea
	Supports secondary (or more) main idea(s)
	Writes conclusion, tying ideas together
	Spelling mostly conventional
	Punctuation conventional
	Usage standard
5	Name and date on paper
	Title
	States main idea in opening paragraph
	Supports main idea, or at least discusses it
	Has more than one paragraph with separate ideas
	Conclusion, but may not tie all ideas together
	Spelling mostly conventional, but some problems with words that are presumed known by now
	Mostly correct punctuation
	Mostly standard usage
4	Name and date on paper
	May or may not have title

FIGURE 3.13

Partial Generic Rubric for a Writing Assignment

Score	Descriptors
6	Name and date
	Title
	Gives at least three sources
	Synthesizes ideas from sources
	Introductory paragraph
	Subheadings
	Main idea for each subheading
	Supporting ideas for each subheading
	At least two visuals to support ideas
	Facts are accurate
	Conclusion pulls together ideas
	Correct spelling
	Correct punctuation
	Correct language use

FIGURE 3.14

Partial Rubric for "Our State" Report, Fourth Grade

interview reports, and others. If a report is to be assessed, students need to know in advance what is expected of them. This can be done by developing a rubric for the report. If students help draw up the rubric and guidelines, they can follow these guidelines as they complete their reports.

RESEARCH REPORT CHECKLIST

Name _____   **Date** _____

Title of Report _____

	You	Teacher
1. Topic appropriate		
2. Cluster or other graphic organizer		
3. Three or more references		
4. Information synthesized		
5. Appropriate paragraphing		
6. Rough draft(s) showing revision		
7. Editing (with editor identified)		
8. Cover page		
9. Bibliography		
10. Work submitted on time		
11. Final copy reflecting all of the above		

FIGURE 3.15

Checklist Used for Research Project in a Fourth Grade

Another way to proceed is to use a checklist on which you itemize each component of the project that will be assessed. Children can check each item, and you can check the same items. The child's checklist can be submitted along with the report.

Figure 3.15 shows a sample checklist for a research project. The components are simply to be checked as absent or present. You could also assign a number of points to each component, allowing yourself to make a judgment regarding the quality of each in addition to its presence or absence. This may also show students a level of importance or priority as they plan their report.

Of course, you and the students will have discussed exactly what each item on the list means. For example, the first item in Figure 3.15, "Topic appropriate," might mean that the topic was narrow enough to research thoroughly, that it fit the overall theme, and that it was introduced in the first paragraph.

If you use a class checklist, particular instructional needs might become clear. For example, one item might call for using a cluster or other organizer prior to writing a rough draft. If many children did not do this, or seemed unable to do it in a way that truly aided their writing, you would know you needed to teach more about this step in the writing process.

A checklist such as the one in Figure 3.15 helps students learn what to think about as they gather information and formulate a report. However, children can satisfy each of the listed items and still need further instruction. For example, if a child has the required number of references but has chosen them unwisely, you might provide lessons on locating and evaluating references for authenticity and suitability.

We have seen arbitrary requirements such as "Must have three revisions." We don't believe this kind of stipulation leads to thoughtful writing. Instead, we urge you to help your students learn how to judge when they have revised sufficiently. If you keep your goals and objectives in mind, you will establish guidelines that truly lead to better writing.

OTHER TYPES OF WRITING

Some other kinds of writing you may want to assess include journals, learning logs, and letters. If your children write in personal journals every morning you will read these journals and respond to the ideas expressed. That is one of the joys of journaling with children.

You might also keep anecdotal records of a child's growth in fluency chronicled in his or her journal. Duane might have only drawn a picture at the beginning of the year, whereas now he is adding a sentence about his picture. Lois might have written only stilted sentences a couple of months ago ("I did this."; "We had fun."), whereas now she is writing such things as "The coolest thing I did this weekend was teach my little brother how to tie his shoes. He was so proud of himself, and I was proud of him and of myself. It feels good to teach someone something."

Along with fluency, you can note increased complexity of language use. For example, note when a child has begun using dependent clauses at the beginning of sentences, when an awareness of audience begins to emerge, or when figurative language and fresh metaphors turn up.

You could also note the growth of conventional spelling and punctuation, even though these are not emphasized in journals. This is, of course, the true test of acquiring skill in these areas: competence even when it doesn't "count."

We suggest that you ask children to note such growth about themselves. Say to a student, "You have grown so much in your writing this year. Let's talk about what you are doing now that you didn't do at the beginning of the year." This kind of discussion is particularly valuable with a child who is feeling discouraged about writing.

Conventions of Writing

Conventions of writing are agreed-on standards: ways of doing things that are judged to be "correct." For example, we agree that proper names should begin with a capital letter (in English, at least), that a complete sentence needs both a subject and a predicate, that there is (generally) one correct way to spell a word, and that noun and verb should agree in number; that is, we shift from "he goes" (singular) to "they go" (plural). The number of conventions is almost endless. For the most part, they are not open to debate, nor are they subjective.

Some conventions apply to both oral and written language. Some, however, such as spelling and punctuation, apply only to written language. Conventions for written language are important because they allow others to read what we write. Computer programs can help writers catch many spelling and grammar errors.

Although the use of conventions may emerge only when children begin to attend school, many children have begun writing long before then. The urge to express oneself in writing is strong. Little children don't let their lack of knowledge of writing conventions inhibit them. They make marks that look sort of like what they see others do and call it writing. And it *is* writing because they know it "says" something.

The difficulty with conventions arises from differences of opinion about how and when children learn to do these things. Should we encourage them to write whatever they want to say, even before they know how to spell all the words or use punctuation? Or should we teach conventions early on? This is not a debate we can resolve here, but we do want to give you some idea of how to assess children's use of writing conventions.

Spelling in authentic writing, not on a spelling test, is the best way to assess where a child is developmentally. You may give tests that purport to assess usage and punctuation, or use a daily language exercise that involves correcting the grammar, mechanics, and spelling of an incorrect sentence written on the chalkboard. While this and other group editing tasks may be helpful, true assessment should be of the children's own writing. When assessment matches curriculum, teachers can be sure they are measuring what is taught (Salvia & Ysseldyke, 2007). You will find specific assessment ideas in Chapters 8 through 12. In this section, we discuss grammar/usage, mechanics, and spelling.

DIVERSE LEARNERS

Some children may not acquire the conventions of writing as soon as others. These may include children with learning disabilities and those with delayed language. If you suspect a student has one of these conditions, document with anecdotal records and checklists, and note exactly what the student is doing. Try direct and explicit teaching of the absent skills. If your attempts fail, you will probably want to consult with special teachers to discuss further assessment.

Children for whom English is a second language may also lag in their use of the conventions of writing. Not all languages construct sentences with words in the same order as in English. In some languages, the adjective follows the noun rather than preceding it. In some languages, each noun is designated masculine or feminine and requires a different article. In some languages, verb endings are derived differently than in English.

Spelling may be particularly difficult for some English-language learners who already spell in their first language. If a student's first language has a strict one-to-one correspondence between a sound and the letter that represents that sound, the multiple ways to spell sounds in English (difficult for most people!) will undoubtedly be confusing.

One of your jobs is to help children move toward the use of conventional English by paying attention to what they are doing now and planning instruction to help them learn what comes next.

GRAMMAR/USAGE

Conventions for grammar/usage include rules on noun-verb agreement, run-on sentences, sentence fragments, and misplaced modifiers. A checklist drawn from your local list of objectives probably is the best way to track your students' acquisition of these skills.

MECHANICS

The area of mechanics includes capitalization and punctuation (periods, exclamation points, question marks, commas, semicolons, dashes, apostrophes, and so on). Again, a simple checklist may be the best way to keep track of your students' skills in this area. You may want to use individual checklists to show when children acquire each ability. Or you may use a class checklist to point to overall instructional needs.

SPELLING

In our college classes over the years, the teaching of spelling has sparked more heated discussion than almost any other aspect of literacy. Those preservice teachers who are "good" spellers are convinced that whatever method was used to teach them made them that way. Those who consider themselves poor spellers are convinced that if only their teachers had used a different method, they wouldn't have trouble spelling.

Most published reading programs have a language program with a spelling component woven in. Some schools use this as their sole language/spelling program. Some schools use a separate language program that includes spelling. Some use a separate language program, and yet another separate spelling program. Some teach spelling directly, some indirectly. Some prefer programs based on high-frequency words, some on word families, some on high-utility words, and some on self-selected words.

The school system in which you teach will likely mandate a certain methodology. Yet it will be up to you to become informed and remain open to emerging research. If you feel strongly about the best method, perhaps you will be a change agent in your school.

Spelling acquisition often begins before children enter school and extends over many years, throughout the literacy stages. Many view spelling ability as essentially developmental (Bear, Invernizzi, Templeton, & Johnson, 2004; Gentry & Gillet, 1992; Henderson, 1990); that is, even without formal instruction, children who write every day will grow in their ability to spell conventionally. Some children seem able to spell virtually any word they can say from kindergarten on. Others seem perpetually unable to spell conventionally, even into adulthood, despite their best efforts (Gentry, 1987).

Stages of Spelling Acquisition. While the terminology differs among researchers, and the ages of acquisition vary, the *stages* of spelling acquisition are remarkably similar for nearly everyone. Before producing anything that looks like a letter, children begin making scribble marks. The marks may be made from right to left, left to right, or top to bottom. As children see others writing and moving their hands from left to right, they begin producing scribble lines in left-to-right order. Then they begin making marks that look rather like letters. Soon after, children begin to use actual letters, though these seem to be random because they don't yet consistently represent sounds. However, this use of letters marks the beginning of spelling development; children have come to understand that all writers must use the same set of marks to enable others to read what is written.

From then on, children progress through several more stages as they move toward spelling words conventionally—that is, correctly. Each child moves through the acquisition of spelling competence idiosyncratically in terms of speed, but almost all go through these stages in sequence. As with all learning, most children are partly in one stage and partly in another, or at one point on one day and another on another day. Furthermore, second-language learners may be in one stage in one language and a different stage in the other (Rubin and Carlan, 2005). Learning is not tidy.

The following list of labels and descriptions of the developmental spelling stages is drawn from Gentry and Gillet (1992). As you read through the stages, think how your knowledge of spelling acquisition might affect decisions about teaching spelling. It has been said that not until a child has reached the conventional stage will he or she benefit from formal instruction. You may decide, however, that there is appropriate instruction for every stage as long as one does not try to teach something to a child who is not developmentally ready to learn it.

1. Precommunicative Stage
   ✓ The writing represents a message, though only the writer can read it and only immediately after writing it.
   ✓ Children do not yet know the **alphabetic principle** that letters represent sounds.
   ✓ Children use letters and marks that resemble real letters.
   ✓ Letters may or may not seem to follow a left-to-right organization.
   ✓ Children mix upper- and lower-case letters and may prefer upper case.
   ✓ Letters are in random order.
   ✓ Children may include numerals with letters.
   ✓ Children may use a few letters or many.

2. Semiphonetic Stage
   ✓ Children begin to acquire the alphabetic principle. This is a stunning discovery for them.
   ✓ Letters represent words, but there is not a complete representation of each sound in a word. Words may often begin with a consonant. In fact, a whole word or syllable may be represented by the initial consonant.
   ✓ The sounds of words are often represented by the sound of a letter's name rather than the sound the letter stands for. For example, the word "elephant" may begin with the letter *L,* and the word "are" may be spelled "R."
   ✓ There is increasing evidence of left-to-right arrangement of letters.
   ✓ Character formations look more like actual letters.
   ✓ There may or may not be spaces between words.

3. Phonetic Stage
   ✓ The next major step in a child's acquisition of spelling ability is the realization that certain letters stand for certain sounds and that all words can be represented with symbols for the sounds. This understanding grows by leaps and bounds as children learn to read.

✓ Particular sounds may always be spelled the same way.

✓ Words are spelled on the basis of sound alone.

✓ As children write, they say words to themselves, listening for the sounds. We say they have developed **phonemic awareness** when they can segment a word into individual sounds. When they write, they use letters for each sound.

✓ Children may use visual memory for some words because of exposure or drill, but mostly they spell words the way they sound. This is what is meant by *invented spelling:* spelling a word the way it sounds. This spelling may not be correct, but it is usually close enough that others can read it. Once children realize they can write this way, they usually increase their writing fluency and the amount they write. If the word is in their heads (they can say it and know what it means), they feel free to write it, matching sound segments with written letters.

4. Transitional Stage

✓ Writers begin to pay attention to what words look like as well as to the sounds, though they may not yet recognize when a word is spelled incorrectly.

✓ Vowel sounds are represented in every syllable.

✓ Writers begin to know alternative spellings for various sounds.

✓ Writers begin to rely on their knowledge of **morphology,** that is, the meaningful parts of words, such as verb endings, prefixes and suffixes, and root words.

✓ Writers begin to discover the more mysterious aspects of spelling: for instance, doubling final consonants or dropping them; spelling the past tense *-ed* even when it doesn't sound that way, except when the verb has an irregular past tense.

✓ Common patterns appear. Sight words are spelled correctly, and those patterns are applied to the spelling of other words.

✓ Writers begin to understand what to do with syllables and how spelling sometimes needs to be changed when a syllable (representing a meaning change) is added. Some examples are "glad" and "gladdest," "happy" and "happier," "live" and "living."

5. Conventional Stage

✓ Most words are spelled correctly.

✓ Writers are catching on to the fact that if they know how to spell a word such as "compete," they need not struggle with what letter to use for the second vowel sound in "competition." The words are related both in meaning and in spelling, so even though the sound is a long *e* in "compete" and a schwa in "competition," the spelling remains *e.*

✓ Writers have developed a "spelling conscience" (Hillerich, 1977), a positive attitude toward spelling and a desire to spell conventionally.

✓ Writers have developed a sense of when a word just doesn't look right and can vary the spelling as they search for the conventional spelling.

TABLE 3.2

Student Spelling Responses Indicating Stage of Development

WORD	PRECOMMUNICATIVE	SEMIPHONETIC	PHONETIC	TRANSITIONAL	CONVENTIONAL
1. monster	random letters	MTR	MOSTR	MONSTUR	monster
2. united	random letters	U	UNITD	YOUNIGHTED	united
3. dress	random letters	JRS	JRAS	DRES	dress
4. bottom	random letters	BT	BODM	BOTTUM	bottom
5. hiked	random letters	H	HIKT	HICKED	hiked
6. human	random letters	UM	HUMN	HUMUM	human
7. eagle	random letters	EL	EGL	EGUL	eagle
8. closed	random letters	KD	KLOSD	CLOSSED	closed
9. bumped	random letters	B	BOPT	BUMPPED	bumped
10. type	random letters	TP	TIP	TIPE	type

Source: Gentry, J. R., & Gillet, J. W. (1992). *Teaching kids to spell.* Portsmouth, NH: Heinemann.

✓ Writers show increased understanding of the spellings of affixes, contractions, compounds, and homonyms (words that sound alike but are spelled differently).

✓ Writers benefit from systematic spelling instruction.

Assessing Spelling Development. In addition to outlining the stages of spelling acquisition, Gentry and Gillet (1992) have suggested a developmental spelling test that allows you to use just ten words to determine an individual child's stage. Table 3.2 presents the ten words along with possible responses indicative of each spelling stage. If you decide to use this assessment, we suggest that you consult the source cited. Chapter 8 presents other ways to look at spelling assessment.

You may decide to analyze each child's spelling at the beginning of the school year. If so, you can use a recent piece of spontaneous (that is, unedited) writing. Make a list of misspelled words, and match them to the characteristics of each stage.

C O M M E N T S

In any one classroom, you may find children at various stages of spelling development and also using the other conventions inconsistently. For example, a child might be at the transitional stage in spelling but apparently ignoring punctuation altogether and still expressing himself or herself with immature or nonstandard language.

(continued)

While a few children seem to have acquired all conventions by age six or seven, others are still struggling as they finish middle school and even into adulthood. Some students can acquire conventions through diligence, good teaching, and support. Others try just as diligently but seem unable to reach the conventional stage even with all the support you can give them.

We believe children should be free to write whatever they have to say regardless of their ability to follow writing conventions, just as they are encouraged to express ideas orally regardless of articulation problems, mispronunciations, or occasional wrong words. Read first without a red pencil. Respond to the child's ideas. Then make notes about development in writing conventions and any instruction you think may be needed.

Techniques for Organizing Assessment Information

To be useful, data must be organized. The point of gathering information—assessing—is to help you meet the needs of your children. Students change from day to day: some move away while new ones move in; some children who seemed unable to do something one day can magically do it the next, while others who have been able to do something one day suddenly seem unable to do it at all. So your data are continually changing—and thus your plans have to continually change. We will suggest a few ways to organize data, but there is no one right way. You are the only one who can judge if a method of organization is working for you. The following sections describe portfolios, file folders, notebooks, cards, and computer programs.

Portfolios

A **portfolio** is a collection of a student's work gathered over time. It shows both progress and achievement. It includes self-assessment and reflection. It can be kept electronically or in any kind of folder or container, such as a box or plastic pocket. It includes items the student has chosen, with reflections about why those choices were made. It includes both formative (showing progress) and summative (showing achievement) items.

The portfolio content represents collaboration between the student and the teacher, and it should be accessible to both at all times, but to no one else. Portfolios are particularly useful during student-teacher conferences, teacher-family conferences, and three-way conferences (student-teacher-family).

The school system in which you teach may direct how you should use portfolios. If not, the following steps should help you get started.

See more with TeachSource Video Case, "Portfolio Assessment: Elementary Classroom."

1. *Introduce the concept and perhaps show a portfolio from a previous year or one you keep for yourself.* Elicit ideas from children about a portfolio's purpose. Talk about how you and they will work to build the portfolio.

2. *Identify the categories of information to be included.* Use students' ideas as well as your own. For young children, you may want only two or three categories to start with, such as work samples, records of independent reading, and some checklists you have used. Later you may decide to add student self-evaluations, your anecdotal notes, tests, and other records related to assessment of reading and writing.

3. *Establish a procedure.* Pick a place to store the portfolios that is easily accessible. Decide the following and make a chart:
   a. How to select materials
   b. How to place them in the portfolio
   c. How to use entry and reflection slips for each student-selected item (see Figure 3.16)
   d. How and when to use the portfolio; when to file and retrieve items
   e. How to use the portfolio in conferences
   f. When to review, reevaluate, and weed the contents
4. *Inform the child's family* about the purpose, the process, and the procedures of portfolios.
5. *Plan regular times* with each child to review the portfolio.

You don't want children to spend time on portfolios that might better be spent on reading and writing. Children must see the value in the portfolio; otherwise, it will become a chore—an end in itself—rather than a support. Children should be able to peruse their portfolio contents and feel proud of what they have accomplished and how much they have grown.

PORTFOLIO ENTRY SLIP

Name _____ Date _____

Work placed in portfolio _____

I included this in my portfolio because _____

_____

_____

It shows that I am good at _____

_____

_____

It shows that I need to work on   _____

_____

_____

FIGURE 3.16

Sample Entry and Reflection Slip for Placing Items in a Portfolio

File Folders

You may choose to keep file folders of information. One set might contain a folder for each child. Another set might contain class results of tests, checklists, or other kinds of records. Still another set might be grouped by skill, each with a cover sheet on which you identify which children are using the skill and which still need to acquire it.

Notebooks

A notebook can have a section for each child. Record sheets for each child can be duplicated. Even if your children use portfolios, you may want to duplicate reading logs and put them into a notebook. As with all record keeping devices, each page should include the child's name and the date(s). Anecdotal records that were written on self-stick labels or sticky notes can be peeled off and put into the notebook.

Cards

Some teachers keep records on note cards, usually a 5″ × 8″ card for each child. The cards may be taped in alphabetical (or any other logical) order, overlapping, onto a clipboard so that the entire set can be carried around easily. When a card is filled, it is removed, filed in a box, and replaced with a new card.

Computer Programs

More and more computer programs are becoming available to help teachers keep records and organize information. But the cliché is true: the program is only as good as the person using it. Once you decide a program will be useful, enter data in a timely manner, double-check accuracy, and be sure you are using the information in a way that helps the children, not just produces statistics. You may also create your own electronic forms to help you organize information.

COMMENTS

Organizing information and record keeping may seem like a far cry from what drew you into teaching in the first place. It will take more time than you think. Accept that you will forget things unless you write them down. Establish habits of attention to detail. Make a checklist to remind yourself of the steps you must take to organize information.

Summary

- In this chapter, we have described tools specifically aimed at helping you assess children's literacy: oral language, reading, and writing.
- To assess a child's oral language development, you pay attention to both listening and speaking. You may use any of a variety of techniques, such as observing, checklists, and conferences.

- For second-language learners, you should be aware of the stages of language production that people typically pass through as they learn a new language.

- Reading assessment focuses on several areas: fluency and word recognition, retelling, discussions, and written responses.

- To assess oral reading fluency and word recognition strategies, you have the child read aloud a selection to you. You take a running record, noting the words read correctly and the miscues. Later you analyze the child's overall score and also the types of miscues he or she is prone to make. You use this information to plan appropriate instruction.

- Retelling involves having a student read material and then tell you about it. You record the results and analyze them to determine the child's needs.

- Classroom discussions allow you to assess reading comprehension abilities such as retelling and summarizing, as well as discussion behaviors. To learn how to conduct a good discussion, children frequently need teacher modeling and guidelines.

- Children's written responses to what they have read can help you assess their construction of meaning, their self-concepts, their attitudes, and more. You can have students write in journals, learning logs, or a variety of other formats.

- Sometimes you will assess children's use of the writing process: prewriting, drafting, revising, editing, and publishing. During a project that involves the writing process, each student should store every stage in a writing folder.

- For final products, holistic scoring yields a single score based on the overall quality of both content and mechanics. You must develop clear rubrics and anchor papers to which students can refer as they work.

- The types of writing you assess will be varied. For reports, you will want to develop a rubric or checklist by which students can judge their own progress. You'll also want to look at journals, learning logs, letters—virtually everything your students write.

- Assessment and instruction for the conventions of writing: grammar/usage, mechanics, and spelling is controversial. Many researchers see spelling ability as largely developmental, pointing out that nearly all children go through the same stages of learning to spell no matter how they are taught. Understanding these stages can help you determine when instruction is needed and what precisely you should teach.

- For all literacy assessment, you will need an efficient means of organizing the information you gather. You can use portfolios (collections of an individual student's work over time, with reflections and self-assessments by the student), file folders, notebooks, cards, and computer programs.

- The tools from this chapter, as well as those from Chapter 2 and Chapters 4 and 5, will be used as you learn about assessing the stages of literacy development in Chapters 8 through 12. We will show you how to use these tools to assess benchmark behaviors and plan instruction.

 Please visit the premium website for *Literacy Assessment*, Fourth Edition to access the TeachSource Video Cases, chapter web links, For Additional Reading, tutorial quizzes, glossary flashcards, online checklists, downloads, and much more! Go to www.cengage. com/login to register your access code.

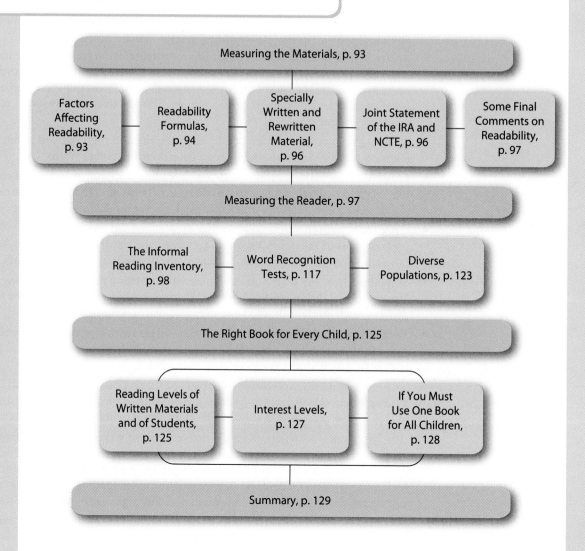

Measuring the Materials, p. 93

Factors Affecting Readability, p. 93

Readability Formulas, p. 94

Specially Written and Rewritten Material, p. 96

Joint Statement of the IRA and NCTE, p. 96

Some Final Comments on Readability, p. 97

Measuring the Reader, p. 97

The Informal Reading Inventory, p. 98

Word Recognition Tests, p. 117

Diverse Populations, p. 123

The Right Book for Every Child, p. 125

Reading Levels of Written Materials and of Students, p. 125

Interest Levels, p. 127

If You Must Use One Book for All Children, p. 128

Summary, p. 129

4

Matching Readers with Text:
Measuring Materials and Readers

- decodable text
- frustration reading level
- independent reading level
- informal reading inventory (IRI)
- instructional reading level
- interest level (IL)
- listening level
- readability (readability level)
- readability formula
- reading level
- sight word
- significant miscues

A new student, Bobby, is joining Ms. Kim's fourth-grade class today. Records from his previous school haven't yet arrived. Ms. Kim introduces Bobby to the class, finds him a desk, assigns him a buddy, and suggests that he just observe how the class begins the day, joining in whenever he feels comfortable.

Bobby sits quietly, looking around. He sees student projects about global warming on the walls and hanging from the ceiling. A couple of students straighten books. Bobby smiles as he spies the computers. After the morning routines, the other students take out folders and begin writing. Bobby is, apparently unsure of what he should be doing.

Another adult enters the room. Ms. Kim greets him warmly and speaks quietly to him. He hangs up his coat and begins circulating, stopping to chat with various students about their writing. Sometimes he pulls up a chair and talks at greater length with a student.

Ms. Kim whispers to Bobby, "Come with me, Bobby. Let's get to know each other." Looking a bit uneasy, Bobby clutches his jacket and follows Ms. Kim to the back room. After they chat for a few minutes, Ms. Kim points to an array of books on the table and asks Bobby to choose one and read it aloud. Ms. Kim listens, relaxed and smiling. After Bobby finishes the book, he and Ms. Kim talk some more. Bobby returns to his seat, and the class prepares for math.

Later, during reading time, Bobby is attentive but does not volunteer anything. Ms. Kim makes eye contact occasionally as if to invite him to respond, but she does not call on him. During independent reading time, Bobby leafs through books about space and astronauts and chooses one.

Later, Ms. Kim has Bobby join a group that has just completed reading various biographies. Ms. Kim asks the group members to share their books and discuss what makes an interesting and worthwhile biography. She tells Bobby the group will help him find a biography to read so that he can participate in this group, which will be together for another week or two.

Ms. Kim has been marking various checklists throughout the day during all blocks of literacy instruction.

The next day, Bobby participates more fully in the morning routines. He has been given a folder for independent writing and is writing busily. An aide enters the classroom to work with students, while Bobby and Ms. Kim go back to the workroom. Ms. Kim has several items ready. Bobby begins reading from lists of words as she marks a paper on a clipboard. Then, he reads short passages and answers questions while Ms. Kim makes notes. They seem relaxed but focused. Bobby is cooperative. They work together again later when the other students read independently.

After school, Ms. Kim looks at the information she has gathered so far about Bobby's literacy, making notes and analyzing results. She then makes notes in her plan book.

The next day, during whole-class reading, Ms. Kim asks Bobby a question calling for an opinion about an event in the story. Bobby ventures an opinion and looks around apprehensively. Ms. Kim nods and invites others to respond to Bobby's idea. Another boy paraphrases Bobby's idea and adds another way of looking at the matter.

During small-group time, Bobby joins the group that is reading biographies. The discussion picks up where it left off yesterday, this time without teacher supervision. The others invite Bobby to talk about the subject of his book and how far he has read. Bobby talks freely and asks to read one of the other books as soon as it is available. Ms. Kim glances over at the group often. When she sees Bobby entering into the discussion, she smiles to herself.

From the classroom described, you can see that although the tools, techniques, strategies, and instruments you have already learned about will be sufficient for most of your ongoing daily instructional decisions, sometimes you need more options to assess students' needs and monitor progress:

- When a new student enters your class and you have no information about the student's reading ability
- At the beginning of the school year
- When a student's reading seems to be dramatically below or above that of the rest of your class
- When a student's reading behavior is puzzling to you for some reason, and you have not been able to figure out what's going on using your usual assessments
- When you need more specific information to make a referral for special placement, extra help, or a staffing (a meeting among all people concerned with a child's learning)
- When you need additional information to help you clarify a student's reading performance for the family

In this chapter, we will discuss some informal measures related to reading. First, we will discuss readability: the concept of measuring the difficulty of reading materials. Then we will discuss measuring the reader, using an informal reading inventory (IRI) and other tools. Finally, we will examine some issues related to matching readers to reading materials.

Measuring the Materials

You would probably agree that to teach effectively you must provide reading materials the child is interested in, with words the child can recognize or figure out, and ideas he or she can understand. To do so, you want to know both the reading level of the student and the reading level of the materials she or he will read. But how can you know how "hard" a given piece of reading material is? The answer isn't as simple as it might seem.

The term **readability,** or **readability level,** is often used to refer to the difficulty of a piece of written material (Harris & Hodges, 1995). Readability is stated as a grade level. For example, a book at third-grade readability is presumably just right for a reader with third-grade reading ability; the reader can both recognize the words and comprehend the ideas.

Readability is a far broader concept than a grade level attached to a piece of text, however. It encompasses all the factors involved in whether or not a given piece of text is comprehensible to a given reader. Only some of these factors are measurable.

Factors Affecting Readability

We group the factors affecting readability into three interconnected categories: the reader, the text, and the environment (see Figure 4.1). We discuss each in turn.

THE READER

Difficulty is idiosyncratic; that is, individual experiences with a text depend on our interests, moods, attitudes, abilities, prior knowledge, and so forth. You probably find that your judgment about how difficult something is to read varies from day to day.

For example, you may find that you can study a certain textbook with concentration and understanding when you are rested and well fed, but if you try to read it when you are hungry or sleepy, you can't make any sense out of it. Similarly, you may have found a novel difficult when you were wrestling with a personal problem; then, when you tried again to read it at a more serene time, you were delighted with it.

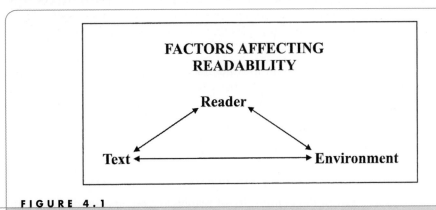

FIGURE 4.1

Interrelated Factors Affecting Readability

Your personal growth also influences your perception of difficulty. Sometimes we reread a book that at a younger age we found puzzling. After acquiring more life experience and maturity, we find the book satisfying and comprehensible. A text that you couldn't understand (though you knew all the words) because you didn't know the underlying concepts makes sense after an instructor provides conceptual support.

Finally, there is the ability of the reader to recognize or figure out the words and put the ideas together. This depends in part on the skills the reader has acquired, either independently or through instruction.

THE TEXT

Some things just seem easier to read than others because of the way they are written. For example:

- A textbook that is arranged logically, has graphic aids such as charts and tables, explains new terms in context, and has pages with wide margins is easier to read than one without these features.
- Stories that are told in straight sequence from a single point of view seem easier than those that use a great deal of flashback or multiple viewpoints.
- Stories that tap into feelings and experiences you share are easier for you to read than those in which you can't relate to the characters or the problems.
- Beautiful language, while sometimes "difficult," is so rewarding that we stick with it. We enjoy nonsense rhymes for the pure pleasure of the sounds, not looking for meaning at all.
- Many features are unique to reading online. These include hypertext, menus, links, advertising, narration, color, moving parts, and how to "turn a page."

THE ENVIRONMENT

Text can be made less difficult for a reader, or more accessible, through the intervention of the teacher. A teacher can support both the reader and the text by accessing or providing background experiences, discussing concepts, introducing critical terms, encouraging prediction, discussing, questioning, and using the many other instructional strategies that support success. Other important environmental factors include these:

- A classroom in which reading is treasured and celebrated inspires students to read more. A teacher who models his or her own pleasure in reading helps children see that making sense of print is worth doing.
- Students who come from a home that values reading have the additional advantage of support for reading both at school and at home.

Readability Formulas

Given the complexity of readability factors—and the fact that you can't measure most of them consistently and reliably or adjust instruction for each child based on individual constellations of factors—it isn't surprising that educators have wanted an easy, quick way to measure the difficulty of text so that they can choose reading material to match the ability of the child.

As early as the 1920s (Klare, 1988), efforts were made to develop a **readability formula** that educators could apply to a text to determine how "hard" the text was. Since then, many formulas have been developed. They differ slightly from one another, but all are based on counting certain features of the text and converting the resulting numbers to a grade level.

Other ways that do not necessarily use a grade-level designation are discussed in Chapter 6. Here we give you some background on readability formulas.

FEATURES OF READABILITY FORMULAS

Readability formulas are based on this assumption: long sentences with hard (or long) words are more difficult than short sentences with easy (or short) words. Formulas commonly rely on two features: syntax (the sentence structure) and semantics (the words).

The difficulty of the syntax is usually measured by sentence length; that is, the longer the sentence, the harder it is to read. The difficulty of the semantics is measured in one of two ways. With some formulas, words are checked against a given list of high-frequency words—that is, words that occur so often in print that you would expect a reader at a certain level to recognize them. For other formulas, words are counted as "hard" depending on their length, often as measured by the number of syllables. The presumption is that words with more than one syllable are harder than one-syllable words.

EXAMPLES OF READABILITY FORMULAS

The professional literature and the Internet contain thousands of references related to readability. One of the easiest formulas to use is the Fry Readability Formula, first published in 1968 and used widely ever since. It is based on the average sentence length and average syllable count of three 100-word samples from different places in a selection. The averages are plotted on a graph that shows the approximate grade level of the material. (This graph and instructions for using it are in the Resource File following the last chapter.) The Fry formula is meant to provide a quick way to judge the approximate grade level of a selection when you have no other information.

Different formulas may yield different results (Klare, 1995). For example, we used three different readability formulas (Fry, 1968; Harris & Jacobson, 1982; Spache, 1953) to check the readability of two books. Notice the variability in the scores (grade-level difficulty):

	Fry	*Harris-Jacobson*	*Spache*
The Paper Crane, by Molly Bang (1987)	5.0	5.2	3.2
A Bicycle for Rosaura, by Daniel Barbot (1990)	4.0	5.4	2.9

This variability means you should be cautious about relying on the results. Some people like to take more than three samples to better gauge difficulty. Some sources of computer programs that perform readability calculations are listed in the Websites section for this text online.

Specially Written and Rewritten Material

Published reading programs sometimes include selections specially written for the beginning reader. These selections are meant to capture children's interest in terms of content and to match the reading development of the beginning reader. Selections may be especially crafted to provide extensive practice with certain words or with certain decoding elements that beginning readers are learning. The rationale for such materials is that readers will more successfully build fluency and confidence when the text challenges they meet are controlled. These materials are frequently called **decodable texts;** they will be discussed further in Chapter 6.

Trade books that young children love to listen to may be too hard for children to read for themselves, so publishers sometimes edit stories to make the text conform to a certain readability level. That is, they choose a story that seems just right for a certain grade level or age in terms of appeal and content and apply a formula to sample passages. If the selection is found to be "too difficult," long sentences may be broken into shorter sentences, one-syllable words substituted for polysyllabic words, and "hard" words—those not on a given list—replaced with synonyms that are on the list.

While it is possible to adjust a book's readability down to the desired grade level, much may be lost, including the original language of the author. Sometimes, breaking up long sentences into shorter ones may result in text that is actually harder to understand. Consider the following example from *The Wonderful Wizard of Oz* (Baum, 1900/1990):

Original text: *But it is a long way to the Emerald City, and it will take you many days. The country here is rich and pleasant, but you must go through rough and dangerous places before you reach the end of your journey.*

Simplified text: *It is a long way to the Emerald City. It will take you many days. The country here is rich and nice. You must go through hard places before you get there.*

As you can see with this example, breaking long sentences into shorter ones loses the connecting words that make the relationship between ideas clear. In this case, because publishers don't like to begin a sentence with the word "but," the contrast between ideas is lost. The passage becomes a series of short, unconnected declarative sentences. The reader has to infer how the ideas are related. The result is a loss of clarity as well as a loss of the beauty of the language, which is further damaged by the substitution of "easier" words. Sadly, editing a story for readability often results in a story that is no longer worth reading at all.

Joint Statement of the IRA and NCTE

In 1984, the International Reading Association (IRA) and the National Council of Teachers of English (NCTE) issued a joint statement that continues to provide guidance in estimating reading difficulty (IRA/NCTE, 1984). Even though this statement is almost twenty-five years old, the two organizations summarize the factors influencing difficulty, many of which we have already addressed, and the problems with reducing the issue of difficulty to a formula. They then suggest the use of three alternative procedures:

1. Teacher judgment of proposed textual material
2. Observation of children using the material
3. Checklists that address such things as student interests, text graphics, new concepts, and line length

The procedures for leveling books discussed in Chapter 6 reflect the principles of this joint statement.

Some Final Comments on Readability

We believe you should take published readability levels with the proverbial grain of salt, knowing they have been determined through the use of at least one formula and remembering that they are based on limited factors. Keep in mind all the other factors affecting readability that a formula does not take into account.

Short sentences are not necessarily easier than long ones. Consider the often quoted "To be, or not to be" from Shakespeare's *Hamlet*. This is a short phrase made up of easy words, but what first grader would understand them? Similarly, long words are not necessarily harder: consider the long names of dinosaurs that very young children learn with delight.

We suggest that you pay attention to the other ways books are being leveled (see Chapter 6). Along with readability levels, use your common sense and your knowledge about children in general—and your children in particular.

Don't sacrifice a wonderful book because a formula says it will be too hard for the child. If the book is exactly right in all respects except for the difficulty level, make it work by reading it aloud to the child, providing more support before reading, or doing shared reading.

On the other hand, a wonderful story is never "too easy." We acknowledge that for growth to occur there must be challenge, but a book that a child finds easy and interesting builds fluency and confidence. This in turn leads to what all teachers have always wanted: children who not only can read but also choose to do so.

Measuring the Reader

Imagine it is the beginning of the school year. You are facing a room full of students and wondering how you can meet the needs of each one when all you know about them is their scores from last year's standardized tests (to be discussed in Chapter 5). You might know which books the child (presumably) read the previous year, but not how successfully, or how much was forgotten during the summer.

Should you give everyone the grade-level book and assume they will be able to read it? How do you know which book to put in the hands of which child? How can you begin to plan lessons? It can be an overwhelming feeling even for experienced teachers.

For kindergarten and first grade, we recommend that you simply ask which children can already read. Tell those children to select a book to read to you. Arrange for an aide, a volunteer, or an upper-grade student to be in your classroom for an hour or two each day for the first two weeks of the school year so you can work individually with each child. Be alert; you may have a child who can read competently but is reluctant to tell you so for one reason or another. You may also have some who say they can read but only recognize a few words. However, if a child *is* already reading fluently, you will want to assess his or her ability further.

From second grade on (or with younger children who are already reading), we recommend that you assess each child using an informal reading inventory, some of which may include materials for assessing early literacy. Or, use an instrument such as the *Developmental Reading Assessment* (DRA) (Beaver, 2002; Beaver & Carter, 2003). The DRA uses a series of little books that have been leveled in terms of difficulty on the basis of language and story structure, concepts, vocabulary, pictures, layout, print size, and other factors. Running records and retelling procedures are used for the lower levels; silent reading and retelling are used at higher levels.

The IRI

An **IRI** is an individually administered instrument designed to sample a child's reading on passages that are graduated in difficulty from very easy to more difficult. Accuracy in word recognition, comprehension, and fluency are taken into account. This instrument is designed to give you initial estimates of placement as well as diagnostic information.

To give an informal reading inventory, you will need thirty to forty-five minutes for each child. During this time, the other children can be monitored by another adult or engage in independent work. If you have thirty students and administer three each day, you will finish in two weeks.

See more with TeachSource Video Case, Literacy Assessment: Administering an Informal Reading Inventory.

BACKGROUND AND DEVELOPMENT OF THE IRI

In 1946, believing that standardized tests tended to place students in material that was too difficult, Betts suggested concepts about assessing reading ability that continue today. According to Betts (1946/1957), each reader has three **reading levels:**

Independent: the level at which children are able to read fluently without assistance and with virtually full comprehension

Instructional: the level at which children are able to read capably with good guidance and instruction

Frustration: the level at which children are incapable of either fluent oral reading or good comprehension, regardless of the teacher's skill

Virtually all published informal reading inventories, including those accompanying published basal reading programs, are based on Betts's original concept, though there have been extensive refinements. Every IRI will provide specific, detailed directions for use, along with the history of its development; a rationale for the particular passages and the criteria for establishing levels; and other support material, such as how the IRI was field-tested.

Often IRIs provide two or more equivalent forms; these can be used for various purposes, which we will discuss later in this chapter. For example, one form might be used to assess the **listening level,** the level of material the child can comprehend when text is read to him or her.

Some IRIs also provide guidelines for analyzing the nature of the child's word recognition and ability to answer questions, and some provide additional diagnostic assessments related to word recognition and comprehension.

READING AND LISTENING LEVELS AND PERCENTAGES

Following are typical definitions and percentages for the reading and listening levels, conforming to Betts's original criteria. When a published inventory deviates from these percentages, an explanation and rationale will be found in the manual.

* *Independent reading level.* This is the highest level the child can be presumed to read accurately, with good understanding, and without assistance. This is an appropriate level for homework assignments and for pleasure reading. The typical percentages for defining this level are 99 percent word recognition (no more than 1 significant error in 100 words) and 90 percent comprehension. Reading should be smooth, free of signs of anxiety or stress, and fluent. Teacher judgment determines which miscues are significant—that is, which miscues "count." For example, substituting "a" for "the" is not usually considered significant.

* *Instructional reading level.* This is the highest level the child can read with teacher guidance and support. When this level is used for instructional activities, you can expect growth in reading ability. The student is challenged but not frustrated. Difficulties are dealt with through appropriate instruction, and the child feels he or she can read the material with the teacher's help. Word recognition accuracy should be 95 percent (no more than 5 significant miscues in 100 words), and comprehension should be at least 75 percent (fewer than 3 questions missed out of 10).

* *Frustration reading level.* This is the level of material the student should not be asked to use at all. When material is at a child's frustration level, he or she is having so much trouble with word recognition or comprehension that learning is not possible. The child then feels incompetent, which compounds the difficulty. Overt behaviors may include finger pointing, squirming, squinting, word-by-word reading, and lack of expression. The percentages indicating frustration are less than 90 percent word recognition (more than 10 words missed out of 100) and less than 50 percent comprehension (5 questions missed out of 10).

* *Listening level.* This is the highest level of material that the student can understand when it is read *to* him or her. The criterion is at least 75 percent comprehension (70 percent in some inventories). If a child can understand text at a certain level when listening, you can assume she or he has sufficient vocabulary and background experience to handle the material. If the child is unable to *read* material at that level, there should be a potential for reading growth with appropriate instruction.

Later in this chapter, we will discuss how to deal with scores that do not fall neatly into the given percentages, such as 99 percent word recognition but only 60 percent comprehension.

TABLE 4.1

Informal Reading Inventory Criteria

	WORD RECOGNITION		COMPREHENSION
Original criteria (Betts, 1946/1957)			
Independent	99%+	and	90%+
Instructional	95%+	and	75%+
Frustration	Less than 90%	or	Less than 50%
Revised criteria (Burns & Roe, 2007)			
Independent	99% or higher	and	90% or higher
Instructional			
Grades 1 to 2	85% or higher	and	75% or higher
Grades 3 to 12	95% or higher	and	75% or higher
Frustration			
Grades 1 to 2	Below 85%	or	Below 50%
Grades 3 to 12	Below 90%	or	Below 50%

VARIATIONS IN IRI PERCENTAGES

The upper portion of Table 4.1 sums up the typical IRI percentages based on Betts's criteria. It has been suggested, though, that at the lower grade levels, a lower word recognition percentage should be tolerated because these children are just beginning to read (Clay, 1985). The lower portion of Table 4.1, based on the IRI published by Roe and Burns (2007), reflects such an adjustment. In the Roe and Burns version, the word recognition expectation is lower for grades 1 and 2 at the instructional level. If you use a published IRI, the percentages will be dictated by the particular publication chosen.

The suggested percentages are just guidelines to help you estimate a child's reading levels. As you will see later, percentages are only part of the picture an IRI yields.

COMPONENTS OF THE IRI

All IRIs are made up of the same basic components:

- *Graded word lists.* These are sample lists of words at each grade level, beginning with preprimer and going up to the highest-graded passage covered by the particular IRI. Some teachers use these lists to judge which passage to have the child read first. Some teachers analyze errors from these lists to see which parts of words the child seems to miss most often.

- *Graded passages.* These are passages of text beginning with the preprimer level and proceeding up. Some go to grade 6; some continue to much higher grades. Comprehension questions and, sometimes, a retelling guide are provided for each passage. Most published inventories provide at least two equivalent sets of passages. Some include one set of narrative passages and one set of expository material. Some include a set of longer passages for alternate use. These multiple sets of passages allow a number of options:

  One set (or form) can be used to assess oral reading (word recognition in context) and comprehension, while another set is used for silent reading comprehension.

  One set can be used at one time and another at a later time to assess growth.

  One set can be used to estimate a child's listening level.

- *Summaries and analyses.* These include various ways to record and analyze a child's performance after administration of the inventory. These may include the following:

  A summary form to pull all information together

  A method for analyzing a child's miscues or errors

  A method for analyzing the types of comprehension questions missed, comparing comprehension on oral passages with comprehension of passages read silently and considering reading performance in light of listening level

The following sections will discuss these IRI components in more detail and offer illustrations of each. The sample forms we will use are from Johns's *Basic Reading Inventory, Ninth Edition* (2005). See the References section for information on the available Tenth Edition.

IRI PROCEDURES

Each published informal reading inventory provides extensive, detailed steps for administering, scoring, and analyzing performance. Although there are many differences between IRIs, the basic steps are similar:

1. Decide what level of passage to have the child read first.
    - We recommend starting one year below the child's grade placement for children in grades 1 and 2 and two years below for children in grade 3 and up to avoid starting them at a frustration level.
    - Alternatively, to estimate which passage the child should read first, you can administer the graded word lists. Each list usually has twenty words. The lists are duplicated for you to mark on and can be photocopied for such purposes without permission. Figure 4.2 shows a sample graded word list. The following procedure is typical:

    Have the child read the words on the list quickly.

    Mark + or ✔ if read correctly. If a word is incorrect, write what the child said.

    Have the child return to the missed words and try to figure them out.

Form A • Graded Word Lists • Performance Booklet • Student Copy is on page 143.

List A 7141 (Grade 1)	Sight	Analysis	List A 8224 (Grade 2)	Sight	Analysis
1. here*	✔		1. ten*	✔	
2. down*	✔		2. poor	p⁻	pour
3. then*	than	then ✔	3. city	k⁻	—
4. how*	who	how ✔	4. teacher	✔	
5. saw*	was	saw ✔	5. turn*	✔	
6. pocket	—	p⁻	6. fight	✔	
7. hello	✔		7. because*	✔	
8. aunt	✔		8. soft	✔	
9. never*	✔		9. open*	✔	
10. puppy	✔		10. winter	✔	
11. could*	couldn't	could ✔	11. joke	j⁻	✔
12. after*	✔		12. different	—	
13. hill	✔		13. say*	✔	
14. men	✔		14. quiet	quite	quit
15. gone*	✔		15. sister	✔	
16. ran*	✔		16. above	✔	
17. gave*	✔		17. seed	seen	✔
18. or*	✔		18. thought*	though	✔
19. way	✔		19. such	✔	
20. coat	cat	coat ✔	20. chase	chose	✔

*denotes basic sight word from Revised Dolch List

			*denotes basic sight word from Revised Dolch List		
Number Correct	14	5	Number Correct	12	4
Total		19	Total		16

Scoring Guide for Graded Word Lists

Independent	Instructional	Frustration
20 19	18 17 16 15 14	13 or less

From *Basic Reading Inventory: Pre-Primer Through Grade Twelve and Early Literacy Assessments,* Ninth Edition, by Jerry L. Johns. Copyright © 2005 by Kendall/Hunt Publishing Company. Used with permission.

FIGURE 4.2

Sample Graded Word List (Johns, 2005)

(Note: The "Scoring Guide for Graded Word Lists" shown at the bottom is not an indication of actual reading level.)

Credit all words read correctly plus all those the child reads correctly when given time to analyze them.

Have the child begin reading the passages at the highest grade level on which he or she read nineteen or twenty words fluently on the graded word list.

2. Decide how to have the child read (silently or aloud) and present the first passage at the determined level.

Silent first: Students above grade 3 should read silently first and then read the same passage aloud. This will save time, as you do not use separate oral and silent reading tests. It is also most like classroom reading tasks.

Oral first: Children below grade 3 or students who have shown word recognition problems should read the passage aloud at sight.

- You may be told to introduce the passage in some way, perhaps by asking the child to predict on the basis of the title. This procedure helps to check for prior knowledge.

- The child reads aloud from a page with only the passage on it. You have a copy with the passage, the comprehension questions, and other information.

- You mark every deviation from the exact text, using the marking system presented in the IRI manual or one you already know, such as the one we presented in Chapter 3 (Figure 3.1). Figure 4.3 shows a sample of a marked form. Note the place to analyze miscues.

- As you mark miscues, you also record observations of the child's behavior, such as fidgeting, word-by-word reading, long pauses, nervousness, frequent requests to be told the word, and other indications of attitude and mood. Some teachers return to passages after administration of the inventory to probe for students' explanations of their behaviors.

Student Copy is on page 154.

A 8224 (Grade 2) Activating Background: Read the title to yourself; then tell me what you think will happen.

Background: Low ├───┼───┤ High

Billy
~~Bill~~ at Camp

MISCUES							
Substitution	Insertion	Omission	Reversal	Repetition	Self-Correction of Unacceptable Miscue	Meaning Change (Significant Miscue)	

Passage	#								
It was the first time ~~Bill~~ *Billy* went to	8								
camp. He was very /*very* happy to be there. ~~Soon~~ *So*	17								
he went for a walk in the woods to look for	28								
many kinds of leaves. He ~~found~~ *saw* leaves	35								
from some maple and oak trees. As ~~Bill~~ *Billy*	43								
walked in the woods, he /*also* saw some animal	51								
tracks. At that (moment) a ~~mouse~~ *moose* ③₀ ran into	59								
a small hole by a tree. ~~Bill wondered~~ *Billy wandered* if the	69								
tracks were made by the mouse. He looked	77								
(around) for other animals. He ~~did not~~ *didn't* see	85								
any. The last thing ~~Bill~~ *Billy* saw was an old	94								
bird nest in a pine tree.	100								
TOTAL									

Didn't count
mispronunciation
of name

Total Miscues [9]   Significant Miscues [1]

Didn't time

Word Recognition Scoring Guide

Total Miscues	Level	Significant Miscues
0–1	Independent	0–1
2–4	Ind./Inst.	2
5	Instructional	3
(6–9)	Inst./Frust.	4
10 +	Frustration	5 +

Oral Reading Rate	Norm Group Percentile
WPM)6000	☐ 90 ☐ 75 ☐ 50 ☐ 25 ☐ 10

From *Basic Reading Inventory: Pre-Primer Through Grade Twelve and Early Literacy Assessments,* Ninth Edition, by Jerry L. Johns. Copyright © 2005 by Kendall/Hunt Publishing Company. Used with permission.

FIGURE 4.3

Sample Marked IRI Passage (Johns, 2005)

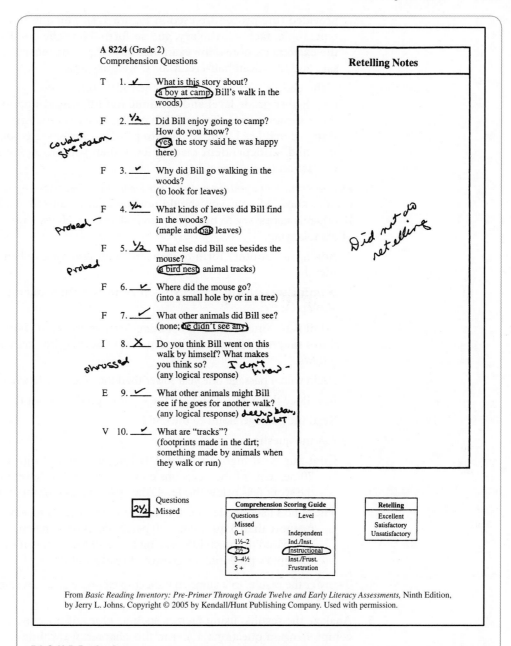

A 8224 (Grade 2)
Comprehension Questions

T   1. ✔ What is this story about?
       (a boy at camp; Bill's walk in the woods)

F   2. ½ Did Bill enjoy going to camp?
       How do you know?
       (yes, the story said he was happy there)

couldn't give reason

F   3. ✔ Why did Bill go walking in the woods?
       (to look for leaves)

F   4. ½ What kinds of leaves did Bill find in the woods?
       (maple and oak leaves)

Probed —

F   5. ½ What else did Bill see besides the mouse?
       (a bird nest; animal tracks)

Probed

F   6. ✔ Where did the mouse go?
       (into a small hole by or in a tree)

F   7. ✔ What other animals did Bill see?
       (none; he didn't see any)

I   8. X Do you think Bill went on this walk by himself? What makes you think so?
       (any logical response)   *I don't know —*

shrugged

E   9. ✔ What other animals might Bill see if he goes for another walk?
       (any logical response)   *deer, bear, rabbit*

V   10. ✔ What are "tracks"?
       (footprints made in the dirt; something made by animals when they walk or run)

Retelling Notes

Did not do retelling

2½ Questions Missed

Comprehension Scoring Guide	
Questions Missed	Level
0–1	Independent
1½–2	Ind./Inst.
2½	Instructional
3–4½	Inst./Frust.
5 +	Frustration

Retelling
Excellent
Satisfactory
Unsatisfactory

From *Basic Reading Inventory: Pre-Primer Through Grade Twelve and Early Literacy Assessments,* Ninth Edition, by Jerry L. Johns. Copyright © 2005 by Kendall/Hunt Publishing Company. Used with permission.

FIGURE 4.4

Sample Record of Comprehension on a Graded Passage (Johns, 2005)

- After the child finishes reading the passage, remove it and follow one of two procedures (see Figure 4.4). (1) Ask the child to retell what is remembered, followed by questions addressing content not recalled. Most IRIs give information about how to use this procedure. (2) Ask the questions provided (the procedure used in Figure 4.4). The questions are labeled by type: topic, fact, vocabulary, and so forth. Note the child's responses and the examiner's notes; the examiner has circled or recorded what the child said and has given half-credit for three questions.

- If the child's performance is at the independent level, you proceed to the next higher grade level and continue until the child's performance falls to the frustration level. If the child's performance on the first passage is at the instructional level, you go back to passages for lower grades to determine the child's independent reading level; then you proceed upward until the frustration level is reached.

3. *Decide whether to administer any other form.* This decision depends on what you need to know. Mostly, you should not spend any more time administering an IRI than is necessary to begin to plan instruction. However, you might do one of the following:

- Administer another form to measure comprehension when the child reads silently.

- Administer a form with expository rather than narrative material (if available).

- Administer one form as a listening-level assessment. For this, the procedures may vary from one inventory to another, but they are basically as follows:

  Begin with a passage one year lower than the child's instructional reading level.

  Introduce the passage and ask the child to predict about the content.

  Read the passage aloud to the child.

  Ask the questions.

  Continue with higher passages as long as the child gets 75 percent (or 70 percent) of the questions correct (misses 3 or fewer out of 10). When the score falls below this level (the child misses 4 or more questions), stop.

  The child's listening level is the highest grade level at which he or she missed no more than 3 questions (70 percent comprehension). This level is then compared to the child's reading levels so that you can hypothesize about the child's potential for growth in reading ability.

4. Transfer the results to a summary sheet to estimate levels. A sample is shown in Figure 4.5.

5. Analyze the results, using factors such as types of miscues and categories of comprehension questions. Later in this chapter, we will discuss some ways to do this kind of analysis.

ESTIMATING LEVELS

When you transfer results to a summary sheet, you have data from each marked passage the child has read. You record the number of miscues and questions missed, along with the associated levels for word recognition and for comprehension of

| Ninth Edition | **BASIC READING INVENTORY PERFORMANCE BOOKLET**
Jerry L. Johns, Ph.D. | Form A |

Student _Gordon_   Grade _4_   Sex (M) F   Date of Test ___

School ___   Examiner ___   Date of Birth ___

Address ___   Current Book/Level ___   Age _9_

SUMMARY OF STUDENT'S READING PERFORMANCE

Grade	Word Recognition						Comprehension		Reading Rate	
	Isolation (Word Lists)			Context (Passages)			Form A		Words per Minute (WPM)	Norm Group Percentile
	Sight	Analysis	Total	Level	Miscues	Level	Questions Missed	Level		
PP1										
PP2										
P					0	Ind	1	Ind		
1					0	Ind	3	Inst/Fr		
2					3	Ind/Inst	2	Ind/Inst		
3					4	Ind/Inst	0	Ind		
4					5	Inst	4	Inst/Fr		
5					15	FR	6	FR		
6										
7										
8										
9										
10										
11										
12										

Significant

ESTIMATE OF READING LEVELS

Also gave silent IRA – see notes below.

Independent _1_   Instructional _2-3_   Frustration _4_

LISTENING LEVEL

Form ____

Grade	Questions Missed	Level
1		
2	0	
3	3	
4	2	
5	3 ←	
6	5	
7		
8		

ESTIMATED LEVEL: _5_

GENERAL OBSERVATIONS

NOTE: On silent passages G. was PP-Ind, P-Inst, I-Inst/F, 2-Ind and 3-FR. Asked for bathroom break on Gr. 1, liked Gr. 4 story, was tired at Gr. 3 and seemed determined _not_ to answer questions.

ORAL ? Reading is flat-monotonal.
Says Gr. 1 story was babyish
Gr. 3 ? volunteered info about bears.
Gr. 5 ? tired. Wanted to stop.

Attitude positive. Wants to read better.

INFORMAL ANALYSIS OF ORAL READING

Oral Reading Behaviors	Frequency of Occurrence			General Impact on Meaning		
	Seldom	Sometimes	Frequently	No Change	Little Change	Much Change
Substitutions						
Insertions						
Omissions						
Reversals						
Repetitions						

From *Basic Reading Inventory: Pre-Primer Through Grade Twelve and Early Literacy Assessments,* Ninth Edition, by Jerry L. Johns. Copyright © 2005 by Kendall/Hunt Publishing Company. Used with permission.

FIGURE 4.5

Sample Results from an Informal Reading Inventory of a Fourth Grader (Johns, 2005)

silently and/or orally read passages. Most summary sheets also provide a place for other information, such as listening level, most prevalent type of word recognition error, and rate (if you timed the readings).

Then you look at the total picture of reading performance and estimate the child's three reading levels. If scores fall neatly into the given percentage ranges, your job is easy. If not, you have to make a decision. Look at Figure 4.5, which shows a summary sheet for Gordon, a fourth-grade student. How would you determine his reading levels?

Gordon's teacher was concerned about his reading, so she followed the procedure for a younger child, using separate passages for oral reading and silent reading. She suspected that Gordon's word recognition needs justified the additional time required.

To estimate Gordon's reading levels, we will use the summary of miscues and comprehension questions missed as well as the information related to attitude and behavior recorded in the box labeled "General Observations." This information comes from notes the teacher made during the administration of the inventory. Notice, too, these other features of the summary page in Figure 4.5:

- The grade levels are listed down the left side of the form.
- On this form one records the *number* of miscues and the *number* of questions missed, not the percentages. In the following discussion, we will refer to the percentages as well.
- Although the teacher will have marked all miscues for later analysis, only significant miscues are counted for the purpose of figuring reading levels. **Significant miscues** are miscues that were not self-corrected and that affect syntax or semantics, resulting in a loss or change of meaning.
- When a score falls between two levels, this fact is indicated with a slash mark; "Ind/Inst" means the child's score fell between the independent and the instructional level.

We estimate Gordon's reading levels to be as follows:

Independent grade 1

Instructional grades 2–3

Frustration grade 4

The following sections explain these choices.

Independent Reading Level. Gordon's independent level is not immediately clear. While his word recognition was at the independent level through grade 1, his comprehension at grade 1 was only 70 percent ("Inst/Fr") for the oral passage and 60 percent (again "Inst/Fr") for the silent passage. However, look at the higher-level passages: his oral passage comprehension was 100 percent at grade 3 (0 questions missed), and his silent passage comprehension was 90 percent (only 1 question missed) at grade 2.

Several things could account for this inconsistency:

- Gordon thought the grade 1 oral story was "babyish."
- The syntax of the preprimer and primer passages is so unlike natural speech that it may have inhibited his comprehension.

- He may have been unused to silent reading.
- He asked for a bathroom break right after the grade 1 silent passage (as noted in the General Observations) and probably was uncomfortable as he read it.

Considering that Gordon is in fourth grade, that his word recognition is independent at grade 1, and that his comprehension is independent at the third-grade level for oral passages and at the second-grade level for silent passages, we would assign him grade 1 material for independent reading to begin with. You might find that he can handle higher-level material when he is focused, interested, and not being assessed.

You would plan instruction in silent reading strategies and metacognition. As you begin work, you might find that you under or overestimated Gordon's independent reading level. Then you would adjust up or down as needed.

Frustration Reading Level. We next like to determine the frustration level—the level at which you should never put the student. For Gordon, we would say grade 4. Why?

- Although his word recognition was still at the instructional level at grade 4, his comprehension was not: on the oral passages his comprehension bordered on the frustration level at grade 4, and on the silent reading passages he was at the frustration level at grade 3.
- Consulting our notes on the grade 3 silent reading passage (not shown in the figure), we recall that Gordon simply shrugged when asked the three questions that called for inference or judgment. He forgot a detail (where the first steam engine was built) and could not give a definition of *steam*. Five questions missed out of ten—clearly the frustration level. However, it may turn out that he is reluctant to venture a response unless he is absolutely sure of being right. This could account for his shrugging and not responding to the questions that had no clear right or wrong answers. With encouragement, he may comprehend better than the numbers indicate.
- Most work in the fourth grade requires strong comprehension and silent reading. A frustration level of grade 4 means that Gordon cannot be expected to learn well from grade-level material. For subjects such as science and social studies, Gordon needs easier materials on the same topics, both for instruction and for independent work. If such materials are not available, he will need extraordinary support to learn from the grade-level materials. For example, he may need to listen to the material read aloud, or he may need study guides or a study buddy. He will need additional prereading instruction to build concepts and teach new vocabulary, as well as more guidance during silent reading, with the text broken into small, meaningful chunks. With extra help, Gordon will be able to participate in a discussion even if the material is challenging for him to read.

Instructional Reading Level. Appropriate books for Gordon to apply skills and strategies should be at his instructional level, which falls between the independent and frustration levels. Often the instructional level involves a range, as it does for Gordon. Since his independent level is grade 1 and his frustration level grade 4, his instructional level is grades 2 to 3.

- Instruction should begin with second-grade material, where Gordon's word recognition is strong (just 1 percent below the independent criterion), and his comprehension is strong on both oral and silent passages. Because Gordon will not need to struggle with word recognition or comprehension, he will probably quickly build fluency, stronger comprehension, and self-confidence and be ready for grade 3 materials.

● Gordon has a listening level of grade 5, which shows his ability to deal with higher-level concepts and language. He also has a positive attitude. He will probably make rapid growth when instructed with materials at the appropriate level.

Remember, an IRI yields a quick estimate of a child's reading ability so you can begin instruction. You may need to make an adjustment almost immediately. From then on, you will use the kinds of informal assessments discussed in Chapters 2 and 3 and Chapters 8 through 12.

ANALYZING MISCUES AND COMPREHENSION

Using information from the IRI, you may want to do a detailed analysis of the student's miscues and comprehension. Often, published informal reading inventories provide a method for such an analysis and help you interpret your analysis and use it to inform instruction. As new evidence occurs during instruction, you will continually revise your conclusions.

Miscues. As you know, a miscue is any oral response to print that differs from the actual print—saying something else instead of exactly what is on the page. Everyone miscues occasionally, even you! If your miscue doesn't upset your ability to construct meaning, you probably read right on without being aware of having miscued. For example, if you substitute "a" for "the," meaning is not affected significantly, and you read on. If you substitute "want" for "went," meaning is lost and you probably catch yourself and self-correct. If you substitute "emerge" for "immerge," you may or may not know that you've miscued, depending on whether you know the difference between the two words.

Educators used to talk about mistakes or errors. But the concept of "miscue" is a better one. It suggests that when a reader's oral response isn't a perfect match for the print, it is because the reader has not paid attention to all the cues in the print: the meaning of the passage, the parts of the word, the graphic symbols and their associated sounds, the punctuation, and so forth. Looking closely at a reader's miscues may give us a hint about the mysterious, unobservable processes one uses to make sense of print.

Although the principles for analyzing miscues are similar, procedures vary from one IRI to another; you should follow the instructions for your chosen IRI. Some manuals direct you to analyze only the miscues that occur during the reading of the passages (not the word lists) and only those from passages at the independent or instructional level for word recognition. Not everyone agrees on the latter point; some IRIs have you analyze miscues from all passages attempted. You can find detailed discussion about analysis of miscues by entering the term in a search engine or consulting books intended for reading specialists.

When a reader struggles with material at the frustration level, the miscues may not be typical and little may be learned. The reader may:

● Guess wildly.
● Miscall words that were read accurately on an earlier passage.

- Ignore word recognition strategies that he or she would usually use.
- Exhibit physical indications of frustration, such as sweating, fidgeting, finger pointing, word-by-word reading, and losing one's place.

Procedures for Analyzing Miscues. For purposes of analysis we use all miscues, including those that were self-corrected and those that were not counted as significant (such as "house" for "home") when estimating levels.

The first step is to transfer the miscues and the corresponding text from each oral reading passage to the summary sheet. Figure 4.6 shows an example of a child's miscues recorded on a form for the *Basic Reading Inventory* (Johns, 2005). Detailed instructions are given in the manual; our discussion here is meant only to give you an idea of how such an analysis is done.

Next, you examine each miscue in terms of several qualities. For example, the "Graphic Similarity" columns ask you to compare the miscue (what the child said) with the text (what is on the page) in terms of letters at the beginning, middle, and end of the word. The "Context" columns ask that you judge whether a miscue was "acceptable in context," which requires that you refer to the passage in which the miscue occurred. There is also a place to record which "unacceptable in context" miscues were self-corrected by the child. The coding in Figure 4.6 uses a check mark if the category applies to a particular miscue, a dash if it does not, and an X if the child did not attempt to say the word. The check marks in each column are then added to produce the totals at the bottom of the form. We have done the arithmetic, the procedures for which are provided in the manual. The column totals are then transferred to the graphs at the right of the form.

The Prediction Strategy, shown at the right of Figure 4.6, has two parts. The "Graphic Similarity" graphs show whether the child relied more heavily on one part of the word than another and to what extent. The "Miscues Acceptable in Context" graph shows instantly what percentage of miscues analyzed did not result in loss of meaning. A comparison of these two graphs may (we realize we may be overgeneralizing) show something helpful in terms of planning instruction. For example, high, graphic similarity and low acceptability in context might mean that a child relies on phonics to the exclusion of what makes sense. The "Correction Strategy" graph at the lower right of Figure 4.6 helps you see at a glance whether a child frequently recognizes when meaning is lost and self-corrects.

Interpretation of Miscues. How might you interpret the information in Figure 4.6? The pattern of this child's miscues reveals several bits of information that could help you make instructional plans:

- The percentages of graphic similarity were low for all parts of the words, indicating that the child pays little attention to the letters on the page.
- A third of the miscues did not result in a loss of meaning; that is, the child's substitutions fit the story. This child seems to say the word he expects in terms of meaning, and if it works, he reads on.

Qualitative Summary of Miscues on the Basic Reading Inventory

Jerry L. Johns, Ph.D.

MISCUE	TEXT	GRAPHIC SIMILARITY			CONTEXT		Self-Correction of Unacceptable Miscues
		Beginning	Middle	End	Acceptable	Unacceptable	
come	some	—	✔	✔		✔	✔
beautiful	pretty	—	—	—	✔		
opened	opening	✔	✔			✔	✔
—	kitchen	✗	✗	✗		✔	
lots of	some	—	—	—	✔		
vant	went	✔		✔		✔	✔
Column Total		2	2	2	2	4	3
Number of Miscues Analyzed		5	5	5	6		
Percentage		40	40	40	83		75

PREDICTION STRATEGY

Graphic Similarity
B M E

Miscues Acceptable in Context

40% 40% 40%   33%

CORRECTION STRATEGY

Unacceptable Miscues Self-Corrected

75%

From *Basic Reading Inventory: Pre-Primer Through Grade Twelve and Early Literacy Assessments,* Ninth Edition, by Jerry L. Johns. Copyright © 2005 by Kendall/Hunt Publishing Company. Used with permission.

FIGURE 4.6

Sample Miscue Summary, Basic Reading Inventory (Johns, 2005)

- Of the miscues that did result in loss of meaning, 75 percent were self-corrected. Meaning is clearly of highest priority for this child. The only miscue not self-corrected was "kitchen," a word he refused to attempt.

- Despite the strengths of self-correction and acceptable miscues, this child needs to pay closer attention to the words on the page. This will be increasingly important as he reads more factual material in content areas such as social studies and science.

For this child, a good instructional strategy would be to let him read into a tape recorder and then assess himself. This would help him become more aware of accuracy. At the same time, support his very real strength in constructing meaning.

Table 4.2 shows examples of what might have been learned about other children through the analysis of miscues and what initial instructional plans might be appropriate.

Comprehension. When you have completed the IRI, you have the reader's responses to several kinds of questions. Many IRIs label each question as to type, such as main idea or topic, vocabulary, literal or factual, inferential, and evaluative. Using information only from passages at the child's independent and instructional levels, you may note which kinds of questions the child consistently answers acceptably and which kinds consistently give trouble.

COMMENTS

Often so few miscues occur that it is risky to draw conclusions about typical strategies the child might be using. However, we believe the IRI miscue analysis can provide enough information to get you started with instruction that is on target.

Also, doing such analysis helps you realize what can be learned from miscues whenever a child is reading, not just during an assessment. It will help you resist the temptation to judge a child harshly for not recognizing a word you think he or she "should" know.

If you think you do not have enough miscues from an IRI to provide a useful analysis and appropriate instruction for a given child, you can take a running or fluency record, as described in Chapters 3 and 10, to generate more miscues to analyze. More elaborate types of miscue analysis also exist (Goodman, Watson, & Burke, 1987, 2005; Rhodes & Shanklin, 1990; Rhodes, 1993). A reading specialist or clinician might choose one of these, but you would want to weigh the time involved against the potential for improved ability to meet the child's needs.

Figure 4.7 shows one summary of a student's comprehension performance on an IRI. Such an analysis makes it easier to look at the total picture of a reader's responses to certain kinds of questions. The manual for this IRI gives detailed directions for filling out the summary, doing the arithmetic, and drawing conclusions. For both oral and silent reading forms, you record how many of each kind of question

TABLE 4.2

Summary, Interpretation, and Instructional Plans Based on Miscues of Three Children

NAME	SUMMARY OF MISCUES	INTERPRETATION	INSTRUCTION
Jorge	Most miscues were semantically and syntactically acceptable, but little attention was paid to graphic clues. Examples: "pony" for "horse," "kids" for "children." Self-corrected most miscues that resulted in loss of meaning.	Obviously understood the text, but needs to learn that such substitutions may not always work and that accuracy is important.	Have him audiotape himself and then check his own tape to raise his awareness of how often he substitutes his own words for those of the author.
Heather	Miscues were graphically similar in most cases: "when" for "where," "ever" for "every," "house" for "horse." Meaning was seldom maintained. Syntax sometimes was appropriate. Few miscues were self-corrected.	Seems so intent on figuring out the sound of the word that she neglects to think about meaning.	Provide many books at her independent reading level to relieve the need to decode every word and allow focus on meaning. Build prior knowledge and encourage prediction. Chunk guided silent reading to help her monitor meaning. Model monitoring: "Does it make sense? Does it sound the way the language is supposed to sound? If it doesn't, I need to reread to see if I miscued."
Wesley	Few miscues and efficient use of strategies when reading narrative material, but not when reading expository text, for which he seemed to use only phonics.	May not have sufficient background information for content material.	Teach strategies for reading content material such as science texts: previewing, predicting, reflecting and retelling to self, summarizing, and reviewing. Deal carefully with new vocabulary and concepts before reading.

Summary of Student's Comprehension Performance on the Basic Reading Inventory

Jerry L. Johns, Ph.D.

	ANALYSIS BY TYPE OF QUESTION									
Grade	**Fact**		**Topic**		**Evaluation**		**Inference**		**Vocabulary**	
	Oral	Silent	Oral	Silent	Oral	Silent	Oral	Silent	Oral	Silent
P	/6	/8	/1	/1	/1	/1	/1	/1	/1	/1
1	/6	/6	/1	/1	/1	/1	/1	/1	/1	/1
2	0/6	0/6	0/1	0/1	0/1	0/1	0/1	0/1	0/1	0/1
3	1/6	0/6	0/1	0/1	0/1	0/1	0/1	0/1	0/1	0/1
4	1/6	2/6	0/1	0/1	0/1	0/1	0/1	0/1	0/1	0/1
5	2/6	3/6	0/1	0/1	0/1	0/1	1/1	1/1	1/1	0/1
6	/6	/6	/1	/1	/1	/1	/1	/1	/1	/1
7	/6	/6	/1	/1	/1	/1	/1	/1	/1	/1
8	/S	/6	/1	/1	/1	/1	/1	/1	/1	/1
9	/6	/6	/1	/1	/1	/1	/1	/1	/1	/1
10	/6	/6	/1	/1	/1	/1	/1	/1	/1	/1
11	/6	/6	/1	/1	/1	/1	/1	/1	/1	/1
12	/6	/6	/1	/1	/1	/1	/1	/1	/1	/1
Ratio Missed	4/24	5/24	0/4	0/4	0/4	0/4	1/4	1/4	1/4	0/4
Percent Missed	16%	20%	0%	0%	0%	0%	25%	25%	25%	0%
Total Ratio Missed	9/48		0/8		0/8		2/8		1/8	
Total Percent Missed	19%		0%		0%		25%		12½%	

ANALYSIS BY LEVEL OF COMPREHENSION				
	Lower-Level Comprehension (Fact Questions Only)		**Higher-Level Comprehension (All Other Questions)**	
	Oral	Silent	Oral	Silent
Ratio Missed	4/24	5/24	2/16	1/16
Total Ratio Missed	9/48		3/32	
Total Percent Missed	19%		9%	

From *Basic Reading Inventory: Pre-Primer Through Grade Twelve and Early Literacy Assessments,* Ninth Edition, by Jerry L. Johns. Copyright © 2005 by Kendall/Hunt Publishing Company. Used with permission.

FIGURE 4.7

Sample Page for Summarizing and Analyzing Comprehension from an Informal Reading Inventory (Johns, 2005)

a child missed out of how many possible for each passage read. You then use these numbers to derive percentages.

Interpretation of Comprehension Scores. First, see if there are gross differences between the student's performance on oral and on silent forms. The performance summarized in Figure 4.7 showed little difference. Next, compare the student's response to literal (fact) questions with all the other (higher-level) questions; here a higher percentage of factual questions were missed. You can also note the percentage missed of each kind of question.

Initial instructional planning may flow directly from your analysis. If the child missed many factual questions, your instruction will focus on the strategy of identifying important details. If the child missed more higher-level questions, focus on inferential and evaluative comprehension. If the performance is fairly even, continue to emphasize all areas of comprehension.

You will not have very large numbers, so drawing conclusions is risky. Say a child scored 67 percent on "topic" questions. That sounds dreadful—but if the child read only three passages at the independent and instructional levels, there were only three "topic" questions altogether and the child missed only one. You can't make a sound judgment based on only three responses and a single error.

However, if you find on analysis that a child has answered every literal question correctly and missed almost all the inferential questions, you have a pattern, and this is useful information for planning instruction.

INTERPRETATION OF ALL DATA

When you interpret the information gathered from an IRI, you look at the total picture of the reader's performance. We have shown you several pieces to look at first separately and then together: the percentages of word recognition and comprehension accuracy, the listening level, the analysis of miscues, and the summary of comprehension. Along with these, you must also consider behavior, attitude, interest, and any other information you have gleaned.

Remember that this instrument gives you an *estimate* of the child's reading levels and an *estimate* of needs in word recognition strategies and comprehension, along with information about a child's strengths. On the basis of all these bits and pieces, you begin to work. If the estimates turn out not to be appropriate—for example, the child isn't working well at the instructional level you estimated—you make an adjustment. Literacy cannot be measured with the accuracy of a ruler.

USING RESULTS TO PLAN AND ADJUST INSTRUCTION

Because the IRI gives you a quick estimate of reading levels as well as strengths and needs, you can place a child into an appropriate book immediately for applying skills and strategies. While this may not be a complete picture of a child's reading, it is a beginning.

- You will know the probable extent to which the child can participate when reading grade-level books.
- You are ready to help the child find books to read during independent reading time.
- You know what the reader is already doing competently, so you can capitalize on that strength.

- You also know what the child seems not to do, ignores, or does poorly. You can prepare minilessons to help the child acquire and build new strengths. For example, if miscues showed a high percentage of graphic similarity but mostly resulted in a loss of meaning, you do *not* need to urge the child to use phonics more often; instead, encourage the child to use his or her sense of language and meaning.

- If the child was unable to respond acceptably to evaluative questions but answered virtually all fact questions accurately, you do not need to urge the child to pay attention to detail. Rather, you will emphasize personal response to text, reading critically, and building confidence in voicing opinions.

- If the child has read haltingly, unwilling to try unfamiliar words, ignoring punctuation marks, and "attacking" one word at a time, you might decide to build fluency at the child's independent reading level by using a tape recorder, a reading buddy, or a volunteer, deferring more challenging reading until the child has built confidence at this level.

PRECAUTIONS

The informal reading inventory will continue to play a role in assessing reading. However, you need to bear in mind a number of concerns:

- Informal reading inventories are based on an assumption that it is possible to accurately determine the reading level of a piece of text, that is, that one can judge a piece of writing to be of second-grade difficulty, sixth-grade difficulty, or whatever. Earlier in this chapter, we discussed some of the complexities involved in this concept of readability.

- Estimates based on an IRI presume that it is possible to establish clear reading levels for a given child. In fact, though, all of us read with more accuracy and deeper comprehension on some days than on others, and we read some types of material better than other types.

- Estimates of the child's reading levels are based on a limited sample of performance. It is a contrived situation, calling for a child to read under conditions that may be stressful.

- Passage content may be a poor match for the child's oral vocabulary, background experiences, and interests. That is, given two passages of equal (according to a formula) reading difficulty, a child may read more competently when material matches his or her interests and background than when it doesn't.

- Many factors may impinge on a child's performance on an IRI on any given day: health, weather, noise, mood, hunger, and so forth. Too often, only numbers are used for decision making or reporting to parents. The careful notes that might explain those numbers are set aside.

Word Recognition Tests

In this section, we briefly discuss three kinds of specific tests of word recognition. *Sight word tests* assess a child's instant recognition of a given body of words. *Phonics tests* purport to isolate which phonic elements a child knows and uses to figure out the probable pronunciation of unfamiliar words. *Structural analysis tests* assess a child's knowledge of and ability to use the structure of words, such as prefixes, suffixes, inflectional endings, and, sometimes, syllabication. We discuss informal assessment of these aspects of word recognition throughout this book.

SIGHT WORD TESTS

A **sight word** can be defined in any of the following ways:

- A word recognized instantly ("at sight"), without analysis or decoding
- A word taught as a whole, without attention to its parts
- A word from a published list of words that occurs with high frequency in all written material and therefore needs to be recognized by any reader

We discuss each of these definitions and then focus on procedures for administering and interpreting sight word tests.

Recognition of a Word "at Sight" Without the Need to Analyze or Decode It. When a child can read a word instantly, without hesitation, you say that word is a sight word for that child. Instant recognition of words on the lists provided with an IRI indicates that those words are sight words for the child in question. However, because such lists are made up of a sampling of words taken from passages at each grade level on the IRI, performance on them cannot be taken as an indication of a child's general sight-word knowledge.

Words Taught as a Whole. Some words are taught or must be learned by sight rather than through analysis of the parts. Sometimes such words do not follow phonic or structural generalizations and therefore do not lend themselves to analysis or decoding. At other times, the child has not yet learned the necessary skills for analysis.

For example, analysis of the word "Titanic" will result in a close approximation of the pronunciation, but six-year-olds have not yet been taught the skills for such analysis. To teach the word to them, you'd present it as a whole word, maybe noting the initial sound.

Words Determined to Be Necessary for All Reading Because of Their High Frequency. A broader and more common meaning for the term *sight words* is "a group of words that children 'should' recognize at sight by a certain grade." Lists of such words have been made by examining children's reading material, counting how often each word occurs, and identifying the "high-frequency" words—the ones that occur so frequently that fluent reading cannot take place without instant recognition of them.

The *Dolch Basic Sight Word Test* (Dolch, 1942) consists of 220 high-frequency words divided into lists from preprimer to third grade. Many teachers use this list to assess children's familiarity with basic sight words. Johnson (1971) reexamined the list and found that it continued to have value. Other lists are also available (Fry, 1980; Fry, Kress, Fountoukidis, & Polk, 1993). The Resource File following the last chapter provides samples.

Procedures for Sight Word Tests. There are two simple ways to administer a sight word list to a child: with flash cards or with a printed list. In either case, words should be exposed for about one second. This is easily done with flash cards. If the child is reading from a list of words, you may need to use an index card to cover and then briefly reveal each word. While the child reads, you mark responses on another copy of the list. After the child has finished a list, you may present the missed words again to see if they are recognized on second look or whether the child can analyze them. If a child begins to miss one word after another, some teachers then ask the child to silently look at the list and find words he or she knows.

As with any test, reassurance is important; tell the child you just want to find out which words he or she already knows and which you both still need to work on.

Figure 4.8 shows a partial-marked list. A + indicates the word was said correctly. When the child misread a word, the teacher attempted to record what the child said instead. The "Flashed Word" column indicates the child's first try; the "Second Look" column records the child's efforts when the missed words were presented again. The teacher also noted behaviors.

Analysis and Summary. If you record the child's exact responses as shown in Figure 4.8, you can analyze the nature of the words not known or miscalled. You might look at such things as the following:

- Were words often skipped? Did the child attempt the word on the second look?
- Did errors increase with each list or occur evenly on all lists?

Very soft voice
Rising inflection on
each word-unsure

Sight Word List

	Flashed Word	**Second Look**
1. the	+	
2. of	+	
3. and	+	
4. to	+	
5. a	+	
6. in	t	it
7. that	what	then
8. is	+	
9. was	saw	+
10. he	she	+

FIGURE 4.8

Partial Sample of a Marked Test of Sight Words

- Were substitutions mostly at the beginnings of words? Middles? Ends?
- Was there any other pattern of errors?
- How did behavior change as the task increased in difficulty?

While not precise, these analyses give you a picture of a child's miscues that might not have been apparent had you relied solely on classroom reading experiences. Recording results only helps if you follow up with an analysis and a summary that lead to improved instruction.

The following is a summary and analysis of third-grader Brian's sight-word test. He was given a second look at words he missed the first time. For these purposes, it is not necessary to know the specific words Brian read or missed. Each summary statement is followed with an instructional note.

SUMMARY STATEMENT	INSTRUCTIONAL NOTE
Read instantly all words on preprimer, primer, and first-grade lists.	Concentrate only on second- and third-grade words. All earlier words are known and will continue to be practiced in any daily reading.
Missed fewer words at second-grade level (12) than third-grade.	Show Brian how he is gradually mastering the lists and is close to "knowing" all the words.
Positive attitude: thinks he'll know all the words "before fourth grade."	Support his positive attitude.
Attempted to pronounce (sound out) all unknown words when given a second chance. Persistent. Kept apologizing, saying, "I should know that word."	Get "should" out of the issue. Focus on his strength and persistence.
Most errors occurred at the middle or end of a word. That is, Brian always began his attempts to decode the words by associating an appropriate sound with the letters at the beginning of the word.	Devise practice activities that call for distinguishing words by middles and ends. Further assess his knowledge of medial and final sounds if necessary.
Once Brian assigned a sound to a vowel, he seemed unable to try an alternative sound when the first one did not produce a recognizable word. For example, he pronounced the word "great" as /greet/. He asked if he was right, and I said, "Not quite, try again," but he could not think of an alternate sound.	Plan specific lessons on vowel digraphs as well as strategy lessons about trying alternative pronunciations when the first attempt fails to result in a real or correct word.

(continued)

SUMMARY STATEMENT	INSTRUCTIONAL NOTE
Several miscalled words may have been read correctly in context. Lack of context seems to inhibit Brian. He kept saying, "I'd know that word if it was in a sentence."	Keep a list of miscalled words handy, and try to notice whether they are known during normal classroom reading activities.
Sometimes Brian strung together close approximations of each syllable of a word without ever having the "Aha!" experience of recognizing what he had just said. Example: *un-i-ted.* He kept saying these syllables over and over, pronouncing *un* with a short *u* sound and using a short *i* in the middle. He didn't want to give up; he kept saying, "I can get it. Just a minute." Finally, when we were finished and I pronounced the word for him, he grinned and said, "Oh, yeah, like the United States of America. Right! I just didn't know it without a capital *U*."	Build on Brian's persistence and expectation that print should make sense.
We discussed his performance. Brian thought he did "pretty good." I agreed. He said he could learn the rest of the words: "Easy—piece of cake." I asked him what he thought would help him learn the words. He said he thought he would write them while he said them. Then he would ask a friend to test him. I told him I thought that was a good plan, and we made a date to retest in two weeks.	Use Brian's ideas and check frequently to be sure he and his friend are working well together. Retest in two weeks.

Interpretation and Planning. Instructional plans should be based on the kind of summaries and instructional notes just illustrated. For Brian, such plans might be as follows:

- Use his idea of saying and writing words. Help him choose a friend to test him.
- Encourage fluency by helping him locate books at his independent reading level to tape-record.
- Plan minilessons based on vowel digraphs and alternative sounds of vowels. Teach him steps to think through if his first try isn't a word he recognizes. For example: "If a word ends in *e,* try the long sound for the other vowel first. If that isn't a word I know, try the short sound. If that isn't a word I know, make a schwa sound and reread the sentence for clues."

Results on the day of testing merely sample a child's reading behavior and are useful only for beginning planning. From then on, daily observation and the use of checklists may be sufficient to monitor progress, though you could readminister a sight word test to track progress.

A Caution. We do not recommend paper-and-pencil, group-administered tests of sight words. Such tests call for a child to look at a row of several words, listen to a word the teacher says, and mark that word. This procedure tests only whether the child can find the word the teacher says. It does not test whether the child can read the word.

PHONICS TESTS

We believe phonics needs to be taught early and taught well. You need to know which children are "getting it" and which are not. Beyond first grade, you need to know who may need reteaching.

We believe the best way to assess a child's knowledge of and ability to use phonics is through careful observation during classroom reading experiences. As you saw earlier in this chapter, analyzing miscues on an IRI can also provide insights into a child's use of phonics.

What about specific tests of isolated phonics elements? A child may do well on a test of isolated phonics skills but fail to apply this ability while reading. The true test of phonics ability occurs as the child is actually reading. Nevertheless, you may have occasion to use some phonics tests in your classroom.

If you are using a published reading program or a stand-alone phonics program, frequent assessment will be built into the program. Your school system may have devised its own assessment or have selected a certain published test that may also assess other aspects of reading.

Some published tests are listed in "For Additional Reading" at the premium website for this text. See Norman and Calfee (2004) for a description of the Tile Test, designed for very young children through mid-first grade.

Most phonics assessments attempt to isolate which phonics skills a child is able to use successfully. Some do this using nonsense words or syllables; the use of real words may be misleading because there is no way to predict which children may already recognize a word at sight. Sometimes one part of the word is held steady while another is manipulated. For example, assume the child either knows the word (rime) *-in* or is taught it. Then various initial consonants (onsets) are added to that rime— *hin, jin, lin, vin*—and the child attempts to pronounce the resulting words aloud. If a child finds it difficult to deal with the notion of nonsense words, you'll need to provide examples of what is expected. Keep in mind that such an assessment is devoid of context.

Remember that phonics is one tool for helping a reader predict the probable pronunciation of an unknown word (or helping a writer predict the probable spelling). It has no end other than that.

A Caution. Assessments that are entirely paper and pencil may not be helpful. These might require children, for example, to listen to a word the teacher says and circle a word (or picture) from a list that starts with the same sound. Unless the child is actually applying phonics to the oral pronunciations, this kind of test will not reveal his or her ability to use phonics.

Interpretation and Planning. Information regarding a child's needs in terms of phonics skills must be used to plan for instruction and determine his or her needs in order to meet needs for RTI. Match the skill against your own school system's scope and sequence of skills or its standards to see which phonic elements your students are expected to have mastered at this point. Children who already use a skill do not need isolated drills. Rather, they should be using the skill in reading connected text.

For children who are not yet using a skill effectively, you must plan specific lessons to teach or reteach it. Pay attention to whether the child can hear the phonic element you are targeting. If a student beyond the Emergent Literacy stage does not seem to hear the sound, or cannot associate the sound with the symbol and use that to figure out unfamiliar words, you may want to consider a conference with a special reading teacher or a referral for additional diagnosis from an exceptional education specialist.

STRUCTURAL ANALYSIS TESTS

Most published reading programs include tests of structural analysis ability. Diagnostic and standardized tests often include aspects of structural analysis as well. The abilities tested include recognition and application of affixes such as prefixes, suffixes, and inflectional endings. They also include the use of patterns of vowels and consonants, such as CVC (a vowel between two consonants) and CVVC (a pair of vowels between two consonants), to predict vowel sounds and accents.

We believe you will be able to note which children are using structural analysis in the course of everyday reading activities. For example, as you review a calendar with second graders, you might talk about how to figure out the pronunciation of "September" by applying the CVC pattern and breaking the word into syllables, then pronouncing each syllable to get close to the exact pronunciation. Then you would encourage children to consider the context in confirming that "September" is a likely pronunciation.

Interpretation and Planning. For each structural analysis element found lacking, plan a lesson for those children who need it. For example, if several children are having trouble with words beginning with the prefix un-, plan a lesson about this. Present the concept of prefixes, the specific prefix and its meaning, examples ("unhappy"), and nonexamples ("under"); then provide guided practice with isolated words, followed by practice in reading words in context. Call attention to (or ask the children to note) examples of words in their day-to-day reading that have, or could have, the prefix. Guide them to think about how the meaning of each base word is affected by the prefix.

Diverse Populations

Measuring the reader should also include attention to the diverse populations represented in your school and your classroom. Here are some ideas for assessing children with special needs as well as those from diverse language and cultural backgrounds.

CHILDREN WITH SPECIAL NEEDS

Within any classroom, you will likely have some children who are or will be classified as part of a special population of one kind or another. These may include students with learning disabilities as well as those with various emotional, mental, or physical challenges.

When you think you have such a child who has not yet been identified, we recommend that you consult your school policies about the proper procedures to follow. Usually these will include keeping careful anecdotal records based on observation, completing certain checklists, consulting with specialists, and trying one or more interventions within your classroom.

More information on assessment in exceptional education can be found at "For Additional Reading" at the premium website for this text.

At some point, the special education teacher may begin additional testing with instruments not used routinely for all children. These are special diagnostic tests used to further define a child's needs and help prescribe a suitable instructional plan. While you will not be expected to administer or interpret these assessments, you may want to inform yourself about them since you will participate in staffings and parent conferences.

LANGUAGE AND CULTURAL DIVERSITY

Cultural and language diversity will influence your interpretation of children's miscues, their retelling, and their responses to comprehension questions. Counting correct items and assigning levels is not enough. You need to give weight to the child's culture and first-language patterns as you decide how to interpret test results.

Miscue or Language Difference? Two basic kinds of language differences may affect a child's oral reading: pronunciation and syntax. A child whose first language assigns a different sound to a letter or combination of letters may retain that sound while pronouncing English words. For example, if a child gives a /th/ sound to the letter *c,* this may not be a miscue; it may reflect a pronunciation difference arising from the child's first language. If you are uncertain whether or not a miscue is the result of a simple pronunciation difference, ask the child for clarification to see if she understood the word she said (Garcia, 1994).

Similarly, if a child reverses the order of words in a sentence, it is not likely that he saw the words in mixed-up order. Rather, the child may be changing the syntax to match his first language. In some languages, for example, the adjective follows the noun rather than preceding it, as in "the sweater yellow" rather than "the yellow sweater."

Comprehension Difficulty or Cultural Difference? As a student retells what he or she has read or answers questions, think about why the child might give a certain response. You want to know whether the child is able to read the words and grasp the ideas sufficiently to construct meaning from the passage. Your procedure is predicated on the assumption that readers will have a somewhat shared background of experience and frame of reference through which to consider the content. Yet a child who has grown up in a different culture from that reflected in your classroom and community likely has quite different experiences and, therefore, a different frame of reference. This could affect recollection of facts in a passage as well as the kinds of conclusions the child might draw.

We all respond to text out of our own cultures, backgrounds, and life experiences. Your job is to try to decide whether a deviation from the expected response is based on failure to construct meaning or on cultural differences.

COMMENTS

If students can read in their first language, you should assess them in that language if possible. Obviously, those who are already literate in some language have a grasp of how language systems work, even if theirs is quite different from English. Conceptual knowledge about print as well as the ability to draw on one's own experiences is universal across languages.

(See Farr and Trumbull, 1997, pp. 138ff., in "For Additional Reading" on the premium website for this text.)

Far more is involved in communication than a simple sharing of the phonological and syntactical aspects of language. Just think of how many misunderstandings arise between two people who speak the same language and share the same household!

The Right Book for Every Child

We want to put the right materials in the hands of each child. To that end, we have discussed procedures for measuring the difficulty levels of materials and the reading levels of children, and we have pointed out some of the limitations of these procedures.

In this section we further explore these concepts. We also discuss the so-called reading and interest levels often provided by book publishers. Finally, we briefly discuss ways to accommodate varying reading abilities if you are required to use a single text for all children regardless of reading level.

Reading Levels of Written Materials and of Students

It would be nice if you could simply determine the readability of the books you have available, assess the reading levels of your children, and then match one to the other. You have already seen, however, some of the complications involved. In this section we address that matter further.

USING THE PUBLISHED READING LEVELS OF WRITTEN MATERIAL

For many children's trade books, the publisher defines the readability by means of a reading level, sometimes abbreviated RL. When a book is given a certain reading level—for example, 2.5—it means that a formula of some kind has been used. The 2.5 means second grade, fifth month—in other words, just right for children who read at the second-grade, fifth-month reading level (a questionable notion).

Some publishers of trade books indicate the reading level on the books themselves. For example, *Piano Lessons Can Be Murder* (Stine, 1993) has "RL4" on the back cover, which means fourth-grade reading level. *Anastasia Krupnik* (Lowry, 1979) says "RL: 6.0," meaning a reading level of sixth grade, zero months. *Amelia Bedelia* (Parish, 1963/1981) has a note on the copyright page stating that a third-grade reading level was determined using the Fry Readability Formula, thus telling the purchaser not only the presumed difficulty level but also the means by which it was determined.

As you deal with reported reading levels of books, keep these ideas in mind:

- The notion that there is a significant difference in text difficulty and in a child's reading ability from one month to the next—that is, that 2.4 is significantly different from 2.5—is misleading. Is it meaningful to say that a child can read at second grade, fourth month, but not at second grade, fifth month? Does such a child even exist?

- Even if ability does change significantly from one month to the next, the notion that we can know a child's reading level with such precision is questionable. A child who has a reading level of 2.5 usually acquired that "score" through an averaging of his or her performance on several discrete parts of a standardized test—a process that many consider to yield a child's *frustration* level. (Standardized tests are discussed in Chapter 5.)

- The readability level reported is the result of taking several samples from a book and averaging them. This is misleading; if a sample from the beginning of a book is found to be at the sixth-grade difficulty level, a sample from the middle at the second-grade level, and a sample from the end at the fourth-grade level, it

This book has captured this student's complete attention.

© mnieves/
istockphoto.com

doesn't make sense to average them and call the whole book fourth-grade level. The fact is, for a child who reads at the fourth-grade level, some of it will be difficult, some quite easy, and some about right.

- Readability levels on published books cannot, of course, take into account an individual reader's interest in or prior knowledge of the content.

USING THE ASSESSED READING LEVELS OF THE CHILD

We have presented the concept of finding a child's three reading levels: independent, instructional, and frustration. For example, Suzy is independent with materials written at the second-grade level, instructional with third- and fourth-grade materials, and frustrated with fifth-grade material. While this information may be more useful to you than a single reading level of 2.5 on a standardized test, you should keep the following ideas in mind:

- The IRI passages used to determine the child's reading levels were presumably graded for difficulty using one formula (this information is given in the manual of the IRI). So you must be willing to accept that a *passage* can indeed be graded for difficulty.

- Then you must accept that performance on said passages can reflect a child's reading ability on other material that has been graded for difficulty using the same or another formula.

COMMENTS

Despite the pitfalls of using readability levels for written material and reading levels for children, we think the effort is worthwhile. Paying attention to both can save time and give you a better shot at a good match between materials and reader.

Interest Levels

When publishers provide information related to interest, they usually report it as **interest level,** or **IL.** Sometimes this is specified by grade level(s) and sometimes by an age range.

When you see an IL, you know that someone—one hopes someone who knows children, child development, and children's literature—has judged the age or grade of a child who might be interested in a given book regardless of how "difficult" it might be. This information can be helpful, because you can read a book to children who are interested in the subject even when they cannot yet read it to themselves. For example, the book, *How Many Seeds in a Pumpkin?* (McNamara & Karas, 2007) reports a reading level of 4 to 8, which is probably more of an age or interest level rather than a reading level. This is true of many picture books. The language, subject, story line, and art are suited to a child who is not yet reading independently; it is assumed that an adult or other reader will read the book aloud.

This same information is also provided for many chapter books meant to be read by children. For example, *Where the Red Fern Grows* (Rawls, 1961/1974) bears the designation "RL 6, IL age 10 and up." This book has been determined to be at sixth-grade difficulty level, but children from about fifth grade (age ten) on may be interested in the story. As the classroom teacher, you would be comfortable reading this chapter book aloud to your fifth-grade class. Even those who might read it on their own will enjoy hearing it. All will benefit from sharing the ideas and the beauty of the language.

You are the expert on your students. If you think a book would interest your children, share it with them no matter what interest level is given. Remember that if a book is judged to be of interest to a certain age of reader, that doesn't imply that all children of that age will be interested. You will soon know if you have misjudged your students' interest.

If You Must Use One Book for All Children

What if you must use the same book for all children, including those who cannot read it? Some teachers try to accommodate the frustrated children by using the social studies (or other) text as round-robin oral reading. Their rationale is that the children who cannot read the text at least hear the content. We do not agree with this practice, for two reasons. First, if those who cannot read it are expected to benefit from listening, the text must be read well by someone who has previously read it and already knows the content. Second, there is little reason to make the entire class sit through the oral reading of a text in social studies or other content area.

If you must use the same text with all students, we suggest you find other ways to accommodate the children for whom the text is at the frustration level. Here are some suggestions:

- Have the text recorded by a volunteer or use a study-buddy system.

- Expand your prereading activities: building or accessing background, presenting new concepts, using prereading overview and study guides, and presenting new vocabulary.

- Have a competent reader summarize during discussion following silent reading. Then the child who was unable to read the text should be able to participate in the higher-level activities of drawing conclusions and predicting. In this way, even children who were frustrated by the text can learn the important information.

- During discussion, direct questions to the struggling readers that they can answer successfully. For example, assume there is only one date in a certain paragraph and you know Johnny knows how to read dates. After the class has read the paragraph silently, you can say, "Johnny, find and read for us the date when _____ _____ happened." The point is to find a way to ask specific questions that a specific child can answer from the text. This allows the child to participate at a level that almost guarantees success.

Even your best efforts may not be enough to help students connect with written text that is beyond their ability. If you are teaching in a situation where you must use the same text with every reader, you will want to read further about teaching reading in the content areas.

Summary

- In this chapter we have presented some tools, techniques, and ideas that go beyond the ordinary daily assessments you will use with all students in your classroom. We have looked at ways to measure the difficulty of reading materials, measure a child's reading ability, and create a good match between reader and material.

- Measuring the materials typically involves the concept of readability. Actual readability depends on the interaction of reader, text, and environment, including factors that are not measurable. Readability formulas, however, concentrate on the text itself, analyzing certain features and converting the resulting numbers to a grade level. These formulas are convenient, but a number of risks are associated with depending on them.

- The joint statement from the International Reading Association and the National Council of Teachers of English (NCTE) urges educators to use methods other than formulas to estimate the difficulty level of text.

- Measuring the reader often involves use of an informal reading inventory to provide information about a student's three reading levels—independent, instructional, and frustration—as well as the student's listening level.

- You can also use the IRI results to analyze miscues and comprehension performance to get an overall picture of a child's reading performance and decide how to plan appropriate instruction.

- Tests that focus on word recognition strategies such as sight word tests, phonics tests, and structural analysis tests are available. All of these measures, however, have limitations and pitfalls.

- When assessing diverse populations in your classroom, take into account difficulties that may arise from language and cultural differences rather than true reading problems.

- Publishers often supply reading levels and interest levels for their books. These may be useful as a quick guide, but you are in a better position than the publisher to judge a book's suitability for your students.

- Assessment tools and techniques are a starting point (as well as a way to monitor progress). As you work with your students to develop their literacy, you will need to make continual adjustments in light of new information.

 Please visit the premium website for *Literacy Assessment*, Fourth Edition to access the TeachSource Video Cases, chapter web links, For Additional Reading, tutorial quizzes, glossary flashcards, online checklists, downloads, and much more! Go to www.cengage.com/login to register your access code.

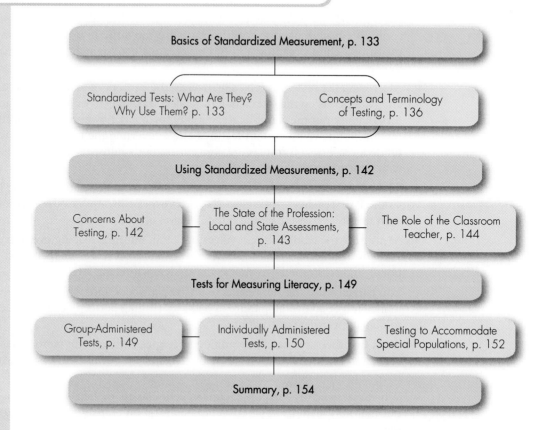

5

Published Standardized Measures:
An Overview for Classroom Teachers

A sign hangs outside Mr. Singh's fourth-grade classroom: TESTING—DO NOT ENTER. Inside, the children sit with booklets and pencils in front of them, as Mr. Singh holds up a copy of the test booklet and demonstrates what they are to do. Some children fidget and roll their eyes. Others are alert and focused. It is achievement test day.

Each day for several weeks the children have been preparing for the state test, taking one practice test after another. They have been told to do their best on the test, but not be anxious about it. No matter what anyone says, the children know the test matters. Some children will, in fact, do their best. Others may not, because they already feel defeated.

Now Mr. Singh has set his timer, written the start and stop times on the chalkboard, and signaled the children to begin. Almost immediately, several hands shoot up. Mr. Singh tiptoes around, whispering to the individual children, reassuring them, pointing to where they should be, reminding them that he cannot help them on this test. They must do the work on their own.

Let's imagine we can see inside each child's mind during the testing. Here are a few examples of how children (and adults) might approach a standardized test.

Sam sits up straight, both feet on the floor, takes a deep breath, and reads the directions on the first page. He looks neither right nor left. Now he turns to the first test passage. The passage has several paragraphs, followed by a series of multiple-choice questions. Sam reads the questions first. After reading two or three, he begins reading the passage. Soon he stops reading with a kind of "Got it!" smile on his face and marks the answer to the second question. Then he returns to the passage until he finds the answers to the first and third questions. He continues moving back and forth between passage and questions until the passage is completed. He checks each answer and makes sure he has recorded it in the right place. He smiles and moves to the next item. He doesn't look up. He doesn't fidget. He works straight through the test.

Sally skips the directions and reads the first passage, with her nose close to the page, moving a finger under the print. Then she answers the questions without referring to the passage. She leaves two questions unanswered and moves on to the next passage. Her brow is furrowed and her feet are twined around the chair legs.

Stuart lounges back, tipping his chair on two legs and draping one arm over the back. At the signal to begin, Stuart looks around to see what everyone else is doing. He skips the directions and glances at the passage. He skips even that and goes directly to the questions. He fills in the bubble for the first answer and doesn't look at the test booklet again. He just fills in bubbles on the answer sheet, making a pattern of them.

Shirley gets about halfway through the passage and stops. Her lips move as she apparently tries to sound out an unfamiliar word. She raises her hand, but of course Mr. Singh can't help her. She continues to try to figure the word out. She is fighting tears and hiding her eyes. She raises her hand and begs to be excused to go to the bathroom. She says she is sick to her stomach. Mr. Singh smiles, but all he can do is murmur words of encouragement.

If asked, Mr. Singh would tell us that he wants to better prepare students to do their best without increasing their anxiety. He wants to help his students think like test makers so that they can be more successful test takers.

All over the country, children like those in Mr. Singh's class are taking similar kinds of tests every year. Some take several such tests in a single year. These are standardized tests designed to measure how well children have achieved in various areas of learning and to compare one group of children to the rest of the children in the school system, county, state, or country.

Such tests consume precious instructional time. The results may or may not seem to be used in any productive way. The published results may cause consternation or gloating, depending on the scores. Low performance sometimes causes schools and even whole states to scrap everything they've been doing and completely revamp their curriculum.

Even when both educators and the public question the usefulness of standardized tests, schools continue to administer them. Why? The answer actually may be simple, understandable, and defensible: taxes support schools. Taxpayers deserve to know that their money is indeed educating children. They want tests that measure what children are supposed to have learned—and want schools to be compared with each other. Thus, we know (or think we know) that children in Arkansas and in New Hampshire, in Oregon and in Tennessee—in fact, all the children—are meeting the same standards of achievement.

In this chapter, we will:

- Introduce some basic concepts concerning the standardized testing of reading.
- Discuss the purposes of standardized testing and the limitations.
- Give you some historical perspective, define some terms, explain how results are reported, and offer advice on interpreting such reports.
- Discuss the state of the profession in standardized testing and the classroom teacher's role in preparing children to take standardized tests.
- Describe several standardized tests and provide sources you can explore for further information.
- Discuss testing to accommodate special populations.

Basics of Standardized Measurement

Considering the amount of money allocated to providing an education for every child, it is important to know whether or not goals are being met:

- Are educators teaching children successfully?
- What are children learning? Is it the right stuff for now and the future?
- Will our children grow up to be adults who are capable of holding their own in a global economy?
- Before we can figure out if anything needs to be changed in our instruction, don't we have to try to determine the results of our present methods?

Clearly, what is assessed must be linked to what is taught. That is, schools must establish educational objectives: what students should know and be able to do. Then educators can plan curriculum: what, when, and how to teach in order for children to meet the established objectives. Logically, then, educators need to find out if children are reaching those objectives. This might be easier if every school system had the same objectives. But they do not—and we're certainly not suggesting that they should. Still, there seems to be some agreement that schools should assess all children using the same or like instruments to compare them. Some states have developed their own tests, or their own norms (norms will be discussed later in this chapter), but even in those states the individual school districts may not have identical educational objectives. Every time one aspect of standardized testing seems clear, another becomes muddied.

Some say that the notion of standardized testing began with the work of Binet and Simon, the authors of an intelligence test for draftees for the armed forces in 1905 (Glazer, 1998). These tests were designed to separate those who were mentally capable from those who were not.

Eventually various instruments were devised to test elements of the reading process, such as word identification, comprehension, study skills, and fluency. Today many published tests purport to measure achievement in every aspect of literacy. The test items cover what each child *should be doing* at each grade level in each area of literacy. To allow for children who are performing below or above that grade level, some test items are much easier and others are much harder.

Every classroom teacher needs to know some basics about standardized tests (Afflerbach, 2007). This book is not a forum for debate about the issue of standardized testing. Instead, we hope to provide enough information for you to begin thinking independently about the issue.

Standardized Tests: What Are They? Why Use Them?

When classroom teachers carry out informal assessment and testing, they try to be objective, but there is variation from one teacher to the next. The classroom climate, the testing conditions, the support the teacher offers, and even the score deemed "passing" may differ from school to school, from classroom to classroom, and from teacher to teacher.

Standardized tests, in contrast, are administered under identical (or nearly identical) conditions every time, no matter where or by whom. This means the same time limits, the same directions, and the same testing circumstances. Since standardized tests are designed to allow comparison between one child or group of children and another child or group, everything about the conditions of the test must be kept identical except for the child's performance.

Absolute standardization is virtually impossible because there are too many variables to control, but if the tests are to have any meaning, the only thing that should vary is student performance. Therefore, test publishers dictate many things, including what to say to the children as you give directions.

The following sections will define and describe three major types of standardized tests: norm referenced, criterion referenced, and diagnostic.

NORM-REFERENCED TESTS

A **norm-referenced test** compares the performance of an individual to that of the group on which the test was standardized. When the scores of such a group are displayed, they distribute in a **bell curve.** A bell curve shows a very few scores at the upper end, a very few at the lower end, and most in the middle. If you plot all the scores on such a graph and draw a line connecting them, the shape resembles a bell—hence the name of the curve.

Figure 5.1 illustrates a bell curve. The horizontal axis indicates the range of scores, from the lowest scores on the left to the highest scores on the right. The vertical axis, labeled "Frequency," shows how often each score occurs in the population. Scores distributed in this way are said to follow a **normal distribution,** and the regularity of the curve allows us to calculate the percentages shown on the graph: for instance, 68 percent of the scores will fall in the center portion of the graph, only 2 percent will be at the extreme right side (very high scores), and 2 percent will fall at the extreme left (very low scores).

How do test makers determine which **raw score** (the number correct) on a test corresponds to which position on the curve? They try out the tests on a **norming population,** often consisting of children from various socioeconomic backgrounds; in cities, suburbs, small towns, and rural communities; and from every part of the country. Test publishers then determine the average score of children at various

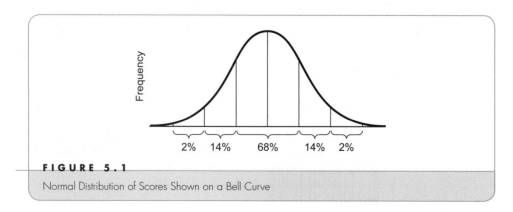

FIGURE 5.1

Normal Distribution of Scores Shown on a Bell Curve

points in their schooling (which grade and sometimes even which time of year), and the resulting scores become the reference for various derived scores (to be discussed later in this chapter). Occasionally a school district will develop **local norms** based on its own children rather than comparing scores to the broader population that includes children from many parts of the country.

You may have heard Garrison Keillor on public radio describe the mythical town of Lake Wobegon, where "all the children are above average." While it is possible that the children of one school (or some other defined group) might all be above average, *all* children cannot be above average. It is statistically impossible. If all children achieve at higher and higher levels, the test scores would still distribute in a curve, though the middle or average might then be a higher raw score. In other words, given large numbers of test takers, there will *always* be a normal distribution. Average isn't what "should be"; average is what "is."

To illustrate the concept of average, Figure 5.2 shows a normal distribution of IQ scores. An IQ of 100 is in the middle, at the peak of the bell curve; therefore, an IQ of 100 is "average."

Here are the main points you must understand:

- Test scores distribute themselves as shown in Figures 5.1 and 5.2, reflecting the wide variance of performance within any group.
- Most scores cluster near the middle.
- Only a very few scores occur at the extreme low or extreme high end.

Norm-referenced reading and literacy tests are apt to be broad measures of achievement, yielding little in terms of particular areas of strength or weakness. Norm-referenced tests are designed to show the entire possible range of performance, so there will likely be items that almost no child in your classroom can know.

CRITERION-REFERENCED TESTS

Unlike norm-referenced tests, which measure performance in relation to the entire norming population, **criterion-referenced tests** measure performance in terms of mastery of particular skills that the child is expected to have learned. Although the child who has completely mastered the skills would get every item correct, 80 percent

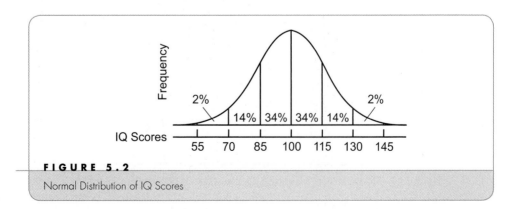

FIGURE 5.2

Normal Distribution of IQ Scores

correct is usually considered acceptable evidence of mastery. You will not know if a child can perform beyond the scope of the test, since the test items are restricted to skills that have been taught.

Published criterion-referenced tests may have a number of subsections, each intended to measure a subskill of reading or literacy. Levels of performance corresponding to mastery are indicated by the publishers. If a child does not achieve mastery, review or reteaching is needed. After reteaching, the same test (or an alternate form) may be readministered.

When a criterion-referenced test matches your own objectives for your students, it may be considered diagnostic if it helps you identify trouble spots for children and plan instruction.

DIAGNOSTIC TESTS

Diagnostic tests are designed to lead to specific instructional plans. Such tests are standardized in that you, the test giver, are told exactly how to administer them. Unless you use the standard procedures, the results are not considered valid. These tests sample many components of an area of achievement, and the scores show which areas need instruction for the child. The test publishers may suggest teaching strategies and techniques to improve each area found deficient.

As you no doubt have realized, the informal assessment we discussed earlier in this text is diagnostic; that is, all of it leads to instructional planning and will help you as you develop your RTI plans. Here, however, we are considering published tests with parameters determined by the publishers, not by you. While such tests may be helpful in screening and in planning educational experiences for some special populations, they may not be necessary for the grade level classroom teacher. Later in this chapter, we will give you the names of some specific diagnostic tests.

Concepts and Terminology of Testing

The following discussion will remind you of concepts and terminology that you must understand in order to use standardized tests, interpret their results, and discuss the implications with colleagues, families, and members of your community. We will also define and explain some of the several ways scores are reported.

STATISTICAL CONCEPTS

The following common statistical concepts are important: validity, reliability, and standard error of measurement.

Validity. A test has **validity** if it measures what it says it measures. Three types of interrelated validity are content validity, criterion validity, and construct validity. The publisher's technical manual will explain how validity was determined for any particular test.

Content Validity. **Content validity** is the degree to which a test's content reflects the content it is intended to measure. The content of the test should be related to what your students have had a chance to learn, and the items should be directly related to what you want to measure.

Criterion Validity. **Criterion validity** refers to how well a particular test compares with other measures. The comparison is reported as a statistical correlation ranging from $+1.0$, which is perfect correlation, to -1.0, which indicates no correlation.

Construct Validity. **Construct validity** is more complicated; suffice it to say that it relates to (1) the likelihood that the score on the test actually reflects what you wanted to test and, conversely, (2) the likelihood that inability to score well on the test cannot be accounted for by any factor other than inability to do that particular task. In other words, the test must have been conceived with a clear notion of what it aimed to test; then it should test that and only that.

Reliability. **Reliability** has to do with consistency. It helps you answer the question, Would Johnny get the same score if he took this test another day? A high degree of reliability indicates a high degree of likelihood that the person tested would receive the same score if the test were repeated. The degree of reliability is reported as a score: 1.0 is perfect reliability; 0.80 is usually considered an acceptable degree of reliability (though some programs require 0.90). The publisher's technical manual will report how reliability was determined for any particular test.

Two common kinds of reliability are test-retest and internal. To determine *test-retest reliability,* test developers give the same tests to the same group two times; they then correlate the two sets of scores to see whether individuals perform close to the same on both testings. To determine *internal reliability,* test developers correlate items within a test; one way of doing this is to correlate performance on one-half of the test items (say, even-numbered items) with performance on the other half (odd-numbered items).

Standard Error of Measurement. Since no test is absolutely perfect, the **standard error of measurement,** sometimes written **SEM,** allows you to say that a score can be trusted, give or take a certain number of points. Based on the normal distribution, the SEM allows you to say that 68 percent of the time the "true" score will fall within the range of plus or minus 1 SEM of the actual score.

For example, let's say a child scores 83 on a test with an SEM of 6. Most likely, the child's "true" score is 83 plus or minus 6, or somewhere between 77 and 89. However, since this is true only 68 percent of the time, 32 percent of the time the "true" score might be even further from the actual score of 83. If you wanted to be even more confident that you were being truthful about results, you could expand your interpretation to include plus or minus 2 SEM; this would give you a 95 percent degree of confidence. In our example with the score of 83 and SEM of 6, you could be 95 percent certain that the true score would be 83 plus or minus 12—that is, somewhere between 71 and 95.

The SEM means that no test is completely accurate. The best it can do is yield a score for the day the student took the test; a score in the middle of a range of possible scores the child might receive. The publisher's manual will provide the SEM for each test.

TEST SCORES

What if Susie's raw score (items correct) is 88 on a standardized test? We have no idea whether to cheer or moan. Too many things are unknown: How does her score compare to those on whom the test was normed? Did this test cover what has been taught in Susie's class? What's average for someone her age or in her grade? How reliable is that score? We need a score that allows us to make inferences and draw conclusions.

To that end, test publishers provide what are called *derived scores* for each possible raw score. These derived scores allow you to look at an individual or at your class in terms of larger groups, from your school to your state to the whole country. Derived scores also allow you to compare one year's scores to those from prior years. While derived scores are presented in tables in the manuals accompanying tests, schools usually return tests to the publisher for scoring; the publisher then sends a report with the raw scores and the requested derived scores.

The most common derived scores are percentile rank, standard scores such as stanine and normal curve equivalent (NCE) scores, and grade- and age-equivalent scores. Figure 5.3 will help you compare some of these derived scores as we discuss them.

Percentile Rank. The test publisher converts each raw score to a **percentile rank** that indicates a student's performance on that test in relation to the comparable group (same age or grade/month) on which the test was normed. The percentile rank tells how an individual score compares in terms of the percentage of students in the norming group who scored above or below that individual score. On the bell curve shown in Figure 5.3, note that the 50th percentile is precisely in the middle: exactly average.

If Susie's raw score of 88 has a percentile rank of 70, it means that 70 percent of the students in the reference group (the group on which the test was normed) had a raw score of 88 or lower. Another way to look at it is this: Susie's score was the same as or higher than the scores of 70 percent of the norming group.

Cautions. Do not confuse percentile with percentage. A percentile rank of 70 does *not* mean that Susie had 70 percent of the items correct; a percentile rank of 70 could be associated with many different raw scores, depending on the group with which Susie's score was being compared. Percentile rank also does *not* compare Susie

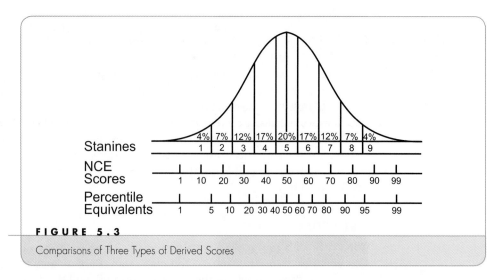

FIGURE 5.3

Comparisons of Three Types of Derived Scores

with the other children in her class; that is, it does not mean she scored higher than 70 percent of her classmates. It compares her *only* with the norming group.

A limitation of the percentile rank score is that the units are not equal. This can be important when cutoff scores are established for eligibility for special programs. Because percentile equivalents are clustered around the middle of the bell curve and lie far apart at the extreme upper and lower ends (see Figure 5.3), a difference of only one or two raw-score points in the middle might mean the difference between being at the 45th percentile and being at the 55th percentile. At the ends of the curve, in contrast, a difference of several raw-score points might not alter the percentile score.

Therefore, if your school has a special program that admits children with percentile scores, say, "at or below the 40th percentile," it is important to consider how many raw-score points put a child on one side or the other of that magic number. Let's assume a child's raw score converts to the 41st percentile, making the child ineligible for a special program according to the 40th-percentile cutoff. If the SEM is taken into account, perhaps the child might be eligible after all.

We don't mean to suggest that percentile ranks are not valid or valuable ways to consider scores; they are very good when you want to look at large numbers of children or at trends. We do want you to learn what such numbers mean (or don't mean) in terms of looking at individual children. But we don't want you to risk making a judgment about an individual child based on a percentile rank without taking into account the limitations of percentile numbers.

Standard Scores. **Standard scores** differ from percentile scores in that the difference between one score and the next represents the same raw-score interval at the extremes that it does in the middle, expressed in terms of standard units of measurement. Two commonly used standard scores are the stanine and the normal curve equivalent. Publishers provide tables that allow you to convert any raw score into these standard scores.

Stanine Scores. The **stanine score** places pupils in one of nine bands from the lowest stanine of 1 to the highest of 9. Stanine scores are assigned to represent a normal distribution, so most students will be in the 4th, 5th, or 6th stanines (around the middle), while only a few will be at the extremes. You can see in Figure 5.3 which percentiles compare with each stanine.

Stanines are widely used and may be more understandable than percentile rank. Each stanine encompasses a range of raw scores, and a child whose performance falls in stanines 4 through 6 is usually considered to be doing average work.

Significant improvement (or decreased performance) is reflected by a change in either direction of two or more stanines. For example, if Joe was in the 5th stanine last year and in the 4th this year, those scores are not sufficiently different to be cause for alarm. If his score this year falls in the 3rd stanine, however, it would be considered a problem that needs exploring.

NCE Scores. **NCE scores** range from 1 to 99 and are equal units; the difference between the 40th and the 45th NCE is the same number of raw-score points as the difference between the 90th and the 95th. While the numbers 1 to 99 might suggest that the NCE is the same as the percentile, the equal (standard) units show that it is not.

Grade- and Age-Equivalent Scores. **Grade-equivalent scores,** often reported to the community and to families, are perhaps the most commonly misunderstood scores.

Grade-equivalent scores are derived from the performance of students in the norming group on a particular test. Let's say the test is designed for fifth graders at the beginning of the school year. The tests are given to a large number of students and scored. The average raw score obtained by the fifth graders at the beginning of the school year is then given a grade-equivalent score of 5.0 (fifth grade, zero months). Tests may be normed at various points in a school year so that publishers can establish grade-equivalent scores for other months as well: for instance, the norming might indicate raw scores equivalent to a grade-equivalent score of 5.4 (fifth grade, fourth month) or 5.7 (fifth grade, seventh month). Sometimes the fifth-grade test is also "normed" on fourth graders and on sixth graders. As long as the grade-equivalent scores are roughly at the child's grade level, little misunderstanding probably occurs.

Age-equivalent scores are derived similarly. The difference lies in the way the score is reported. Rather than by grade and month, the score is reported in terms of an age and a month. While grade-equivalent scores conform to a school year in that they run from 0 months (5.0) to 9 months (5.9), age-equivalent scores conform to calendar years, running from 0 months to 11 months.

Cautions. Grade-equivalent scores have several problems; in fact, some publishers no longer publish these scores. The problems have to do both with how the scores are derived and with how they are misunderstood.

Publishers use average student scores at the intended grade level to estimate equivalent performance at higher and lower grades. That is, grade-equivalent scores are mathematically extrapolated both down to lower grades and up to higher grades.

During the taking of this standardized test, both students and teacher are silent.

© Tony Freeman/
PhotoEdit

Thus, publishers can provide tables showing that a given raw score might correspond to a grade equivalent much lower or higher than the actual grade for which the test was intended, even though the test wasn't actually administered to students in those grades.

Let's say George, a fifth grader, has a raw score of 34 with a grade equivalent of 5.2 on a fifth-grade reading test. His score is the same as that of the average fifth grader in the second month in the norming group.

Now let's look at Jimmy, another fifth grader, whose raw score on the fifth-grade test has a grade equivalent of 8.5. You can probably say that Jimmy reads above grade level. However, you *cannot* say that Jimmy reads at the eighth-grade level; he wasn't reading eighth-grade material. All you can say is that, *on this fifth-grade test,* Jimmy performed the same as the average student in the eighth grade would probably have done *on this fifth-grade test* if the test had actually been given to eighth graders.

By the same token, if fifth-grade classmate Sheri receives a raw score with a grade equivalent of 3.5, it does not necessarily mean that she is a third-grade reader or that she should be given third-grade material. The test wasn't made up of third-grade reading material, and it probably wasn't normed on third graders. The only thing one can say about her score is that Sheri performed on this fifth-grade test the way the average child in the third grade, fifth month, would probably perform on this test. It will be obvious to the teacher (and family) that she is struggling and not doing "average" work, but that's all the score means.

An additional problem occurs because grade-equivalent scores are not standard. That is, growth from one grade equivalent to the next might not mean the same thing from one year to the next or from one test to the next.

Moreover, reading scores on formal measurements may not be consistent with a child's actual reading performance in the classroom. You will remember that in our discussion of informal reading inventories in Chapter 4, we explained that it is important to determine a child's instructional reading level—the level at which the child will grow with good instruction. The score an individual child obtains on a standardized norm-referenced assessment probably does *not* reflect his or her instructional level (Betts, 1949) and is not a reliable guide to placement in reading material. If anything, the score may be closer to the child's frustration level. This is what the child did on a day when trying his or her hardest, perhaps—and made a few lucky guesses.

Practicing What You Have Learned. Following are derived scores for three children. Read each derived score and try stating what you know and what you don't know from the given information. Then read the discussion of each student.

- BILLY: *third grade; percentile rank 66.* Percentile rank compares an individual's score to the curve of the norming population. Billy read as well as or better than 66 percent of the students on whom this test was normed, which puts him slightly above the middle. The percentile rank does not compare him to his classmates, nor do we know how it compares to his previous performances. Remember that a percentile difference of 5 or even 10 in the middle of the curve represents a much smaller difference in test performance than it would at the extreme high or low ends.

- JILL: *fourth grade; stanine 4; last year's stanine 6.* Stanines are nine bands of scores, with 4, 5, and 6 representing average performance. Jill's score this year is within the average range for students in her grade in the norming group, but

> it is two stanines lower than last year's score. We will look at Jill's classroom performance to see if this score seems reasonable. We will also do informal diagnostic assessment to determine how we can help.
>
> * *CARLA: second grade; grade equivalent 5.8.* The grade-equivalent score compares an individual score to the average score of children in the norming population at different grade levels; it is expressed in terms of years and months. This test was normed on second- and third-grade students. A mathematical formula was used to project how children at higher or lower grade levels might perform on this test. Carla's grade-equivalent score of 5.8 reflects such a projection. We know that Carla reads well above grade level, but this does not mean she should be reading fifth-grade material. Rather, we can say that she performed on this second-grade test the way a student in the fifth grade, eighth month might have performed on this second-grade test.

Using Standardized Measurements

In the following sections, we will summarize some of the concerns, discuss current thinking, and show you some ways to handle standardized assessment in your classroom while helping your students perform to the best of their abilities.

Concerns About Testing

Many educators have reservations about the norm-referenced testing that is part of almost every school system. However, decisions about such testing are often in the hands of politicians and school boards, and the content of the tests is largely in the hands of publishers.

Each school system must know its purpose for testing and decide how best to report the results to the public or to whatever regulatory authority required the tests. In all such reporting, it must be remembered that standardized test scores can be misinterpreted.

A related problem arises when schools allow curriculum to be driven by performance on assessments. Much of what is done in each classroom, then, is directed toward nudging students to score better on the test. In an effort to ensure that students will make adequate yearly progress, curricula are often revamped to align with tests and huge blocks of time are devoted to preparation for test taking. Local standards and benchmarks may be rewritten to conform to whatever test is chosen. This, in effect, hands curriculum over to politicians and test publishers.

You, as a classroom teacher, may have little to say about which tests are given to your students, but you can vow to be involved in such decision making. Assessment should be a good match with your local standards. Further, once a test is chosen, careful decisions must be made about how to report the results honestly and in a way that is clear to the community:

* Are all derived scores for each school reported in the newspaper?
* If so, are the scores accompanied by an explanation of what they mean?

- Will it be clear that the 40th percentile is average and what being average actually means?

- Are scores of some children omitted, and, if so, which scores and why?

- Are the scores of special education students left out of the report? Those of bilingual students?

- What kinds of decisions are being made as a result of a single child's score, an individual teacher's class scores, a school's scores, or a county's scores?

The State of the Profession: Local and State Assessments

Widespread, state-mandated testing affects almost every aspect of education. Schools, and by association teachers, are being measured by the results of such tests and, in some cases, even being assigned a grade. "A" schools are rewarded, often with additional funds. "F" schools are punished, often by not being given additional funds.

This testing is sometimes called "high-stakes" because a child's future may rest on test performance. For example, test results can dictate whether a child will be promoted to fourth grade or spend another year in third grade, despite research showing that neither repeating a grade nor moving on to the next grade (often called "social promotion") is apt to provide support for students who are at risk (Jimerson & Kaufman, 2003). Instead, intervention is needed to help those students deemed at risk.

Other consequences relate to the effect of such testing on minority students. For example, in Texas, which has had state-mandated testing for twenty years or more, data revealed that African American and Mexican American students had a significantly higher failure rate on the Texas Assessment of Academic Skills (TAAS) than their white peers. Several of these minority students decided to sue the state of Texas, since each had taken and passed all the required courses for graduation and felt they should not, and could not, be denied a high school diploma.

Read a discussion of this issue in Valencia and Villarreal (2003), listed in "For Additional Reading" on the premium website for this text.

We suggest that you learn your state's requirements for testing and how your local school system is complying with state mandates. Opinions about mandated testing appear in newspapers (and online) with increased intensity. Hardly anyone—educator, politician, parent, or layperson—is neutral. All have strong opinions, and you may find little agreement except on the most basic of issues: all children have the right to a good education; literacy (reading) is of paramount importance; we need to assess whether we are helping all children progress toward literacy (and other goals); and we need to find ways to help those children for whom such progress is difficult.

As results of widespread testing are reported in a community, you will notice a groundswell of reactions. If the scores have fallen or have failed to improve significantly, a scapegoat is sought. We, as a profession (and as members of the taxpaying community), may want to find something or someone to blame when children are not learning what we think they should be learning. Remember that events are seldom caused by a single event or condition; and remember that two events that may exist together, or correlate (such as single-parent homes and low reading scores), do not necessarily indicate cause and effect. Correlation is not the same as causation. There are many ways to look at data and infinite ways to interpret those data.

You will want to keep reading and learning about standardized testing in your school system as well as in the nation. Also look at test results of high school students;

these students are products of your elementary and middle school programs. Significant decisions based on the results of such testing include, but are not limited to, the following matters: special funding from the state; the right reading program to use; how children are assigned to special classes; changes in mandated materials; and, in some states, whether students in a given school will be eligible for a public or private school voucher to use for a different school.

Relevant websites are listed on the premium website for this text.

Besides staying informed about local and state policies, you will want to read professional journals and visit websites. Ask questions. Be a part of change that grows out of the concerns of educators; do not be someone who passively allows decisions to be handed down from the top. Learn about the existing state of assessment in your community; then either support it if you agree with it or work for change if you do not.

The Role of the Classroom Teacher

In an ideal world, there would be a perfect fit between what you teach and what is tested. We would teach what we test and test what we teach. This is not a perfect world, of course; therefore, you must help your students demonstrate what they have learned on whatever assessment you are required to use.

Standardized testing may be quite unlike your students' regular daily activities. The tests are paper and pencil. They may require filling in bubbles on a separate answer sheet. They may require reading a short, decontextualized paragraph and answering a series of questions. They may require connecting items or circling items. They may emphasize recall and details.

Also, your behavior during testing will differ from your daily behavior. You will be required to use the publisher's language to explain what your students are to do. During the test, you will not be allowed to answer questions, nudge children toward using skills, or ask stimulating questions. Time limitations will be rigidly imposed.

As in Mr. Singh's class described at the beginning of this chapter, your children will display a range of behaviors in response to the demands of testing:

- Some children are extremely anxious; no matter how much you reassure them, they will feel they should be perfect.

- Some children cannot really understand why the test publisher would put items on the test that are clearly too hard for most of them.

- Some children may decide the test has little to do with their real lives, so they scarcely look at the test items. Rather, they just make interesting designs as they fill in bubbles on the answer sheet or pick C for every multiple-choice item.

- Some capable, hard-working, agreeable children work slowly and methodically; they are thrown into a near panic when time limits are imposed.

- Some children rush through everything they do and see no reason to work differently on a test.

- There may be physical symptoms of stress: stomachache, headache, coughing, crying, or excessive thirst. Your heart will ache especially for these children.

Many teachers spend some time each year teaching their students how to take the required tests. Such preparation can take quite a bite out of instructional time.

Glazer (1998) reports studies showing that each child in the United States faces, on average, two thousand test items a year. In addition to the test time, teachers spend an average of fourteen hours a year preparing children to take tests. Special education students spend even more time being tested.

Let's begin with the assumption that your students will spend some time each year taking standardized tests. We think you can help them perform to the best of their abilities. We suggest that you teach them about the formats, layouts, constrictions, and language of such tests. This is not cheating; you are not using actual test items. You are teaching your students to think like test makers, so that they can become good test takers.

HELPING YOUR STUDENTS PREPARE

Your students may be used to demonstrating their understanding of what they have read in a number of interesting and personal ways. However, there is no choice about one's response on a standardized test, nor is there room for divergent opinions. For example, a common format requires the student to answer a series of questions by choosing from several options: the familiar (to you) multiple-choice item. Students are expected to give or identify "the" correct answer—the one the test makers had in mind.

Simply leading students through practice tests is not true preparation; such practice does not help them learn how to think as they take the test. Following are some simple ways you might plan instruction and teach students how to take tests:

- Examine past tests to discover which formats are commonly used. Examples might be close (fill-in-the-blank) passages, multiple choice, and matching.

- Take the test yourself, and think about the strategies you used to determine the "correct" answers. Compare your strategies with those of colleagues.

- Observe students as they take tests, and make notes of various strategies you see them using. Then, make evident to students what they do as they take tests. Discuss their behaviors. Ask questions, examine incorrect answers, and ask students to explain why they chose the answer they did.

- Invite students to share ways to read and respond to an item.

- Examine each possible response to each item with your students, clarifying why it is or is not the best choice.

- Replicate the testing conditions, and let students get used to working silently and independently within the time limits— without asking questions.

- Share things you and others do that help you, and urge students to try these strategies, reassuring them that they may or may not choose to adopt them. For example, you may prefer reading the questions before you read a test passage so that you can look for answers as you read. This may seem the most sensible approach in the world to you, but it may not be the best for everyone. Some test takers prefer to read the passage first while holding in their minds the thought "What are they [the test makers] looking for?" There is no one right way to perform successfully on every test. Each person must find his or her own best way.

- Teach students how to use answer sheets. Begin with how to fill in the personal information. Then show them how the page is set up: how each row of choices matches

This teacher is having a conference with a student and her mother about her achievements.

© Bill Aron/PhotoEdit

items in the test; whether one should move across or down; what to do if there are five possible bubbles but some test items have only four options; how to keep their place as they move back and forth from the test booklet to the answer sheet.

• Stress to students that the goal in responding on a test is to get right answers, not to be creative or personal, even though this may be quite different from what you emphasize in everyday responses to reading.

You will undoubtedly get better at helping your students become competent, confident test takers as you learn more about the tests they will be taking and more about your individual students' responses to testing.

TALKING TO FAMILIES

Another important job is helping families understand what test scores mean. Your school may have a particular way of reporting test results, but you may want to do more. The families of your students may appreciate a letter informing them of upcoming testing as well as a later letter explaining, with examples, exactly what their child's score means in terms of her or his performance in this school in this grade on this particular measure.

Figure 5.4 shows a sample of a letter you might send home to explain upcoming standardized testing. Figure 5.5 is a sample letter you might send explaining an individual child's score on a standardized test, putting the derived score into words that a layperson can understand.

You could create a template on your computer to minimize the time it takes you to write individual letters; with a template, you can insert individual pieces of information and write a personal statement for each student. Figure 5.5 shows the individualized information for Jeremy in **boldface.** (In the actual letter, of course, you would not use boldface.)

Dear Family,

Standardized testing will take place next week on [insert dates and times]. This letter explains why we give these tests and how you can help your child handle them with as little stress as possible.

Why? Standardized tests help us know how our students are doing in comparison to [insert whatever norming population is used in your system: national (the rest of the country), state (other schools in the state), local (other schools in this district)]. Results of this testing also help us plan future instruction in our school.

After the tests have been scored, which will take several weeks, we will report schoolwide results to the public. Your child's scores will be reported to you by letter [and conference, if appropriate].

What can you do? We need a clear picture of how our students are doing, which means each child must be able to do his or her best on test days. Children need to take the tests seriously but also not panic about them. This is a tough balance to achieve, and you can help in the following ways.

Tell your child you know about the tests and are sure the child will do his or her best work. Talk about the purpose of the tests: to help teachers help kids. Fooling around on the answer sheet or guessing wildly spoils the results.

Explain that there may be some things your child won't know on the test. Point out that "they make the test hard enough for the smartest kid in the whole world."

Tell your child not to be "creative." For example: When asked to "pick the best title," your child should simply pick the answer that tells what the passage or story is about, even though real titles often don't tell what a story is about. Unlike some of our class work, on standardized tests, children need to try to find "right answers."

Be sure your child is well rested and well fed. Sleepy, hungry children can't think well.

Telling a child "don't worry" or "don't be nervous" doesn't help much. Testing IS stressful. It's best to acknowledge it.

Reassure your child that you are proud of him or her . . . no matter what.

Thank you for all of your support.

Sincerely,

FIGURE 5.4

Sample Letter About Standardized Tests

Dear family of **Jeremy,**

Here is **Jeremy's** score from the standardized test he took in **February** and an explanation of what that score means. I've also made some comments about how these scores fit with what I'm seeing in the classroom every day.

At our next conference we'll talk about these scores, **Jeremy's** daily work, and any concerns you or I have.

Jeremy's percentile rank on the reading test was **45.** This means that he did as well as or better than **45** percent of the students on whom this test was developed. It DOES NOT compare him to the rest of this class. His percentile rank of **45** shows him to be **an average reader. Jeremy's** percentile rank this year is **slightly higher than** it was last year.

Jeremy has worked very hard this year. This test may not have given him a chance to show everything that he can do. For example, there is a time limit on the test and Jeremy likes to work slowly and carefully. He might have had a higher score if he could have worked longer.

One thing that always delights me about Jeremy is his imagination. When he reads, his mind leaps from one interesting idea to another. We certainly don't want him to curb his imagination, but on a standardized test it may have kept him from concentrating on the "right answers" such tests demand.

I look forward to our conference. Please call 555-5555 and leave a message. I'll call you back to schedule a time for us to meet.

Sincerely,

FIGURE 5.5

Sample Letter Reporting an Individual Child's Test Results (Boldface Indicates Individualized Additions to the Basic Template)

The tone of the letter should always be positive. For those children whose performance is worrisome, try to find a way to reassure the family. For example, tell them that you see evidence of growth in the child's daily activity that is not reflected on the test. Of course, you must be truthful; don't hide your concerns if you have them.

Even if you have communicated with families via letters, at certain times you will probably want to talk face to face. In a conference following the reporting of test results, you should try to do all of the following:

1. Give family members a chance to say how they feel about the child's learning at this point.

2. Share work such as writing, reports, projects, checklists—the kinds of informal assessment we suggested earlier in this book.

3. Give a report and review of the child's performance on the standardized test and an interpretation of what the score means. Explain what is meant by a percentile rank, grade equivalent, or stanine. Explain where the child falls. Compare the child's score to his or her previous scores (not to the rest of the class).

4. Encourage questions and welcome concerns.

5. Describe your reaction to the child's test performance and how it matches (or fails to match) the child's daily performance in the real world of the classroom.

6. Together with the family, draw up a plan to support continued growth.

Chapter 7 contains additional suggestions related to working with families.

Tests for Measuring Literacy

This section briefly describes several tests for measuring literacy. We have organized the tests into three types: group tests, individual tests, and tests for special populations. We describe some achievement tests, which are designed to measure how well students can do what the test publisher has deemed appropriate for a certain population. We also describe some diagnostic tests, which are designed to measure specific subskills of literacy to support a prescription for teaching.

Some reading tests are part of an achievement test (sometimes called a *survey* test) that covers other aspects of literacy, such as spelling or language (grammar). Some are part of a battery of tests that also includes math. Some include specific skills involved in reading, such as phonics or structural analysis. Some are standardized but not normed.

This is not a comprehensive list; we are simply naming and briefly describing some tests to give you an idea of what is published. Inclusion of a test here does not imply recommendation.

Group-Administered Tests

Group-administered tests (survey or achievement tests) are the most common tests used in schools. These are chosen by the administration and are used to assess progress in reading (and perhaps other subjects), to target children who may have problems, and/or to provide evidence regarding the success (or failure) of a particular program. These tests are norm referenced, so each individual score, class average score, or school average score can be compared to a large norming sample. (Sometimes local norms are developed as well.) A survey test usually has several levels so that it can be used with students in every grade. Sometimes one level is designed to be used with more than one grade. Often there are alternative, equivalent forms for the same level to allow pre- and post-testing.

Don't forget: the tasks required on the achievement test may be quite different from the kind of reading your children do on a daily basis. In addition, the test situation itself often inhibits children and keeps them from doing what they might normally do easily.

Remember, too, that group survey tests may be unsatisfactory when used with children who are having reading problems; the test that is appropriate for the child's grade may be much too difficult for the child to read. Let's say you teach fifth grade, and you know Johnny will be unable to read most of the fifth-grade test. In many cases, you can't give Johnny a lower-level form such as the second-grade test (which he might be able to read) because no norms are provided for fifth-grade children on the second-grade test, and therefore the score Johnny obtained would have no meaning. Some publishers do, however, provide norms for students on either side of the grade level for which the test was written. This allows a certain amount of "out-of-level" testing. In such a case, you might be able to make better sense of Johnny's performance.

The following are some examples of group-administered tests:

- GRADE: Group Reading Assessment and Diagnostic Evaluation (2001)
  American Guidance Service
  PreK to Adult
  Measures reading skills and gives reading levels.

- Iowa Tests of Basic Skill (ITBS) (Form A, 2001; Form B, 2003; Form C 2007)
  Riverside Publishing Company
  Grades K to 8
  Series of tests includes measures of literacy areas. Yields usual derived scores.
  Both norm and criterion referenced.

- Metropolitan Achievement Tests (MAT), 8th edition (2000)
  Pearson
  Grades K to 12
  Series of tests covers several disciplines, including reading. Criterion-referenced scores available as well as practice and locator tests (to allow testing out of grade level).

- Stanford Diagnostic Reading Test, 4th edition (1995)
  Pearson
  Grades 1.5 to 12; several levels from grades 1.5 through 12.8
  Assesses various components of reading from auditory discrimination through scanning and skimming. Provides all usual derived scores. Norm and criterion referenced.

- TerraNova, 3 (2001)
  CTB/McGraw-Hill
  Grades K to 12; group or individual
  Tests listening comprehension, basic understanding, text analysis, reading strategies, and knowledge of sound/symbol relationships.

- Gates-MacGinitie Reading Test, 4th edition (2000)
  Riverside Publishing Company
  Grades K to Adult; several forms
  Subtests include various aspects of reading, from concepts and oral language at the lower level to vocabulary and comprehension. Provides usual derived scores.

Individually Administered Tests

Individually administered tests are often designed to yield diagnostic information. Though some group tests claim to provide diagnostic information, we believe such information is better learned through individually administered tests such as those described here and, of course, through the many informal assessments

The publishers' addresses are listed in "For Additional Reading" on the premium website for this text.

described throughout this text. Following are a few examples of some of the more widely used tests in this category:

NORM-REFERENCED TESTS

- Dynamic Indicators of Basic Early Literacy Skills (DIBELS), 6th edition, Revised (2007)

  Center on Teaching and Learning, University of Oregon.

  Grades K to 6

  Students from kindergarten through grade 3 are given benchmark assessments three times a year that measure phonemic awareness, phonics, fluency, comprehension, and vocabulary. Students in grades 4 through 6 are assessed in fluency and comprehension. For students with reading difficulties, monitoring assessments are given as often as needed. Schools can download DIBELS free of charge by going to https://dibels.uoregon.edu/measures/.

- Test of Early Reading Ability (TERA–3), 3rd edition (2001)

  Pearson

  Ages 3 to 8

  Norm referenced. Administration takes about thirty minutes. Tests construction of meaning, including logo and environment reading, alphabet knowledge, reading words and comprehension, and conventions of written language. Raw scores can be converted to various derived scores.

- Comprehensive Test of Phonological Processing (CTOPP) (1999)

  Pearson

  Grades K, 1, 2, 3, and higher

  Requires approximately thirty minutes per student for administration. Norm referenced on a nationwide sample.

- Test of Phonological Awareness (TOPA 2+), 2nd edition (2004)

  LinguiSystems

  Ages 5 to 8

  May be individual or group administered. Normed on a large sample in twenty-six states.

- The Phonological Awareness Test (2007))

  LinguiSystems

  Grades K, 1, 2, and 3

  Requires twenty to thirty minutes per student for administration. Covers the major skills of phonological awareness. Raw scores can be converted to age-equivalent scores, percentile scores, and standard scores.

CRITERION-REFERENCED TESTS

- BRIGANCE Comprehensive Inventory of Basic Skills, Revised (1999)

  Curriculum Associates

  PreK to 9

  Several inventories assessing early development, basic skills, and essential skills. A Spanish-language assessment is also available. The inventories are criterion referenced and helpful in writing individual education plans for exceptional education students. Software for IBM and Macintosh is available.

- Diagnostic Assessments of Reading (DAR), 2nd edition (2005)

  Riverside Publishing

  Elementary to adult

  Assesses key areas of student learning in reading and language, including word analysis, oral reading accuracy and fluency, silent reading comprehension, spelling, word meaning, word recognition, letters and sounds, print awareness, and phonological awareness. Individually administered; takes about forty minutes.

- Texas Primary Reading Inventory (TPRI) (2006-2008.)

  McGraw-Hill

  Grades K, 1, and 2

  Provides a screening section and an inventory section at each level covering appropriate graphophonemic knowledge, phonemic awareness, book and print concepts, listening comprehension, reading accuracy, word reading, and reading comprehension. An intervention activities guide provides helpful suggestions for the teacher.

RELATED FORMAL ASSESSMENTS

The publishers of the tests just cited also publish other individually administered assessments in related literacy areas. These include language development, oral language, spelling, writing, intelligence, cognitive functioning, and school readiness. As a classroom teacher, you will be unlikely to administer them, though you may need to understand reported scores for children who have been given such tests. To that end, you will want to acquaint yourself with the assessments used in your school system.

Testing to Accommodate Special Populations

Have you ever done poorly on a test of some kind and said to yourself, "But the test wasn't fair!"? Perhaps in a physical education class you were supposed to clear a hurdle, but you were much shorter than the others. Maybe you thought the height of the hurdle should have been proportionate to your height. Everyone has had the experience of feeling judged unfairly because of being held to a standard of performance that did not take into account individual differences. Accommodating differences does not mean making excuses; it does mean trying to adjust for an uneven playing field.

STUDENTS IN EXCEPTIONAL OR SPECIAL EDUCATION

Testing plays a critical part in special education programs: tests help educators decide what a program for students with disabilities should look like, how the program might be carried out, and whether or not it is successful. Every program planned for a special population must address several questions:

- Who needs the help?
- How will we identify those children?
- What do we need to teach them?

- How will we teach them?
- How will we know if we have been successful?
- What will we do if we have not been successful?

Moreover, as with any other program funded by tax dollars, there must be accountability for the use of the funds. This becomes even more important when funds are limited and schools must compete for them by showing greater need or by demonstrating greater success.

As a classroom teacher, you may not need to choose or administer any formal tests other than those required by your school for all students to meet the requirements of RTI. However, schoolwide standardized tests may be the first signal that a child should be tested further to determine whether she or he needs special services of some kind. Further tests will probably be administered by special school personnel. If such a need is determined to exist, an individual education plan will be written, and your job will be to provide instruction in your classroom that supports what the special teachers are providing.

You will want to keep informed about the assessment of special populations even though you don't administer the tests yourself. This is part of your development as a professional, a subject we will consider in detail in Chapter 7. Reports of investigations and research are often summarized in professional publications, and we recommend that you consult such publications regularly.

TITLE I AND READING FIRST STUDENTS

Another special population is students who participate in Reading First and Title I programs, both of which are designed to help students who have difficulty learning to read. There are mixed opinions among educators and lay persons as to whether or not these programs are successful (National Center for Technology Innovation, 2008). You will want to find out about these programs in your school and community so that you can know what is available to help your students.

SECOND-LANGUAGE LEARNERS

A major concern, of course, is using assessment to make wise decisions about the education of every student, no matter what element of our diverse population the student represents. A child who is not yet proficient in English cannot demonstrate what he or she knows when the test is written in English, just as a child from a minority culture may not understand test items reflecting only mainstream culture.

Many of the published tests mentioned here (and many others as well) are available in a Spanish version. Consult publishers' catalogs or websites to find out which provide tests in another language. When you have the opportunity, you will want to assess literacy without limiting that assessment to English. It is important to learn which children are already literate in another language and to what extent they are using literacy skills in that language.

Although students may develop conversational proficiency in English fairly rapidly, it takes much longer to develop academic literacy skills. According to Collier (1992), it takes five to nine years for English-language learners to reach grade level on many standardized tests.

CONCLUSIONS

Accountability, a term that comes up repeatedly in discussions of assessing diverse populations, is not a bad word; it means that educators need to continue to find ways to demonstrate what children are learning, support what is being taught, monitor whether what is assessed matches what is taught, and show that schools are doing the job they are supposed to be doing. When students are living with differences that inhibit the use of the usual assessment instruments and procedures, educators must find ways to accommodate those differences without contaminating the results. Educators must be especially vigilant when considering evidence that can lead to potentially life-altering decisions about a child.

Summary

- This chapter introduced basic information about formal and standardized assessments.

- Standardized tests, designed to be administered under identical conditions every time, are often used to measure how well schools are teaching and also how well children are achieving.

- A norm-referenced test compares the performance of an individual to that of the norming population, the group on which the test was standardized. Plotted on a graph, the scores on such tests take the shape of a bell curve, with the largest portion of scores concentrated near the middle (the "average") and very few at either the high end or the low end.

- Criterion-referenced tests differ in that they measure performance in terms of an absolute mastery of particular skills the child is expected to have learned; that is, they are tied directly to specific areas of curriculum.

- Diagnostic tests, another major type, are designed to lead directly to instructional decisions.

- Critical for all these tests are validity (the extent to which a test measures what it is supposed to measure) and reliability (the consistency of results). Another important statistical concept is the standard error of measurement, which tells us how confident we can be that a particular score is a child's "true" score.

- In addition to a student's raw score on a test, publishers usually provide one or more derived scores. Common derived scores include the percentile rank, standard scores such as the stanine and the normal curve equivalent, and grade- and age-equivalent scores. All of these have benefits as well as disadvantages. Teachers need to be careful not to misinterpret derived scores or to foster confusion among students and their families.

- Besides the risks of misinterpretation, concerns about standardized testing include the degree to which tests may drive the curriculum. Partly because of such concerns, many changes are occurring in standardized testing across the United States—changes about which you will want to keep informed, especially as they affect your own district.

- Your role as a teacher will include helping students prepare for standardized tests and conveying the results to students and families in a positive, helpful way.

- For measuring literacy, many formal tests are available. They include group and individual tests, norm- and criterion-referenced. In this chapter, we have listed some specific tests, though this is in no way a comprehensive list.

- A major concern in all standardized testing is the degree to which it may be unfair for special populations. Accommodations may be needed for students in special education programs, Title I students, and students for whom English is a second language. At the very least, educators should be aware of the pitfalls in using a single test for a diverse population.

- The information in this chapter is intended simply to introduce some very basic terms and concepts for an area of testing with which all classroom teachers must deal. Ideas about such testing are being challenged daily, and decisions about how best to assess all students fairly are always evolving.

Test Publishers

American Guidance Service, Inc., 4201 Woodland Rd., Circle Pines, MN 55014. 1–800–328–2560; **www.agsnet.com/**

Center on Teaching and Learning, University of Oregon, Eugene, OR 97403 1–888–497–4290 **https://dibels.uoregon.edu/measures/**

CTB/McGraw-Hill, 20 Ryan Ranch Rd., Monterey, CA 93940. 1–800–538–9547 **www.ctb.com/**

Curriculum Associates, Inc., P.O. Box 2001, North Billerica, MA 01862–9914. 1–800–225–0248 **www.curriculumassociates.com/**

LinguiSystems, 3100 4th Ave., East Moline, IL 61244–9700. 1–800–776–4332 **www.linguisystems.com/**

Pearson, One Lake Street, Upper Saddle River, NJ, 1–800–477–3269 Assessments **www.pearsoned.com**

www.proedinc.com/

Riverside Publishing Company, 425 Spring Lake Dr., Itasca, IL 60143–2079. 1–800–323–9540 **www.riverpub.com/products/**

Texas Education Agency, 1701 N. Congress Ave., Austin, TX 78701. 521–463–9734 **www.tea.state.tx.us/**

Please visit the premium website for *Literacy Assessment*, Fourth Edition to access the TeachSource Video Cases, chapter web links, For Additional Reading, tutorial quizzes, glossary flashcards, online checklists, downloads, and much more! Go to www.cengage.com/login to register your access code.

Standards Focus (See inside back cover)
Standards for Reading Professionals: 1, 2, 4

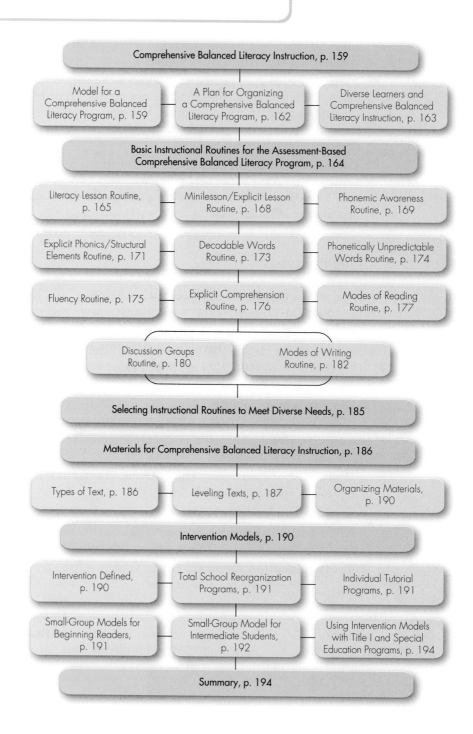

Comprehensive Balanced Literacy Instruction, p. 159

Model for a Comprehensive Balanced Literacy Program, p. 159

A Plan for Organizing a Comprehensive Balanced Literacy Program, p. 162

Diverse Learners and Comprehensive Balanced Literacy Instruction, p. 163

Basic Instructional Routines for the Assessment-Based Comprehensive Balanced Literacy Program, p. 164

Literacy Lesson Routine, p. 165

Minilesson/Explicit Lesson Routine, p. 168

Phonemic Awareness Routine, p. 169

Explicit Phonics/Structural Elements Routine, p. 171

Decodable Words Routine, p. 173

Phonetically Unpredictable Words Routine, p. 174

Fluency Routine, p. 175

Explicit Comprehension Routine, p. 176

Modes of Reading Routine, p. 177

Discussion Groups Routine, p. 180

Modes of Writing Routine, p. 182

Selecting Instructional Routines to Meet Diverse Needs, p. 185

Materials for Comprehensive Balanced Literacy Instruction, p. 186

Types of Text, p. 186

Leveling Texts, p. 187

Organizing Materials, p. 190

Intervention Models, p. 190

Intervention Defined, p. 190

Total School Reorganization Programs, p. 191

Individual Tutorial Programs, p. 191

Small-Group Models for Beginning Readers, p. 191

Small-Group Model for Intermediate Students, p. 192

Using Intervention Models with Title I and Special Education Programs, p. 194

Summary, p. 194

6

Instructional Routines for a Comprehensive Balanced Literacy Program: An Overview

r. Aroyo's fifth-grade class consists of thirty-one students: eighteen girls and thirteen boys. Nine students are Hispanic; their families are from Mexico, Central America, and Puerto Rico. All of these Spanish-speaking students have achieved the level of intermediate fluency in English (as described in Chapter 3) and have made the transition from reading Spanish to reading English. They participate in all class activities, even though twice a week they still go to English as a second language tutoring for work on academic English.

Today the class has divided into three groups; each group is reading a different book related to catastrophes, the theme the class has been studying. Mr. Aroyo first meets with the group reading *Predicting Earthquakes* (Vogt, 1989). He introduces the semantic map shown in Figure 6.1, and he models for students how to use it to organize the information they will gain from reading the text.

Next, Mr. Aroyo moves on to another group reading *Emergency* (Gibbons, 1994). He guides and talks students through the first six pages of the book to prepare them for better comprehension of the text. The students then read silently. This group is reading considerably below grade level, and Mr. Aroyo is trying to accelerate their reading development by using highly structured lessons. He follows a method known as *reciprocal teaching*, an interactive process in which teacher and students take turns modeling reading strategies. (See Chapter 11 for a detailed discussion of this method.)

Mr. Aroyo moves on to the third group, where he participates and observes as students discuss their book using written prompts that he has previously given them. As students complete their discussion, Mr. Aroyo makes notes on his clipboard about each student's response. At the conclusion of their discussion, he tells the group, "You identified almost all of the main points!"

This brief glimpse into Mr. Aroyo's classroom shows how he operates a Comprehensive Balanced Literacy Program in a classroom of students from several different cultures, reading at different levels. On this day, his students read **developmentally appropriate books.** Such

NEW TERMS

• shared reading
• shared writing
• teach
• teacher-modeled writing
• teacher read-aloud
• text walk
• word bank

books are at the students' instructional reading levels, so they can read capably with good guidance and instruction. On other days, we might see the entire class reading the same book, in which case Mr. Aroyo uses different types of instructional activities to meet the individual needs of students.

We saw Mr. Aroyo use three instructional strategies. When he used the semantic map shown in Figure 6.1, he was employing a type of **graphic organizer,** a visual representation of the way a text is organized. (The story maps mentioned in Chapter 3 are another type of graphic organizer.) When Mr. Aroyo talked students through the first six pages of *Emergency* before they began reading, he was using a technique known as a **text walk.** The students who talked about their book using Mr. Aroyo's prompts were in a **discussion group** (also known as a **discussion circle**). As he participated in and observed the discussion group, Mr. Aroyo was assessing how students were using previously taught skills.

Most of Mr. Aroyo's students were functioning at the Almost Fluent Reading and Writing Stage, though we noticed some variation. There was also variation in their fluency in English. Yet Mr. Aroyo accommodated all of the children's needs comfortably in the same classroom.

This chapter will provide an overview of a Comprehensive Balanced Literacy Program and will review eleven key instructional routines that you can use with students at all stages of literacy development. We will refer to these routines frequently in Chapters 8 through 12 as we consider each stage of literacy development.

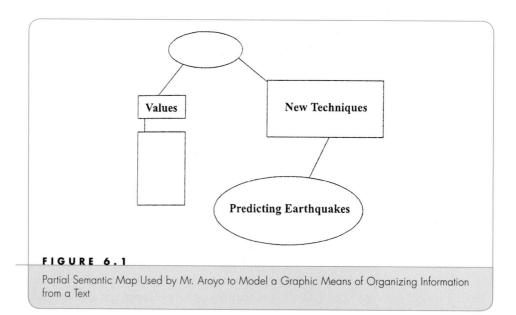

FIGURE 6.1

Partial Semantic Map Used by Mr. Aroyo to Model a Graphic Means of Organizing Information from a Text

Comprehensive Balanced Literacy Instruction

See more with TeachSource Video Case, "Elementary Reading Instruction: A Balanced Literacy Program."

Comprehensive Balanced Literacy Instruction is a widely supported concept (Armbruster & Osborn, 2001; Au, Carroll, & Scheu, 1997; Fountas & Pinnell, 1996, 2001; Freppon & Dahl, 1998; National Reading Panel, 2000; Pressley, 1998; Snow, Burns, & Griffin, 1998; Strickland, 1994). Despite some differences and perhaps other wording, educators mostly agree that a Comprehensive Balanced Literacy Program places emphasis on the right combination of elements each student needs to achieve success in literacy. These elements include both direct instruction in skills and strategies for those who need it (Delpit, 1986; National Reading Panel, 2000) and indirect instruction through a variety of meaningful instructional literacy experiences.

Model for a Comprehensive Balanced Literacy Program

Figure 6.2 presents a model for an effective way to think of a Comprehensive Balanced Literacy Program or what is sometimes referred to as core instruction. As you recall from Chapter 1, the foundation for RTI is good core instruction (Taylor, 2008). Figure 6.2 illustrates that a literacy program must give equal attention to both reading and writing (within which areas oral language will flourish), and that time must be provided for instruction, for practice, and for provision of extra help to those who need it. This figure should help you as you organize your assessment-based literacy classroom on a daily basis.

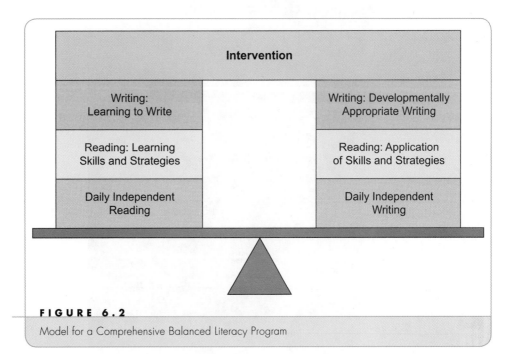

FIGURE 6.2

Model for a Comprehensive Balanced Literacy Program

Figure 6.2 shows that there are six blocks that *all* students receive in a Comprehensive Balanced Literacy Program:

- Daily Independent Reading
- Daily Independent Writing
- READING: Learning Skills and Strategies
- READING: Application of Skills and Strategies
- WRITING: Learning to Write
- WRITING: Developmentally Appropriate Writing

These six blocks require a minimum of three hours per day in kindergarten and a minimum of two hours per day in grades 3 through 8. *Intervention instruction for struggling readers is in addition to these times.* Now let's take a closer look at each block.

INDEPENDENT READING AND WRITING BLOCKS

Daily Independent Reading and *Daily Independent Writing* make up the first two blocks of the Comprehensive Balanced Literacy Program and must be provided daily. These blocks provide students with the practice they need to become effective, fluent readers and writers. An average of ten to fifteen minutes per day should be allotted for *each* block, with adjustments for the grade level you teach.

During Daily Independent Reading students are free to choose from bins of books.

© Michael Newman/ Photo Edit

Research is not conclusive about whether independent reading helps to develop fluency (National Reading Panel, 2000). However, we believe that beginning readers and struggling readers need more fluency practice (at least five to ten minutes per day from the independent reading block), and more able readers just need a strong component of independent reading to develop adequate fluency (Pikulski & Chard, 2003). A routine for directly focusing on fluency is presented later in this chapter.

Independent reading does much more than just build fluency. During the Daily Independent Reading block, students read self-selected books, magazines, and newspapers. At the beginning literacy stages, children may look at pictures. You may read to yourself to model independent reading during part of the block, but you should also monitor students' reading and hold conferences with individuals.

Similarly, during the Daily Independent Writing block, students choose what to write. You also monitor and confer with students during this block, though you may do some personal writing to model for students that you value writing, too.

READING INSTRUCTION BLOCKS

Reading: Learning Skills and Strategies, one of the two blocks for reading instruction, is the block in which you systematically and explicitly **teach** students the designated grade-level skills and strategies they need to become independent decoders and comprehenders. During this block, students use an **anthology** if you are using a published basal program, or they use designated core books with which they can practice and apply the skills and strategies you have taught.

By **core books,** we mean books that are used by all students in the class. Using the same book for all students during this block serves three main purposes:

1. It helps all students see that they can learn from a common book, even though everyone may not do the same kinds of activities with the book. This helps to elevate self-esteem.

2. The core book provides a basis for developing a common body of prior knowledge, vocabulary, and background.

3. Through the use of **minilessons** (described later in this chapter), key skills and strategies are taught within the meaningful context of the literature using direct, explicit instruction.

For the majority of the class, the book used for the core book should be *slightly* more difficult than the students' reading levels (Snow, Burns, & Griffin, 1998). For a few students, the core book will be less challenging. For others (for instance, some English-language learners who lack English proficiency), the book may be more challenging. Through the use of small groups, you meet the needs of these students by providing different types of instruction. This process is further illustrated in Chapters 10 through 12.

Reading: Application of Skills and Strategies is the block of instruction in which students apply the skills and strategies they learned from reading the core book—and develop their skills and strategies by reading texts appropriate to their reading levels. (For a discussion of reading levels, see Chapter 4.) The skills and strategies students need are taught with minilessons. Students work in small groups that change as students grow in their ability to read. *Groups are never static or constant.*

In the beginning of kindergarten and first grade, the two reading instruction blocks usually take place daily. As students progress through the grades and stages and read longer texts, it is appropriate to alternate between these two blocks.

WRITING INSTRUCTION BLOCKS

In the *Writing: Learning to Write* block, you teach children how to write. At the Pre-K and kindergarten levels this includes teaching students to form letters and write words and sentences. Writing plays an important role in developing students' knowledge and use of concepts of print, phonemic awareness, and letter-sound associations. During this block you also model different types of writing, such as stories and informational pieces. Spelling and grammar are taught as a part of writing. This block may be provided to small groups or to the whole class.

Writing: Developmentally Appropriate Writing is the block in which students write their own pieces. By **developmentally appropriate writing,** we mean that students do the type of writing that was modeled in the Learning to Write block, but they *select their own topics*. In the beginning, students may write only sentences or captions for their pictures. Gradually, they begin to write stories and even informational pieces. This block provides time for practice and application of spelling and grammar.

INTERVENTION

For a thorough discussion of a Comprehensive Balanced Literacy Program, see Cooper (2006), Chapter 2, listed in "For Additional Reading" at the premium website for this text.

Intervention is the additional block that provides support only for students who are experiencing difficulty in learning to read or who have special learning needs. This block encompasses all the Tiers of Intervention included in Chapter 1's discussion of RTI that is designed to stop or prevent failure. Students receiving intervention also take part in the six other blocks. Later in this chapter, we will discuss intervention in more depth.

A Plan for Organizing a Comprehensive Balanced Literacy Program

In your classroom you will have students at more than one stage of literacy development. Each needs instruction that meets his or her needs. A *daily blocked plan* provides the structure that allows you to carry out that instruction.

The *minimum* suggested times for literacy are:

Kindergarten	3 hours
Grades 1 to 2	2 to 3½ hours
Grades 3 to 5	1 to 2 hours
Grades 6 to 8	1 to 2 hours

These times include a minimum of ninety minutes per day for reading and a minimum of thirty to forty-five minutes per day for writing. Intervention instruction for struggling readers requires an additional thirty to forty-five minutes per day. Table 6.1 presents a sample daily blocked schedule for a Comprehensive Balanced Literacy Program. No one schedule works for all classrooms. Further, your school

TABLE 6.1

Outline of a Sample Daily Blocked Plan for a Comprehensive Balanced Literacy Program

BLOCK	TIME RANGE IN MINUTES
Daily Independent Reading	10 to 20
Daily Independent Writing	10 to 20
Reading	
Reading: Learning Skills and Strategies	
• Literacy lesson	15 to 40
• Explicit phonics/structural elements routine *or* explicit comprehension routine	15 to 20
Reading: Application of Skills and Strategies	
• Guided reading *or* other modes of reading	15 to 40
Writing	
Learning to Write/Writing or *Developmentally Appropriate Writing*	15 to 40
• Minilessons for writing procedures	5 to 15
• Minilessons for grammar and spelling	5 to 15
TOTAL MINUTES	**90 TO 210**

may mandate certain time parameters for certain instruction. Within your restrictions, you need to work out a schedule, post it, discuss it with your students, and revise it when necessary. Any plan must be flexible enough to allow you to organize and manage your Comprehensive Balanced Literacy Program. In Chapters 8 through 12 we present examples of plans at various stages of literacy development.

Diverse Learners and Comprehensive Balanced Literacy Instruction

The concept of a Comprehensive Balanced Literacy Program and the instructional strategies presented in this chapter are all appropriate for diverse learners, if adjusted to accommodate students' needs.

When planning an instructional program for ELL students, we believe you should give serious consideration to the recommendations of the Committee on the Prevention of Reading Difficulties in Young Children (Snow, Burns, & Griffin, 1998, p. 325):

- *If language-minority children arrive at school with no proficiency in English but speaking a language for which there are instructional guides, learning materials, and locally available proficient teachers, these children should be taught how to read in their native language while acquiring oral proficiency in English and subsequently taught to extend their skills to reading in English.*

• *If language-minority children arrive at school with no proficiency in English but speak a language for which the preceding conditions cannot be met and for which there are insufficient numbers of children to justify the development of the local capacity to meet such conditions, the initial instructional priority should be developing the children's oral proficiency in English. Although print materials may be used to support the development of English phonology, vocabulary, and syntax, the postponement of formal reading instruction is appropriate until an adequate level of oral proficiency in English has been achieved.*

Delaying reading instruction too long puts English-language learners further and further behind. The most widely accepted line of thinking is to do lots of reading to and with students, having them write from the beginning to develop academic English as well as conversational English (Krashen, 1993). Instructional routines such as shared reading (discussed later in this chapter) support language development in a nonthreatening way. In addition, see Young and Hadaway (2006) in References for suggestions on how to work with English-language learners in all classrooms.

We suggested some adaptations for assessment procedures to meet the needs of diverse learners in Chapters 2 through 4. *A Comprehensive Balanced Literacy Program is an assessment-based literacy program.* In other words, as you work with your students, you will continually think about their performance in relation to the stages of literacy development and will use a variety of tools and techniques to determine students' strengths, needs, and progress. Without such continual assessment, you cannot maintain a balanced program.

In our classrooms, we made changes in our instructional programs on the basis of what we observed. At times we grouped, at other times we taught the whole class, and at still other times we worked with individuals. Our literacy classrooms changed as students grew and changed. This will happen in your own classroom as you develop your teaching skills. The next section will present eleven instructional routines to use as you adapt your program to meet the needs of your diverse learners.

Basic Instructional Routines for the Assessment-Based Comprehensive Balanced Literacy Program

In previous chapters, we presented a variety of tools and techniques for assessment and stressed the need to be selective about which ones to use. As you make decisions about students' instruction, you will similarly need a variety of instructional routines and techniques. **An instructional routine** is a pattern of instruction that is used repeatedly. These routines will help you provide the much-needed ingredient in a successful classroom, **explicit teaching** (Hancock, 1999)—the process of clearly modeling for students what they are to learn. In this section we present eleven routines you will use over and over in your classroom:

1. Literacy lesson routine
2. Minilesson/explicit lesson routine
3. Phonemic awareness routine

TABLE 6.2	
The Place of Routines in Comprehensive Balanced Literacy Programs	
ROUTINE	**WHERE TO USE**
1. *Literacy Lesson*	Any reading instructional block
2. *Minilesson/Explicit Lesson*	Any reading or writing instructional block
3. *Phonemic Awareness*	Reading: Learning Skills and Strategies
4. *Explicit Phonics/Structural Elements*	Both instructional reading blocks
5. *Decodable Words*	Both instructional reading blocks
6. *Phonetically Unpredictable Words*	Both instructional reading blocks
7. *Fluency*	Both instructional reading blocks
8. *Explicit Comprehension*	Both instructional reading blocks
9. *Modes of Reading*	Both instructional reading blocks Daily Independent Reading block
10. *Discussion Groups*	All reading blocks
11. *Modes of Writing*	Both instructional writing blocks Daily Independent Writing block

4. Explicit phonics/structural elements routine
5. Decodable words routine
6. Phonetically unpredictable words routine
7. Fluency routine
8. Explicit comprehension routine
9. Modes of reading routine
10. Discussion groups routine
11. Modes of writing routine

We define and describe each routine, provide procedures, and offer some additional comments. In Chapters 8 through 12 you will find repeated references to these basic routines.

Table 6.2 shows where each routine fits within the blocks of the Comprehensive Balanced Literacy Program. You will use one or several of these routines every day no matter what age you teach.

Literacy Lesson Routine

The **literacy lesson** provides a framework for planning instruction using a piece of text for reading and writing instruction. It has three parts (Cooper, 2006): Introducing, Reading and Responding, and Extending. Table 6.3 identifies these parts, outlines their basic procedures, and explains their rationale.

TABLE 6.3

The Literacy Lesson: An Instructional Framework

LESSON PART	PROCEDURES	RATIONALE
Introducing	• Activate and develop prior knowledge and background for the text. • Help students set purpose for reading.	• Utilizes the research-based findings that prior knowledge/background and a purpose for reading are essential to effective comprehension.
Reading and Responding	Students: • Read text using one or more of the modes of reading (described later in this chapter). • Respond to the text through discussion and/or writing. • Apply decoding and comprehension strategies and skills. • Discuss which strategies and/or skills helped them read the text successfully. • Summarize orally and/or in writing what they read.	Builds on these research-supported ideas: • Readers must receive scaffolded support, moving toward independence as they learn to read. • Talking about strategies and skills used helps students apply what they are learning and make the strategies and skills their own. • Responding and summarizing lead to improved comprehension.
Extending	• Students use the knowledge and information gained in a follow-up activity. • Writing is taught on the basis of the type of text being read.	• Using knowledge gained from reading helps students see the value in learning to write. • Writing and reading are best taught together.

You can use the literacy lesson whenever you have students read any type of book for instructional purposes. As you can see from Table 6.3, the lesson also involves writing. At times you will model how to write the particular type of text students are reading. For example, if students are reading a story, you will model for them how to write a story (in the Learning to Write block) and then have them write their own story (in the Developmentally Appropriate Writing block). You will not need to model a new type of writing every time you do a literacy lesson because the writing is likely to extend over several days.

PROCEDURES

The literacy lesson framework is appropriate throughout your literacy program. While maintaining the basic structure, you can adjust the lesson to your students' needs and to the types of text they are reading. The following procedures can help you plan your lessons:

1. Look at your students' strengths and needs; consider where they are in the stages of literacy development (discussed in Chapters 8 through 12). Decide what skills and strategies will help them move on to the next stage.

2. Select the type of text your students need at this point. You will probably use a published program that has an anthology as a core book, as well as a variety of other types of text.

3. Read the text and the suggestions given in the manual that accompanies it. If the text is narrative, outline on paper or in your mind the story map (the setting, characters, problem, actions, and outcome). If the text is expository, outline the main ideas and supporting details. Also note key concept words that may need to be taught in advance of reading. This information helps you identify the key background concepts that need to be developed and helps you see what big ideas should be brought out in the reading. Also, look at the text to identify places that give students the opportunities to **practice** (use when reading with teacher guidance) and **apply** (use when reading independently) what they need to move to the next stage of literacy.

4. Outline each part of your lesson. Table 6.4 presents a set of questions that can guide you as you develop lessons. In the beginning, you may write out the lessons. As you gain more experience, you will outline your lessons mentally.

TABLE 6.4

Questions to Guide Development of a Literacy Lesson

Introducing	**a.** What key prior knowledge and background concepts need to be brought out or developed? (Look at your story map or main ideas and supporting details.)
	b. How will you develop this prior knowledge in an *interactive* way in a short amount of time (ten to fifteen minutes or less)?
Reading and Responding	**a.** What key skills and strategies do you want your students to practice and/or apply in this text? How will you bring these out after reading?
	b. How do you want students to read this text? (See the modes of reading routine.)
	c. What types of response prompts and/or activities will you use?
Extending	**a.** What types of follow-up activities would give students a chance to use what they have learned in this text? (Follow-up activities are not always necessary; they depend on the text.)
	b. What type of writing will you teach using this text as the basis for your modeling?

Minilesson/Explicit Lesson Routine

Minilessons (Calkins, 1994; Cooper, 2006) are explicit lessons. They are short, focused lessons (five to fifteen minutes) that may be taught to a small group or the whole class. They are used to teach a specific skill, strategy, concept, or process based on students' needs.

Minilessons can be used in any of the four instructional blocks of reading and writing. They may precede or follow a literacy lesson.

PROCEDURES

You can use the following steps to teach minilessons:

1. *Introduction:* Tell students what they are going to learn.

2. *Teacher modeling:* Model the skill or strategy, using text from literature that students have read or from students' own writing. The following is an example of a teacher model for explicitly teaching students how to select a topic for writing:

   When I need a topic for writing, I think about things I know the most about or like the most. I make a list of them. [Write a list for students to see, such as the one below.] Then I look over my list and circle the one I want to write about now. [Circle one topic.] I put the others in my writing folder and save them for later.

3. *Student modeling and guided practice:* Have students model the same procedure you modeled.

4. *Summarizing and reflecting:* Guide students to summarize in their own words what they have learned and tell when they would use the process, skill, or strategy.

5. *Follow-up:* Provide repeated opportunities for independent practice and application of what was taught. Application should take place during the actual process of reading, writing, speaking, or listening rather than in isolated worksheet activities. Draw students' attention to their successful application of what was taught.

When you are planning minilessons for your students, you will find the following procedures useful:

1. Identify what students need to be taught. Do this by referring to your ongoing assessment data in relation to the stages of literacy development.

2. Use the questions in Table 6.5 to guide your planning of the specific parts of the minilessons. (Students' performance during the minilesson is part of your ongoing assessment.)

3. Reflect on each lesson after you teach. What worked well? What would you change?

TABLE 6.5	
Questions to Guide Minilesson Development	
Introduction	What are you going to teach? (Tell or show students directly what you will teach.)
Teacher Modeling	Does this skill, strategy, or concept lend itself to modeling?
	How will you model the process? What "think-alouds" will you use?
Student Modeling and Guided Practice	Where will students be able to find other examples of what has been taught? What questions do you need to ask to guide students in modeling what they have learned?
Summarizing and Reflecting	What questions will you ask to guide students in summarizing and reflecting on what has been taught?
Follow-up	What authentic reading and writing tasks will be used for repeated practice and application of skills and strategies?

For more on minilessons, go to "For Additional Reading" on the premium website for this text.

Minilessons, or explicit lessons, are useful tools throughout your literacy program whenever you need to teach a particular skill or strategy. Such lessons keep the instruction focused and succinct. Whether you use the term *minilesson* or *explicit lesson*, remember that these lessons are always based on students' needs.

Phonemic Awareness Routine

Teach explicit lessons to encourage the acquisition of phonemic awareness, which is the understanding that the syllables and words in speech are made up of individual sounds. Such awareness comes from being able to do several distinct but closely related tasks:

- Identify and produce rhyming words
- Identify and count syllables
- Identify and count individual sounds
- Segment words into syllables
- Blend syllables into words
- Segment individual sounds in a syllable or word
- Blend individual sounds into a syllable or word

Other lessons are available in "For Additional Reading" on the premium website for this text.

Routines to help children develop phonemic awareness should be short (five to ten minutes) and repeated frequently as long as needed. We present one sample lesson in Table 6.6, which can be adapted for other phonemic awareness lessons.

PROCEDURES

Use these guidelines to develop phonemic awareness lessons. You will notice that they follow the same general thinking as for the minilesson/explicit lesson routine presented earlier: tell children what you will teach, model, have students model, and

TABLE 6.6

Phonemic Awareness Routine: Sample Lesson for Segmenting Syllables into Sounds

Teach

1. Select a one-syllable word that is familiar to children, such as "pig."
2. Say the word (pig). Tell children the word "pig" has three sounds.
3. Tell children to listen for the three sounds. Repeat the word, exaggerating each sound and separating them (/p/ /i/ /g/). Then say it normally. Repeat.
4. Say, "This word has three sounds: /p/, /i/, /g/—pig."
5. Use several other words and repeat the procedure, saying, "What is the word? How many sounds do you hear? Say the sounds. Which sound is at the beginning? (/p/) the middle? (/i/) the end? (/g/). Say the word."

Practice

- Sit on the floor in a circle. Say a word with three sounds, and roll a ball to a child to repeat the word, segment it into individual sounds, and roll the ball back to you. Repeat with other words and children.
- Have three volunteers stand in a row. Say a word with three sounds, and have each child give a sound in order. When children are comfortable with this activity, substitute other sounds in one position. For example, if three children are standing for the sounds in "pig" (/p/ /i/ /g/), say the word "fig" and ask where the sound is different. Then have a volunteer make the new beginning sound (/f/) and come up to replace the beginning /p/.

provide practice. The steps for teaching one phonemic awareness lesson, segmenting individual sounds, are presented in Table 6.6.

1. Identify what needs to be taught.
2. Gather examples, words that are in the children's oral language.
3. Have children listen as you model the target element with one word.
4. Have children identify the element you are teaching.
5. Repeat steps 3 and 4 with other words.
6. Have children distinguish the element from others.
7. Have children generate examples.
8. Provide practice activities.
9. Repeat lessons as often as needed.
10. Continue practice activities as long as needed.

Keep lessons designed to develop phonemic awareness short and fun. The procedures in the sample lesson can be used with any words, and the format is appropriate for any of the abilities. Remember that phonemic awareness need not involve associating specific letter names or symbols with sounds. The skills being developed are precursors to phonics.

Explicit Phonics/Structural Elements Routine

The five-step *explicit phonics/structural elements routine* builds on the best research we have to date on explicitly teaching sound elements (Adams, 1990; National Reading Panel, 2000). It incorporates five steps: (1) awareness, (2) segmentation, (3) association, (4) reading, and (5) spelling. This routine provides a pattern that you can use repeatedly for explicitly teaching phonic and structural skills. Teachers often teach a phonics/structural routine for certain sound elements before having students read text that contains examples of those elements. Other teachers use the routine following the reading of the text. Research does not offer a definitive answer as to which way is best.

PROCEDURES

We recommend the procedures outlined in Table 6.7 to explicitly teach phonics and structural skills. Each of the five steps should be incorporated within every lesson. However, each step can be given more or less emphasis as needed.

TABLE 6.7

Routine for Explicitly Teaching Phonics: Sample Lesson for Initial Sound /b/

STEP	PROCEDURES
1. *Awareness*	**a.** "Today you will learn to use the sound for the letter *b* at the beginnings of words to help you read and spell."
	b. "Listen to this word (pronounce "boat" slowly, each sound slightly exaggerated) /b/-/ō/-/t/. ("Say it again slowly.") How many sounds do you hear in this word?" (Students respond, "Three.") "What is the first sound you hear?" (Repeat using the words "big," "boy," "box.")
	c. If students respond correctly, move on to the next step. If students do not respond correctly, do further work in phonemic awareness.
2. *Segmentation*	**a.** "The first sound in 'box' is /b/. What is the first sound in 'barn'?" (Students respond, "/b/.") Repeat using the words "bet," "bang," "bake."
	b. If students respond correctly, move on to the next step. If they do not, provide more teaching and practice in segmentation.
3. *Association*	**a.** Write the words "box," "boy," and "bear" on the chalkboard. Underline the *b*. Say, "Each of these words begins with the same letter and the same sound. The letter is *b*; the sound is /b/." Say each word slowly, emphasizing the /b/ sound. Have children repeat with you.
Bb	**b.** Show a picture card with a bear. Say, "This bear's name is Boris—Boris Bear. He will help us remember the sound for *b*: /b/."
Boris Bear	**c.** Write groups of words on the chalkboard. Have students read the words with you and decide which ones begin with the same letter and sound as Boris Bear:
	band, car, bell
	hat, beg, big
	top, Bob, cap

(continued)

TABLE 6.7

Routine for Explicitly Teaching Phonics: Sample Lesson for Initial Sound /b/ (continued)

STEP	PROCEDURES
4. *Reading*	**a.** Write a few words on the chalkboard that students are likely to know: "funny," "say," "pig."
	b. For the first word, say, "This word is 'funny.' If we change the beginning letter to *b*, what sound will be at the beginning of this word?"
	<div align="center">b ƒunny</div>
	(Students respond, "/b/.") "What is the new word?" (Students respond, "Bunny.")
	c. Repeat using the other words.
	d. Write a silly sentence on the chalkboard:
	<div align="center">**Big bear went to box the baby boy.**</div>
	Ask students to read it, emphasizing the sound for *b*.
5. *Spelling*	**a.** Using small chalkboards, magic slates, or sheets of paper, ask students to write the following:
	• the letter that stands for the sound you hear at the beginning of "bake"
	• the letter that stands for the sound /b/
	b. Dictate several words, mixing in words that begin with other sounds that students know ("bank," "best," "cup," "zoo," "box"). Have students write the words. Look for accuracy in using the *b* and any other sounds that have previously been taught.

The following guidelines will help you plan explicit phonics/structural element instruction:

1. Using your ongoing assessment data, identify students who need instruction in a particular phonics or structural element or elements.

2. Use the explicit phonics/structural elements routine as outlined in the example in Table 6.7.

3. Follow the instruction with practice by having students read and reread books containing the element numerous times.

COMMENTS

The use of routines for explicit teaching of phonics is not new (Cooper, Warncke, Shipman, & Ramstad, 1979). Many teachers have found them effective for years. Placing the use of such routines within the framework of a Comprehensive Balanced

Literacy Program helps to make them more effective. We believe that when they are taught within this kind of framework, explicit phonics routines are important for all students, including those with special learning needs (Chard & Osborne, 1999; Cooper, Chard, & Kiger, 2006). ELLs first need to develop adequate understanding of the English sound system before these routines will be helpful. For more information on phonics routines, see "For Additional Reading" online.

The texts used for step 3 are often called decodable texts because they contain mainly words with phonic elements students have been taught. Sometimes these texts are created to focus on certain sound elements, and at other times they are trade book literature. As students begin to read more natural-language texts, encourage them to apply what they have been learning and practicing in decodable texts.

Decodable Words Routine

The *decodable words routine* is used to teach high-frequency words and any other words that are completely decodable (such as "at," "it," "prefer," "dissatisfied") as soon as students have learned the decoding elements involved in the word.

Before students read a text for instructional purposes, it may be necessary to teach some key-concept or high-frequency words that may cause them difficulty in reading. In such a case, the decodable words routine becomes a part of the literacy lesson routine discussed earlier.

PROCEDURES

As an example of the decodable words routine, assume you are teaching the word "fan." You will follow these procedures:

1. *Review the sounds.*

   Show the key pictures for sounds needed to decode the word.
   Ask students to give the sounds /f/, /ă/, and /n/. (Note: If they are unable to do so, use the phonetically unpredictable words routine described in the next section and re-teach the sounds later.)
   Say, "We are going to use these three sounds to read a new word."

F f

fish

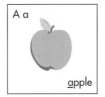
A a

apple

N n

nail

2. *Sound and blend.*

   Print the new word on the board:

   fan

   (Do not say the word.)

Point to each letter. Ask students to give the sound. Model or coach as needed. Say, "Now, let's blend the sounds to read the word" (or "Let's read the word"). Sweep your hand under the word as children blend. Model or coach as needed.

3. *Read the word.*

Print the word in a sentence:

The fan is red.

(All words in the sentence except "fan" are known words or are decodable.) Ask children to read the sentence.

COMMENTS

Following the reading of the word in the sentence, you can give each child a 3″ × 5″ card. Tell the child to copy the word on one side and the sentence on the other side. Then each child should place the word in alphabetical order in his or her **word bank,** a personal file of words the child has learned or is interested in learning:

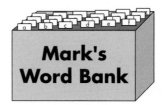

Two or three times each week, have children play games with words in their banks. For instance, they can draw words from another person's bank and read it, or they can play a game like FISH.

Phonetically Unpredictable Words Routine

Students will often encounter **phonetically unpredictable words** or words for which they do not yet have the necessary decoding knowledge. The *phonetically unpredictable words routine* can be used as part of the literacy lesson to teach vocabulary needed before reading a selection.

PROCEDURES

You can use the following procedures for the phonetically unpredictable words routine. Imagine you are teaching children the word "the."

1. *Read the word.*

Write a sentence on the board with the word:
The car is red.
Read the sentence aloud to the group. Ask the children to read the sentence with you.

2. *Match the word.*

> Distribute several 3″ × 5″ cards containing the word. Ask each child to find the word in the sentence, match it by holding the card under it, and read the sentence aloud. Have the other children clap their hands softly if the child is correct.

3. *Write the word.*

> Hold up a word card containing the word, or point to the word in the sentence. Say, "This word is 'the,' *t-h-e*."
> Say, "Now you say and spell it."
> Ask children to write the word on their papers or slate boards, saying and spelling the word as they write.

You should follow your instruction with many opportunities for children to read the text containing the words you have just taught. You will want to provide repeated practice like that described for the decodable words routine.

Fluency Routine

See also Hasbrouck and Tindal (2006), listed in "For Additional Reading" on the premium website for this text.

Fluency refers to the ability to read quickly and accurately. Children develop fluency by having many planned opportunities to read and reread material that is familiar and easy (National Reading Panel, 2000). This is known as repeated reading. Assessment of fluency was discussed in Chapter 3; here we focus on building fluency. Norms for judging fluency are given in Chapter 8.

PROCEDURES

1. Either you or the child may choose a familiar book to practice fluency.

2. Each child reads his or her book silently. Note that very young children usually read softly aloud when reading to themselves.

3. Move around the classroom listening to individuals read a segment of text. Encourage rereading of sentences and pages until the children know their reading is smooth. Remember that second-language learners may take longer to build fluency even with familiar material.

4. Children may tape their oral reading and critique their own performances.

5. Give children time to share their books with each other.

6. Children may enjoy reading to younger children, to peers, to aides, or to volunteers.

COMMENTS

For emergent and beginning readers, the fluency routine should take place daily. Allow children to continue using the same book as long as they feel their fluency is increasing. Children are good judges of when it is time to choose a different book. Fluency practice can take place during the Daily Independent Reading block; the Reading: Learning Skills and Strategies block; and the Reading: Application of Skills and Strategies block.

Explicit Comprehension Routine

In the *explicit comprehension routine*, the teacher models a comprehension strategy at each of three levels: concept, listening, and reading.

PROCEDURES

You can use the procedures outlined in Table 6.8 to teach comprehension strategies. The guidelines that follow will help you plan comprehension strategy lessons.

1. Identify students who need explicit instruction in a comprehension strategy. (You will learn how to do this in Chapters 7 through 11.)

2. Use the minilesson framework to teach the strategy. Incorporate the routine outlined in Table 6.8.

3. Provide repeated practice and application through reading until students are comfortable using the strategy.

TABLE 6.8

Explicit Comprehension Routine: An Example Based on the Strategy of Inferencing in Narrative Text

STEP	PROCEDURES
1. *Concept*	**a.** Begin by developing the concept of inferencing. Use concrete materials and examples: Say, "Look outside. Is the sun shining? Is it cloudy?" and so on. (Students respond.) "What do these things indicate the weather is likely to be in a few hours?" (Students respond, depending on the conditions.) **b.** Discuss with students how they arrived at their answer (important information they gained by looking outside, prior knowledge they had, logic). Tell students that this process is called *inferencing*.
2. *Listening*	**a.** Read aloud a short paragraph that requires students to infer. Say, "Listen to this paragraph and tell what happened about Mr. Lind's appointment": Mr. Lind only had fifteen minutes to make his appointment. He hurried from his office and pushed the elevator button, but the elevator didn't come. Finally, after some nervous moments of waiting, it arrived. Down the forty-two floors and out into the parking garage he ran. As he got into his car, he noticed it was leaning to the right. He got out and went to the other side to find a flat tire. Mr. Lind looked at his watch and saw that he had five minutes and eight miles to go (Cooper, 1986, p. 208). **b.** Recall the purpose for listening to this passage: "What happened about Mr. Lind's appointment?" Note that because of all his problems, he was likely to be late. Discuss students' responses. If they have difficulty with this process, provide more models using a think-aloud and repeat the process using several additional examples.
3. *Reading*	**a.** Select a piece of text students have read that requires inferencing. (Note: All texts require inferencing; some, however, have more opportunities than others for students to use this strategy.) **b.** Model the use of inferencing with a think-aloud.

COMMENTS

The routines for teaching comprehension have been refined, as our knowledge about comprehension has increased (McLaughlin & Allen, 2002). These strategies are important for all learners, including diverse learners with special needs, such as English-language learners (Young & Hadaway, 2006). The seven most significant strategies are *visualizing, inferencing, identifying important information, monitoring, summarizing, synthesizing,* and *generating questions.*

Modes of Reading Routine

For more information on teaching comprehension routines, see Cooper (2006), listed in "For Additional Reading" on the premium website for this text.

The **modes of reading** concept helps you provide appropriate scaffolding of instruction as students read texts. Each mode provides a different level of instructional support. By varying the way students read a text, you vary the amount of instruction given.

The five modes of reading are **teacher read-aloud, shared reading, guided reading** (observational and interactive), **cooperative/collaborative reading,** and **independent reading.** Figure 6.3 shows how these modes of reading provide decreasing instructional support and increasing independence. This concept is based on what Pearson (1985) calls the "gradual release of responsibility."

Within your literacy lessons, you will use different modes of reading to meet students' needs. Even after students read some text independently, you will return to other modes as needed to deal with more challenging ideas and texts.

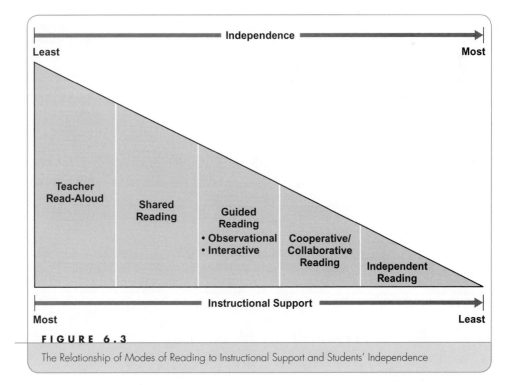

FIGURE 6.3

The Relationship of Modes of Reading to Instructional Support and Students' Independence

PROCEDURES

Table 6.9 presents a summary of the basic procedures and the purpose for each mode of reading.

TABLE 6.9

Procedures for Using Different Modes of Reading

MODES OF READING	TYPE OF TEXT AND GENERAL PROCEDURES	TIME TO USE
Teacher Read-Aloud *Purpose:* Develop concepts, vocabulary, sense of story, text structure, and comprehension	Use with any type of text. • Teacher reads text aloud; students do not have a copy of text. • Teacher and/or students set a purpose before reading. • Discussion follows to check purpose and summarize what was read.	• When text is beyond students' independent or instructional levels (see Chapter 4 for a discussion of these levels). • When the greatest amount of teacher modeling and support is needed.
Shared Reading *Purpose:* Model reading; develop concepts of print, decoding skills, and comprehension skill	Often used with big books; may be done with any book. • Text is usually predictable or patterned. • Teacher reads aloud from book, tracking lines of print with hand or pointer • Children are encouraged to join in as they can. • Texts are reread many times to build fluency and comprehension. • Skills are taught using examples from the text.	• When students need heavy teacher support and modeling. • As a way to introduce reading when students are at the Early Emergent Literacy, Emergent Literacy, and Beginning Reading and Writing stages. May be used with older students who are having difficulty with a particular type of text.
Guided Reading • *Observational Guided Reading Purpose:* Have students apply strategies and let teacher observe students' use of strategies	Texts are at students' instructional level with just a few new words and/or concepts • Teacher introduces text by building background. • Students make some predictions. • As students read, teacher observes to see how they are using various skills and strategies. • Follow-up discussion is held to check predictions and talk about text. • One or two new skills or concepts may be taught.	• When teaching literacy lessons. • When students are in the beginning stages of reading. Students may read the text aloud softly as a group, each reading at his or her own pace.

TABLE 6.9

Procedures for Using Different Modes of Reading (continued)

MODES OF READING	TYPE OF TEXT AND GENERAL PROCEDURES	TIME TO USE
• *Interactive Guided Reading* *Purpose:* Help students read a challenging text successfully	Any texts. • Teacher divides text into meaningful chunks. • Teacher introduces text. Together students and teacher make predictions or pose questions. • Students read first chunk silently. • Discussion is held to check predictions or answer questions. • New predictions or questions are posed. • Silent reading continues.	• At all stages of literacy development. • When teacher support and scaffolding are needed.
Cooperative Collaborative Reading *Purpose:* Practice reading with limited partner support	Any texts. • Teacher introduces text. • Students read meaningful chunks with a partner; reading may be done orally or silently, followed by discussion. • *Note:* Mix student pairs. Don't always put a better reader with a less able reader.	• When students are approaching independence at their current level of development but still need some support. • When motivation is low for students. Working with another student can be encouraging.
Independent Reading *Purpose:* Practice reading by oneself	Any texts. • Teacher introduces text. • Students and/or teacher make predictions or pose questions. • Students read silently. • Follow-up discussion is held.	• When students are independent at their current level of development. • When students need to try using strategies on their own. • At all stages of literacy development.

Teacher Read-Aloud. Reading a text aloud for instructional purposes is an important strategy to use when concepts or ideas might challenge students. However, be cautious; don't use texts that are so difficult that you always feel you need to read the texts aloud. Teacher read-alouds for instructional purposes should not be confused with read-alouds for enjoyment, which take place at a variety of times during the classroom day.

Shared Reading. The concept of *shared reading* was introduced by Holdaway (1979) as a way to start beginning readers, but it can be equally effective with older students and second-language learners. Basically, the teacher reads a text aloud as students look at the text and follow along. Students are encouraged to join in when they can. Chapter 8 describes the process in more detail.

Guided Reading. The practice of *guided reading* has been used to teach reading for many years (Betts, 1946/1957). As the name implies, the teacher guides students' reading. Many variations of the concept exist. We present two basic types: observational (Fountas & Pinnell, 1996) and interactive (Cooper, 2006).

During *observational guided reading,* students read a text that requires a minimum of new skills or concepts. They construct meaning while using strategies to decode words and solve other problems. A complete text is usually read. The teacher observes and coaches.

During *interactive guided reading,* students read text that has been divided into meaningful chunks. Under the teacher's guidance, students make predictions or pose questions that become their purpose for reading. After they have read each chunk, the teacher guides discussion, helps students look at any difficult words, and supports students as they make predictions about the next chunk to be read.

Cooperative/Collaborative Reading. In *cooperative/collaborative reading,* students read with a partner. Though some teachers set up cooperative reading groups of three, this often results in an "odd person out." Therefore, we believe it is best to use partners for this type of reading. Cooperative reading is generally used as a follow-up to shared or guided reading. During this time, the teacher moves among partners and coaches as needed.

Independent Reading. In this mode, students read alone. They have reached a point in their development at which they are able to independently apply decoding and comprehension strategies when given text appropriate for them. All students at every stage of literacy development need experience with independent reading.

Independent reading for instructional purposes is different from (and in addition to) the Daily Independent Reading block in a Comprehensive Balanced Literacy Program. In the Daily Independent Reading block, students select reading materials *they* want to read; instructional independent reading is sometimes not self-selected.

C O M M E N T S

Learning to think about reading in the modes concept helps you see how the various types of reading function together in the instructional process. All modes of reading should be used for all students at numerous times throughout their stages of literacy development. By observing your students, you will be able to determine when a particular mode is needed to help them continue to gain power in reading. You will learn to vary the mode on the basis of student needs, developmental stage, and materials being read.

Discussion Groups Routine

Discussion groups provide time for students to talk about what they have read. We saw one in Mr. Aroyo's class described at the beginning of this chapter. Small groups of students (usually three to five) meet together to talk about what they have read. Initially, these discussions are prompted by the teacher, who participates and observes as the students discuss. As students become more proficient in discussion, they decide for themselves what to discuss, and the teacher's prompts are not needed.

In the Comprehensive Balanced Literacy Program, discussion groups can be used in all of the reading blocks. A discussion may focus on a core book that all students have read or experienced, or it may be used following small-group reading of developmentally appropriate books. Discussion during the Daily Independent Reading block includes telling others about each book; it may also involve comparing such things as characters, events, and authors' techniques.

Students should always have some time to discuss what they have read. This is an important part of developing students' ability to comprehend.

PROCEDURES

The following steps will help you organize and manage discussion groups:

1. Introduce the concept of discussion groups. Role-play the procedures. Develop with students a list of guidelines for class behavior during this time, and post the guidelines where everyone can see them. For instance:

   CLASS GUIDELINES FOR DISCUSSION TIME
   (1) Move quickly to your groups.
   (2) Listen while others share.
   (3) Think about what each person says. Add your comments.
   (4) Stick to your task. Watch your time.

2. Form groups of three to five students; do this by random assignment, your assignment, or student choice. Vary the way in which groups are formed.

3. In the beginning, give two or three written discussion prompts. For *A River Dream* (Say, 1988), the prompts might look like these:

   TODAY'S DISCUSSION
   TALK ABOUT …
   (1) how Mark and Uncle Scott differed in their feelings about fishing.
   (2) what Mark learned about fishing.
   (3) anything you feel is important about this story.

4. As students discuss, circulate among the groups, observing and/or participating.

5. As you become more comfortable with the procedure, use it as a form of assessment. Use a simple checklist like the one in Figure 6.4 to observe students as they discuss.

6. A time limit for discussion groups will keep students focused. Usually three to five minutes is enough in preschool, kindergarten, and first grade. In grades 3 through 8, five to ten minutes is generally sufficient. Use your judgment about the amount of time your students need; it may be more or less than we recommend.

7. Have students share and discuss as a whole class.

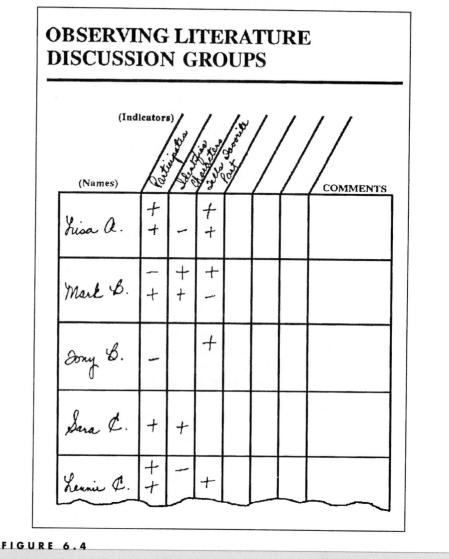

FIGURE 6.4

Sample Observation Checklist for a Discussion Group

Modes of Writing Routine

The **modes of writing** concept is a way to think about different types of writing in terms of their instructional support and student independence. The five modes of writing are: **write-aloud, shared writing, guided writing, cooperative/collaborative writing,** and **independent writing.**

Figure 6.5 shows how these modes of writing move from heavy teacher support to student independence, with write-aloud having the greatest amount of teacher

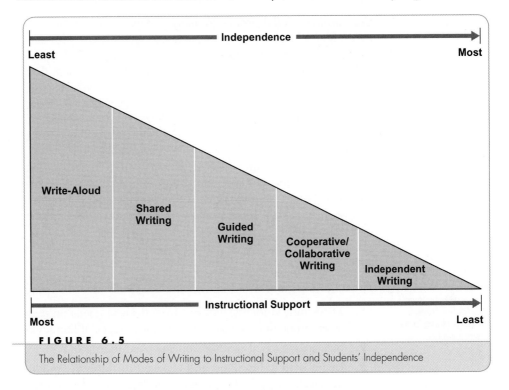

FIGURE 6.5

The Relationship of Modes of Writing to Instructional Support and Students' Independence

support and modeling. Again, this concept is based on Pearson's (1985) idea of gradual release of responsibility. Writing is taught by moving through the modes of writing concept. The following sections explain the main features of each mode.

Write-Aloud. In the *write-aloud* mode, the teacher thinks aloud while writing something to model thinking that occurs during the writing process.

You may do this with students at all stages of literacy development to show them how to use a particular type of writing.

Shared Writing. *Shared writing* is a process in which students and teacher write a piece together. The teacher does some of the writing, and the students do some of it, by dictating to the teacher in beginning grades. Later, when students actually write the words on the chart or transparency, it becomes **interactive writing.**

The key to shared writing is that both teacher and students have input into the piece. The teacher models how to write in a particular domain of writing, such as persuasion or simple description. Shared writing is an effective way to model and teach writing for any age level and is appropriate whenever a difficult concept or task is introduced. The child who writes a report independently in grade 3 may need shared writing again in grade 4 while learning to write more complex reports.

Guided Writing. *Guided writing* takes place when students work on their individual pieces of writing and the teacher models, coaches, and prompts the students, serving as editor as well.

Cooperative/Collaborative Writing. *Cooperative/collaborative writing* occurs when two students work as partners on developing a single product. They take turns writing things down and contributing to the overall piece of writing. The teacher continues to model, coach, and support the students as needed. Cooperative/collaborative writing is especially motivating for students who dislike writing.

Independent Writing. *Independent writing* is used when students are ready to write on their own, using all the processes, strategies, and skills they have learned. The product from independent writing is usually evaluated.

In this context, independent writing refers to a way of scaffolding teacher instruction. This form of independent writing, used in the Developmentally Appropriate Writing block, should not be confused with what occurs in the Daily Independent Writing block, when students are writing for power and practice on topics and products of their own choosing.

PROCEDURES

For more on the various modes of writing, see Au, Carroll, and Scheu; Calkins; and Cooper in "For Additional Reading" on the premium website for this text.

The following guidelines will help you use the modes of writing concept:

1. Determine students' writing strengths and needs on the basis of your ongoing assessment and your knowledge of the stages of literacy development.

2. Select the type of writing students need to learn.

3. Begin with write-aloud and proceed through the modes of writing until you achieve student independence with the type of writing you are teaching. This process will take from several days to several weeks, depending on the age and grade level you are teaching.

4. Remember that progression from one mode of writing to the next will not necessarily be smooth and continual. You will often find that you do shared writing and move on to guided writing, only to discover that students need more

These students help each other during this collaborative writing project.

© Andersen Ross/ Jupiter Images

modeling through shared writing. This process once again illustrates that literacy development is a jerky continuum. The nature of the writing process and tasks also dictates moving back and forth among the modes.

C O M M E N T S

The modes of writing concept give you a clear way to see how to actually teach writing. By moving students through the various modes of writing, you will be able to provide the direct instructional support they need to progress through the stages of literacy development. The modes of writing concept also provide the framework you need to meet the individual needs of diverse learners.

Selecting Instructional Routines to Meet Diverse Needs

You will use the eleven key instructional routines we have presented throughout your assessment-based literacy program. As you develop your teaching skills, you will learn other routines to help meet the needs of your students. But how will you select which routine to use?

Think back to Mr. Aroyo's classroom, which we visited at the beginning of this chapter. How did he know what to teach his students? How did he decide which instructional routines to use? He had to make some important decisions about what to teach and how to teach it. Mr. Aroyo considered several factors:

- *The strengths and needs of his students.* He was continually assessing what his students could do well in literacy and where they needed to grow and improve their literacy development.
- *Each student's stage of literacy development.* As Mr. Aroyo identified students' strengths and needs, he thought about each student's stage of development and what was coming next.
- *Students' levels of English proficiency.* Mr. Aroyo adapted his instruction to the level of academic English proficiency of his second-language learners. If we had visited his classroom daily, we would have seen him provide extra help for ELL students in reading content-area texts and we would have noticed them responding in a variety of ways, including labeled pictures, graphics, and short writing assignments.
- *Difficulty of texts in relation to students' achievement levels.* Mr. Aroyo knew his students' reading abilities, and he was able to match students to texts that were appropriate for them.
- *How students had learned with previously used instructional routines.* Each time Mr. Aroyo used an instructional routine, he was aware of how well it worked with his students. This information helped him decide what to do next.
- *Students' interests.* Mr. Aroyo knew his students' likes and dislikes in terms of reading. He used this information to help him select the books to use with the instructional routines. Sometimes students selected the book they read or the group with which they worked.

Sometimes Mr. Aroyo was pleased with his decisions; sometimes he wasn't. He made adjustments daily. He built his knowledge and experience through trial and error. This is the same process you will use in selecting instructional routines for your classroom. It all takes place through ongoing assessment.

Throughout Chapters 8 through 12, we will illustrate how you can use assessment to help you make decisions in planning instruction and selecting instructional routines for students at each stage of literacy development.

Materials for Comprehensive Balanced Literacy Instruction

Part of your decision-making process will involve choosing materials appropriate for your students. We introduced this topic in Chapter 4; here we introduce some ideas about the types of text you will use, how you will level them (that is, decide their calculated degree of difficulty), and how you can organize your materials.

Types of Text

Different texts are used for different purposes. Texts can be divided broadly into two types, authentic literature and decodable texts:

- **Authentic literature** (or text) refers to any piece of text that is in the original form as written by the author. This includes narrative text (stories), expository text (information), and procedural text (directions). Authentic literature can be used for any aspect of reading instruction.

- *Decodable texts* are those specifically written to use only certain decoding elements and high-frequency words that students have been taught. These are often called *controlled vocabulary texts* or *created texts*. They are short, and they are used for immediate practice and application of decoding skills, whether related to phonics or to structural analysis.

In the beginning stages children may benefit from texts that let them "try their wings of reading" by immediately using the skills they are learning. Decodable texts are used for this purpose.

As children develop independence in decoding (most will by the end of grade 1), decodable texts become less important, though many teachers will continue to use decodable texts through third grade to provide students with practice in fluency. These texts are used along with authentic literature as the core for literacy instruction.

You will hear many other terms related to types of text, including the following:

- *Anthology:* a collection of texts bound in one volume. Some collections may not include all the illustrations of the original work.

- *Literature sets:* books that you have in multiple copies. These are often called *class sets* or *small-group sets*.

- *Library books (trade books):* authentic literature books available in single copies. Usually they are the books students select for independent reading. Literature sets may be multiple copies of such books.

Knowing these terms will help you as you read and listen to what is being said about literacy instruction.

Leveling Texts

Leveling texts—that is, placing them in order of their difficulty—is important in beginning reading instruction because students need to ease gradually into the process of reading until they become independent in decoding (Clay, 1991). Clay calls this creating a "**gradient of difficulty**" for books.

There is no one right or absolute way to level or sequence texts. We do not believe, however, that the use of the traditional readability formula is the best way to level texts in light of what we know about literacy learning . Table 6.10 presents one set of criteria for leveling and sequencing texts at the beginning stages of reading (Peterson, 1991). These criteria can be used through about second grade. These leveling guidelines simply give you a way to order texts from simple to complex; the level numbers do *not* equate with grade levels.

Even beyond the beginning stages of literacy development, it is often helpful to level texts, especially for students who are experiencing difficulty in learning to read. Table 6.11 presents a set of leveling criteria that were developed for grades 3 through 6 (Cooper, Boschken, McWilliams, & Pistochini, 2000). Again, the category numbers do not equate with grade levels; they just provide a framework for putting texts in order of difficulty.

TABLE 6.10

Criteria for Leveling Texts for Beginning Readers

LEVELS 1 to 4	• Consistent placement of print
	• Repetition of 1 to 2 sentence patterns (1 to 2 word changes)
	• Oral language structures
	• Familiar objects and actions
	• Illustrations provide high support
LEVELS 5 to 8	• Repetition of 2 to 3 sentence patterns (phrases may change)
	• Opening, closing sentences vary
	• Or, varied simple sentence patterns
	• Predominantly oral language structures
	• Many familiar objects and actions
	• Illustrations provide moderate to high support
LEVELS 9 to 12	• Repetitions of 3 or more sentence patterns
	• Or, varied sentence patterns (repeated phrases or refrains)
	• Blend of oral and written language structures

(continued)

TABLE 6.10

Criteria for Leveling Texts for Beginning Readers (continued)

LEVELS 9 to 12
- Or, fantastic happenings in framework of familiar experiences
- Illustrations provide moderate support

LEVELS 13 to 15
- Varied sentence patterns (may have repeated phrases or refrains)
- Or, repeated patterns in cumulative form
- Written language structures
- Oral structures appear in dialogue
- Conventional story, literary language
- Specialized vocabulary for some topics
- Illustrations provide low to moderate support

LEVELS 16 to 20
- Elaborated episodes and events
- Extended descriptions
- Links to familiar stories
- Literary language
- Unusual, challenging vocabulary
- Illustrations provide low support

Source: © Peterson, B. (1991). Selecting books for beginning readers. In D. E. DeFord, C. A. Lyons, & G. S. Pinnell (Eds.), *Bridges to literacy: Learning from reading recovery* (pp. 119–147). Portsmouth, NH: Heinemann.

TABLE 6.11

Criteria for Leveling Texts for Grades 3 through 6

Category I
- Small amount of print per page. (The majority of pages have one to three sentences.)
- Pictures/illustrations are clear and uncluttered, and they directly support the text.
- Text for both fiction and nonfiction is narrative, with a clear, easy-to-follow story line.

Category II
- Still a small amount of print per page, but text can increase to one or two paragraphs on the majority of pages. Short lines of dialogue may increase the amount of text per page.
- Pictures/illustrations still give direct text support; two or three spot vignettes on a page are appropriate.

TABLE 6.11

Criteria for Leveling Texts for Grades 3 through 6 (continued)

- Expository nonfiction on highly focused topics with simply stated main ideas and few supporting details. (Often a picture or photograph illustrates each main idea.)
- Short captions (a word, a phrase, or one sentence) may accompany pictures. Simple diagrams with clear labels are appropriate.
- Narrative story lines remain simple.

Category III

- Increasing print with several paragraphs per page. Books themselves become longer.
- Pictures/illustrations are less supportive of text. Captions may increase in length.
- Narrative texts have a clear story line, but now multiple characters are appropriate.
- In expository texts the topics may broaden; main ideas increase in complexity with more supporting details.
- Text may contain a secondary element, such as sidebars or speech balloons.
- More inferencing is required by the nature of the text.

Category IV

- Text increases to fill the page.
- Narrative story lines become more complex: there may be subplots, mysteries, or multiple problems that require critical thinking.
- In expository texts the topics expand to include subtopics, which may be organized by chapter; main ideas increase in complexity and contain more details, requiring readers to organize and analyze information.
- Picture support is less direct; pages may be designed more for visual effect than to help readers with the text. Chapter books may contain spot art or none at all.

Category V

- Number of chapters increases.
- Size of print decreases as amount of text per page increases.
- Picture support is minimal or nonexistent. Book length may increase to 80 to 100+ pages.
- In narrative texts, greater inferencing skills are required to follow complex story lines containing multiple characters. Problems, which are multiple, are more sophisticated.
- In expository texts, an increasing amount of new information is presented with more complex text organization. Readers may be required to sift through information and make decisions about how relevant each detail is to the topic at hand.

Source: Cooper, J. D., Boschken, I., McWilliams, J., & Pistochini, L. (2000). *A study of the effectiveness of an intervention program designed to accelerate reading for struggling readers in the upper grades—Final report.* Boston: Houghton Mifflin Company.

Organizing Materials

Having instructional materials organized for easy access and use within a school is especially important when selecting books that are developmentally appropriate for students. We recommend that criteria similar to those presented in Tables 6.10 and 6.11 be used to organize all of the sets of books within a central location in a school. If your school isn't doing this, you might want to try it within your own class and then encourage other staff members to consider the idea for the entire school.

Intervention Models

See more with TeachSource Video Case, "Teaching Struggling Readers: Key Strategies for the Inclusive, Elementary Classroom."

Recall the Response to Intervention concept introduced in Chapter 1 and the Comprehensive Balanced Literacy Program (refer to Figure 6.2) which includes instruction, practice, and additional support for those students who are experiencing difficulty in learning to read or who have special learning needs. The extra instruction they receive, called *intervention,* is provided *in addition to* the regular core instruction given in the classroom. Let's examine the concept of intervention.

Intervention Defined

Intervention, according to *The American Heritage Dictionary,* is the act of coming into or between to hinder or alter an action. A **reading intervention program** provides students with additional instruction in reading that is designed to accelerate their reading to an age-appropriate level. The primary goal of reading intervention is to prevent or stop reading failure. Students who receive intervention instruction are given the program *only for as long as they need it.*

You cannot think about reading intervention, however, without considering the entire Comprehensive Balanced Literacy Program, in which a major goal is to prevent failure in literacy learning. According to existing research, *all* children need the highest-quality literacy instruction to learn how to read and write; however, *some* children need all of this instruction *plus* intervention to achieve success in literacy, especially reading (Snow, Burns, & Griffin, 1998).

Reading intervention can be provided in three ways:

- *Within the classroom:* This can be done by the classroom teacher with a small group at some time during the day, or a specialist may come into the room to teach the small group. All existing evidence suggests that intervention should be provided by certified teachers (Snow, Burns, & Griffin, 1998). If an aide or assistant is available, the teacher should provide the intervention while the aide monitors the remainder of the class.

- *Pullout program:* With this model, students leave your classroom for a period of instruction. Many problems exist with this model (Allington & Walmsley, 1995), the major one being, *When* do students leave the classroom? The only acceptable answer to this question is *any time other than when literacy instruction is being provided in the classroom.*

- *Extended-day program:* In this model, students come to school early or stay later for additional instruction. A certified teacher provides the instruction.

Regardless of the model used to provide intervention, the intervention support must be consistent with the overall classroom literacy program. Most intervention programs focus on the beginning reading levels because evidence supports the idea that the earlier the intervention is provided, the better it is for students (Snow, Burns, & Griffin, 1998). Although this is true, some students beyond the beginning reading levels are still reading considerably below their age-appropriate level (Mullis, Campbell, & Farstrup, 1993; NAEP, 1995). Therefore, models for intervention are needed for upper-grade students as well.

In the rest of this section, we present brief descriptions of four types of reading intervention programs that have solid research evidence supporting their effectiveness: total school reorganization programs, individual tutorial programs, small-group models for beginning readers, and a small-group model for intermediate-level students. Refer to the references cited in the chapter to find further information on the programs of interest to you.

Total School Reorganization Programs

Success for All (Slavin et al., 1996) is an example of a reading intervention program that requires total school reorganization in grades 1 through 3. Students are regrouped homogeneously across the three grades and given ninety minutes of direct instruction daily. Individual tutoring sessions are provided for students who show signs of falling behind. This model has been implemented in many inner-city school districts throughout the United States.

Individual Tutorial Programs

Another type of intervention program focuses on tutoring of individual students. *Reading Recovery,* for example, is an individual tutorial program for first-grade children developed in New Zealand (Clay, 1985) and transferred to the United States (Pinnell, Fried, & Estice, 1990). Each student receives thirty minutes of instruction per day for twelve to twenty weeks in addition to comprehensive classroom instruction. The goal of the program is to get students up to level; if the program doesn't work, a different alternative is sought after the set number of days.

A great deal of research has been conducted with Reading Recovery (Swartz & Klein, 1997). While the program usually seems effective in its initial stages, issues have been raised about its lasting gains and transfer effects (Snow, Burns, & Griffin, 1998). Even in light of these questions, Reading Recovery is a very strong, effective model for intervention.

Small-Group Models for Beginning Readers

There are many small-group models for reading intervention (Hiebert & Taylor, 1994). Three that have received much attention are *Early Intervention in Reading* (Taylor, Frye, Short, & Shearer, 1992), *Right Start* (Hiebert, Colt, Catto, & Gury, 1992), and *Facilitating Reading for Optimum Growth* (Hall, Prevatte, & Cunningham, 1992). All three of these small-group models are designed for first and second-grade students.

A comparison of these and other models (Pikulski, 1994) revealed that they have many common characteristics:

- Small-group instruction (three to five students)
- Intervention instruction provided in addition to quality classroom instruction
- Simple texts with natural language, leveled and sequenced in difficulty
- Structured, fast-paced lessons
- Repeated reading of texts
- Instruction on word parts
- Writing
- Ongoing assessment
- Home-school connections
- Strong teacher preparation

Small-Group Model for Intermediate Students

Project SUCCESS (Cooper, Boschken, McWilliams, & Pistochini, 2000) is a small-group (five to seven students) intervention model designed specifically for students in grades 3 through 8. While it builds on what has been learned from early intervention programs, it has special features that accommodate the needs of below-level readers in the upper grades.

Project SUCCESS has a system for leveling and sequencing literature that is used in structured lessons incorporating the research-proven strategies of reciprocal teaching (Palincsar & Brown, 1986) and graphic organizers (Pehrsson & Robinson, 1985). Table 6.12 presents an outline of the lesson structure for Project SUCCESS,

TABLE 6.12

The Project SUCCESS Instructional Model

KEY FEATURES
- Forty minutes per day in addition to regular classroom instruction
- Fast-paced lessons using reciprocal teaching and graphic organizers
- Instruction by certified teachers

COMPONENT	DESCRIPTION	RATIONALE
Revisiting (5 minutes)	• Students reread, alone or with a partner, previously read SUCCESS books. • Teacher takes a running record of a retelling or coaches individuals. *or* • A group conference about independently read books is held.	• Builds fluency. • Develops comprehension. • Builds connection between learning to read and independent reading.

TABLE 6.12

The Project SUCCESS Instructional Model (continued)

COMPONENT	DESCRIPTION	RATIONALE
Reviewing (5 minutes)	• Students summarize previous day's reading using graphic organizers. • Students and teacher discuss strategies used and share examples of use beyond SUCCESS.	• Develops comprehension. • Keeps students focused on the same four strategies. (See the Reading section later in this table.)
Rehearsing (10 minutes)	• A quick text talk, guided preview, cooperative preview, or independent preview is done for new text to be read. • Students may predict, question, or start a K-W-L chart.	• Builds background, specifically for the text to be read. • Sets purpose for reading.
Reading (15 minutes)	• Students silently read a predetermined meaningful chunk of text to verify predictions or answer questions. • Following reading, reciprocal teaching is employed, with students and teacher taking turns assuming the role of teacher modeling for these four strategies: *Summarize Clarify* *Question Predict*	• Applies strategies and develops comprehension. • Develops students' ability to construct meaning.
Responding/ Reflecting (5 minutes)	• Students do one or more of the following: Make a written response Complete graphic organizers Reflect on strategies Discuss and share	• Develops comprehension. • Develops use of strategies.
Home Connection	• The completed book is sent home with a letter to be signed and returned with the book.	• Shares student success with home. • Builds self-esteem.

which is taught by a certified teacher forty minutes per day in addition to the balanced classroom program the students receive.

Research with Project SUCCESS using fourth graders in a national study showed that statistically significant gains were made after an average of seventy-six days of instruction (Cooper, Boschken, McWilliams, & Pistochini, 2000). Project SUCCESS has been used as the basis for a published program, *Soar to Success* (Cooper, Boschken, McWilliams, & Pistochini, 1998), which has also been very effective for English-language learners.

Using Intervention Models with Title I and Special Education Programs

All the models of intervention described in this section are appropriate for use with special education students. The same is true for children in Title I programs (federally funded programs for students in high-poverty schools and other at-risk children). The intervention models provide the type of structured, fast-paced, focused instruction that will help students with special needs achieve success.

When considering the use of an intervention model for Title I or special education, remember that intervention is *in addition to* the basic core program. Look back at Figure 6.2. Note that the bar of intervention is supported by the six blocks in the classroom. For example, if your school has a pullout concept for special education, sending students to a resource room for part of the day, those students should *never* miss their reading or language arts instruction in the regular classroom. This is also true for English-language learners. Students who are having difficulty learning to read need good instruction in the classroom *plus* good intervention instruction (Snow, Burns, & Griffin, 1998).

Summary

- A Comprehensive Balanced Literacy Program contains components to meet the needs of diverse learners. Using this model, the teacher continually thinks about students' performance in relation to the stages of literacy development and uses assessment information to plan further instruction.

- The model includes six blocks of time that provide assessment-based instruction in reading and writing.

- A seventh block, the intervention block, provides additional support for students who are experiencing difficulty in learning.

- We have described eleven basic instructional routines that are important in such a program: the literacy lesson routine: the minilesson/explicit lesson routine, the phonemic awareness routine, the explicit phonics/structural elements routine, the decodable words routine, the phonetically unpredictable words routine, the fluency routine, the explicit comprehension routine, the modes of reading routine, the discussion groups routine, and the modes of writing routine.

- Instructional routines can be used repeatedly with students at various stages of literacy development. You can select among the routines on the basis of your students' strengths, needs, and interests.

- A Comprehensive Balanced Literacy Program requires a variety of materials. These include both decodable texts and authentic literature of various types.

- Books should be leveled in terms of difficulty according to an appropriate set of criteria.

- A reading intervention program, such as RTI and others, helps to prevent reading failure. Intervention programs may involve total school reorganization, individual tutorial programs, or small-group models.

- Intervention is always given in addition to, not in place of, the regular literacy instruction.

Please visit the premium website for *Literacy Assessment*, Fourth Edition to access the TeachSource Video Cases, chapter web links, For Additional Reading, tutorial quizzes, glossary flashcards, online checklists, downloads, and much more! Go to www.cengage.com/login to register your access code.

Standards Focus (See inside back cover)

IRA Standards for Reading Professionals: 5

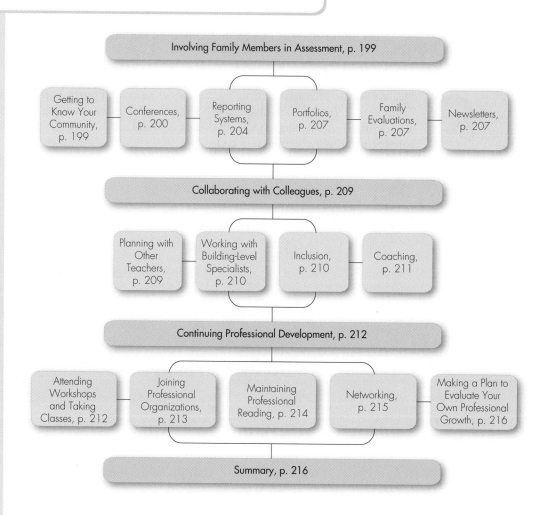

7

Collaborating with Families, Peers, and Other Professionals

Today we are following Mr. Bingham, a second-grade teacher, on the afternoon of a released day at his school. The released day is for home/family conferences and professional committee meetings, including the Response to Intervention team. First, we see a part of Mr. Bingham's last family conference; then we see him attend the school's Professional Development Committee meeting.

As we catch up with Mr. Bingham, he is meeting with his student Fred and Fred's grandmother, Mrs. Higgenbottom. He begins by telling Mrs. Higgenbottom that he feels Fred has made a great deal of progress in figuring out words and reading more smoothly, which were the two goals set for Fred at their last conference.

Mr. Bingham then asks Fred to show his grandmother the two best pieces of reading work he has done during the past two months. Fred shows her two pictures: each is of a different bird, and each has three sentences written below the picture. Fred says these are pictures of the birds that he liked best in a book he finished a few weeks ago. His grandmother asks Fred to read aloud what is written under each picture. Fred smoothly and accurately reads what he has written. You can tell that Fred is proud of his drawings and his reading—and so is his grandmother.

Next, Mr. Bingham asks about Fred's reading at home. Mrs. Higgenbottom says that Fred reads a little each night to her or to his grandfather. She notes that Fred reads the words but can't always remember what he reads when she asks him questions.

At this point, Mr. Bingham takes out the benchmark checklist for Fred (the one for the Beginning Reading and Writing stage). He tells Mrs. Higgenbottom that he and Fred look at this checklist every two weeks. He says that Fred is doing fine with figuring out the words, but he is still struggling with getting the meaning of what he reads. (The checklist shows that Fred has pluses or checks in most word recognition categories, but has only a few checks and several minuses in the constructing meaning categories.) "What Fred does with you when he reads at home," Mr. Bingham says, "It is the same thing he does at school."

After some discussion about understanding what one reads, Mr. Bingham, Fred, and Mrs. Higgenbottom decide that the goal for Fred should be reading for understanding. Mr. Bingham suggests that Fred do all his home reading silently and then practice retelling what he has read. He suggests that Mrs. Higgenbottom and Fred take turns retelling sections of the story to each other. In this way, Mrs. Higgenbottom will serve as a model for Fred. At first, Mr. Bingham says, Fred should retell while looking at the book. After he is comfortable with this, he should try to retell from memory. Mr. Bingham further points out that when Fred retells, he should give only the most important, or "big," ideas; he does not need to give all the details. The conference concludes with everyone agreeing that Fred's goal should be to improve his understanding of what he reads by doing silent reading and some retelling at home.

After completing this family conference, Mr. Bingham goes to the Media Center to meet with the four others on the Professional Development Committee: Ms. Liong, who teaches special education for grades 3 to 6; Mr. Anders, a fifth-grade teacher; Ms. Washburn, who teaches first grade; and Ms. Fishbein, the assistant principal. The committee is finalizing plans for two **inservice** meetings—meetings of practicing teachers that will form part of the school's **staff development** program, its ongoing training for teachers and other professionals in the school.

The two upcoming meetings will be about ongoing assessment and inclusion for students in grades 1 to 6. Ms. Washburn has contacted Dr. Garcia, a professor at the local college who specializes in managing inclusion programs in elementary schools. She has a list of suggested workshop topics, ideas, and available dates from Dr. Garcia. After some discussion, all the members agree that Dr. Garcia's suggestions should be followed.

Ms. Liong, however, expresses her concern, as she has before, about how teachers will accept these new ideas about inclusion. She suggests that the committee meet with Dr. Garcia prior to the inservice to discuss how the teachers in the school think about assessment.

Consider some of the things that took place in our opening scenario:

THE FAMILY CONFERENCE

- The teacher, student, and grandparent participated in the conference.
- Mr. Bingham operated from a positive point of view.
- Mr. Bingham focused on goals set at the last conference and tried to build on and connect to what Mrs. Higgenbottom said.
- Mr. Bingham was careful to use terminology that Fred's grandmother understood rather than educational jargon that might be unfamiliar to her. For example, he talked about Fred's "getting the meaning of what he reads" rather than about "constructing meaning."

THE COMMITTEE MEETING

- Teachers were collaborating, working together to plan and implement the school's programs.
- The staff development and inservice planning involved topics of critical importance to the classroom.
- Teachers assumed part of the responsibility for seeing that staff development was implemented properly.

As you can see from this scenario, teachers must work together to support an ongoing, assessment-based literacy program. No one should simply close the classroom door and work alone. To rephrase a common saying, "It takes a whole school" to create literate students.

In this chapter, we will focus on the importance of collaboration in maintaining a Comprehensive Balanced Literacy Program. We will examine three main issues related to collaboration:

1. Involving families in the ongoing literacy assessment process
2. Working together with colleagues, other classroom teachers, administrators, and specialists throughout the instructional process
3. Maintaining one's own professional development through study and collaboration with colleagues

Involving Family Members in Assessment

See more with TeachSource Video Case, "Communicating with Parents: Tips and Strategies for Future Teachers."

Research over many years clearly shows that when parents and other family members are involved in their children's education, the benefits for improving learning are great (National PTA, 1998). When family and school work together, some of the research-proven benefits are as follows:

- Children achieve more, regardless of their socioeconomic level.
- Students get better grades and have higher test scores.
- Students have more positive attitudes about school and learning.

One aspect of family involvement is to have parents and other family members participate in the ongoing assessment. There are many ways to do this effectively, such as through conferences, reporting systems, portfolios, family evaluations, and newsletters. First, however, you must begin by getting to know your community.

Getting to Know Your Community

Your process of collaborating with families should begin at the community level, which includes the entire spectrum of local diversity. The more diverse our classrooms, the greater the opportunities to provide better instruction for all students.

You can contact various organizations and groups representing different cultures within your community. You can find out about special programs, festivals, and materials they might have to help you bring particular cultures into your classroom. You can also invite family members of students in your room or your school to give talks and share their customs and traditions. They might talk about their food, dress, language, celebrations, and so on. These visits will help lay the groundwork for good instruction and for the involvement of family members in the assessment process for individual children in your class.

This mother shares her South Asian culture with her child's classmates.

Judy Harrison/
PhotoFusion/Learning
Pictures

Conferences

See more with TeachSource
Video Case, "Home-School
Communication: The Parent-Teacher
Conference."

As you saw, family conferences are an important part of the ongoing assessment process. Nearly all schools require that teachers have a certain number of such conferences each year. Some schools provide released days when students go home early so that teachers can hold conferences. At other schools, conferences are held in the late afternoon or evening.

Usually the school's requirement is one conference per semester or one conference per grading period. In fact, if family members are to be truly involved in assessment, it is best that you have a conference for every grading period or at least for every other grading period. The exact number of family conferences you have will be directly influenced by the size of your class as well as by your school's policies.

We see ten steps to having an effective conference. Study each of these steps, and think about how you can use them in your classroom.

1. *Schedule an appropriate time.* Many family members work outside the home. Sometimes everyone in the household has a job. Therefore, it is important to schedule your conference at a convenient time for the family members attending. This may be before school, during the day, after school, in the early evening, or even on a Saturday. Some schools allow teachers to go to the student's home for a conference. You must adhere to school policies on this matter.

   Notify the family about the conference in enough time to allow for needed adjustments. This notification may be done over the telephone, by mail, by e-mail, or by a note taken home by the student. Figure 7.1 presents a sample

FAMILY CONFERENCE NOTIFICATION

Your family conference for _____ has
been scheduled as follows: (Child's Name)

       Date: _____

       Day: _____

       Time: (from:) _____ (to:) _____

       Location: _____

Please return the bottom of this form by _____.

You should plan for _____ to be present for the conference.
              (Child's Name)

                     _____
                          (Teacher)

                     _____
                      (School Telephone)

- -

Family Conference Agreement

_____ The scheduled time is good for me.

_____ I am unable to attend at the scheduled time. Better dates/times for me
would be:

_____

Here are some things I would like to discuss in the conference:

_____

_____

                     _____
                        (Signature)

                     _____
                        (Telephone)

FIGURE 7.1

Conference Notification Form (Have copies available in other languages as needed.)

notification form. Notice that it provides family members with a way to give alternative times and make suggestions for things they might want to discuss. Also, notice that the form indicates that the student is to attend the conference. When children come from a second-language background, and their parents don't speak or read English, send the notice in the family's native language, if possible.

In advance of a conference, you might send home a notice indicating which particular topics you intend to address; this will give parents time to gather their thoughts and be prepared to share their perception of their child's school experience.

2. *Prepare for the conference.* Advance preparation is critical for a successful conference. Figure 7.2 presents a sample form that many teachers use both to prepare for the conference and to consult during the conference. You should think about the topics you want to discuss and the materials you need to illustrate any points you want to make. Recall that Mr. Bingham had Fred share some samples of his work. It is always important to have work samples, checklists, and so forth to illustrate your points.

There may be times when you want to involve the principal or other building-level specialists in the conference. Plan ahead for this, but don't let so many people get involved that the conference becomes overwhelming to the student or the family.

When working with second-language families, be sure to check in advance to see if family members speak English. If they do not, try to arrange for a translator to be present during the conference. The translator might be an older student or one who is more proficient in English. It is also important to try to learn something about the attitudes toward school and teachers of the culturally diverse family.

3. *Involve the student in the conference.* When students are involved in the critical learning and assessment process, they know that everyone is working together for their benefit. Ask the student in advance to identify some work samples in particular areas to share during the conference. If there are things you and the family member want to discuss between yourselves, you can simply ask the student to go to another area during this time. Have some books, magazines, or computer activities available for students during this period.

4. *Arrange a comfortable, pleasant, professional environment for the conference.* You are a professional. When you have conferences with family members and students, you are sharing your best professional image. Therefore, hold your conference in an area that is neat, clean, attractive, and organized. Usually conferences are held in the classroom, so make sure your room is organized, neat, and attractive. Such a room helps families have confidence in you.

Have comfortable seating available, preferably at a round table. If you do not have a round table, arrange comfortable chairs in a circle. Avoid arrangements with yourself on one side of the table and the family member(s) and student lined up on the other side, which can be seen as threatening or authoritarian.

CONFERENCE FORM

Student's Name _____

Date of Conference _____ Time_____

Persons Attending _____

_____

Topics to Discuss: _____

_____

_____

Materials: _____

_____

_____

Conference Notes:_____

_____

_____

_____

_____

Goals: _____

_____

Next Conference:_____

_____

FIGURE 7.2

Sample Conference Form

5. *Begin your conference on a positive note.* Students and family members should not perceive conferences as a time when the teacher tells what is wrong with the student. Begin your conference with positive points, focusing on the good things the student has been doing. Show good, representative work chosen by you or by the student (or by both of you). If this is a follow-up conference, begin by discussing progress toward goals established at the previous conference.

6. *Build your conference from goals.* Involve the student in setting some goals before the conference. For example, one student said he had two goals for the conference: "Show my mom my good writing, and let her hear my oral reading to show her I can read." Having goals for the conference keeps it focused and on target.

7. *Listen.* Resist the temptation to talk too much. Listen to what family members and students are saying; you can gain some valuable insights. In a conference that one of the authors once held, a parent kept comparing her son (the student) to his older sister. It was easy to see why the child, who was an excellent student, always felt he was not doing a good job. Even when shown his good work, the mother always brought up something that the sister did better. During the year, we worked to help this parent see her son's strengths and understand the danger of comparing one child to the other.

8. *Use nontechnical language.* Recall that Mr. Bingham used language that Mrs. Higgenbottom could easily understand. Family members may not always understand educational terminology. Therefore, use clear, simple explanations without too much "jargon." Just put yourself in the family member's place. If you've ever taken your car to a mechanic who explains the problem using terminology you don't understand, you'll understand how some teachers make family members feel. Avoid this situation. Using educational "lingo" thoughtlessly creates a wall between you and the family.

9. *Give specific suggestions.* Parents and other family members really do want to help their children. Give them suggestions that they can readily follow. Recall that Mr. Bingham suggested that Fred's grandmother have him read silently and retell what he read. He gave her specific ideas for doing this. Avoid vague suggestions like "Teach your child these words" or "Study spelling with your child." These are not helpful.

10. *End your conference with goals.* Just as you started your conference with goals, end it with goals. Conclude with one or two learning goals that the family can focus on at home and that you will work on at school. Keep the goals simple and doable. Recall how Mr. Bingham did this.

See more with TeachSource, Video Case "Parental Involvement in School Culture: A Literacy Project."

Reporting Systems

Another way to involve families in the literacy assessment process is through some type of reporting system. The most commonly known reporting system is the report card, with which everyone is familiar. Ever since we began our careers in education, report cards have been an issue. We remember no school situation in which the report card seemed exactly right. There was always a committee working on a new type of report card.

You probably remember the traditional report card. You were given letter grades in specific subjects: Reading, Math, English, Social Studies, and so forth. The traditional letter-grade system was used: A, B, C, D, and E or F.

Over the years, educators came to realize that these letter-grade reporting systems had little meaning and were not helpful to families, students, or teachers. Schools began to try other alternatives. For example, sometimes a narrative written

Involving Family Members in Assessment

**LOGAN SCHOOL
SIX-WEEK REPORT**

Name _____ Sara James _____   Grade ___ 4 ___

Teacher ____ Mr. Watters ____   Date __ 10-15 __   Report __#1__

Language Arts

Sara is making good progress with her reading, writing, and spelling. She is at the Almost Fluent Reading and Writing stage. She has improved in her comprehension and spelling. She needs to focus more on her writing, especially noun/verb agreement.

Math

Beginning geometry is Sara's favorite area in math. She is grasping the concepts and enjoying what she is learning. She needs to improve in the addition of fractions and in long division.

Social Studies

We have been studying a geography theme. Sara has good understanding of the concepts of continent, country, state, and province. She is beginning to understand the use of a map legend.

FIGURE 7.3

Sample Narrative Report

by the teacher gave information about the student's growth. Figure 7.3 provides an example. Often narratives are used only in the primary grades, though some schools have used them in the upper grades as well. Some schools combine some type of grading-scale system with a narrative, as shown in Figure 7.4. While narrative reports are very helpful, they are also very time consuming for teachers and have been abandoned by many schools.

SCHOOL ————————————————
TEACHER ————————————————
PRINCIPAL ———————————————
SCHOOL YEAR ————————

TEACHER COMMENTS

First Report

Second Report

Third Report

Fourth Report

Growth in School Studies

	First Report		Second Report		Third Report		Fourth Report	
This section reports your child's achievement in studies listed. Items not checked were not evaluated at this time.	Progressing Very Well / Progressing Satisfactorily / Progressing Slowly		Progressing Very Well / Progressing Satisfactorily / Progressing Slowly		Progressing Very Well / Progressing Satisfactorily / Progressing Slowly		Progressing Very Well / Progressing Satisfactorily / Progressing Slowly	

INTEGRATED LANGUAGE ARTS

		First Report	Second Report	Third Report	Fourth Report
1.	Displays comprehension skills and strategies				
2.	Self selects a variety of reading material				
3.	Reads independently				
4.	Reads with fluency				
5.	Reads with expression				
6.	Expands vocabulary				
7.	Identifies elements of a story				
8.	Identifies elements of fiction and nonfiction				
9.	Writes in response to reading				
10.	Uses the writing process				
11.	Writes for a variety of purposes				
12.	Expresses ideas in writing				
13.	Uses capitalization correctly				
14.	Uses punctuation correctly				
15.	Uses grammar correctly in speaking and writing				
16.	Spells assigned words correctly				
17.	Spells correctly in written work				
18.	Forms letters and numerals correctly				
19.	Writes neatly and legibly				
20.					
21.					
	EFFORT				

FIGURE 7.4

Sample Report Card Using a Grading Scale and Narrative

The reporting system used in your school is an important part of the ongoing literacy assessment process and is one important way to involve families in this process. We believe you should consider the following guidelines to help you use your school's reporting system effectively:

- Find out early about the reporting system in your school. Look at previous reports sent home for your students, if they are available.

- Talk with other teachers who are familiar with the system to learn about any issues or problems.

- If a letter-grading system is being used, talk with your principal and, if possible, other grade-level teachers about what each letter grade means and how to determine the criteria.

- At the beginning of the year, find out exactly when reports are to be sent home so that you can make sure you have the information you need to complete them.

- Study the reporting system carefully to make sure you know how to complete each report.

Portfolios

For more on this topic, see Cohen and Wiener (2002) listed in "For Additional Reading" on the website for this text.

We introduced the concept of the portfolio in Chapter 3. Portfolios are a good way to involve family members in the ongoing assessment process. They can be used in family conferences as a way to show a student's progress. Family members can see the type of work a child has done at school and has selected to show in the portfolio. It is also helpful for family members to read the reflections of both the child and the teacher on work the child has done.

Family Evaluations

Another effective way to involve the family in the assessment process is through evaluations of various aspects of a child's literacy activities at home. Figure 7.5 presents a sample home evaluation form.

A form of this type can be sent home at the beginning of the year and as often as you need. You will want to customize the form to suit your own special needs. By using such a form, you will learn about how family members perceive what their child is doing at home. Many times this information will help to explain why a child does or does not do certain things at school.

Newsletters

On the premium website for this text, "For Additional Reading" lists books that provide further ideas.

Newsletters are another good way to involve family members in the literacy learning and assessment process. These can be sent home periodically to keep families abreast of what's taking place in school. Students themselves can contribute to the newsletters. For example, one teacher with whom we work features two or three children in each newsletter. All children are included throughout the year.

HOME EVALUATION

Student's Name _____ Grade _____

Teacher _____ Date _____

Dear Family Member,

Please complete this form and return to school within five days. Think about your child in relation to each item.

1. This student reads a lot at home. ___ Yes ___ No

    Estimate the amount of time spent in daily reading: _____

2. List the types of things you see your child reading at home:

    _____

    _____

3. Circle the words that best describe the quality of your child's reading at home:

    Excellent - Good - Fair - Poor - Does Not Read

4. How often do you read to your child?

    Every Day - Once in a While - Whenever I Have Time

5. This student often likes to write stories, letters, and other things at home. __ Yes __ No

6. Circle the word(s) that best describe(s) the quality of your child's writing at home:

    Excellent - Good - Fair - Poor - Does Not Write

7. Make any comments that would help me work with your child in reading and writing.

    _____

    _____

    _____

    _____

FIGURE 7.5

Home Evaluation of Literacy Activities

Your literacy newsletter might include the following: strategy or skill being taught, theme or topic being studied, trade books related to that theme that families might find at the library, websites for further exploration about the theme, activities the family might carry out at home, tips for how parents can encourage literacy growth outside of school, and anything parents might contribute, such as memorabilia from trips, photographs, and old letters.

If you are using a published reading/language arts series, you may find that newsletters are available as a part of the instructional program. Sometimes these letters are available in other languages as well, such as Spanish, Creole, or Hmong.

Regardless of how you approach the collaborative process with families, you must involve family members in the literacy learning and assessment process. Use some of the ideas presented here. Seek out others from other sources.

Collaborating with Colleagues

See more with TeachSource Video Case, "Teaching as a Profession: Collaboration with Colleagues."

Throughout this text, we have stressed the importance of all teachers building their classroom programs around the stages of literacy development and a Comprehensive Balanced Literacy Program. A significant part of Response to Intervention is collaborating with colleagues. To make the school one that truly prevents failure and promotes success, all staff members must be seen as a team collaborating and working together (Hiebert, Pearson, Taylor, Richardson, & Paris, 1998; Fuchs, Fuchs, & Vaughn, 2008). In this section, we examine the second important part of collaboration: working with colleagues.

To collaborate means to work together in a joint effort. Here we are talking about working together with colleagues in one's school in a joint effort to help all children become successful literacy learners. We address four aspects of collaborating with colleagues: planning with other teachers, working with building-level specialists, inclusion, and coaching. Even though these overlap, we address each separately.

Planning with Other Teachers

A significant part of collaboration within your school involves long-term planning with other teachers at your grade level or related grade levels. This planning focuses on examining the various stages of literacy development within each teacher's class and talking about what each is teaching and how students' learning is progressing. Further, you need to plan with other teachers in order to implement RTI plans effectively.

We suggest that you meet at least once a month with teachers at your grade level or with teachers at related grade levels if you are in a multi-age teaching situation. During these meetings, you should cover such things as the following:

- Talk about the stages of development represented in your class. Review students' progress.

- Discuss instructional procedures that have worked particularly well and those that have not.

- Review individual students who have particular problems. Brainstorm alternative teaching ideas.

- Review assessment data to monitor progress of individual students or for the school as a whole; discuss areas of literacy that seem strong or weak; consider the RTI plans for each student.

Working with Building-Level Specialists

In most buildings, you will find a variety of specialists who operate as part of the educational team and your RTI. These may include a reading teacher or specialist, a special education or resource room teacher, a language specialist, an intervention teacher, a technology specialist, a music teacher, and an art teacher. You may work more directly with some of these teachers than with others. Some specialists may come into your classroom to work (see the next section on inclusion), and others may pull students from your classroom for special classes and programs. Whatever the arrangement, a number of things will make working with special teachers easier:

- Meet with special teachers periodically to let them know where your students are in their literacy development and what the students are studying. This type of information helps the special teacher coordinate his or her instruction with yours. If students are pulled from your room for any type of literacy instruction, you should meet with the special teacher at least once every two weeks to ensure close coordination. For example, discuss how a given student performs in your class and how he or she performs for the special teacher.

- If students are pulled from your room individually or in small groups, make sure they leave your room early enough to get to the special teacher on time. Special teachers work on a tight schedule and have a limited time with each individual or group.

- Include special teachers in family conferences when appropriate or needed. Often what a student does in special classes can provide important information for the family about the student's overall literacy learning.

- Consult with special teachers when completing home reports of any type. Information obtained from the special class may be very helpful in formulating your evaluation.

- If any of the special teachers do demonstration lessons, invite them to come into your class to provide a demonstration in an area where you need particular help with one or more students.

- If possible, visit the special classes from time to time to see how your students are performing. Insights gained by observing students' literacy behavior with a different teacher, in a different setting, and with different materials will help you to better understand each student's literacy development.

Building-level specialists are a part of your educational team. Working with them helps to make your instructional program stronger.

Inclusion

As a classroom teacher, you will deal with *inclusion,* the policy and procedures used in placing students with various disabilities in the regular classroom program for instruction (Lerner & Kline, 2006). This may also be a part of your plans for RTI. **Full inclusion,** a policy followed in many districts, is the placement of *all* children with any and all special needs within the general education program for *all* instruction.

When you have students with special needs or disabilities within your class, remember they may be held accountable for basically the same benchmarks as other students. Your task is to modify instruction as necessary to enable these students to achieve the benchmarks.

Depending on a student's disability, you may often have a paraprofessional or resource teacher to assist you with the instruction. This means that you and any person working in the room with you must plan together using the concepts, ideas, and suggestions presented in this text. Your ability to work with such a colleague will be vital to the student's success in your classroom.

The policies of inclusion and full inclusion are both highly debated topics among general educators and special educators. Recent analyses of existing research do not clearly support any one type of program for *all* students with disabilities. In fact, current data appear to support the idea that pullout programs may be best for some students with disabilities (Swanson, Hoskyn, & Lee, 1999).

For a full discussion of this topic, see Lerner and Kline (2006), listed in "For Additional Reading" on the premium website for this text.

Coaching

An important aspect of collaborating with your colleagues is coaching. **Coaching,** as the term is used here, is the process of helping a teacher internalize a set of instructional strategies through observation and feedback. Research over many years (Murphy, 2000) has shown the importance of this process. As a new teacher, or even as a veteran teacher who is learning some new instructional strategies, it is important that you have a coach to help you internalize what you learn.

For readings on this topic, see Toll (2005), listed in "For Additional Reading" on the premium website for this text.

If your school does not have a plan for coaching, we suggest that you locate another teacher with whom you can establish a partnership in which you coach each other. A full discussion of coaching is beyond the scope of this text. We suggest the following four steps to develop a collaborative coaching model between yourself and your colleague:

1. *Identify areas for growth.* Together, you and your colleague should identify two or three teaching areas you would like to strengthen. For example, you might need help in working with a particular student or in using a particular strategy.

2. *Schedule a time for observation, or make a video.* If possible, schedule a time to observe each other teaching or make a videotape (or an audiotape if video is not available) of a lesson. The observer should make notes about what was observed during the lesson.

3. *Meet to discuss observations or to review videos.* During this time, talk about the things that were taking place during the lesson. Offer each other feedback and suggestions for continued growth. Identify one area on which each of you should focus.

4. *Schedule another observation, or make another video.* Continue this process until you believe you have developed strength in the particular area of concern. Then move on to another area.

Collaboration with colleagues through coaching is an important part of building teaching strength within your school. It is also an important part of continuing your own professional development, a subject that we will now address.

Continuing Professional Development

As you have just seen, collaboration through coaching supports your professional development. Yet in terms of professional development, you will want to do much more than that, because you realize that a good teacher is never finished with learning about children and about teaching. In this section, we discuss four ideas for continuing your professional development: attending workshops and taking classes, joining professional organizations, maintaining professional reading, and networking. You should select the ones that best suit your needs and make a plan to evaluate your own professional growth.

Attending Workshops and Taking Classes

Teachers can maintain a high level of knowledge in their fields and continue to update that knowledge through workshops and classes. Watch school bulletin boards for notices from local colleges and universities. Many school districts also have a full range of workshop and class opportunities.

In addition, there are private groups that offer full-day workshops for teachers on a variety of literacy-related topics affecting instruction and assessment. Following are some groups that present workshops throughout the country:

URLs for these groups are hyperlinked on the premium website for this text.

- Staff Development Resources (SDR)
  2535 West 237th Street, Suite 126
  P.O. Box 3168, Torrance, CA 90505
  1–800–678–8908
  www.sdresources.org/

A teacher shares with her fellow faculty members a culminating project from a unit of study in her classroom.

© Bob Daemmrich/ PhotoEdit

- Bureau of Education & Research (BER)
  P.O. Box 96068
  Bellevue, WA 98009–9668
  1–800–735–3503
  www.ber.org/
- Charlesbridge Seminars
  85 Main Street
  Watertown, MA 02472–4411
  1–800–225–3214

Contact these organizations to get on their mailing lists, and find out what offerings they have in your area.

You will also want to attend professional meetings designed for teachers of second-language learners. Check these sources for meetings and useful materials:

- The National Association of Bilingual Education
  1030 15th Street, NW, Suite 47
  Washington, D.C. 20005
  1–202–898–1829
  www.nabe.org/
- Teachers of English to Speakers of Other Languages (TESOL)
  700 South Washington Street, Suite 200
  Alexandria, VA 22314
  1–888–547–3369; 1–703–836–0774
  www.tesol.org/

Joining Professional Organizations

Becoming a member of some professional organizations is an important part of your professional growth. You will learn about local and state organizations from colleagues in your area. These organizations will help you keep up with the latest research, adopt good ideas from other teachers, and share ideas of your own.

You will also want to join a national organization related to literacy. The two largest national literacy organizations are:

- International Reading Association
  800 Barksdale Road
  P.O. Box 8139
  Newark, DE 19714–8139
  1–800–336–READ; 1–302–731–1600
  www.reading.org/
- National Council of Teachers of English (NCTE)
  1111 W. Kenyon Road
  Urbana, IL 61801–1096
  1–877–369–6283
  www.ncte.org/

When you join one of these organizations, you receive many benefits, such as professional journals, special workshops, and information on political issues related to education.

Maintaining Professional Reading

Reading professional journals and magazines for teachers is also an important part of your continuing professional development. The two professional organizations mentioned in the preceding section offer a number of professional journals. You get one journal of your choice with your membership and can subscribe to other journals for an additional fee:

INTERNATIONAL READING ASSOCIATION

- *Lectura y Vida:* Spanish-language journal for all teaching levels
- *The Reading Teacher:* for preschool, primary, and elementary teachers
- *Journal of Adolescent and Adult Literacy:* for teachers of middle school, high school, and adult learners
- *Reading Research Quarterly:* a journal of reading research
- *Reading Online:* a free e-journal

NATIONAL COUNCIL OF TEACHERS OF ENGLISH

- *Language Arts:* for elementary teachers and teacher educators
- *Primary Voices K to 6:* a journal written by different teams of elementary educators; material through 2002 available online
- *School Talk:* a newsletter for classroom teachers
- *Voices from the Middle:* for middle school teachers

The following are some other widely read magazines published for teachers:

- *Instructor*
  Scholastic Inc.
  557 Broadway
  New York, NY 10012
  1–800–SCHOLASTIC (1–800–724–6527)
  www.teacher.scholastic.com/
- *Early Childhood Today*
  Scholastic Inc.
  555 Broadway
  New York, NY 10012
  1–800–544–2913
  www.teacher.scholastic.com/
- *The Mailbox*
  Education Center Inc.
  3515 West Market Street
  Box 9753
  Greensboro, NC 27403

1–800–334–0298
www.theeducationcenter.com/

- *Teaching K to 8*
  40 Richards Avenue
  Norwalk, CT 06854
  1–800–678–8793
  www.teachingK-8.com/

- *PBS Teacher Source*
  One Lincoln Plaza
  New York, NY 10023
  www.pbs.org/teachersource/

Networking

Networking is the process of getting to know other individuals who do the same or a similar type of work that you do. Networking gives teachers the opportunity to discuss and share issues and problems with others who have similar concerns. Networking within one's own school building is invaluable; in part, this is what we have been discussing in terms of collaboration and planning with other teachers and specialists.

In today's world, however, networking goes far beyond the building where one teaches. Attending conferences at which you can meet and talk with other teachers is also a powerful part of networking. You are able to find out how teachers in another school, district, state, or country handle various aspects of education.

Networking has been greatly enhanced by advances in technology. By using e-mail and the Internet, it is possible to find out what other schools are doing; in fact, with e-mail you can maintain an ongoing dialogue. Many schools and educational programs have their own web pages on the Internet. It is possible to find schools and classrooms similar to yours. Not only can you have a dialogue with the teachers, but also your students can communicate with each other.

Following are some websites that may be helpful to you:

- *The International Institute of Literacy Learning*
  www.tiill.com/
  Click on "Pathways" to find teacher resources, links to professional organizations, a live chat line, and a news forum.

- *Illinois Literacy Resource Development Center*
  www.ilrdc.org/
  Gives information on sites with programs in family literacy, workforce literacy, and adult literacy.

- *Foundation for Comprehensive Early Literacy Learning*
  www.cell-exll.com/
  Helps elementary teachers strengthen their teaching of reading and writing.

- *Co-nect*
  www.co-nect.net/

Provides information on how to become a Co-nect school that focuses on restructuring and planning, using existing resources, and using technology wisely.

Making a Plan to Evaluate Your Own Professional Growth

An important way to cope with the challenges of the classroom is to continuously evaluate your own professional growth and make plans for self-improvement (Cooter, Matthews, Thompson, & Cooter, 2004/2005). Begin by reflecting on your own strengths and needs in teaching. Then identify one or two areas to focus on each year, as well as things you will do to accomplish your goals. For example, if you need new teaching strategies, you can attend a seminar or expand your professional reading. At the end of several months, reflect on what you have accomplished and revise your plan. Professional teachers take responsibility for their own learning.

Summary

- Collaboration is extremely important to successful literacy programs. This collaboration must involve families, peers, and other professionals.

- Involving students' family members in the assessment process is important for effective literacy instruction. You need to begin by getting to know your community in terms of its cultural makeup. Then you can promote family involvement through conferences involving family members and students, the use of family-sensitive reporting systems, student portfolios, family evaluations, and newsletters.

- Collaborating with peers and colleagues entails planning with other teachers and with building-level specialists to develop consistency within your program. Where inclusion is involved, planning and collaborating with others become especially important. Another important aspect of collaboration is the coaching that teachers can provide to each other. Every school needs some type of program in which teachers are coached by peers and other professionals.

- Ongoing professional development can support and deepen what you gain through direct collaboration. You can attend workshops and classes, join professional organizations, maintain your professional reading by keeping up with journals in your field, and network with other teachers and education professionals. Each teacher should develop a plan for self-improvement.

- This chapter concludes the first part of this book, entitled "Tools and Techniques for Assessment-Based Literacy Instruction," which has provided the theoretical basis, background information, and framework necessary for understanding assessment-based instruction in a Comprehensive Balanced Literacy Program. The next part focuses on specific stages of literacy development.

Please visit the premium website for *Literacy Assessment*, Fourth Edition to access the TeachSource Video Cases, chapter web links, For Additional Reading, tutorial quizzes, glossary flashcards, online checklists, downloads, and much more! Go to www.cengage.com/login to register your access code.

PART II

Literacy Stages: Assessment and Instruction

© Jupiterimages/Workbook Stock/Getty Images

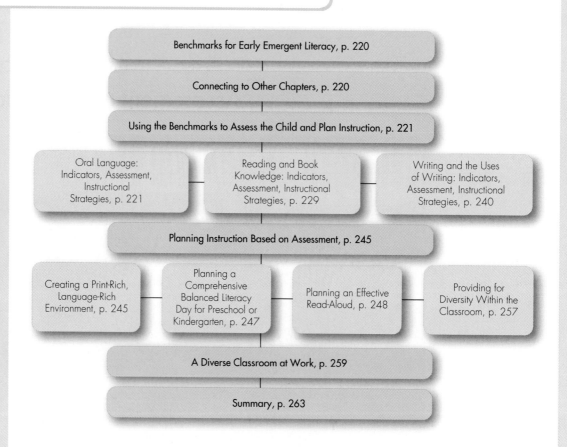

8

Early Emergent Literacy

 e are looking through the doorway into a bustling bilingual prekindergarten class. At first, we don't even see the teacher. Children are busy everywhere.

In one center, a little girl is putting her dolly to bed. She tucks the covers around her "baby's" shoulders and kisses it on the forehead. Then she takes a book and settles down in a rocking chair nearby to read a bedtime story. She turns pages as she tells the story, holding the book for her baby to see the pictures. In another center, children are shopping for groceries, consulting a list, choosing cans and boxes, paying, and putting things in bags. Another group is listening to a story read aloud by an adult who stops from time to time for children to predict what they think will happen next. Two children are in a writing center. They have drawn pictures and are writing captions with markers and signing their names. One child is using the computer in the far corner. She knows how to turn it on and find a game she likes to play. Then she goes back to the screen she started from so the computer is ready for the next child.

Finally, we spot the teacher, Mr. Gomez. He is holding a clipboard and making notes as he observes the children. After a while, he calls all the children to a rug in front of the rocking chair. Together they recite nursery rhymes while Mr. Gomez points to the words in a big-book version.

You can see that this is a busy, diverse, assessment-based preschool. Jeff Gomez, the head teacher, notes what each child is doing throughout the day. In a folder on each child, he records anecdotal evidence of growth in language and literacy as well as in other areas of development.

In this classroom, children explore using all of their abilities, including language. The tools of literacy are everywhere within easy reach. There are books, paper, pencils, crayons, markers, a computer, an old typewriter, magnetic letters, word cards, movable cardboard letters, and alphabet blocks. Wherever the children look, they see print, both in the classroom and in their greater environment. Often this print is in more than one language.

These children already sense that print plays an important part in life, even though they may not yet be able to articulate this understanding.

They are learning which life situations call for the use of print. Children who are steeped in such a rich literacy environment will learn to read and write more easily because they know how the process is supposed to work. They expect print to be an important part of their lives.

For all teachers, this is one of the most thrilling parts of literacy development to witness. It is also the most critical. A thorough review of the research on preventing reading difficulties in young children verifies that what happens during this time influences all aspects of the child's future literacy development (Snow, Burns, & Griffin, 1998).

In this chapter, we focus on the period of development just before the one most commonly called "emergent literacy." We call this Early Emergent Literacy, yet much of what we discuss here could be considered part of Emergent Literacy. The lines are blurry rather than clear-cut; children are emerging into literacy from the day they are born.

Benchmarks for Early Emergent Literacy

The following benchmarks for oral language, reading, and writing are typical of a child in the Early Emergent Literacy phase. Later in this chapter, we will present sample behaviors that indicate the presence of each of these benchmarks. We will show you how to assess these behaviors and then suggest instructional strategies that will encourage development of behaviors not yet evident.

The behaviors you will learn about in this chapter are typical of children ages three to five, preschool through kindergarten. In some rare cases, a child will display some or all of these behaviors as early as age two; in other rare cases, an older child may still be at this stage.

A complete list of benchmarks with related behavior indicators is in the Resource File following the last chapter in the book.

Connecting to Other Chapters

In Chapters 8 through 12, we present assessment information and instructional ideas based on the child's literacy development. Keep in mind that children vary in their literacy development and may not exactly fit the patterns we describe.

Sometimes you may need to use some of the assessments suggested for an earlier or a later stage. For example, if you teach preschool children, you would use the suggestions in this chapter to assess the benchmark behaviors for Early Emergent Literacy. However, if you have a child in your class who already knows some letters and words or is already reading, you would probably omit some of the assessments in this chapter and you use assessments suggested for Emergent Literacy, described in Chapter 9.

The foundations laid in earlier chapters apply as you read about all five phases of literacy development: the framework for assessment-based literacy instruction presented in Chapter 1, the assessment techniques described in Chapters 2 through 5, and the instructional routines presented in Chapter 6.

B E N C H M A R K S

ORAL LANGUAGE

The child shows through both receptive (listening) and productive (speaking) behaviors that language development is occurring.

- ☐ The child shows pleasure in stories, poems, and informational texts.
- ☐ The child shows growing facility with the functions (uses) of language.
- ☐ The child enjoys word play.
- ☐ The child shows increasing knowledge of grammar and other language conventions.

READING AND BOOK KNOWLEDGE

- ☐ The child has acquired many concepts about print.
- ☐ The child is familiar with various genres.
- ☐ The child begins to construct meaning.
- ☐ The child enjoys literature and language.

WRITING AND THE USES OF WRITING

- ☐ The child knows the purpose of writing.
- ☐ The child tries to communicate in writing.
- ☐ The child connects reading and writing.

Using the Benchmarks to Assess the Child and Plan Instruction

Three areas of Early Emergent Literacy can be assessed informally: 1) oral language, 2) reading and book knowledge, and 3) writing and the uses of writing. In this chapter, we will first show you ways to assess benchmarks in each of these areas and then suggest some instructional strategies to promote achievement of each benchmark in those children who are not there yet.

Each benchmark has one or more indicators that will help you determine the presence or absence of the benchmark. Sometimes two or more behaviors are discussed as a group. Occasionally we add commentary about how a behavior, assessment, or instruction might vary for ELL students in whom benchmark behaviors may not occur in the same way or in the same sequence as for those for whom English is the first language. ELL students face a temporary hurdle as they learn English; they should not be treated as having a learning disability (unless that condition coexists with their status as ELL students).

Oral Language: Indicators, Assessment, Instructional Strategies

Most oral language can be assessed in the routine course of your day with your students. You do not need a special activity or a special instrument. Observation is your best tool. There are four oral language benchmarks for Early Emergent Literacy:

- Shows pleasure in stories, poems, and informational texts
- Shows growing facility with the functions (uses) of language
- Enjoys word play
- Shows increasing knowledge of grammar and other language conventions

At the end of the oral language section you will find a sample class checklist that includes all areas of oral language (Figure 8.1).

> ☑ **The child shows pleasure in stories, poems, and informational texts.**
>
>   - Attends to read-alouds
>   - Attends to CD-ROMs and to programs on television and will predict future events during commercials

Assessment. Read-alouds are sessions in which you or someone else reads aloud to children. As you read aloud to a group, or as the children watch a video, DVD, or television, note their behavior. Which children are captivated by the material? Do some pay attention to some things, and not others?

Do some children offer predictions, and are the predictions logical? That is, are they supported by the picture(s), the title, previous story or program events, typical story or program structure, and background experience?

Instructional Strategies. Try to motivate attentive listening by engaging children in predicting. When children cannot make logical predictions, you need to model the process by sharing your own predictions. When illogical predictions are offered, gently examine why they probably are not acceptable. Often children at this stage simply need more experience in being asked to predict and then to pay attention to whether their predictions come true. Other ways to encourage attentiveness are showing a picture, film, or object related to the story; changing seating arrangements; and monitoring the duration of your reading. Be a good listener yourself.

> C O M M E N T S
>
> Unless you are delivering curriculum-dictated content, it may not be necessary for every child to absorb everything you read aloud or to everything shown on television. It is unreasonable to expect all children to like everything.

> ☑ **The child shows pleasure in stories, poems, and informational texts. (continued)**
>
>   - Can retell stories in sequence or tell what a story or an expository text is "about"
>   - Uses book language when retelling a story or informational text

This teacher is conducting a listening activity using good literature.

© Ellen Senisi/
The Image Works

Assessment. When you ask children to retell a story, or when you overhear a child retelling a story to a doll, a stuffed animal, or a friend, is the retelling basically complete and accurate? Did the child use book language, that is, begin with a phrase such as "Once upon a time"?

Instructional Strategies. If retelling is not consistently complete, talk about what is included and what is omitted. Model retelling, first using your own everyday language and then using book language: "Listen to these two ways to begin retelling a story: 'A little girl went for a walk.' 'Once upon a time, a young girl went into the woods to walk.'"

> ◻ **The child shows pleasure in stories, poems, and informational texts. (continued)**
>
> - Likes to make up stories
> - Tells a story or gives information to go with a picture

Assessment. Give each child a chance to make up a story based on an event, an object, or pure fantasy. Invite children to come to you individually when they are ready to tell you the story they have made up. As they tell their stories, listen to see if story elements are present.

You may also ask for a story or descriptive comments to go with a child's artwork. Not all pictures will produce language.

Instructional Strategies. Most children will learn to make up stories if given a chance. If children omit certain story elements, reinforce these during group discussions based on stories you read aloud. Also, guide the children with questions such as "How about giving Susie a problem to solve?" or "Tell us where your story is taking place. What does it look like?"

If a child is unable to make up a story to go with a picture, model by thinking aloud. For example, "What if the people who live in this house had never heard music? One day, they hear some and it frightens them. What might they do?"

> ◘ **The child shows growing facility with the functions (uses) of language.**
>
> - Retains oral directions to do more than one thing; usually can tell the directions back
> - Makes verbal requests or gives verbal orders that others understand
> - Asks questions for information and for permission

Assessment. You will frequently give oral directions in the classroom often related to completing one activity and preparing for the next. When you do so, note which children follow such directions. You could give each child a set of two or more things to do to assess ability to follow directions, but we think this is better assessed in the normal course of activities. Also, note which children can restate directions they have been given orally.

Observe whether or not the child can make herself or himself understood when asking about something and when telling someone to do something.

Instructional Strategies. If a child does not follow directions, ask yourself how this behavior might be explained.

- Was it because the child was so involved that he or she literally did not hear you? If so, have a signal that means "Stop-Look-Listen." The signal can be a hand clap, a rap, a bell, a light, or a chord on an instrument. Before children can follow directions, you must get their attention.
- If the child hears and wants to comply but doesn't understand, demonstrate what is required, model it, explain the rationale, and guide practice. Failure to follow directions for completing a project or worksheet may be due to lack of understanding, lack of coordination, or lack of interest.
- If a child hears and understands but doesn't obey, this is a problem with compliance and not a listening problem, though you will want to explore the behavior.

To help children express themselves more clearly, role-play with them, pretending you are trying to follow a child's orders but failing to understand what she means. This will encourage the children to be more precise.

> ◘ **The child shows growing facility with the functions (uses) of language. (continued)**
>
> - Converses with peers and adults
> - Reports orally on events in his or her life

Assessment. Listen to the children as they talk with each other and with adults. Are they actually exchanging ideas with others, or are they engaged in **parallel talking,** that is, taking turns talking without really having a conversation?

Is the child able to report on daily activities or events that occurred at home in such a way that others understand?

Instructional Strategies. Parallel talking is typical for this age, but you can role-play what conversations should be: an exchange of ideas, taking turns, responding to what the other person says, and so forth.

If a child cannot make himself or herself understood by others, you must try to figure out a possible explanation so that you can attempt to help.

- If the problem is articulation—that is, the child cannot form sounds clearly—start keeping a list of specific sounds. Unless you are a speech specialist, you probably cannot determine whether or not a true speech delay or problem exists. If the articulation difficulty is with certain sounds, such as /l/ or /r/, chances are this is merely immaturity, but monitor it closely. Share what you have noted with a speech specialist. The child may need help beyond what you can give in the classroom.

- If the child is an English-language learner, limited conversation in English is likely related to levels of comfort and competence with the new language. Converse with the child even though she or he may not understand much. This will help vocabulary growth.

- The child who never initiates conversations may be shy. You can help by gently encouraging conversation but not insisting. Some children remain shy. Forcing them to talk may do more harm than good. Patience is the key here.

Give children many opportunities to report on events to others. If a child cannot make other children understand, observe carefully to determine the nature of the problem; then model, paraphrase, and demonstrate. Adequate reporting involves good listening as well.

◘ The child enjoys word play.

- Likes to play word games

Assessment. As you engage in various kinds of word play, note what children do in response and whether or not they participate. For example, play a game such as "I'm going to Grandma's house and I'm taking a . . . book." Each child repeats everything that has been said before and adds one more thing. Most children this age find this fun and enjoy trying to remember the string of items and adding a new one.

Instructional Strategies. Encourage and support children who are reluctant to participate in word games. Some children may be embarrassed or afraid of looking foolish. You may need to act silly yourself to help them relax. Some children may feel they are failing if they cannot remember how to play a game; repeat the directions and reassure them.

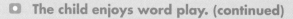

▢ The child enjoys word play. (continued)

● Pretends or role-plays using appropriate language

Assessment. When children role-play independently, observe whether they use language appropriate to the roles. For example, if a child in a housekeeping center is playing at being a parent, note whether the tone and language fit the role.

After you have read a story to children, you can encourage them to act it out. Note which children use appropriate language for the story character they are playing.

Instructional Strategies. Model by taking a role yourself. Before asking children to role-play, talk about character traits, feelings, and events and how a character might react to events in the story.

▢ The child enjoys word play. (continued)

● Repeats and uses (sometimes inappropriately) new words

Assessment. When you use "big" words, notice which children try them out in their own oral language. When you introduce new vocabulary related to concepts in science, music, art, math, and so forth, do children begin using these words with growing confidence? This is a global judgment on your part. You should not "test" vocabulary but simply observe whether each child continues to add to his or her vocabulary.

Instructional Strategies.

● Make a game of "use a new word today." Announce the word early in the day. Make it a useful word, perhaps a concept related to weather (such as "frigid" or "balmy") or ethical behavior (such as "trustworthy" or "truthful"). Use the word often, and ring a little bell or otherwise acknowledge every time someone uses it that day.

● As you complete a group presentation or discussion, make vocabulary part of your review of what was learned.

● After reading a story, ask children to recall words they heard that were new to them. Then locate the words in context and talk about their meaning.

● Elaborate basic sentences. If a child says, "See my truck," respond, "Yes, indeed, I do see your truck. What a beautiful shade of green. I notice it has special windows in the back and a place to carry things." When a child says, "Pretty flower," say, "The flower is a geranium. It *is* pretty. In fact, I think it is gorgeous! Look at the blossoms and the fuzzy leaves." Informally, note whether children are producing more elaborate sentences as a result of your modeling.

> ☐ **The child shows increasing knowledge of grammar and other language conventions.**
>
> - Tells you a sentence doesn't make sense or sound right if incorrect syntax or incorrect facts are presented
> - Is generalizing about such language oddities as irregular plurals and verb forms
> - May be able to identify what is or is not a complete sentence, though cannot tell why

Assessment. Which children are using conventional construction? Can they fix a sentence with incorrect word order (**syntax**) such as "That is a cow big?" Will they tell you if a sentence presents wrong facts? For example, if someone says, "That is a cow" when in fact the animal is a dog, can the child tell you the statement is incorrect? Does the child attempt to correct the statement?

Do your students use irregular plurals such as "feet" and "women," or are they still overgeneralizing their growing understanding of plurals to "foots" and "womans"? Do they affix *-ed* to all verbs, as in "goed," or are they using the irregular past "went"?

As you talk with children, ask them to listen and tell you if what you say is a complete sentence. Make up several examples. Children cannot give grammatical explanations, but their ears tell them whether a sentence is "complete."

Instructional Strategies. Most children have a clear grasp of word order in the English language almost from the time they begin speaking—if English is their first language. If it is not their first language, you need to provide models of syntax, restating and paraphrasing what a child says until he or she can switch to English syntax when speaking English, while retaining the first language's syntax when speaking that language. There is no need to correct immature construction. Rather, repeat the child's idea using the correct form.

When a child uses **nonstandard English,** little is gained by interrupting to "correct" grammar. That tactic is not likely to result in more standard usage; what will more likely result is a decreased willingness to speak to you at all. Continue to attune children to complete sentences by modeling and "catching yourself," using incomplete sentences and fixing them aloud.

C O M M E N T S

Both children's **receptive language** (listening) and their **productive language** (speaking) are, to a great extent, the result of the language spoken in the home. While you cannot change, nor should you denigrate, the language used in the home, you can model appropriate language when the children are with you and support their efforts to use school language.

Figure 8.1 sums up the benchmarks and behavioral indicators for oral language in the form of a sample checklist that you might use in class.

**ORAL LANGUAGE CHECKLIST:
EARLY EMERGENT LITERACY STAGE**

Date _____   Class/age group _____

Key: Y = behavior present consistently   **Student Names**
      S = behavior sometimes present
      N = behavior not yet present

Benchmark

Pleasure in Stories, Poems, Information

Attends to read-alouds

Predicts

Retells:

  story/sequence

  information/main ideas

Uses book language when retelling

Makes up stories

Tells story to go with picture

Functions of Language

Retains oral directions

Makes verbal requests/gives orders

Asks questions

Converses

Reports

Word Play

Likes word games

Role-plays

Uses new words

Grammar

Knows when sentence doesn't sound right

Generalizes irregular plurals and verb forms

Identifies complete sentence

F I G U R E   8 . 1

Sample Class Checklist for Early Emergent Literacy: Oral Language Benchmarks and Behaviors

Reading and Book Knowledge: Indicators, Assessment, Instructional Strategies

There are four benchmarks for reading and book knowledge:

- Has acquired many concepts about print
- Is familiar with various genres
- Begins to construct meaning
- Enjoys literature and language

You will notice that much of the evidence for reading benchmarks parallels the oral language benchmarks previously discussed; you may not need further information. Assess each child early in the school year or whenever a child enters your care. Record which behaviors are present using a checklist and/or anecdotal records or notes. Continue to assess children for behaviors that are absent during your initial assessment and record when they appear consistently. Figure 8.6 at the end of this section presents a sample class checklist for Early Emergent Literacy reading and book knowledge.

> **☐ The child has acquired many concepts about print.**
>
> - Has concepts about books and print

Assessment. Some children may already have acquired some of the concepts about books and print before attending school. They will often realize, for instance, that the marks on a printed page stand for something. When handling a book, they may know where it begins and when it is right side up. You can assess these concepts (see the checklist in Figure 8.2) directly, one on one with each child. The rare child who has acquired all the concepts beyond this phase. Use the following procedures to help you assess this benchmark.

Procedures for Assessing Concepts About Books and Print. (These procedures are based on the work of Clay, 1985.) Use any simple picture book. Sit where you and the child will not be disturbed. Tell the child you are going to read and talk about the book together. Explain that you will be making notes as you talk so that you won't forget anything. Keep your manner friendly but businesslike. Discontinue this assessment if the child becomes frustrated or clearly doesn't understand.

Assessing Concepts About Books. Use the following steps to assess the child's concepts about books:

1. *Front of the book.* Dangle a picture book by the spine and ask the child to take it and show you the front, or where it begins.
2. *Print carries the message.* Tell the child you are going to read the story. Ask the child to point to where you should begin in the book. The child should point to the print, not the picture.

**CHECKLIST FOR CONCEPTS ABOUT BOOKS AND PRINT:
EARLY EMERGENT LITERACY STAGE**

Name_____ Year_____

Key: Y = has concept
      N = does not have concept
      B = beginning signs of concept

Concept		Date					Comments
Books							
• Front of book							
• Print carries message							
• Directionality							
• Voice-to-print match							
• First and last							
• Inverted picture/print							
• Left before right							
• Word order							
Print							
1. Punctuation							
a. period							
b. question mark							
c. exclamation mark							
d. other							
2. Upper-case match							
3. Lower-case match							
4. Upper- to lower-case match							
5. Frame one letter							
6. Frame two letters							
7. Frame one word							
8. Frame two words							
9. Found and named letters							
10. Found and named words							

Comments:

FIGURE 8.2

Sample Checklist for Early Emergent Literacy: Concepts About Books and Print

3. *Directionality.* The concept of **directionality** involves the understanding that print goes from left to right and top to bottom on the page. Ask the child to point to where you should start on a page (should point to the first word), then in which direction to go (left to right), then what to do at the end of the line (move to the left side of the next line down).

4. *Voice-to-print match.* Ask the child to point to the words as you read somewhat slowly but with normal inflection. The **voice-to-print match** tells you whether the child seems to understand that the marks on the page are related to the sounds coming from your mouth. Though an exact match may not occur, the child's finger should move along as you read.

5. *First and last.* Ask the child to show you the first and last parts of the story.

6. *Inverted picture and print.* Present the child with a "page" you have made up on which a picture is inverted (Figure 8.3A). Do not use the term *upside-down*. Ask the child to show you the bottom of the picture. If the child has the concept, she or he will either turn the page or point to the appropriate place. Then show a "page" with inverted print (Figure 8.3B) and ask where to begin reading. The child who has the concept will turn the page or point to the correct place even though the print is upside-down.

7. *Left page before right.* Return to the picture book. Showing a double spread of pages, ask which page to read first.

8. *Word order.* Read a sentence with the words out of order and ask what's wrong (we talked about this with oral language). The child should say it doesn't sound right.

Assessing Concepts About Print. Continue to use the picture book. As the child responds to the following items, you may sense many more questions you want to ask.

FIGURE 8.3

(A) Page with Inverted Picture; (B) Page with Inverted Print

That's perfectly all right. While you don't want to put words in the child's mouth, you do want to find out what the child knows. Sometimes you have to probe gently.

1. Point to random punctuation marks and ask what they are for. Accept any words that indicate the child understands the concept. That is, a child may not name the exclamation point, but he or she may tell you it means to say the words louder or with excitement. Or the child may demonstrate by saying something in that manner.

2. Point to random upper-case letters and for each one ask the child to find another one like it.

3. Do the same with lower-case letters.

4. Point to an upper-case letter and ask the child to find a lower-case one like it. If the child doesn't seem to understand, demonstrate first. You can assess a few letters this way, using the book you have in hand. If the child seems to know many letters, you may want to move on to a more elaborate assessment of every letter, upper and lower case. We will discuss this further in the next chapter on Emergent Literacy.

5. Ask the child to show you one letter by framing it with an index finger on each side. Do this a few more times.

6. Ask the child to frame two letters.

7. Ask the child to frame one word.

8. Ask the child to frame two words.

9. Ask the child to find and name any letters he or she knows.

10. Ask the child to find and say any words in the book he or she knows.

Instructional Strategies. While many children have already acquired the concepts just assessed at home, others may be experiencing them for the first time at school. Concepts about books and print will be taught often during everyday activities such as the following, all of which are discussed in detail later in this chapter: read-alouds, shared reading, shared writing, language experience, and morning message.

Here is a sample scenario of a teaching opportunity as you get ready to read to your class. Hold the book so all children can see. Talk about concepts related to books and print. Be specific:

Teacher: "Here is the spine of a book. It holds the book in shape just like your backbone." (Point to the spine.) "What do we call this?"

Class: "The spine."

Teacher: "Right. Now let's look at the front of the book, called the cover. Here is the top of the cover, and here is the bottom of the cover." (Point as you talk.) "This picture is the art. These letters are the print. Who can point to the art? Who can point to some print?" (Volunteers do so.)

Teacher: "These letters are the words in the title. The name of this book is (read the title). This is the name of the author (read the author's name), and here is the name of the artist, sometimes called the illustrator, the person who did the pictures in this book (read the illustrator's name)."

Continue by having volunteers come up to identify parts of the book you name, to tell you the difference between art and print, and to name parts you identify.

The following scenario shows a way to incorporate teaching a concept about print as you do shared writing. The teacher has written this child-dictated sentence on the chalkboard: "We had three feet of wet snow today."

Teacher: "The first word is 'we.' It has two letters. Who will come and frame the word 'we'?"

(Volunteer does so.)

Teacher: "Who can frame one letter of the word 'we'?"

(Volunteer does so.)

Teacher: "Now who will frame the other letter?"

(A child does so.)

Teacher: "The next word is 'had,' and it has three letters." (Point to each and count.)

"Who will come and frame each letter and then the whole word?"

(A child does so.)

Teacher: "The first letter in the sentence is a capital *W*. Raise your hand if you can find a lower-case *w* in this sentence. Good!" (Have a child frame both letters.)

Teacher: "Now look carefully. Raise your hand when you have found one letter four times in our sentence. Wonderful! . . . You have sharp eyes!"

Teaching continues, reviewing known concepts and introducing those the children have not yet acquired.

> **☑ The child has acquired many concepts about print. (continued)**
>
> - Knows that labels name products or tell something about them
> - Knows the purpose of some print

Assessment. Observe which children recognize some products or objects in the room by the labels. While they may not yet recognize the words on the labels in other contexts, recognition that the words tell about the product or object is an important indicator.

Watch behavior and listen during everyday activities to make inferences about each child's awareness of the purposes of print and books. The following are some examples:

- If you ask, "Shall we have a story?" the child asks for a familiar story or goes to the bookshelf to get a book.
- If you wonder what to watch on television, the child gets *TV Guide* or goes to the on-screen guide.
- If you are making a shopping list, the child says, "Write 'bananas,' please."

FIGURE 8.4

Classroom Showing Labeled Items

- If a grownup is writing a letter, the child says, "Tell Gramma I love her."
- If you wonder aloud about whether a certain animal has more than one baby at a time, the child prods you to "look it up."

Instructional Strategies. Label objects in the room as in Figure 8.4. As you use products with brand names, reinforce with commentary: "There are many kinds of fruit juice in the grocery store. I choose the one I want by reading the label on the can." Children will associate pictures, logos, containers, and print.

Encourage awareness by modeling the use of many kinds of print, commenting on what you are doing, and explaining how the print is helping you. Some examples follow:

- Show children a recipe. Ask them to hypothesize about what would go wrong if ingredients were missing, directions were wrong, or the cookies were baked at the wrong temperature.
- As you read aloud, tell children that a person wrote this funny story so that you could have a good laugh when you read it.

- Send letters, by either regular mail or e-mail. Talk about the many reasons for writing letters.
- When children ask questions about concepts they are studying, ask, "Where can we look it up?"

COMMENTS

Some children grow up in families where reading and writing are an important part of daily life. Their understanding of the purposes of books and writing is as natural to them as their knowledge of the purpose of a bed or a spoon. Other children are not so fortunate; you need to immerse them in literacy. Surround them with print, talk about it, and model its use, giving children the language they need to talk about books and writing.

☐ **The child has acquired many concepts about print. (continued)**

- Likes playing with movable and/or magnetic letters
- Asks questions about print and about own writing, scribbling, or drawing

Assessment. Simple observation will show you which children are interested in playing with various kinds of letters you have in your classroom, moving them around to make words and matching them to words on charts and in books.

Observe which children demonstrate interest in print by asking what letters and words are when they see them. Which children question their own writing? After scribbling, which children ask what they have "said"?

Instructional Strategies. Children who do not show an interest in playing with movable letters may simply have not yet had an opportunity. Make sure many ways of making words are available, such as alphabet blocks, magnetic letters, cardboard letters, and foam letters.

Children will develop an interest in print when an adult or other literate person makes print a significant part of the day. Write while children watch you, thinking aloud, saying what you are writing, helping them make the connection between your spoken and written words.

Reassure them that they, too, will learn to do this.

☐ **The child is familiar with various genres.**

- Knows several/many nursery rhymes
- Knows several/many traditional stories such as fairy tales

Assessment. Note which children chime in as you recite traditional nursery rhymes. Children whose first language is not English may know nursery rhymes in another language. Some native English speakers may know rhymes specific to a particular culture rather than the rhymes you consider traditional. Invite children to share these.

8-28 Gina — knows the movie version of "Beauty and the Beast" but apparently hasn't heard the original version.

8-28 John — did not join in when we did "Jack and Jill." Note whether or not he participates in future nursery rhymes.

8-28 Jamal — told me he had "about a million" books at home and his grandma read to him every night.

8-28 Amy — had all the stuffed animals lined up in front of her and was retelling "Pinocchio" to them. We have not read this in class yet, but she knows it well. Could be she saw the old movie. Ask her.

8-30 Douglas — brought a watered-down version of Pooh story to be read. I substituted the original and read it aloud instead. He had never heard it before, but volunteered the opinion that it was better than his version. Next time, talk with him about what he thinks is "better."

FIGURE 8.5

Sample Teacher Observation Notes for Children's Familiarity with Various Genres

Which children are already familiar with some traditional stories, such as fairy tales and legends (in any language)? Some may know these stories only through a contemporary, rewritten, or cartoon version.

We suggest that you keep anecdotal records as evidence accumulates about each child's familiarity with various genres of literature. Note both global and specific information related to this aspect of book knowledge. Figure 8.5 shows some sample observation notes.

Instructional Strategies.

- Children who already know nursery rhymes will delight in hearing and saying them over and over as others learn them for the first time. Nursery rhymes and other poems develop a sense of rhyme, rhythm, alliteration, onomatopoeia, plays on words, as well as an ear for the sounds in words.

- The classic fairy tales, including modern classics, bear rereading over and over. When children ask for the same story many times, it isn't because they have forgotten what happened. They love the familiarity and the story language. We sometimes talk about "anchoring the sounds of language in the child's ear." Children who know these favorites and have heard them many times are acquiring a sense of book language.

- Read aloud (and suggest that parents do likewise) the rich, authentic versions of stories. When you read a watered-down version of any classic fairy tale such as "Beauty and the Beast," you deprive children of the richness of the language. It doesn't matter that they don't yet understand every word; when they begin to read for themselves, they know what book language should sound like.
- Encourage children to talk about their favorite stories and why they like them.
- Encourage children to compare new stories with their favorites.
- Talk about your own favorite stories.

> **▢ The child begins to construct meaning.**
>
> - Predicts what will happen next or what word or phrase comes next during a read-aloud

Assessment. As you read aloud, stop at certain points to ask what might happen next. Can the child predict a reasonable event? Can the child tell why he or she is making a certain prediction? The child who consistently makes reasonable predictions—based on story events or characters, knowledge of story structure, awareness of human nature, or personal experience—has achieved this benchmark. For example:

- When hearing a folk tale about a child who goes off into the woods, many children will predict that something bad will happen to the child. They explain their prediction by telling you that woods are dangerous or that that's what happens in stories like this.
- If a character does something naughty, children can predict that the child will be sorry and may get punished because that's what happens to them when they do something naughty.
- If a character is walking down the street and the picture shows a banana peel on the sidewalk, children predict that the character might slip and fall because they've seen that happen in a movie.

Ask ELL students who are still at the silent phase of English production to give predictions in their first language or to mime their predictions.

Instructional Strategies. Model predicting by thinking aloud as you read to children or watch videos with them. Explain what leads you to think as you do: "I bet he's going to surprise her with a ring, and then she'll have to tell him she . . ." or "He's never going to get her that ring she wants, because . . ." Give children many opportunities to predict and talk about why a prediction is logical on the basis of story events and personal experience.

Also talk about the author's task of deciding what to have happen in a story. An adult concept of a good story is one in which events surprise us yet seem inevitable. Even little children can think about and talk about such things: Why did the author have the character do that? Could the author have made a different decision? How would that have changed the story? Why couldn't the character behave in a certain way? When children explore these ideas with you, their ability to think about story grows enormously.

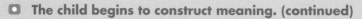

> **◘ The child begins to construct meaning. (continued)**
>
>   • Makes up stories to go with pictures
>   • Can retell a story he or she has heard

Assessment. Ask children to make up a story based on a picture they have seen or drawn. Note whether story elements are present: character, setting, problem, events, and solution.

After a story is read aloud and the book is closed, ask what the story was about. Children on the brink of Emergent Literacy can remember the main characters, what the problem was, some of the events, how the problem was solved, and how the story ended. Even if they leave out some of these elements, they usually can recall them with a little prompting.

Read aloud an informational book or watch a video. Then ask, "What did you learn?" Does the child say something such as "It was about penguins. It told where the penguins live and what they eat and how the daddy holds the eggs on his feet"? Children are apt to talk most about the part they found most interesting, but with prodding they usually can remember other information.

Instructional Strategies. Reinforce children's growing awareness of story by tying stories they hear to stories they make up. Model making up stories. Omit an element, such as setting, and ask children to tell you what is missing. Probe to get children to expand stories by asking, "Why?" as they tell you what a character does.

Children may also enjoy describing a picture or giving information about what is portrayed. For example, children can be encouraged to describe and tell about pictures of animals, food, or space shuttles.

Make retelling of stories and information a regular part of your day-after read-alouds and viewings. Applaud all efforts, even when they include every single little detail. Improve retelling through prereading activities that help children focus as they listen. After listening, probe for recall of additional information.

If a child cannot retell at all, model, collaborate, prod, guide, support—and then do it all over again—as often as needed for as long as needed. You are the scaffold, providing whatever support your students need for as long as they need it.

> **◘ The child begins to construct meaning. (continued)**
>
>   • Can play games such as "What if . . .?"

Assessment. Can the child hypothesize an alternative story that is reasonable? Use a story children know, and ask, "What if . . .?" questions. For example: "What if Goldilocks stayed to live with the three bears? Where would she sleep?"

Instructional Strategies. Play this kind of game frequently. Model by making up alternatives for children. Accept all suggestions while helping children see which could work and which could not and why.

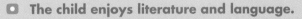

The child enjoys literature and language.

- Enjoys listening to stories read aloud
- Wants favorite stories read over and over
- Looks at books independently
- Pretends to read

Assessment. Note each child's response to read-aloud time. Does the child show interest? Come willingly? Sit attentively? Participate in discussion?

Note whether the child asks for favorite stories and asks to hear them read aloud or to listen to audiotapes.

Does the child look at books during free time? Does the child pretend to read, retelling stories and turning pages?

Instructional Strategies.

- Motivate children by showing enthusiasm.
- Not every child will be interested in every story, but all can learn to sit quietly to accommodate the interests of others.
- If a child is reluctant to join the group, look for a social reason, such as the child's being bothered by others. Invite participation; don't demand.
- Encourage attentiveness by engaging children in predicting and allowing time for talking about pictures.
- Second-language learners will maintain attentiveness better if you not only show pictures but also use gestures, vocal inflections, and facial expression to support the words as you read.
- Allow children to hear their favorite stories as often as requested. As children listen to these stories, they are learning about story structure, character, beautiful language, and human nature.
- Provide time and freedom to engage in looking at books each day. After reading a book aloud, leave it on a shelf where children can choose it.
- Model choosing a book as a free-time activity.
- Provide books in children's first language, if possible.

The child enjoys literature and language. (continued)

- Enjoys playing with sounds and words

Assessment. Does the child show enjoyment of the rhymes, alliteration, and onomatopoeia in poems and stories? Can the child substitute sounds? That is, when you ask for rhymes for "cat," will the child give you such words as "fat," "mat," "rat"?

Instructional Strategies. Games with sounds and words support developing phonemic awareness (see more later in this chapter), and increase delight with the sounds of language. Play such games with children daily; for instance: "A: My name is Alice, my husband's name is Al, we live in Alabama, and we sell apples." Use rhythm instruments, clapping, marching, and other means to reinforce the rhythm of language. Talk about onomatopoetic words you find in stories and poems, and show your own pleasure in such words as "buzz," "hiss," "whoosh," "squish," and "thump."

C O M M E N T S

Some preschool-age children already read fairly fluently. The easiest way to learn about this is to ask if anyone can already read. Invite whoever says yes to choose a book and read it to you privately. Some can indeed read unfamiliar text with accuracy, fluency, and understanding. For these children, use the assessment procedures described in one of the next chapters.

Other children may say yes and run to bring a book to you, but in fact they are not yet reading independently. It is wonderful that these children see themselves as readers, but you should use the assessments suggested in this chapter.

Figure 8.6 presents a class checklist for summarizing reading and book knowledge.

Writing and the Uses of Writing: Indicators, Assessment, Instructional Strategies

There are three writing benchmarks:

- Knows the purpose of writing
- Tries to communicate in writing
- Connects reading and writing

Since there is a great deal of overlap between the reading and writing assessments, you may find that you have enough data from reading assessments to judge this area without separate observations.

Often children attempt to write before they attempt to read. We want to encourage all efforts; therefore, we celebrate each child's attempt and recognize it as an important step forward. Even though Early Emergent Literacy children are not producing what you would call writing, they generally know they are writing.

Some children grasp a crayon, bear down on the paper, and beam, saying, "See what I wrote?" You can't read it, of course, so ask them to tell you about it. Your anecdotal record will note which children are beginning to use writing but are not yet making letterlike marks.

In terms of spelling, this is the precommunicative stage, as described in Chapter 3. Writing is made up of scribbles, letterlike forms full of vertical, horizontal, and diagonal lines and occasional curves, numbers, and some actual letters, usually upper case. As yet there is no connection between letters and the sounds they represent, nor is there a match between the number of letters and the number of sounds in a word. These children have not grasped the alphabetic principle that letters represent sounds. They do not yet have phonemic awareness of the separate sounds in speech, or they have

Reading and Book Knowledge Checklist: Early Emergent Literacy Stage

Date _____   Class/age group _____

Students

Key: P = behavior present
S = some knowledge
L = little knowledge
N = behavior not present

Benchmark

Concepts About Print

Has concepts about books and print*

Recognizes labels

Purpose of print

Plays with letters

Questions about print

Familiarity with Genres

Nursery rhymes

Traditional stories

Construction of Meaning

Predicts

Makes up stories

Retells

Plays "What if . . ."

Enjoyment

Enjoys listening

Has favorite stories

Looks at books independently

Pretends to read

Plays with sounds/words

* See also separate checklist in Figure 7.7

FIGURE 8.6

Sample Class Checklist for Early Emergent Literacy: Reading and Book Knowledge Benchmarks and Behaviors

not used such awareness as they attempt to write. There is often no space between the "letters" to indicate word boundaries. Some children write left to right and top to bottom, while others do not. These variations are normal and developmental.

Little direct instruction in writing is warranted at this time. Rather, your role is to model writing: read to children what you have written and talk about what you are doing and why you are doing it. Ask questions. Guide. For example, when you see a child showing another child something, say, "How else could you share that? . . . Yes, you could write it down." Collect samples of children's efforts frequently, identifying them with the child's name and the date. As these are reviewed later, it is easy to see how the child is growing in writing. Figure 8.7 at the end of this section presents a sample class checklist for writing.

> **▢ The child knows the purpose of writing.**
>
> ● Understands that the marks on a paper mean something
> ● Wants to write messages, letters, greeting cards, and shopping lists

Assessment. You will already know something about the child's understanding from your assessment of concepts about books and print. Informal conversation with the child will reveal whether she or he knows that the print—that is, the "marks"—carries the meaning.

Note if the child attempts to write messages. Does the child draw a greeting card and "write" on it, or make a list of presents she or he wants, or a grocery list while playing in the housekeeping corner?

Instructional Strategies.

● Continue to point to text as you read aloud from big books.
● Point to labels and print in the classroom as you say the words. Reinforce with children why a sign, picture, or product needs to have print to let others know exactly what it is.
● Model the uses of writing in your own life and in the life of your classroom.
● Make lists that the children help you compose.
● Write thank-you letters to visitors; talk about the purpose of the thank-you letter, and let the children help you compose it.
● Let the children see you engage in purposeful writing, and encourage them to contribute to it.
● Encourage families to do likewise.

> **▢ The child tries to communicate in writing.**
>
> ● Uses paper and pencil (marker, crayon, chalk, typewriter, computer) to attempt to write
> ● Arranges movable letters, writes string of letterlike shapes, or hits random strings of letters on a keyboard and then asks, "What did I say?"

Assessment. Observe which children are using writing tools: paper and pencil, markers, crayons, chalk, typewriter, and computer keyboard. Note whether the child asks, "What did I write?" or tells you what the writing "says" or at least knows that the writing should say something.

If a child arranges movable letters or hits a random string of letters on a keyboard and wants to know what the result "says," this indicates understanding that print can help one communicate.

Instructional Strategies. Provide a wide variety of writing tools for children to experiment with. Don't worry about whether they are using the tools correctly (except, of course, to avoid damage or injury). We see no reason to withhold any tools from little children as long as there is reasonable supervision.

- If a child is not at ease with any writing tools, introduce them one at a time, with brief instructions and demonstrations. For example, demonstrate using crayons on paper. Talk about where not to use the crayons. Show the child how to put them away. Then get out of the way.

- Support children's random production of print, whether by hand or on a keyboard. If children ask what the letters "say," you might respond, "You tell me," and also comment that before long they will learn to make marks that others can read and that they will be able to read for themselves.

- Informal comments about the nature of print will help children grasp that print is stable; the same string of letters always says the same thing.

> ☐ **The child connects reading and writing.**
>
> - Wants to label own pictures
> - Understands that stories are made up by a person who thought of the story and then wrote it down, and that he or she can do this also
> - Can spin out a story to go with attempts at writing and with drawings

Assessment. A child's desire to label his or her own pictures is a sign that the child is beginning to understand the connection between print and objects, concepts, and events.

When you read a story, does the child ask who wrote it? Note which children know that a person (the author) makes up a story and writes it for others to read.

Which children are beginning to see themselves as authors—people who can make up stories and write them down or have someone else write them down?

Which children are able to spin out a story to go with their attempts at writing and with drawings? Those who can show they understand that the print carries the words of the story and that the picture usually is not enough to tell the whole story.

Instructional Strategies.

- If a child does not yet show the desire to label his own pictures, demonstrate, doing it for him until he begins to request it or do it for himself.

- Whenever you read aloud or talk about a book, tell children the name of the person who wrote it. Help children see the author as a real person—one who was once a child as they are now. Share information about the lives of authors. As you record stories the children make up, include a short biography so readers will know something about the author.

- Ask children to make up a story, and then write it for them. Let them talk a story onto a tape, and then type it out for them. If you have older children, reading buddies, or other volunteers who come to your class, this is a good activity for them to share.
- Figure 8.7 presents a sample class checklist for Early Emergent Literacy writing.

Writing and Uses of Writing Checklist: Early Emergent Literacy Stage

Date _____   Class/age group _____

Key: P = behavior present
S = some knowledge
L = little knowledge
N = behavior not present

Student Names

Benchmark										
Purpose										
Marks mean something										
Wants to write										
Communicates										
Uses tools										
Manipulates letters										
Connects to Reading										
Wants to label own pictures										
Understands stories are made up and he or she can do this also										
Can make up stories										

FIGURE 8.7

Sample Class Checklist for Early Emergent Literacy: Writing and the Uses of Writing Benchmarks and Behaviors

COMMENTS

Children do not reach literacy through a series of steps that are separate and discrete; they are on a continuum. Another analogy might be a carousel, on which children grab more and more of the brass rings of literacy each time around.

Happily, many—perhaps most—children have numerous literacy experiences before coming to school. For these children, you assess and go on. For those who have missed such experiences, you make up for it by providing a rich environment in the classroom.

Planning Instruction Based on Assessment

You have just learned how to assess individual Early Emergent Literacy children to find out where they are functioning in relation to oral language, reading and book knowledge, and writing and the uses of writing. *Do not delay instruction* in order to complete assessment. As you begin gathering information, establish an environment that supports literacy growth and lends itself to adjustments for individual children. In time, you will gradually tailor instructional experiences to particular children based on your assessment.

Three conditions are necessary for appropriate instruction: (1) a print-rich, language-rich environment; (2) a comprehensive literacy day; and (3) a way to meet the needs of students who require special attention. You were introduced to the concept of a Comprehensive Balanced Literacy Program in Chapter 6. Here we will show you what such a program looks like in a prekindergarten setting, adapting and adjusting the model to meet the needs of individual students. In addition, we will describe a typical day in the kind of classroom we recommend.

Creating a Print-Rich, Language-Rich Environment

The terms **print-rich environment** and **language-rich environment** are used to describe the setting in which literacy growth will flourish. Many families provide this quite naturally in their homes. They read to their children from birth and surround them with all kinds of print. They talk to their children, sing to them, tell them nursery rhymes, write notes to them, and share conversations. They are readers and writers themselves, so their children see reading and writing as a natural part of life.

You'll want to provide for children at school the same rich environment you wish all children had at home. At this stage, children need many "play" opportunities. They need many kinds of materials to experiment with, such as sand tables, water, plants, and blocks. Though we are discussing prekindergarten, most kindergartens and primary grades need the same environment, with some change of materials (for example, sand and water tables are seldom found beyond kindergarten). The materials and physical arrangement described in the following sections are directly related to literacy and should be part of every classroom from prekindergarten through primary grades.

MATERIALS, TOOLS, FURNITURE

Children use many materials and tools independently for part of the day, with teacher supervision but little direct instruction. For reading, here are a few of the items they use:

- Big books
- Picture books
- Wordless picture books
- Books to be read aloud
- Board books
- Manipulative books
- Magazines
- Poetry books
- ABC books
- Counting books
- CD-ROMs
- DVDs
- Comfortable chairs, couches, mats, pillows, or beanbags
- Low bookshelves
- Means for displaying books with the covers facing out, such as racks or plastic pockets

For writing, the tools, materials, and furniture include these:

- Tables and chairs
- Chalkboards
- Paper
- Magnetic boards and letters
- Typewriters
- Computers
- Pencils, crayons, markers, and chalk
- Clay or another substance for shaping letters

PHYSICAL ARRANGEMENT

Early Emergent Literacy children are mostly in prekindergarten settings. The room probably has tables and chairs, though it seldom has desks. The setting is informal and arranged to encourage development in all types of learning, including literacy. In its physical arrangement, the classroom has various areas, including the following.

Learning Centers. **Learning centers** provide one kind of comfortable environment. They may include such areas as housekeeping, doctor's office, grocery store, sand and water tables, tools, painting, pets, clay, reading, and writing.

Put books and writing implements in every center to help children see reading and writing as a part of everyday life. If children find books about animals in the pet center, they will look at them. If they find paper and pencil in the housekeeping center, they will make grocery lists.

Read-Aloud Area. One area, preferably with a rug and a rocking chair, can be a designated read-aloud area. This is where your entire class can gather comfortably while you read aloud to them and do shared writing.

Listening/Viewing Area. Here children can listen with headphones to favorite stories while following the story in a book. They can also listen to music, view videos of books, or use CD-ROMs and DVDs.

Cubbies. Labeled cubbies allow children to store their personal belongings. Also, you may want to have individual mailboxes for messages that are to go home.

THE TEACHER'S PART IN THE ENVIRONMENT

Perhaps the most important thing the teacher can do, besides reading aloud, is talk to children. Most often, this talk is informal; the teacher circulates as children work on various tasks and talks with them about what they are doing.

Such talk gives children the words for the concepts they are learning, expanding their oral language. The growth of oral language in young children is amazing. By ages three to four, children have vocabularies of about 1,500 words and use most language patterns—an astounding feat that they have accomplished without any formal instruction. By ages four to five, the number of words is up to 2,500. By ages five to six, children understand approximately six thousand words. They acquire this vocabulary and language facility by interacting with adults and other children. It is a good example of the principle of the **zone of proximal development:** learning something most easily when there is someone handy who already knows it (Vygotsky, 1978). It is also an example of scaffolding. Teachers provide scaffolding every step of the way as children become literate, only withdrawing support as children become able to work things out independently.

Many teachers collaborate with the children to label virtually every object in the classroom. They don't formally teach the words, but no matter what the object, the child hears and sees the word for it.

Despite differences among classrooms, effective learning environments have some things in common. They are comfortable and inviting. They make it easy for children to use the tools of literacy. They are staffed by adults who delight in children and in literacy.

Planning a Comprehensive Balanced Literacy Day for Preschool or Kindergarten

Though we recommend a great deal of free time for Early Emergent Literacy children to explore the tools of reading and writing on their own, several instructional techniques and strategies are appropriate. Some are so natural that adults often do them without realizing they are teaching. We presented some instructional strategies earlier in this chapter. In this section, we focus on several more strategies that support literacy development.

READ-ALOUDS

Reading aloud to children may be the single most important activity you do to promote literacy growth; this was well documented (Strickland & Taylor, 1989) years ago. We know that children who learn to read on their own usually have been read to repeatedly (Durkin, 1966).

Reading aloud to children is recommended for all children, though one reads aloud differently to three-year-olds than to ten-year-olds. With Early Emergent Literacy children, reading aloud several times a day is appropriate. The books in your classroom should reflect various cultures and include all genres, classics and old favorites, as well as newly published books, books by award-winning authors, and books by lesser-known authors. You will also want to share information about authors' lives with your children. You may want books in other languages. It's hard to imagine a child who will not want to read when he or she is read to by an adult who loves books. In order to keep up with new books, see "Good Books and Where to Find Them" (Cooper & Kiger, 2009) and refer to the website for this text.

The following suggestions will help you plan effective read-alouds.

Planning an Effective Read-Aloud

BEFORE READING

1. Read the story to yourself first so you know it well, can pronounce all the words, know what is important to emphasize, are familiar enough to make frequent eye contact with listeners, and know logical places to stop for talk and predictions.

2. Call the children to sit on the floor for a story while you sit in a rocking chair, positioned so that everyone can see you.

3. Show the cover. Tell the title, author, and illustrator, showing the children where the information is found. You may discuss the publisher, copyright, and any other concepts about books, such as the spine, the front and back, and the top and bottom.

4. You may want to do a **picture walk** before reading. This involves looking at each picture with the children, talking about it, and hypothesizing about the story that goes with the picture. You can do this with a regular-size trade book or with an oversize big book. Of course, you won't show pictures that might give away a surprise ending.

DURING READING

1. Read the book, pausing to show the pictures to the entire group. Be careful not to sweep the book in front of the group; it's hard to look at a moving picture. Rather, hold the book still for one side of the group to see, then for the center of the group, then for the other side. Allow plenty of time. As you read the story, stop whenever it seems appropriate to discuss what has happened so far and what might happen next.

2. If you are reading a big book, it will probably be on an easel, which makes it easy for all the children to see both the print and the pictures.

3. Sweep a pointer or your hand under the words as you read. As you do this, children acquire a solid sense of the connection between your voice and the print. This procedure is an integral part of shared reading, which we describe later in this section.

AFTER READING

1. Talk about the story: what the children liked, what they didn't like, how it made them feel, and anything else they want to say about the story or book.

2. Have the children retell the story, recalling favorite parts, characters, problems, and so forth. If the book was not a story, have them tell what they remember. Though the children are not yet reading, you are teaching thinking skills that they will use in reading.

It is not necessary to perform all these steps every time you read a story, except that you should first read the book to yourself. Sometimes just read a book straight through for sheer pleasure and let it go. If you put the books you have read aloud on a bookshelf that children can reach, you'll see them "reading" the books to themselves and each other frequently. They already know the story, so it's easy for them to retell it to themselves.

ACTIVITIES FOR ORAL LANGUAGE DEVELOPMENT

In every learning center, there is opportunity for talk. Here are some other activities to encourage oral language growth.

Dramatic Play. Children in learning centers often will play roles appropriate to the center. In the store center, for example, children adopt roles as storekeeper, shopper, or stock person. With a supply of costumes, children can be a princess or a firefighter.
  Stories offer perfect opportunities for dramatic play. After hearing *The Three Billy Goats Gruff,* children will become the billy goats or the troll, changing their tone of voice and their actions. Keep props handy so that children can act out stories without supervision. This is not "putting on a play." It is a spontaneous way for oral language to develop.

Puppets. Children develop oral language by using and responding to puppets. These may range from full-size, realistic puppets to tongue depressors, Styrofoam boxes, and old socks.

Music. Singing expands oral language, especially when children have learned songs by heart and then make up their own words to t their lives. For example, after learning "Row, row, row your boat," children may add, "Zip, zip, zip your coat." After learning "The wheels on the bus . . .," they may innovate, "The siren on the truck goes . . ."

Art. Encourage children to talk as they paint, draw, or use clay. Let them watch you and talk about what you are doing.

Poems, Rhymes, Chants, and Finger Plays. Combining movement with language enhances both. Such activities never grow old, either for adults or for children. We've never met a teacher who didn't take continued pleasure in "Itsy, bitsy spider" even after doing it thousands of times over many years.

C O M M E N T S

Children find virtually everything in the world interesting. We can give them the language to talk about that world. Once they have the language in their ears and in their heads, they are on the road to becoming literate. When they meet those same words in print, they will be familiar with them. They will have expectations about how language in print will "sound" because they have had such rich experiences in the sounds of oral language.

SHARED READING

Chapter 6 introduced shared reading as one of the modes of reading. As you read aloud, invite children to share the reading task with you whenever it feels comfortable. Continue to "revisit" the story as many times as you and the children are interested.

While there are many ways to do shared reading, the following steps will provide guidelines as you conduct a shared-reading experience with young children.

INTRODUCING THE BOOK

1. Bring the children together so they can all see the book. (This may be a big book; however, that is not necessary.)
2. Discuss the cover, title, author, illustrator, and other book elements.
3. Look at and talk about pictures, unless doing so gives away the ending.
4. Encourage predicting. If children are reluctant to predict or predict wildly, model the process, explaining how a picture or the title supports your prediction. You may record the predictions that you and the children make and read them aloud when you discuss the story later.

READING AND RESPONDING TO THE BOOK

1. Read the story aloud. Be sure the children can see each page. Run a pointer under the words as you read them, being careful not to block the print. Allow children to chime in if they want to. This is especially likely in stories that have a repetitive refrain.
2. Stop at key points for reactions, but don't linger. Get the story read.
3. Encourage the children to talk about the story. The discussion may be unprompted, or you may ask specific questions, such as:

Were your predictions right?

What was your favorite part?

How did the story make you feel?

Which character did you like, and why?

REREADING AND RESPONDING FURTHER TO THE BOOK

1. Reread the book, inviting children to join in. For example, during a second reading of *The Gingerbread Man,* children might chime in for the repeated refrain, "Run, run, as fast as you can. You can't catch me. I'm the gingerbread

man." Repeat the rereading as often as children want. Each time, they will participate more because they have the story almost memorized. As you point to the words, the children will connect the oral words to the print.

2. Encourage other responses to the book besides discussion. Examples:

Draw a picture.

Tell the story to a friend.

Make up a new ending and tell a friend.

Dramatize the story.

During shared reading, you will also find many opportunities to emphasize the sounds of language, such as beginning sounds in alliterative poems or ending sounds in rhymes.

SHARED WRITING

Shared writing is powerful throughout literacy development. By modeling the purposes and pleasures of reading and writing at this stage, you help children see where they are going in their development. Here we describe two shared writing activities: morning messages and collaborative stories and reports.

Morning Message. A **morning message** is just what the term implies: a written activity with which to start the day. There are almost as many ways to do morning message as there are teachers. We describe two here; others will be described in Chapter 9.

Teacher-Written Morning Message. The teacher writes a message on the chalkboard before the children arrive (see Figure 8.8). He or she names the day and date, tells what will happen that day, and gives other information. When the children are settled, the teacher reads the message to the group, sweeping a pointer under the words. Sometimes she or he rereads it. Then teacher and children talk about the message, thus combining oral language, reading, and writing. Table 8.1 shows a sample of dialogue related to the message in Figure 8.8.

A conversation such as the one in Table 8.1 is instruction, even though informal. The things you call attention to, ask children to locate, or include in your morning message will depend on your assessment and on what the children have been learning. If your children

> Today is Tuesday, October 14.
> We are going to visit a farm today.
> Kristen is 4 years old today. It is her birthday.
> We will make decorations for our room this afternoon.

FIGURE 8.8

Sample of a Teacher-Written Morning Message

TABLE 8.1

Samples of Dialogue After Morning Message

(The teacher has read aloud the morning message shown in Figure 7.8 and then reread it with the children.)

Teacher: Tell me something you notice about the message.

Child 1:   Some dots.

Teacher: Point to them. (Child does so.) These are periods. We put them at the end of each sentence. A period shows that the sentence has ended.

Child 2:   Big letters.

Teacher: Yes, they are called capital letters. Point to each one. (Child does so.) We need capitals at the beginning of each sentence. Where else do you see capitals?

Child 3:   (Points to "Tuesday," "October," and "Kristen.")

Teacher: Right! The names of some things begin with capital letters. (Points.) This is the name of the day, Tuesday. This is the name of the month, October. This is the name of a person, Kristen.

(Dialogue can continue as long as children are interested.)

have no knowledge yet of the kinds of writing conventions mentioned in Table 8.1, you may be more didactic. For example, pointing while talking, you might say:

> *When we write, certain words need capital letters at the beginning. Sometimes we call these "big letters," but the correct term is "capital letters" or "upper-case letters." Watch where I point. We use a capital letter for the first word of every sentence (pointing to each). We also use a capital letter for the names of the day, the month, and a person (pointing to each). Who can tell me one place where we need a capital letter?*

Child-Dictated Morning Message. You may write the morning message with your children. Begin by asking the children to discuss what they want to include in their message. After several ideas are put forth, ask a child to dictate a sentence. Use this opportunity to reinforce a sense of what makes a complete sentence. For example, if a child dictates, "Tuesday, October 14," prompt, "Let's make that a complete sentence." If the child doesn't understand, prompt further by cuing with the beginning, "Today is . . ." Children acquire a sense of what is or is not a complete sentence long before they can tell you anything about subjects or predicates. Use the morning message to instruct children about writing features they do not yet know and to reinforce those they do. Focus on a few conventions at a time. Keep up a running commentary as you record the children's dictated sentences. For example, say such things as:

> *I'm beginning this word with a capital because it is the name of a month. . . . I need an apostrophe here to form the contraction "isn't." . . . I start the word "tomorrow" with the same letter that starts Tim's name. . . . That's a question, so I use a question mark to let whoever reads this know it is a question.*

There is no prescribed set of steps. You simply comment about what you are do-ing and why. If it seems appropriate, you ask the children to tell you what to do and why. If they know, fine. If not, tell them. It is an informal, comfortable, risk free—and very powerful—way to teach.

Eventually, you can use the children's own message to develop phonemic awareness (discussed later in this chapter) and a sense of how phonics will help them figure out words. For example, let's say the children had dictated, "We are going to visit the farm today." You might say the following:

> *Let's look and listen as we read this sentence: "We are going to visit the farm today." (Teacher and students read it together several times as the teacher points to the words.)*
>
> *(Pointing to "we") I hear two sounds, and the first one almost isn't a sound—it's a way I make my mouth when a word begins with the letter w. (Teacher exaggerates slightly and confirms the two sounds.)*
>
> *When we write, every sound in a word we say has at least one letter to stand for that sound. When we say the word "we," we hear two sounds. The letter w stands for the first sound, and the letter e stands for the second. In this word, there are two sounds and two letters.*

This is not an explicit lesson: nor should it be. Children at this stage are developing their phonemic awareness and getting ready to use phonics to help them decode words when they read as well as figure out what letters to use when they write. Virtually every sound in the English language will turn up within a few days in any dictated message or story. Use these words from the children's mouths to call attention to the separate sounds in words and the letters that can stand for those sounds.

Collaborative Stories and Reports. Almost any event during the day is reason for shared writing. Let's say a storm has blown up with thunder, lightning, and hail, causing outside recess to be canceled. What more perfect time to write a story?

- Ask the children to describe what the weather was like and how it made them feel. Put your own ideas in, too; collaboration means everyone has input.
- After you have talked about the storm, suggest writing a story.
- Take ideas from several children.
- Talk with the children about each idea before you write it to be sure you are writing just what you and they want to say.
- If you write on the chalkboard or a transparency, you can revise.
- As the children observe you write, think aloud about what a writer needs to consider. What are we trying to say? Are we saying it the best way we know how? Will our words make the reader know how the storm frightened us? Talk about choosing certain words to express certain ideas.
- Also talk about some of the mechanics of writing: the capitals, the punctuation, the choice of letters for certain sounds, and the need to form the letters carefully so others can read them.

Throughout the day, lead children to grasp the many purposes for writing. For example, if you are planning a field trip, ask children, "How can we remember everything we have to do?" You hope the children suggest making a list. Then have them dictate what should go on the list and help you put the tasks in logical sequence. Or say, "How can I let your families know about our party?" The children should suggest a letter to go home and then help you compose it.

LANGUAGE EXPERIENCE

Language experience is a beginning reading approach closely related to shared writing (Allen, 1976; Stauffer, 1969) that is still effective. There is a critical difference, however, between the two. In the language experience approach, the teacher serves only as the scribe, not as a collaborator; that is, the teacher writes exactly what the child says and then uses it as reading material for the child. This is a useful instructional technique with those at any age who are not yet fluent readers, as well as with bilingual students, struggling middle-school students, and adult nonreaders (Dorr, 2006; Mulligan, 1974; Sharp, 1990).

The language experience approach is based on the theory that one learns to read most easily if what one reads sounds like the same language one speaks and is about something one knows. When a child dictates a story about his or her experience, and the teacher writes exactly what the child says, the child has a better chance of reading the resulting story successfully than if the language and topic are unfamiliar.

Language Experience Procedures: Individual. The purest use of language experience is with individual stories, since no two children share exactly the same experience or have exactly the same oral language. Table 8.2 shows the basic steps.

Older children often reread a copy each day for a number of days, underlining the words retained and putting them into a word bank. Language experience can be

---

TABLE 8.2

Basic Steps for Language Experience Story with One Child

1. The teacher and child have a brief discussion and decide on a topic.

2. The teacher and child sit side by side, with the teacher on the right so the child can see the teacher as she or he writes (unless the teacher is left-handed).

3. The child dictates and the teacher records what the child says, saying the words aloud as they are written and commenting on conventions of print. The teacher accepts and records the child's exact language even though it may be nonstandard. Rewording into standard language takes away from the pure expression of the child's own experience and language.

4. The teacher reads the completed story aloud, pointing to the words as the child follows along.

5. The teacher rereads the story, inviting the child to join in.

6. The child is invited to read the story alone, or more rereadings together take place. This process will vary from child to child.

7. The story can be the basis for lessons about print.

8. A copy is made available to the child for multiple rereadings and for illustrating.

a valuable technique if it is not belabored. Do it from time to time. Enjoy the stories the children dictate. Help those who can to read their own stories. Compile the stories into a book—a sort of anthology. Send them home to families. But *don't* turn this into a formal ritual.

Language Experience Procedures: Group Dictation. Sometimes several children contribute to a dictated story. Unlike the individual story, you can avoid nonstandard usage when taking group dictation, but keep corrections low key: for example, when a child dictates "ain't," comment, "When writing, we use 'isn't.'" You may want to indicate which child contributed which idea by writing, "David said, 'Today we will take a trip to the petting zoo.'"

As with the individual dictated story, many kinds of instruction can flow from the dictation, depending on what the children are ready for and interested in. Copies can be made so that each child who contributed has a personal collection of stories to reread as well as to illustrate.

Reading a familiar story, written with one's own words and about one's own experience, almost guarantees a high degree of success. The more times children reread a story, the more likely they are to recognize words from their stories when they see them in other places.

PHONEMIC AWARENESS

Phonemic awareness refers to the child's understanding that the syllables and words in speech are made up of individual sounds. This awareness and the eventual ability to segment words into sounds and to blend sounds into words are a necessary part of learning to read and write (Armbruster & Osborn, 2001). Even though there are no Early Emergent Literacy benchmarks associated with phonemic awareness, the Comprehensive Balanced Literacy classroom must provide activities to encourage it to emerge.

Phonemes are the speech sounds of language. They have no meaning in themselves. A single phoneme may be represented in print by one or more letters. For example, the word "cat" is made up of three phonemes, or sounds. In this case each phoneme is spelled with one letter. The word "that" is also made up of three phonemes, but the first one is spelled with two letters: *th*. When we talk about knowing which letters are associated with which sounds, we are talking about phonics, a topic we will discuss further in later chapters.

How Phonemic Awareness Develops. There is solid, unrefuted research evidence to show us how children develop phonemic awareness, and why it is so important in learning to read and write (Adams, 1990; Armbruster & Osborn, 2001; Ehri et al., 2001). Many children acquire phonemic awareness and concepts about print naturally. Chances are these children have been read to a great deal and have seen both reading and writing modeled in their homes. They recognize and make rhymes. They play with sounds in words. They have probably been "writing" for some time. When you listen to such children talk to themselves as they write, you will hear them segmenting speech sounds. For example, /c/ – /a/ – /t/. They will write a letter (or letter-like shape) for each sound. They will slow down and deal with one word at a time, often repeating what they have said before going on.

All successful readers and writers have acquired phonemic awareness and concepts about print, but this is not like learning to tie one's shoes. Learning to tie shoes involves a huge leap of manual dexterity; after fumbling and total failure, suddenly one day you can do it and you can continue to do it forever. Acquisition of phonemic awareness is gradual.

For example, little children who know fairy tales may tell you that the first word is "onceuponatime." They hear that group of words as a continuous sound—and, in fact, it *is* continuous sound when we say it. (Try it!) We do not pause between words in this phrase or in most groups of words. The group of words also has semantic unity for children: it tells them about the kind of story that will follow. Therefore, children may write these four words as one when they write stories. We applaud all such efforts to express oral language in writing, and we call attention to the conventional writing of "once upon a time" the next time we share a story with the children. After a while, the children's writing will reflect awareness of the separate words and, eventually, of individual sounds in each word.

What to Do in the Classroom. Direct instruction in phonemic awareness is seldom needed for young Early Emergent Literacy children. (Older children who have not yet acquired phonemic awareness may need such instruction.) Rather, informal, indirect teaching is most appropriate.

Following are some ideas for developing phonemic awareness throughout the day's activities.

Rhymes. A regular part of every day should include reciting many familiar rhymes, emphasizing the rhyming words (in a poem) and then adding other words that also rhyme. This helps children develop an ear for rhyme.

You may call attention to print also. For example, take the words "bed" and "head" from a nursery rhyme and begin a **word wall** (a space on the wall where words are posted) of rhyming words. As you build an ear for rhyme, you also build awareness for segmentation of sounds, separating *b-e-d* and *h-ea-d* as you write them. You may note the two spellings for the same sound in the middle of the two words.

Finger Plays. Finger plays help children build phonemic awareness because of the rhythmic nature of the recitation. If you do "Five little monkeys jumping on the bed" with gestures, each word, and sometimes each syllable, gets attention.

Singing. Because each word, and sometimes each syllable, is a separate note, songs reinforce concepts about words. It is a short leap from this awareness to awareness of individual sounds.

Clapping and Other Action. Clap as you recite rhythmic poems. Then say the words and have children clap the syllables, stamp their feet, snap their fingers, or shrug their shoulders.

Playing Games with Words. Turn learning activities into games throughout the day. For example, "I'm thinking of a word that begins like 'baby' and is what I take to get clean," or "I'm thinking of a word that rhymes with 'hot' and is something to cook in."

We suggest weaving instruction that will develop phonemic awareness into everything you do all day long. Yopp (1995) reminds us that phonemic awareness is not acquired through drill-type activities. Later we will discuss more formal instruction for children who do not seem to be acquiring the skills naturally.

SCHEDULING THE COMPREHENSIVE BALANCED LITERACY DAY

The literacy model presented in Chapter 6 covers preschool through grade 8. At the preschool level, the model is adjusted to meet the developmental needs of the students. Schedules will vary widely depending on a number of factors: how long the children are in a school setting (whether a half-day, full day, or extended day), the nature of the physical facility (whether part of a public school or a separate preschool), the philosophy of the school, the availability of aides and volunteers, the materials on hand, and much more.

While this text is focused on literacy, other equally important development is taking place. Children are having experiences with numbers and shapes, with animals and plants, with art, and with music. Children are learning to get along with others, to follow rules, to pay attention, to work and play with new materials, to visit new places, to relate to new adults, and perhaps to relate to children who are culturally quite different from them. Each teacher must find a way to schedule time so that all aspects of a child's development are supported, including, but not limited to, literacy.

A preschool day does not look like a traditional primary-grade classroom. However, literacy activities may very well glue the day together. For example, each day may begin with children looking at books quietly (or drawing or writing) for a short period of time. This may be followed by the morning message and a read-aloud. More read-alouds take place throughout the day, along with other writing. Later in this chapter, we will look at a sample schedule.

Providing for Diversity Within the Classroom

In this section, we offer some ideas concerning very young children with exceptionalities and children who are learning English as a second language.

EXCEPTIONALITIES

Development varies widely from the time children are born. Some variations are attributable to the natural differences in the population and some to specific difficulties in language development or intellectual, behavioral, or physical development.

Some young children may not yet exhibit all of the behaviors given as benchmarks in this chapter. Usually, this does not require special attention; for most children, all the behaviors will emerge naturally with time.

If a child lacks *most* of these behaviors, however, you may need to initiate steps to get special help. Follow the suggested procedures for your school. You will usually begin by keeping careful anecdotal records, checklists, and other documentation. After you have gathered the requisite information, you will probably refer the child for further assessment by a specialist.

When a child is referred for special assessment and possible special placement, he or she will likely remain with you for at least part of the day as part of a mainstreaming or inclusion policy. Educators are a long way from settling issues regarding the identification of learning differences (including giftedness) and how best to help children who exhibit some kind of exceptionality. For the purposes of this book, we are concerned with how *you* help these children *while they are with you.*

- You are responsible for doing for each child whatever that child needs to the best of your ability.

- You must not assume that others will take care of children who fall outside the parameters of "normal" on either end. In any given classroom, you are the teacher for the entire range of development found in the age group you teach. If you are a prekindergarten teacher, most children will exhibit Early Emergent Literacy behaviors, but some may have almost no oral language and some may already be reading and writing independently.

- If some of your children are pulled out for special attention, you must find out what is being done for them and reinforce it while the children are with you.

- You must continue to learn about the kinds of challenges your children face.

- You must get to know the families of your children so that you can encourage and support them.

    You may need to adapt some procedures or materials for certain children in your class. You will want to accommodate differences without isolating those who need special attention. You may need to accommodate a wheelchair, for instance. You may need large-print books for visually impaired children or microphones for those with hearing impairments. You may need special computer programs. But whatever special attention your children need, you are not alone; you will have help and support from your colleagues, special teachers, the child's family, and professional organizations.

    We believe that good teaching is good teaching, regardless of the recipient. So if some of your children have not yet begun to show the behaviors typical of this stage, assess them carefully, refer them to specialists if appropriate, and keep on teaching them every single day, giving them the language they need.

SECOND-LANGUAGE LEARNERS

To be certain that second-language learners are receiving the special attention they may need, you should focus both on what the school does and on what you as an individual teacher can do.

What the School Does. You will need to learn how your school system addresses this need. For example, your school system may have a series of questions that are asked about each child at enrollment. Examples:

- What is the primary language spoken in the home?

- Does the child speak English or the first language at home?

- Does the child speak English outside the home?

- What degree of oral English fluency does the child demonstrate?

- Are the parents bilingual?

- Is the child already literate in any language?

Depending on the answers to such questions, the child may be assigned to a class for English as a Second Language or to a bilingual classroom in which the child is taught in his or her native language while concurrently being taught English.

What You Do. Even when a child in your class is assigned to a special program, you should do your own assessment using the levels of language production discussed in Chapter 3. Listen and observe carefully as the child interacts with other children and with adults. Many factors impinge on a child's oral language usage, not the least of which is fear of a new situation. The child who refused to speak at all during enrollment may show a more advanced level of production when relaxed in the safe environment you provide in the classroom.

A simple technique to encourage speech is to expand what a child has said. For example, the non-English speaker points to the water fountain and grunts or says, "Agua." You reply, "Water. You want a drink of water." You elaborate and rephrase, but keep it simple. The other children will mimic you, of course, so you will soon hear them all doing the same kind of elaborating and rephrasing. As the non-English speaker reaches for paper and crayons, another child says, "Do you want some paper? Here is a piece of paper. You may use my crayons, too. What color do you want? The yellow one?"

The first thing the child needs is the words for necessities in the environment: bathroom, lunch, drink, home, bus, coat, book, paper, hurt, cold, hot, sick, tired, teacher, and so forth. The other children in the class are probably the best teachers.

At the same time, you will continue to label orally (and in print) objects in the room, and the labels may be in more than one language. In addition, you will find opportunities to embed labels in elaborated sentences: "This is the window. Look out the window. See the bird? The bird is in the tree. We can look out the window and see a bird in a tree." This technique will benefit all the children and will be especially helpful for second-language learners.

Be sure to have audio versions of stories. These are tireless—retelling stories over and over, building language in the process.

Most classrooms welcome the ESL child with open arms, the teacher bubbling with speech. It doesn't matter that the child doesn't understand all the words. What matters is that the child feels a part of the class.

We believe all learners need the same thing: instructional support that is developmentally appropriate—in other words, pleasure in where they are now and scaffolding or support in helping them grow. ELL children need to be steeped in the English language. Therefore, all the usual activities are appropriate: reading aloud, rereading, finger plays, songs, nursery rhymes, acting stories, drawing, building, splashing, and stirring—all accompanied by language.

A Diverse Classroom at Work

Let's return to Jeff Gomez's prekindergarten classroom, described at the beginning of this chapter. Table 8.3 shows his daily schedule for his 4-hour preschool program. Look at the schedule, and then read the descriptions that follow.

TABLE 8.3

Daily Schedule for Mr. Gomez's Class: A 4-Hour Preschool Program

8:00–8:20	Arrival; check-in; independent activity
8:20–8:40	Calendar; world and local news; personal news
8:40–9:00	Child-dictated morning message
9:00–9:15	Independent reading and writing
9:15–9:30	Rug time; story
9:30–10:00	Centers
10:00–10:15	Snack and rest
10:15–11:00	Centers
11:00–11:15	Rug time; informational book
11:15–11:40	Science/math experiment or manipulatives
11:40–12:00	Clean-up; story/song/poem/finger play

8:00–8:20: Arrival; check-in; independent activity. As children enter the room, they turn over their name tags on the big attendance chart so that Jeff Gomez can tell at a glance who is here. The tags have the children's photos as well as their names. The children put their wraps in individual cubbies and check their mailboxes.

Next, the children engage in quiet literacy activities. There are no desks or assigned seats. Children settle wherever they are comfortable. There are pillows, beanbag chairs, writing tables, an old sofa, and, of course, the floor. Some children look at books independently. Some talk quietly in pairs as they share a book. Some are writing. Some are drawing and writing captions. While there is a hum in the air, the atmosphere is quiet and focused.

During this time, and at other times when children are working quietly, classical music is played softly.

8:20–8:40: Calendar; world and local news; personal news. Mr. Gomez first talks about the calendar—the month, the day, special events—then the weather, and finally news. He reports these in English and in Spanish, which is the first language of several children. All the children are *invited* to share something they heard on the news or something their parents read to them from a newspaper. Some days they share personal news, such as the birth of a baby sister or brother. Children are encouraged to use their first language if they are not fluent in English.

8:40–9:00: Child-dictated morning message. Teacher and children compose the morning message together. Mr. Gomez writes on chart paper using a felt marker. Once a week, a bilingual aide composes a morning message with the Spanish-speaking children. All morning messages, in either language, are read and discussed by all children.

9:00–9:15: Independent reading and writing. The children continue independent activities while Mr. Gomez completes daily "housekeeping" chores. This time may also be used for individual assessment of one or two children.

9:15–9:30: Rug time; story. The children come to sit on the rug in front of Mr. Gomez's rocking chair. This is a time for shared reading of some kind. Mr. Gomez has English books, Spanish books, and some books that show both English and Spanish.

9:30–10:00: Centers. Children work at assigned learning centers. Each child has a clothespin with his or her name written on it. The centers are listed by name and with a picture on a large chart. Mr. Gomez clips each child's clothespin to the center where the child should go. Every child is assigned to each center at least twice a week. Some of the centers are art, housekeeping, water and sand, store, listening, blocks, book nook, dramatic play, pets, and computer. Some of the activity at centers is "free," while at other times a specific task may await the children.

Some days, Mr. Gomez leads the children in whole-class music during this time. Many instruments are available, though not always in free reach of the children. There are a piano and a guitar in the room. Even when no particular music activity is planned, Mr. Gomez finds odd moments for songs and dancing.

10:00–10:15: Snack and rest. Family members take turns providing healthful snacks each day. Children distribute the snacks. Following snacks, all close their eyes and rest for a few minutes.

10:15–11:00: Centers. Mr. Gomez circulates as the children work at centers, using this time to make notes and occasionally pulling a child aside for individual assessment.

On some days, this long period is scheduled tightly. On other days, it is broken into a defined period of assigned centers and a longer period of free time. The children spend a great deal of time at the beginning of the year learning procedures for conducting themselves during this kind of activity.

Books are everywhere, including many books in Spanish and some with English text as well as Spanish. The children are free to choose and read any book in the classroom. It is clear from the way they handle the books that they have been taught to respect them. Some books are in plastic tubs, grouped by topic and labeled. For example, the tub that holds books about snakes and reptiles has a picture of a snake on the front, and the ABC book tub has letters on the front. There are also shelves with picture books, both with print and wordless. Books accompanied by audiotapes or CDs are in the listening center.

Writing tools and paper are available in several places. Each child knows where things are and knows the procedures for getting and returning materials.

Each child also has a take-home envelope for special things to share at home.

By next year, Mr. Gomez hopes to have at least two computers for the children to use.

11:00–11:15: Rug time; informational book. Mr. Gomez and his students are very interested in science and math. Every day he reads aloud an informational book about a topic in one of these areas, following up with an activity related to the book content.

11:15–11:40: Science/math experiment or manipulatives. This time is directly related to the book Mr. Gomez has just read. He may demonstrate a physics principle or present children with a problem and lead them to hypothesize. Often these activities stretch over several days. They may be related to matter, plants, the elements, weather, motion, animals, or any other area of science. They may also be related to counting, shapes, quantities, estimating, or anything related to mathematics. This period ends with shared writing of some kind.

Sometimes the activities from 11:00 to 11:40 are reversed. Mr. Gomez may begin with an experiment, demonstration, or problem and end the period with a book. The time is flexible, but it always includes an activity, a book, and writing.

11:40–12:00: Clean-up; story/song/poem/finger play. After everything is cleaned up and put away, Mr. Gomez takes a few minutes to review the day. The children talk about what they did that day and what they learned. This is, of course, exactly what families will ask when the children get home: "What did you learn in school today?" The children also talk a bit about what they will be reading, writing, and doing the next day.

Finally, there is a story, a poem, a song, or a finger play that Mr. Gomez has planned in advance. The Spanish-speaking children have taught the others many songs, stories, and poems in Spanish, and these are included frequently. By the end of their year with Mr. Gomez, these children will know hundreds of stories, songs, poems, and finger plays.

ACCOMMODATING VARIATIONS

The day in Jeff Gomez's classroom flows from one thing to the next, and many deviations from the posted routine occur. All kinds of things may disrupt the regular

After these children finish working at the water table, they will talk about the experience and then dictate a story about it.

© H. Mark Weidman Photography/Alamy

schedule: a thunderstorm, a butterfly, a new sprout in a garden, baby guinea pigs—all are good reasons to vary the usual agenda.

The exact activities in any class vary widely, of course, but some things are common to all language-rich classrooms. Children talk a lot—to the adults, to one another, and to themselves. They spend a lot of time with print: books, magazines, computers, maps, signs, packaged and canned goods, and so on. They write a lot. Perhaps most common is the frequent request they direct to any adult: "Will you read us a story?"

Summary

- We presented benchmarks and behaviors that are typical of the Early Emergent Literacy child. We suggested how to informally assess oral language, reading and book knowledge, and writing, and presented some appropriate instructional strategies for use in your classroom.

- It is important to create a language-and print-rich environment with appropriate materials, tools, and furniture. The physical arrangements in your classroom—for example, learning centers and a listening/viewing area—can help support literacy development.

- ou can foster literacy development by reading aloud, talking constantly to the children to expand their oral language, labeling objects in the classroom, and making the environment comfortable and inviting.

- Several instructional strategies are especially important for a Comprehensive Balanced Literacy Program: read-alouds; oral language activities, including dramatic plays, puppets, and poems; shared reading; shared writing, including morning messages as well as collaborative stories and reports; language experience activities in which children read something they themselves have written; and phonemic awareness activities.

- Although schedules may vary a great deal, literacy activities should take place frequently throughout each day.

- Some students with exceptionalities may need adaptations in procedures and materials.

- Children who are learning English as a second language need to have their production of English encouraged on an everyday basis.

- Overall, the instruction for diverse students differs little from what you have already learned about teaching reading and language arts.

- Good teaching is good teaching; meeting the needs of each child is mostly a matter of matching appropriate instruction to the child's development.

 Please visit the premium website for *Literacy Assessment*, Fourth Edition to access the TeachSource Video Cases, chapter web links, For Additional Reading, tutorial quizzes, glossary flashcards, online checklists, downloads, and much more! Go to www.cengage.com/login to register your access code.

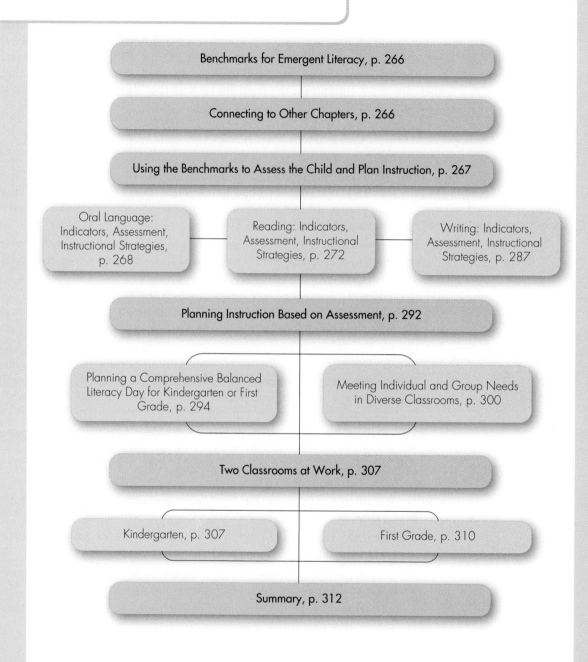

Emergent Literacy

- Author's Chair
- connected text
- context
- decoding
- environmental print
- graphics
- onset
- predictable texts
- rime
- word structure

We are looking into Mrs. Bullock's kindergarten class. The twenty children in this class are engaged in various independent literacy activities. Over in the reading corner, two boys sit side-by-side on floor cushions, sharing a book. As we watch, one boy turns the pages and seems to be pointing to and talking about the pictures. The other child adds comments and points to other things, then continues turning pages. The two boys go through the entire book this way, talking about the pictures. Then they turn back to the beginning, and one boy appears to be reading the story. He points to words as he reads. We cannot tell whether he has memorized the story or actually recognizes the words, but he seems to be matching his words with the print on the page.

We glance around the room to see what else these kindergarten children can do. Two are sorting alphabet cards to match upper- and lower-case letters. Another is paging through a child-made personal dictionary with both words and pictures, naming the picture and pointing to the word on each page. Another bends low over a piece of paper, the tip of his tongue moving back and forth between his lips, fiercely concentrating on what he is writing. A little girl is telling two friends about a book she just heard on an audiotape.

During these independent activities, Mrs. Bullock moves about the room, observing and making notes. She also uses this time to hold individual conferences with five children. A chart tells, with both words and pictures, which children are to have conferences today and what to bring to the conference. Today each child is to bring his or her writing folder to the conference.

Later in the day, the children come to the rug at the front of the room, where Mrs. Bullock sits in a rocking chair and reads aloud Library Mouse (Kirk, 2007). The children talk about what the mouse does in the library and then discuss with Mrs. Bullock what stories they might write as a group.

In Mrs. Bullock's classroom, we saw that the children are in the process of growing toward literacy: the Emergent Literacy stage. They already see themselves as readers and writers. Reading and writing is an important part of their daily lives. They make good use of the reading and writing materials that surround them and are available to them throughout the day. They are, in fact, readers and writers.

Some teachers believe this is the most exciting stage of literacy to share with children. The students joyfully embrace their growing literacy. Most are experiencing success. As teachers provide solid instruction for these children, they identify those who are struggling and provide the extra scaffolding they need to keep from faltering.

Benchmarks for Emergent Literacy

No matter where you teach, your school system is likely to have its own set of benchmarks or standards, beginning with kindergarten. These standards represent what each child (and his or her teacher) is held to in terms of achievement each year.

No two sets of benchmarks will match exactly; however, most agree on the big ideas. Children develop mostly in the same sequence, though not always at the same rate. Think of the process as crossing a creek on steppingstones—one stone for each stage. We slip occasionally. We may have one foot on one stone and one on the next. As we reach for the next stone, we may fear slipping and retreat to a previous, more secure stone. But having had a glimpse of things to come, we try again, and this time we are more confident because we know where we are going.

We present behaviors that will indicate to you that a child is indeed *at* a particular stage of literacy development, thus helping you plan appropriate instruction for that child. The following benchmarks are typical of children ages five to seven, kindergarten through first grade. Some children are already beyond this stage when they begin kindergarten. Others may still be at this stage beyond first grade.

Connecting to Other Chapters

Literacy development occurs along a continuum; therefore, it is impossible to isolate literacy behaviors and address them in only one stage. They give hints that they are coming before they appear consistently. They also sometimes disappear briefly long after we have thought they were secure. Your assessment-based instruction must reflect this understanding.

Although the Emergent Literacy stage usually occurs when children are in kindergarten or first grade, some children in these grades will be at the previous literacy stage, while others will be at a subsequent stage. Children who display few Emergent Literacy behaviors need the assessment and instructional ideas presented for Early Emergent Literacy in Chapter 8. Children who already exhibit all of the Emergent Literacy behaviors need the assessments and instructional strategies discussed for Beginning Reading and Writing in Chapter 10, or beyond.

In this chapter we are talking about children who are at the Emergent Literacy stage, regardless of their grade or age, and that your assessment and instruction must be adjusted to fit each child.

B
E
N
C
H
M
A
R
K
S

ORAL LANGUAGE

- The student exhibits behaviors of Early Emergent Literacy to a greater degree.
- The student uses standard sentence construction and grammar.
- The student's facility with oral language is growing.
- The student's oral language reflects literature to which he or she is exposed.
- The student shows pleasure in language.

READING

- The student exhibits behaviors of the Early Emergent Literacy stage to a greater degree.
- The student has acquired most or all of the concepts about print.
- The student is using print in everyday life.
- The student is learning decoding skills: letters and words.
- The student shows evidence of phonemic awareness and the alphabetic principle.
- The student is beginning to use phonics; knows many letter-sound associations, both consonants and vowels.
- The student is beginning to use other decoding strategies to begin to build fluency: sight words, context, graphics, and word structure.
- The student is constructing meaning.

WRITING

- The student exhibits continued growth in many of the Early Emergent Literacy behaviors.
- The student knows and writes his or her name and some letters and uses some other writing conventions.
- The student is using phonemic awareness in writing.
- The student is using sound/symbol association in writing.
- The student is using writing for own purposes.
- The student is becoming familiar with the writing process.
- The student is constructing meaning in writing.

Using the Benchmarks to Assess the Child and Plan Instruction

In this section, we show you how to assess informally the three major areas of literacy—oral language, reading, and writing—building on the Early Emergent Literacy stage and adding the new benchmarks for Emergent Literacy. Following the assessments, we suggest instructional strategies to help children who do not yet exhibit the sample behaviors consistently.

If your school system requires you to use its benchmarks, you may want to supplement that assessment with some of the assessments presented here. In fact, many of these tools may be used to assess local benchmarks.

You should begin both instruction and assessment on the first day of school using the kinds of materials, methods, and routines that you know promote literacy development in all children. As the days pass, you gather information about each child in each of the areas. In other words, assessment takes place as you teach.

Sample individual checklists can be downloaded from this text's website.

Sample class checklists are presented at the end of our discussion of each of the three areas.

Oral Language: Indicators, Assessment, Instructional Strategies

Children's oral language continues to grow rapidly as they move from Early Emergent Literacy into Emergent Literacy (Resnick & Snow, 2009). Much of the development is refinement of language begun earlier. With the influence of school, some new behaviors begin to emerge. We do not recommend using a specific assessment instrument: rather your assessment will be largely based on observation during whole class, small group, and individual activities. We address the following major areas:

- Continued development of behaviors from Early Emergent Literacy
- Standard usage and grammar
- Facility with oral language
- Reflecting literature experience
- Pleasure in language

A class checklist for oral language (Figure 9.1) appears near the end of the section.

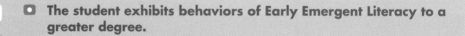

▢ The student exhibits behaviors of Early Emergent Literacy to a greater degree.

Most of the oral language benchmarks in the Early Emergent Literacy stage will be present with increasing consistency and maturity as children move into Emergent Literacy. This growth is not a leap. Nor is it a sudden "aha" experience such as a child might have in math when suddenly grasping the principle of multiplying by zero. This growth is gradual and mostly steady, given continued good support.

▢ The student uses standard sentence construction and grammar.

- Is recognizing use of nonstandard language in self and others
- Is developing a sense that school/book language is perhaps different from home or neighborhood language

Assessment. Listen to children who have come to school using nonstandard English, whatever its root. Note which are beginning to "catch themselves" in such usage and change their wording to standard usage. When you ask direct questions, perhaps during a collaborative writing activity, which children can suggest a way to word ideas using standard language? Note which children are beginning to switch language from playground usage, which reflects home or neighborhood, to classroom usage, which reflects school and book language.

Instructional Strategies. This may be one of the most ticklish and divisive areas of teaching. You must walk a path between two somewhat conflicting notions. On the one hand, you know it is important for all children to eventually be able to use standard English comfortably. On the other hand, you value whatever language a child brings to school as reflecting the child's culture and family.

Interrupting a child's speech to correct his or her usage may not result in more standard usage; on the contrary, it may make the child reluctant to speak at all. Instead:

- continue to model standard usage.
- when revising and editing written work that requires standard English, focus on the work, not the child, so that changes make the work stronger rather than appearing to denigrate the child's language.
- praise specific instances of self-correction.
- remember that some students are adjusting to regional or cultural differences or dialects of English.
- remember that second-language learners face the dual task of learning a new language and distinguishing between informal, conversational language and book language.

> **◘ The student's facility with oral language is growing.**
>
> - Makes self understood by peers and adults
> - Follows "rules" for conversation and discussion
> - Paraphrases what others have said
> - Participates in sharing
> - Retains oral directions
> - Can ask questions for clarification

Assessment. Most children can communicate with classmates and adults without difficulty. Note whether children are comfortable in informal conversations as well as during discussions. If you note some children struggling, ask yourself questions such as these:

- Does the child have trouble articulating the sounds of English?
- Should I consider referral to a language or speech specialist?
- Is the problem lack of vocabulary? Is it social—that is, do the other children not listen to this child for some reason?

The ability to paraphrase relates to the child's understanding of what was heard as well as the child's own language for putting something "into his or her own words." Also, note if any children are not willing to participate in sharing time. Remember that second-language learners may acquire the vocabulary and grammar of English long before they are comfortable with possible cultural differences related to conversations with adults.

Many of these students are raising their hands, anxious to share their answers with their teacher.

© Monkey Business Images Ltd/Photolibrary

Observe which children can remember a series of oral directions, such as "First finish your rough draft and put it in your writing folder. Then you may work on your math or read with a buddy. Check the schedule for your computer time." Equally important, note whether children are aware of when they do not understand something and ask questions for clarification.

Instructional Strategies. If you have children who struggle to make others understand, and the problem is not rooted in difficulties with articulation or cultural/language differences, build more opportunities for children to communicate directly with each other. For example, if a child relates something to a group, the other children should be free to ask questions of the speaker. Such talk should not be filtered through you but instead should be directly child to child.

- Discussion guidelines established by you and your students can support participation by everyone in the class. Such guidelines can be amended as needed. Children should be encouraged to verbalize the reasons for having guidelines and gradually learn to monitor their own and their group's behavior during discussions.

- Help children become good conversationalists by modeling the process of exchanging thoughts with others. As you participate in conversations with children, model paraphrasing. Demonstrate the difference between repeating someone's exact words and putting ideas into one's own words. Help children see how paraphrasing helps others know we have understood them.

- Since paraphrasing may be difficult for some second-language learners, at first accept virtual repetition of what was said and ask questions to be sure of understanding. Gradually encourage ELLs to restate ideas in their own words.

- If a child never wants to share ideas with others, try to determine the reason. Is it shyness? Would sharing in a small group or even with just one friend be easier? Perhaps you need to provide some structure for sharing time. For example, if you have show-and-tell, teach a routine such as this: Show your item. Name it. Tell what it is for. Tell why you wanted to share it. Ask for questions.

- If children cannot remember oral directions, consider writing the directions on the chalkboard so everyone can refer to them. As children begin to write with more ease, introduce the habit of taking notes about what to do.

- We want children to be aware of when they don't understand something and to ask questions as needed. Be sure children feel free to ask questions. Don't assume that the child who has questions wasn't listening.

- Some children are not aware they do not understand. When you ask, "Are there any questions?" no hands go up, but as a child begins to work, she or he is full of questions. Children cannot always anticipate what will be difficult to understand in advance of beginning the task. One way to help children monitor their own understanding of directions is to ask them to retell what to do.

- Some children, in contrast, ask more questions than needed, seemingly because they need the special attention from the teacher. You find that when the child asks for clarification, he or she understands perfectly and can tell you exactly what to do, but needs reassurance. In this case, give whatever support is needed while gradually working to build the child's confidence.

> ☑ **The student's oral language reflects literature to which he or she is exposed.**
>
> - Uses new words from stories
> - Uses "book language" when appropriate; that is, storytelling narrative is clearly different from conversation or simply relating an event
> - Enjoys "making a play" of a favorite story

Assessment. Note that children are incorporating words from stories they hear into their everyday language. Observe which children experiment with new words and which do not. As children retell stories, note whether they are using story language. Which children enjoy making stories into a play? Which are comfortable using the story and character language? The ability to assume the role of a character in a story shows both a grasp of the story's meaning and oral language facility.

Instructional Strategies. Discuss words as you engage in read-alouds and in shared reading. Encourage children to use story words both during discussions of the story and at other times during the day. Acknowledge those who do so with specific praise: "That word was in the story we read this morning." Share your own experience of learning new words and beginning to "try out" new words first orally and then in writing.

Model retelling that uses book language. Demonstrate the difference between retelling in your own language and using book language. Both are important, of course, but you want to encourage sensitivity to book language. Help children see the differ-ence between "Pooh wasn't very smart, and he was always wanting to eat honey" and "Pooh was a bear of very little brain. When he was hungry, he always said it was 'time for a little something.'" If such story language was a part of your family language, share that with children.

Allow children time and space to role-play stories, both under your supervision and on their own. Consider taking a part yourself to model using the language of a story character.

> ☐ **The student shows pleasure in language.**
>
> - Enjoys jokes related to words, such as puns
> - Enjoys tongue twisters
> - Enjoys hearing humorous books related to idioms
> - Is proud of learning new words
> - Tries out new words and asks what words mean

Assessment. Note which children are enjoying language-related jokes such as puns. Which are beginning to enjoy tongue twisters and books whose humor depends on un-derstanding idiomatic language? You might see an example of this behavior when you read aloud a book like *Amelia Bedelia (Parish 1963/1981)* when children understand that Amelia took "change the towels" literally and she changed the towels by cutting holes in them. Children at this stage understand that she should have changed them by replacing them with fresh towels. Some humorous books are particularly based on knowledge of homonyms or homophones—*The King Who Rained* (Gwynne, 1988), *Homonym or Homophone*, (Loewen, 2007), and *Eight Ate* (Terban & Maestro, 2007).

For second-language learners, absence of the behaviors discussed in this sec-tion should not absolutely indicate that a child is at an earlier literacy stage. Jokes are among the most difficult things to understand in another language.

Note which children are pleased to use new words, trying them out and freely asking what unfamiliar words mean. Such pleasure indicates an active interest in lan-guage that contributes to growth in all aspects of literacy. The child meets a new word through listening or reading and begins to get an idea of its meaning. Next, the child begins trying out the word orally. If that seems successful—that is, people understand—the child may begin using the word in writing.

Instructional Strategies. No direct instruction is necessary beyond your usual vocabulary-building instruction. Vocabulary develops best through wide reading (and listening), along with risk-free opportunities to try out new words. Everyone misuses a word now and then, and no one should be made to feel embarrassed.

Figure 9.1 presents a class checklist for the Emergent Literacy oral language benchmarks.

Reading: Indicators, Assessment, Instructional Strategies

Much reading assessment informally can take place as you teach and observe children during their regular daily activities. Some assessments require one-on-one time with

Oral Language Checklist:
Emergent Literacy Stage

Teacher_____   Date_____   Grade_____

Student Names

+ = behavior present
- = behavior absent
✓ = somewhat present

Benchmark										
Early Emergent Literacy Behaviors										
Standard Usage and Grammar										
Recognition of nonstandard usage										
Sense of school/book language										
Facility with Oral Language										
Makes self understood by peers and adults										
Follows "rules" for conversation and discussion										
Can paraphrase what others have said										
Participates in sharing										
Retains oral directions										
Can ask questions for clarification										
Reflecting Literature										
Uses new words from stories										
Uses "book language" when appropriate										
Enjoys "making a play" of a favorite story										
Pleasure in Language										
Enjoys jokes related to words										
Enjoys tongue twisters										
Enjoys hearing humorous books										
Is proud of learning new words										
Tries out new words										

FIGURE 9.1

Sample Class Checklist for Emergent Literacy: Oral Language Benchmarks and Behaviors

each child and are best accomplished during conferences. These are usually sprinkled throughout the day and week, giving you time alone with perhaps five children each day. There are eight areas of reading:

- Continued development of the Early Emergent Literacy behaviors
- Concepts about print

- Use of print in everyday life
- Use of decoding (letters and words)
- Phonemic awareness and the alphabetic principle
- Use of phonics
- Use of other decoding strategies and build fluency
- Construction of meaning

A sample class checklist for reading benchmarks appears in Figure 9.2 at the end of this section.

>
>
> ◻ **The student exhibits behaviors of the Early Emergent Literacy stage to a greater degree.**

Recall the benchmarks for reading and book knowledge in Early Emergent Literacy, described in Chapter 8. Whereas at that stage a child is just beginning to demonstrate the behaviors, now the behaviors are exhibited consistently. All of the suggested instructional strategies in Chapter 8 are also appropriate for children at this stage and beyond.

> ◻ **The student has acquired most or all of the concepts about print.**
>
> - Handles book in correct position; knows where to begin reading and in what direction to read
> - Can point to a word, two words, a letter, two letters
> - Knows that print should match the voice of the reader
> - Knows about such book parts as title, author, and illustrator

Assessment. Observe children to see whether they are handling books in right-side up position, starting at the beginning, and turning pages appropriately. When they are pretend-reading and point to the print, note whether they are moving their fingers from left to right and from top to bottom. As you interact with children individually, ask them to point to a word, to two words, to one letter, and then two letters. As you sit with an individual child, ask him or her to point to the words as you read, noting whether the child seems to understand the connection between the words you say and the marks on the page.

During group activities as well as individual conferences, you can determine each child's knowledge of book parts. Even though a child may not be able to read the titles or the names of the author or illustrator, look for understanding of book parts by asking questions as you point: What does the title tell us? Where do we learn who wrote this book? Who drew the pictures? Show me the spine of the book. Where is the front? The back? Here is a glossary; what is that for?

Instructional Strategies. If children do not yet exhibit the behaviors related to book handling consistently, demonstrate and verbalize frequently. For example:

Watch how I hold the book so the pictures and print are right side up. I begin here, the front of the book. I turn the pages this way. When I read the words, I start at the top and move my eyes from left to right like this. (Move your finger to demonstrate.) When I come to the end of the line, I move down to the beginning of the next line and go from left to right again.

By verbalizing as you demonstrate, you give children important concepts, such as *up, down, left, right,* and *front,* as you model them. As children become comfortable with these concepts, you can have them take turns showing these things to the other children as you read a big book together.

Children who cannot yet isolate letters and words in print may simply need to be shown. Don't wait for children to "catch on." Use any text, such as a big book or the morning message. Point to one letter and then frame it with your two index fingers, saying:

This is one letter (you can name it if you like, but doing so isn't necessary). This is two letters (move your fingers). This is one . . . This is two . . . one . . . two. Now you do it.

The same activity can be done with one word and two words.

If a child doesn't yet seem to have made this connection between voice and print, he or she will benefit from many experiences of shared reading during which you move a pointer, finger, or marker under the words as you read aloud. In addition, the child will be aided in grasping this concept through one-on-one read-alouds with you, an aide, a volunteer, or a reading buddy.

Research shows that a child's eventual ability to finger point to words being read depends on prior letter knowledge and phonemic awareness (Ehri & Sweet, 1991). Demonstrating that there is such a connection between voice and print is worthwhile, however, even before the child can point to the words independently.

Children who don't have knowledge of book parts probably haven't been taught about them yet. The knowledge is easily taught (and learned) through your continual reference to book parts as you conduct activities such as read-alouds and shared reading.

> **◘ The student is using print in everyday life.**
>
> - Can locate a specific book, record, CD, audiotape, and so forth
> - Recognizes some **environmental print,** such as brand names and fast-food restaurant signs

Assessment. Children at this stage of development begin to show in various ways that they understand some of the many ways print is used in daily life. Assessment is informal and observational.

Note which children are able to go to the bookshelf or audio/visual storage and select a particular item. The child knows that the print tells which book or tape it is, even before being able to read the words on it.

Note also which children recognize environmental print in newspapers, television commercials, products, and so forth in the classroom. A child may first think

Crest says "toothpaste." While that is not the right word, this behavior shows that the child knows the print tells what the product is.

Instructional Strategies. Demonstrate frequently your own use of print to inform you about items in the environment. For example, read to children from newspapers and magazines, look up the time of a television program, locate a word in a dictionary to verify pronunciation, check the daily menu to see what's for lunch, and note the manufacturers of items such as sneakers, book bags, and other personal items.

Scaffold instruction. For example, when a child points to the word *Crest* and says "toothpaste," use this to build understanding: "Yes, it is Crest toothpaste and this word is Crest. Let's say the letters together. What do you hear at the beginning?"

> **◘ The student is learning decoding skills: letters and words.**
>
> - Recognizes and can name most letters
> - Can match many upper- and lower-case letters

Decoding is what the reader does to determine what a printed word is. Some words are recognized instantly (at sight): they have been memorized. Words that are not recognized instantly require the use of one or more strategies for decoding. The reader must use his or her background knowledge and vocabulary, phonics, the structural nature of words (such as prefixes, suffixes, and roots), surrounding text (what you may think of as "context clues"), and graphics (such as illustrations) on the page. Keep in mind that phonemic awareness, phonics, and knowledge of the structure of words also play a large part in attempts to spell.

Readers must be able to decode unfamiliar words. The child who has to struggle to figure out each and every word has little chance of constructing meaning. Without meaning, the child is just saying words. Therefore, fluent decoding is necessary, but not sufficient, for acquiring literacy.

Most of the words that emergent readers will meet in print are already in their oral vocabulary. They understand the word when they hear it and may use it when they speak; they just don't yet recognize it in print. If the child is reading meaningful text of some kind, the pronunciation arrived at through the application of word recognition skills, even if not exactly correct, probably will trigger the correct word in the child's mind.

Assessment. You need to know which print letters each child can name and find. Following is a set of individual assessments. Begin with task 1, which shows the most knowledge. Each time, if the child seems unable to do the task, go to the next assessment. You can quickly tell if you need to discontinue a task and move to the next. Do so casually: "Let's do something else now. How about . . . ?"

1. Use a set of alphabet cards, both upper and lower case and in mixed-up order. Go through the stack (or train an aide to do so), asking the child to name each letter. Sort into two piles: known and unknown. If most are unknown, use the next task.

2. Use the same set of cards. Ask the child to find and name as many letters as he or she can and put them in a pile.

3. Use the same set of cards. Display a few at a time, and ask the child to point to the letters you name.

4. Use the same set of cards, but separated by upper case and lower case. Ask the child to match upper- and lower-case cards.

5. Use two sets of upper-case cards and then two sets of lower-case cards. Display in groups of eight or so letters at a time. One at a time, hold up a letter card and ask the child to find one on the table just like the one you are holding.

6. Display cards randomly (in small batches), and ask the child to find and name any he or she knows.

Group assessment of letter knowledge may seem quicker, but the information obtained is not as precise. A paper-and-pencil assessment presents rows of randomly ordered letters. You ask the children to circle or put a mark on the letter you name. This gives you a broad notion of your entire class, but not enough to be truly helpful, in our opinion. Most such paper-and-pencil assessments do not assess every letter, both upper and lower case. Furthermore, they test only whether a child can find a letter when you name it, not whether the child can name the letter.

Instructional Strategies. The same tasks you used for assessment can be used for children to play games of matching letters. Besides the lessons you may routinely use to teach the alphabet, many daily activities offer opportunities to teach and reinforce letter knowledge. Here are just a few:

- Name aloud the letters you use to write on the chalkboard, chart paper, or computer.
- Call attention to "new" letters as you revisit stories you have read during shared reading.
- Hold up a letter and ask a child to come to the big book or morning message, name the letter, and find where else it appears.
- Have available and share ABC books.
- Provide tactile experiences as needed: sand, salt, pudding, bumpy rubber manipulative letters, sandpaper, or flocked letters.

The relationship between letter knowledge and ease in learning to read is strong (Durkin, 1966; Snow, Burns, & Griffin, 1998; National Reading Panel, 2000). Though it is possible for a child to begin reading before knowing the names of all the letters, letter knowledge is required for grasping the alphabetic principle—the notion that letters systematically represent phonemes. However, do not hold up instruction because some children do not yet know the names of *all* the letters. Proceed with teaching letter recognition, letter names, and the sounds associated with letters, along with other aspects of word recognition.

> **◻ The student is learning decoding skills: letters and words. (continued)**
>
> - Recognizes and can name some words
> - Recognizes own name in print and perhaps other names

Assessment. At this stage, there is no set of words that all children "should" know. Many children, of course, can read some words, their own names, and perhaps the names of some family members or classmates. You will learn this informally within a couple of days as children find their cubbies or collect their drawings from a pile.

You want to find out if children can recognize and read other words besides their names and, if so, which words. We see little value in the group paper-and-pencil assessments that ask children to mark a word you say aloud. What you need to know is whether the child can recognize and say the word when he or she sees it. How you assess this depends on your first observation of each child's interaction with books. If item 1 in the following list isn't true of a child, proceed to item 2 or 3.

1. *If a child is reading books independently from the first day:* Arrange an individual conference and have the child read to you. If the reading is fluent, find a book with which the child is unfamiliar. If the child is fluent with this book as well, take a running record of fluency.

2. *If a child frequently looks at books and appears to recognize some of the words there and in the environment:* Have a conference. Ask the child to bring a book and either read to you or find words that are familiar and say them. If the child knows quite a few, you might assess his or her knowledge of what are called *basic sight words* using word cards. (A list of basic sight words appears in the Resource File.)

3. *If a child spends little time with books, or pages through quickly looking only at the pictures:* Spot-check any words recognized as you do daily activities, such as calendar, time, morning message, shared reading, and shared writing.

Instructional Strategies. Reinforce the connection between print and the spoken word in your everyday activities. You may or may not choose to teach a group of words before reading a story. Published reading programs may have vocabulary lessons (which are also word recognition lessons) built into each selection's instruction.

Also, provide many opportunities for children to become familiar with frequently used words through shared reading and rereading, choral reading, and the use of prerecorded books on tape or CD. Encourage children to read with a friend; each will help the other learn to recognize words. A buddy program that brings older readers into your class is also a fine way for children to build recognition of words through repeated reading of familiar books.

> ◘ **The student shows evidence of phonemic awareness and the alphabetic principle.**

Assessment. This benchmark and the next emerge in order, though with some overlap: first comes an ear for the separate sounds, then the alphabetic principle (the idea that letters represent phonemes, or individual sounds), and then the actual association of certain sounds with certain letters (Stahl, Duffy-Hester, & Stahl, 1998). Each benchmark applies both to reading and to writing; that is, a child who uses phonics to decode an unfamiliar word will likely also use phonics to aid in spelling a word not yet learned.

One test for assessing phonemic awareness in young children is the Yopp-Singer Test of Phoneme Segmentation, which includes lists of words and guidelines for checking phonemic awareness.

You may also quite informally assess each child by saying some individual words and demonstrating isolation of the sounds: "Listen to me say a word: 'cat.' Now listen as I say each sound separately: /c/-/a/-/t/." After giving some examples and doing several with the child, say a word and then ask the child to segment the sounds alone. There is no need to assess every sound, of course. You just want to find out whether the child has the concept—the awareness of the separate sounds in words.

Kindergarten programs often provide activities that combine phonemic awareness with the introduction to letter names and to the sounds associated with letters. Children will begin to use their growing sense of how print works as they decode (read) and perhaps even more as they encode (write). In fact, some children may be segmenting sounds and making a separate mark for each sound before learning all the letters of the alphabet and which letters represent which sounds.

To assess whether a child seems to have a sense that letters represent individual sounds—the alphabetic principle—you must observe two kinds of activities:

1. As the child tries to read unfamiliar words, note the application of known sounds, such as the beginning sounds in the child's name. Similarly, during group activities note which children are able to substitute sounds in rhyming words: "This word is 'cat.' If we take off the beginning sound, /c/, and substitute the sound we hear at the beginning of Mary's name, what word will we have? ['mat']." Children may be able to do this without yet knowing the names of all the letters and which sounds go with which letters.

2. As a child is writing and attempting to spell an unknown word, does he or she segment sounds, writing a letter or letterlike form for individual sounds? (See more about this aspect of phonemic awareness in the section on writing benchmarks later in this chapter.)

Instructional Strategies. Continue the routines given in Chapter 8 for Early Emergent Literacy: rhymes, finger plays, singing, and other games with words. Children can learn to manipulate sounds through games, rhyming patterns, and analogies. For example, the child who can say "book" and can segment sounds into the onset *b* and the rime *-ook* can figure out the new word "took." (The onset is the consonant sound that precedes the vowel in a syllable; the rhyme includes the vowel and any consonant sounds that follow.)

Continue activities that support the development of phonemic awareness through games, songs, and rhymes. Help children break syllables into onset and rime. At a later stage, they will use analogies independently to figure out how to read and write new words with the same rime. At the same time, show children how letters are associated with sounds. This may occur during instruction in letter formation (handwriting), during reading, and during writing.

C O M M E N T S

Phonemic awareness assessment and instruction may not work in the same way for students for whom English is a second language. Until they know English phonology, or sounds, efforts to impose typical phonemic awareness activities (as well as subsequent phonics activities) may not only be inappropriate but actually impede learning. See a discussion of this issue in Freeman and Freeman (2001). Keep this idea in mind as you read about associating sounds and letters in the next section. Also, remember that associating sounds with letters may not result in understanding of a word, even if the child pronounces the word correctly. As with all readers, if the word is not in the child's oral language, it will simply be a meaningless sound, no different from a nonsense word.

> ◘ **The student is beginning to use phonics; knows many letter-sound associations, both consonants and vowels.**

Assessment. Phonics helps children figure out the probable pronunciation of an unknown word by associating letters with sounds. How you assess children's ability to use phonics will depend largely on which approach to phonics (and reading instruction) you are using. Your assessment may be largely observational as children read and write, a stand-alone published test or the assessments that accompany a published program.

Most published basal reading programs incorporate a phonics strand and provide systematic and periodic assessment to check whether children are learning the skills that have been taught. Stand-alone phonics programs also have periodic tests. Keep in mind that performance on a phonics test may not reflect a child's ability to use phonics while actually reading.

Instructional Strategies. We recommend that you apply the explicit phonics/structural elements routine suggested in Chapter 6 when children show a need for it. Whatever program your school uses, such explicit routines will help your children clearly see how they can use phonics to figure out the pronunciation of unfamiliar words in reading and writing. It is a valuable decoding strategy, though not the only decoding strategy readers need.

C O M M E N T S

While this is not the place for a detailed discussion of phonics, we will remind you of some basic ideas to keep in mind as you help children:

- Reading requires constructing meaning; pronunciation of words is not enough.

- It is sometimes possible to infer meaning without pronunciation.

- English is not completely phonetically regular; the same letter can represent different sounds in different words ("cat," "city"); the same sound can be spelled with different letters in different words ("do," "due").

- Readers use phonics even when they don't realize it. Most readers can make a stab at the pronunciation of a word they have never seen. Phonics, the ability to associate sounds with letters, makes this possible.

- You can't treat children like automobiles on an assembly line, stamping the same instruction on all of them. If there were indeed one perfect way to teach every child to decode every word, educators would simply do it and end the debate about a "best" way. What we do know is that some ways seem to work for some children and some for others. Bear in mind that most children learn to read with comparative ease—therefore, any approach would likely work for most children.

That being said, Snow, Burns, and Griffin (1998) summarize how three basic teaching approaches develop phonics skills, but caution that these vary a great deal from teacher to teacher:

1. *Whole language.* The teacher teaches phonics as opportunities arise during authentic reading and writing. The emphasis is on **connected text,** groups of words that convey meaning. Learning regarding the alphabet is assumed to take place implicitly.

2. *Embedded phonics.* Phonics instruction is sequenced according to a list of word families. Children substitute sounds at the beginnings of words and generalize the patterns as they figure out new words. Teachers use trade books that contain the target patterns. They also use the patterns in writing and spelling. This approach appeared to be more effective with disadvantaged students than whole language (Hiebert, Colt, Catto, & Gury, 1992).

3. *Direct code instruction.* Once children understand how print works (concepts of print), letter-sound correspondences and spelling conventions are explicitly taught and practiced. Children read books designed to review the words and phonics lessons they have experienced up to that point. The strategy emphasized is this: if you don't recognize a word, sound it out. Then children use anthologies and trade books to develop reading and writing. According to the report by Snow, Burns, and Griffin (1998) and the National Reading Panel (2000), children taught via this approach improved in word reading at a faster rate and had higher word recognition skills than those taught by the other methods.

Your school system will have embraced an approach to teaching reading that probably includes a position on phonics. You will need to reconcile your beliefs about phonics instruction with your school's stated philosophy. Keep in mind that *all* teachers share a common goal, regardless of philosophy: to help children learn to read and write successfully.

> ▣ **The student is beginning to use other decoding strategies to begin to build fluency: sight words, context, graphics, and word structure.**

Assessment. Other strategies besides phonics help readers when they encounter an unfamiliar word. These will be addressed more fully in Chapter 10. Here we present a brief overview of these strategies. Use of each of these strategies can be assessed informally during regular reading instruction:

- *Sight words.* Words recognized at sight, without the need to apply any other decoding strategy, are known as sight words. As readers become more competent, each builds a body of words that are recognized instantly. The term *sight words* or *basic sight words,* as mentioned earlier, also refers to a given group of high-frequency words. (See the list in the Resource File.)

- *Context.* When a child uses the words surrounding an unfamiliar word to hypothesize about the target word, he or she is making use of **context.** The surrounding text may be a phrase, a sentence, a paragraph, or the entire work. Readers who are constructing meaning as they read have expectations about what words will appear in certain contexts. For example, if the story is about a zoo, the reader expects to find animal names. Thus, even if an unfamiliar animal name appears, context helps the reader at least infer that the word names an animal of some kind. A hypothesis about an unfamiliar word can then often be confirmed or rejected by applying phonics.

- *Graphics.* Any **graphics** available on the page or in the text can help a reader decode the text. Very young children often use pictures to make "guesses" about an unfamiliar word; this is a good strategy up to a point. Readers also use captions under illustrations, tables and charts, maps and other insets, and typographical aids such as boldface and underlining. All of these help to create an expectation of what kind of word might appear in the text.

- *Word structure.* Understanding of **word structure,** especially the fact that certain parts of words carry meaning, is an important decoding tool. The meaningful parts of words include prefixes and suffixes; children learn, for instance, that *un-* before a word often means "not." Word structure also includes inflected endings such as those that denote the tenses of verbs or those that denote plurals, possessives, gender, or comparisons. The child who has learned that *-ed* at the end of a word often means the past tense of an action word can apply that knowledge in figuring out an unfamiliar word.

- *Fluency.* Once students begin to read, you will want to assess their fluency. This can best be done by having children read aloud from a text that they are able to read and noting whether they are reading smoothly and accurately. You should always ask students to tell you what they have read to make sure they comprehend the material. Around the middle of grade 1, begin to compare students' word accuracy on a timed one-minute read using the criteria presented in Table 9.1. These criteria are based on the research of Hasbrouck and Tindal (1992, 2006) and Good and Kaminski (2002).

TABLE 9.1

End-of-Year Grade-Level Criteria for Reading Rate and Accuracy

GRADE LEVEL	END-OF-YEAR READING FLUENCY RATES: ACCURATELY READ WORDS PER MINUTE
1	70–90
2	80–100
3	100–120
4	110–130
5	120–140

Instructional Strategies. The ultimate goal of learning all of these skills and strategies for the student is to develop fluency (Cooper, Chard, & Kiger, 2006). If children are not using these decoding strategies when appropriate or are using them inefficiently, provide direct and explicit instruction using routines presented in Chapter 6. The routines that are particularly helpful are the decodable words routine, the phonetically unpredictable words routine, and the fluency routine. Keep in mind that these strategies are best practiced during meaningful reading experiences.

COMMENTS

Skilled readers use each of these strategies to varying degrees. Emergent readers benefit from having them taught and reinforced as they engage in the appropriate reading and writing activities in any Comprehensive Balanced Literacy Day. Being taught how to approach unfamiliar words helps children build fluency and confidence in their ability to become independent readers and writers.

We believe that meaning must always be central in children's minds as they read; therefore, the first thought about an unfamiliar word probably should be "What would make sense here?" Then children should think about the familiar parts of the word such as endings and prefixes, apply phonics if needed, and confirm that the word fits the context.

☐ The student is constructing meaning.

- Can retell a story page by page
- Can summarize

Assessment. The most authentic way to assess a child's construction of meaning is during actual reading experiences rather than with a test of some kind. As you conduct literacy lessons and minilessons, you will learn which children are struggling to construct meaning. What you learn then changes how you plan your next literacy lesson or minilesson.

Some techniques described in Chapter 3 are particularly useful for assessing construction of meaning: retelling or summarizing, discussion, and personal written responses.

Ask children individually to retell (or summarize) a story or other text as they page through a book. Use a book they have heard read aloud. Children at this stage can look at the pictures, and perhaps part of the print, and tell you what went on during each part of the story. They remember the characters, setting, and events. They can tell you how the story ended. If the text was expository, they can tell you the important ideas and some of the details. This retelling response gives you an idea of children's understanding of story structure or expository structure and usually of whether they can relate the content to their own lives.

Instructional Strategies. You help children learn to construct meaning as they read by providing good basic instruction. The following routines, all of which you read about in Chapter 6, are important:

- Provide the blocks of time necessary for complete literacy learning.
- Use the various modes of reading: teacher read-aloud, shared reading, guided reading, cooperative/collaborative reading, and independent reading.
- Plan and carry out literacy lessons.
- When needed, plan and carry out minilessons.
- Use the explicit comprehension routine when appropriate.
- Provide for response to reading through discussion and writing.

Make retelling part of your daily instructional activities. As you talk with children during shared reading and during and after read-alouds, engage them in recalling and retelling story elements and information from informational text. Encourage personal responses, tying story events to the children's experiences. Encourage broader and deeper thinking through modeling and prompting.

> **▣ The student is constructing meaning (continued).**
>
> - Participates in small-group and whole-class discussions about books and stories
> - Talks about books with others
> - Responds to books in writing
> - Begins to see self as a reader

Assessment. Observe which children talk about the books and stories they have been listening to and reading. For example, note the child who recommends a book to another child or snags another child to listen to a retelling.

At the same time, note how children are participating in group and class discussions. Which children participate willingly, staying focused but sharing personal responses to the story or topic? Which children never participate? Are they shy? Have others ridiculed their ideas in the past? Do they lack background experience for the concepts in the story? Were they not participating during the read-aloud or shared reading? In other words, lack of participation in a discussion may not have a single explanation. Keep looking.

Note which children respond to books in writing. Children who are responding to stories in personal ways always will have something to say. At first, their responses may include or be limited to drawing a picture. They may also keep a log of books they have read, create a response journal in which they record feelings about books they are listening to or reading, write a play, or write an innovation—a new version using the same pattern. Note, too, whether children tell you, "I can read."

Instructional Strategies. If children are not talking about books and stories with each other and in discussion groups, search for a reason. It may have nothing to do with reading but rather with the social dynamics of your class. Establish a climate in which all ideas are valued, while at the same time modeling how to stay focused on the book under discussion and on related experiences. Second-language learners will benefit from very small discussion groups. Sometimes try going around the group and asking each child for a quick response; this may draw out the shy child who will not volunteer.

Even though your students may not yet be able to read, you may want to post some discussion guidelines on which you all agree, such as these:

DISCUSSION GUIDELINES

1. Take turns.
2. Don't talk while someone else is talking.
3. It's okay to disagree, but not to argue.
4. Speak loudly enough for everyone to hear.
5. When you say something about someone else's ideas, talk to that person—not to the teacher.
6. Never say anything bad about anyone else's ideas.

When necessary, you can refer to the chart and read the pertinent item aloud. Continue to show by word and deed that responses to a story are personal and important. Share your own written responses to your own reading. Provide time for children to respond in writing to what they are reading. When you respond to children's written responses, comment on content, not mechanics. If the child writes, "Ths wuz a gd bok," don't correct the spelling. Just say something like "I'm so glad you loved the book. It was a favorite of mine when I was a child." Second-language learners should be encouraged to write in any language or in a mixture of English and their first language. Help all children see themselves as readers even though they may not yet know every word.

Figure 9.2 presents a group checklist for all the Emergent Literacy reading benchmarks.

Reading Checklist:
Emergent Literacy Stage

Teacher _____ Date _____ Grade _____

Students

+ = consistently present
− = not present
✓ = somewhat present; recheck

Benchmark										
Early Emergent Literacy Behaviors										
Concepts About Print										
Handles book correctly										
Points: a word, two, a letter, two										
Knows print matches voice										
Knows book parts										
Using Print in Everyday Life										
Locates specific book										
Recognizes some environmental print										
Decoding Skills: Letters and Words										
Recognizes and names most letters										
Matches upper- and lower-case letters										
Recognizes and names some words										
Recognizes own name and others										
Phonemic Awareness and Alphabetic Principle										
Phonics										
Other Decoding Strategies–build fluency:										
Sight Words										
Context										
Graphics										
Word structure										
Constructs Meaning										
Retells stories										
Summarizes										
Discusses										
Talks about books										
Responds in writing										
Begins to see self as reader										

FIGURE 9.2

Sample Class Checklist for Emergent Literacy: Reading Benchmarks and Behaviors

COMMENTS

You may be used to thinking of meaning construction as *comprehension,* a term that traditionally refers to several discrete skills, such as knowing the main idea, significant details, supporting details, sequence, and cause and effect; drawing conclusions; and distinguishing between fact and opinion. If you use a published reading program, you may find lessons devoted to these separate skills. If you teach such lessons, be sure children integrate their learning into the whole act of constructing meaning. Isolated performance of skills is not enough.

Writing: Indicators, Assessment, Instructional Strategies

As with reading, you will determine if children are at this stage in writing by examining their work and by observing and listening to them as they work. Some information can be gleaned as you observe and work with children in groups or as a whole class. Some is best gathered in individual conferences. We address the following areas in this section:

- Continued development of the Early Emergent Literacy behaviors
- Awareness of spelling and other conventions
- Phonemic awareness
- Sound/symbol association
- Purposes of writing
- Familiarity with the writing process
- Ability to construct meaning

A class checklist (Figure 9.3) appears near the end of the section.

> **The student exhibits continued growth in many of the Early Emergent Literacy behaviors.**

All of the assessment and instructional strategies presented in Chapter 8 continue to be appropriate for children at this stage and beyond.

> **The student knows and writes his or her name and some letters and uses some other writing conventions.**
>
> - Can write own name (perhaps first name only), with all or most of the letters present, though not necessarily formed correctly
> - Can name most letters in random presentation
> - Forms letterlike shapes and some correct letters
> - Uses some punctuation

Assessment. On the first day of school, you can ask children to write their names if they already know how. Tell those who say they cannot that you will help them. Often teachers have premade name cards ready for children to use as a model to copy their names, but first ascertain which children can write their names without copying.

An assessment with alphabet cards, as described earlier in the reading section, will quickly tell you whether students can name letters. Examine children's writing wherever it occurs—on drawings, in journals, in assigned papers. Which children are writing some correct letters and shapes that look like letters? Note, too, which children are putting down some kind of mark to indicate the boundaries of their thoughts. Many children will be using periods at this stage. Some may become especially fond of exclamation points once they discover them.

Instructional Strategies. Names are important. Children should learn to write their own names as soon as possible. Provide models for the children to copy. Regardless of the sequence in which you intend to teach letter formation, help each child learn to write the letters in his or her own name. Gently help children to reform incorrectly formed letters. Remember that children at this stage frequently write letters backward or stroke in a different direction from what you will teach. For most children, this will straighten out in good time; intervention is seldom necessary.

For the formation of letters, the same kinds of activities and games described earlier for reading will help the child in writing. Teaching of punctuation will take place informally every time you write in front of the children, when you discuss morning messages and other collaborative writing, and when you revisit big books. At this stage, we do not believe isolated explicit lessons on punctuation are needed, but we do urge frequent, repetitive commentary, first from you and then from the children themselves.

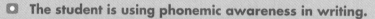

O The student is using phonemic awareness in writing.

- Is using sound/symbol association in writing
- Can give a letter sound or say a word that begins with the letter sound

Assessment. Earlier in the chapter, we discussed phonemic awareness and letter sound connections as decoding skills for reading. Evidence of the use of phonemic awareness to aid in writing is available from two sources: a child's self-talk as he or she writes and the product that results from writing.

1. *Self-talk.* Sit with children individually as they write. Listen to what they say to themselves. You may hear them segment sounds and see them write a letter or a shape to represent each sound as they say the word. This ability will increase as children's literacy grows. Gradually, as they learn both the names of letters and the sounds associated with letters, they will put their ability to segment the sounds in a word together with letter-sound knowledge and move toward conventional spelling.

2. *Product.* As you read what a child has written, segment the sounds in your mind to see if a letter (or letterlike form) has been used to represent each sound. Review the stages of spelling development described in Chapter 3. You will note whether phonemic awareness is demonstrated at all, once or twice, or most of the time. Remember that awareness of separate sounds and acquisition of the alphabetic principle—that letters represent sounds—may precede knowledge of which letters represent which sounds. Here you need to note whether a child is "getting the hang" of how the system works.

Instructional Strategies. Good basic teaching of the sort described in Chapter 8, along with your regular curriculum related to introducing letter names, sounds, and the association between the two, will be sufficient for most children. Children who are not acquiring phonemic awareness as expected will need additional and specific instruction. As you write on transparencies or the chalkboard, encourage children to help you segment sounds, decide which letter(s) to associate with the sounds, and then write those letters. As you circulate while children write, guide them to use their growing knowledge of the alphabetic principle to segment words into sounds and write letters for sounds.

The term *invented spelling* refers to this very process. It is not guessing. On the contrary, it is the thoughtful invention of an unknown word's probable spelling using one's ability to segment words into separate sounds, and one's knowledge of which letters are associated with which sounds. All writers "invent" spelling whenever they write words they are not sure how to spell; some may look up and verify spelling as they write, though many save this process for the editing step. To use a dictionary for spelling, of course, one must first have been able to invent a likely spelling.

COMMENTS

Some children for whom English is a second language may have already begun attempting to spell in their first language. It is likely that spelling knowledge in another language may not develop in the same way it does for native English speakers (Freeman & Freeman, 2001).

The student is using writing for own purposes.

- Can keep a journal that may combine drawing and writing
- Shows interest in practicing writing, often through copying favorite stories from books
- Shares writing with others
- Attempts to read others' writing

Assessment. You may encourage children to keep a journal in which they do personal writing, though at first this may be largely pictures. Note which children willingly comply with this request and show increased interest in expressing personal thoughts and events in writing. You may also notice that some children practice writing by copying favorite stories and poems from books.

Also note whether children are willing to share their writing when you ask for volunteers. No child should be made to read from a personal journal, of course. Note whether a child who might not read aloud to the entire class will share with a friend. At the same time, note which children are attempting to read what others have written, whether by published authors or classmates. Such attempts indicate that the child has grasped that just as he or she can record ideas, so can others—and that all writers share the same system of using symbols (letters) to record words.

Instructional Strategies. You can encourage personal writing by modeling it daily: share your own journal writing with your students. Support their efforts by reading and responding to their journals frequently. This need not be daunting; if you have thirty children, you can easily read and respond to six journals each day, thus reading all journals once a week.

Many children enjoy practicing the physical act of writing as they gain control over their eye-hand coordination. Children need a great deal of practice forming letters, and they may as well gain some of it by copying favorite stories or poems. As they do so, they will also absorb something about the art of composition. Just as wonderful language can be anchored in the ears of a listener, it can also become anchored through copying.

Point out to children that the same words they are using as they write are in the writing of others. As they learn to read their own words, they will also be able to read the words others write.

Sharing writing is risky, as many successful authors will testify, because when you share your thoughts, you expose yourself. Therefore, we believe no child should be required to share personal writing. However, you should encourage sharing of nonpersonal writing such as reports or stories. Many teachers have a special chair, labeled **Author's Chair.** (See the Author's Chair websites listed on the website accompanying this book or input "author's chair" in a search engine.) Children who are ready to share are invited to sit in the special chair as they read aloud and then receive comments and questions from their audience.

> ### ▢ The student is becoming familiar with the writing process.
>
> - Uses the steps of the process appropriately with guidance
> - Understands that the author of what is read has also gone through a process of some kind

Assessment. As you do shared and collaborative writing with children, note which ones are becoming comfortable with the process used for creative writing: generating ideas, making a rough draft, revising, editing, and publishing. Children at this stage may not yet do much independent revising and editing, but they are beginning to understand the process that leads to a finished piece of writing.

Instructional Strategies. Continue to model, demonstrate, guide, and teach the processes used to produce a publishable piece of writing (as opposed to journal writing, logs, lists, and so forth). Use the minilesson format to teach and reteach each part of the process. For example, you may devote several lessons to generating ideas or brainstorming. When children are becoming comfortable with generating ideas, you can begin to present minilessons on producing a rough draft, then revising, then editing, and finally producing a "publishable" piece of writing.

Help children accept that writing is hard work that few people get perfect on the first try—and that it is worth the hard work. There is more about the process of writing in upcoming chapters. Try to find information about how authors write, and read it aloud to children or paraphrase if it is difficult to understand. Many children's authors maintain websites that include information about their lives as well as their writing.

> **◻ The student is constructing meaning in writing.**
>
> - Responds to reading
> - Composes both narrative and expository pieces
> - Expresses and reports on personal events and feelings

Assessment. Readers use information from the text and their own background experiences to assign meaning to a text. They must monitor their thinking, pay attention to their purposes, and understand the text structure. Similarly, writers construct meaning to tell a story or present information in an organized fashion or to express a personal response to something internal or external. Writers also are aware of audience. In other words, much the same kinds of thinking are needed both for reading and for writing.

As children engage in writing tasks, those of their own choosing as well as those you have assigned, you assess their success in constructing meaning by talking with them as they write, examining their efforts, helping them revise, and evaluating their final products.

Instructional Strategies. As with reading, children learn to write by doing it frequently and by receiving good basic guidance and instruction. Examining their writing, including their written responses to reading, should help you determine what instruction they need to improve their ability to construct meaning as they write.

For example, if a child's story is disorganized, with no clear sequence of events, you need to help the child evaluate his or her own work and then teach how to plan and write something in which the sequence of events is clear to the reader. If several children show the same need, you can teach a minilesson to a small group.

With English-language learners, apparently unorganized writing may reflect a different cultural writing pattern than that of English. Children may get ideas started by first engaging in a peer conference in their home language. Then, perhaps with help from the teacher, a friend, or a volunteer, they can rephrase their ideas into English. If several different cultures are represented in your classroom, you probably won't be able to familiarize yourself with the writing patterns of each, but do be aware that differences exist. Provide support as you help students move toward the patterns and forms needed to communicate in English.

As we've said before, many problems may be the result of inadequate teaching. When you find problems with children's assigned writing, again ask yourself some questions:

1. Was the assignment or task clear?
2. Was the assignment or task reasonable for these children?
3. Did I model what I wanted the children to do?
4. Did I provide enough guided practice?
5. What are the particular problem areas (for example, had no clear purpose, lacked a sense of audience, did not stick to topic, omitted one or more story elements, did not support ideas, drew no conclusion)?
6. What do I need to do next?

There is more to teaching writing than what we have discussed here, of course. Beyond these broad aspects of writing are many other important considerations, such as sentence construction, choice of words, misuse or overuse of adjectives and adverbs, tone, mood, color, and research.

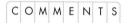

COMMENTS

As you look at a child's written work to judge construction of meaning, you may also note instructional needs in the area of mechanics, conventions, and usage. Do not, however, equate ability in those areas with ability to construct meaning. A child may have advanced ability in those areas but write in a disorganized fashion. On the other hand, a child may write a beautifully cohesive piece that has many problems with conventions. Some children, of course, are skillful at both and some at neither.

Figure 9.3 presents a group checklist for all the writing benchmarks.

Planning Instruction Based on Assessment

This section is arranged around two major concerns: planning the day and meeting individual and group needs in your Comprehensive Balanced Literacy Program.

Within each day, you will provide a classroom environment in which literacy can flourish and a time for literacy instruction, practice, and application. Throughout the day, you will continue to assess children, often while in the act of teaching. On the

Writing Checklist:
Emergent Literacy Stage

Teacher_____   Date_____   Grade_____

Students

+ = consistently present
- = not present
✓ = sometimes present/needs instruction

Benchmark

Early Emergent Literacy Behaviors

Spelling and Other Conventions
Writes own name
Names most letters
Forms letter-like shapes/letters
Uses some punctuation

Phonemic Awareness in Writing

Sound/Symbol Association in Writing
Gives letter sound or says word with the sounds

Purposes of Writing
Keeps a journal
Practices writing
Shares writing with others
Attempts to read others' writing

Writing Process
Uses steps
Knows all authors have used a process

Constructing Meaning
Responds to reading
Composes narrative and exposition
Expresses/reports personal events and feelings

FIGURE 9.3

Sample Class Checklist for Emergent Literacy: Writing Benchmarks and Behaviors

basis of that continual assessment, you will be able to select appropriate routines, techniques, and materials to meet the needs of both individuals and groups, including children with special needs.

Planning a Comprehensive Balanced Literacy Day for Kindergarten or First Grade

We address three areas related to planning the balanced literacy day for kindergarten and first grade: the comprehensive balanced classroom, the blocked schedule, and continuous assessment.

THE COMPREHENSIVE BALANCED CLASSROOM

Children at the Emergent Literacy stage need the same print-rich, language-rich environment as those at the previous stage. The materials, tools, furniture, and overall physical arrangement of your classroom are all important.

Materials, Tools, and Furniture. Materials, tools, and furniture at this stage of literacy development look very much like those described for the previous stage, with just a few differences. You may not have a sand or water table in your kindergarten and almost certainly will not have either in a first grade. All of the same reading and writing materials need to be available, however, and you may want to add ruled paper as children become ready to use it in writing.

By first grade, children may have individual desks or at least tables and chairs. We know of one first-grade teacher who accommodated her children's preferences by lowering one or two large tables so that some children could sit or kneel on the floor as they worked on the table surface. Tables were left at regular height for those children who preferred sitting on chairs.

Physical Arrangement. The physical arrangement of the room will depend on factors such as available cubbies, shelves, display tables, chalkboards, and sinks. What you have in your classroom matters less than what you do with what you have.

Children need a classroom that is inviting and comfortable. They need places where they can work independently without being disturbed, as well as places where groups can collaborate. You need at least one table at which a group can meet. There should also be a place where the whole class can gather to listen to a story or discuss a news item. You'll want to have a place for animals, plants, and science experiments. You need listening posts, computer stations, and centers to meet your curriculum needs. You need a place to display work—walls are not enough. Hang things from the ceiling or clip them to miniblinds if you need to.

Your classroom will be unique: a combination of what is available for you to work with, the size and arrangement of the room, your own ideas of what will work, and your children's wishes. However your room is arranged, it should work for the children. They should know where everything is and, after guidelines are established, be able to function with increasing independence.

THE BLOCKED SCHEDULE

Recall from Chapter 6 that the Comprehensive Balanced Literacy Program is based on blocks of time allocated to three major areas: independent reading and writing, instruction, and intervention as needed. The amount of time allocated to each block and the nature of the activities will vary as children move along the continuum of literacy development. We will discuss the blocks as they look in kindergarten and first grade for children who are at the Emergent Literacy stage. You may need to make alternative arrangements for kindergartners or first graders who are not yet at this stage or are at a subsequent stage.

How much time you devote to your literacy program may depend in part on your school system's requirements. We suggest a minimum amount of time for each block, but scheduling is flexible. Some days you may devote more time to one block and less to another. However, remember that literacy development occurs best in an environment that balances instruction with opportunities for independent reading and writing and provides for these every single day.

Later in this chapter, you will read more about routines, techniques, and materials that are appropriate for this stage. The section "Two Classrooms at Work" suggests both a kindergarten schedule and a first-grade schedule and presents possible activities for each segment of the day.

There are two blocks devoted to independent reading and writing:

Daily Independent Reading. During this time, children choose books that interest them. They also select books for fluency practice; these books should be ones that have been used for instruction. Group books by topic to help children make selections. Quiet time for independent reading at this stage may not be entirely quiet. These children often talk to themselves as they look at books.

Some teachers allow partners to look at books together during this time in kindergarten. You could also schedule individual children to listening stations during this period.

Teachers who read to themselves during this time are providing a powerful message about the pleasure of reading. However, you may also use part of this block to hold individual conferences with children. The Daily Independent Reading block should be at least 10 minutes each day.

Daily Independent Writing. A second block of time is allocated for any writing that the children choose to do. Again, you may spend some of this block doing your own writing and part of it holding individual conferences with children. The Daily Independent Writing block should be at least 10 minutes each day.

COMMENTS

It takes some time to establish independent reading and writing behavior with children in kindergarten and first grade. Don't expect the process to work perfectly at the beginning of the year. You may begin with very short blocks, perhaps only 5 minutes in kindergarten. Gradually expand the blocks as children become able to sustain independent work for a longer period of time.

Talk with the children about what they will be doing during each block. Collaborate to draw up guidelines. Rehearse and role-play such things as the following:

* Responding to a signal that independent reading (or writing time) is beginning, such as playing a classical music tape or CD.
* Behavior during the block: do not bother anyone else, don't talk out loud, don't walk around.
* What to do if . . . (for instance, I need to use the bathroom or I finished my book). Bathroom routines will vary. If a pass is required, work out a system that does not require speaking. If a book is completed, the child should not get up to get another book but should reread the book or enter it in a reading log. This point may require further discussion later about being sure to have enough reading material on hand.
* How to behave if coming to a conference: lift chair to push in, tip-toe, don't touch anyone on the way.
* What to do when signaled that the block has ended: put materials away; stand, stretch, and wiggle; get ready for the next activity.

Figure 9.4 presents a sample chart you might post to help children remember guidelines for the Daily Independent Reading and Writing blocks.

Four blocks make up the instructional part of the Comprehensive Balanced Literacy Day:

Reading: Learning Skills and Strategies. During this block, you use routines to teach explicit lessons on strategies and skills you have determined are needed through your informal assessment. At this stage, the main needs are related to word recognition, and children will read from books specially designed to foster particular word recognition skills. These skills, which will help them become independent decoders, should also be reinforced during other blocks.

Reading: Application of Skills and Strategies. In this block, instruction is carried out with big books (and multiple small-book copies of the same book), read-alouds, shared reading, and guided reading. Students develop their ability to construct meaning by listening and then moving on to reading.

Even though some children may not yet be at the Emergent Literacy stage while others may be at the Beginning Reading and Writing stage or beyond, the same book can be used for instruction some of the time. Together you enjoy the story, predict, explore ideas, discuss literary elements, compare the story with other stories, talk about vocabulary, and examine various components of words. To accommodate the range of literacy development you may have in your group, you can use multilevel prompts, varying the kinds of questions and expected responses according to children's level of development. For example, after reading the big book *If You Give a Mouse a Cookie* (Numeroff, 1985, 1989), you might begin by asking children to look at the first page and tell something they

WORK ALONE

1. Begin to work.

2. Don't talk.
   Don't move around.

3. Follow rules quietly.

4. Conference? Shhh!

5. Off?
   Clean up.
   Stand and wiggle.

FIGURE 9.4

Independent Reading or Writing Chart

notice. Comments will vary depending on the children. Some comments about the words or print on page 1 ("If you give a mouse a cookie,") might include the following:

- The first word has a capital.
- The sentence isn't over because there's just a comma.

- That word (pointing to "mouse") rhymes with "house."
- The word "a" is there two times.
- The *oo* in that word ("cookie") is like the *oo* in the word "book."
- The *ou* in "you" sounds different from the *ou* in "mouse."
- I can hear three sounds in the word "give."

Children need practice in generating these kinds of observations. Begin by modeling and then invite comments. Make it part of your routine. You can also direct observations for particular children:

- You might turn to page 6 and ask Miguel to come up. "Point to all the words on this page that begin with the same first letter as your name," you tell him (the words being "mirror," "make," "milk," and "mustache"). "Now use your two first fingers and frame that letter and tell us its name."
- On page 8, you might ask Susie to "find a word that rhymes with 'deep'" ("sweep").
- You might ask Jonah to explain what the author means on page 9 when she says, "He might get carried away and . . ." (this requires understanding of figurative language).
- Melissa might be asked to explain how the picture of a refrigerator on page 23 helps a reader predict that the word on the next page probably has something to do with eating or drinking something.
- You might ask Greg to respond to the question "How do we know how the mouse liked the story? Read the page that tells us" (page 15).

No matter where each child is on the literacy continuum, every one of them can participate in this book experience. During this block, you may occasionally form groups of children with like needs. Such groups are changed frequently as needs change. This block is 15 minutes or more.

Writing: Learning to Write. You may alternate between this block and the Writing: Developmentally Appropriate Writing block, teaching a lesson one day and then allowing several days for children to work on the type of writing you taught. You teach several related aspects of literacy concurrently:

- You demonstrate a particular type of writing. As you do so, you help children understand aspects of genre, audience, text structure, and story elements, as well as style and tone. You may simply model writing or combine modeling with collaborating. For example, you may demonstrate writing a circular story such as the one you just read. As you progress, children may contribute so that the task becomes collaborative.
- You teach the grammar and spelling needed for the writing. While you may teach separate grammar and spelling lessons during another part of the day, here children discover how these lessons are applied. For example, as you first model and then guide collaborative story writing, you verbalize that you begin each sentence with an upper-case letter and end each sentence with a period.
- You reinforce the phonic and structural patterns the children are learning in reading. Such learning is useful in both reading and writing. As you write, verbalize about how you choose certain letters to represent certain sounds

and about how many sounds a word has. For example: "Our story is about a cat. How many sounds can we hear in the word 'cat'? What letter can I use for each sound?"

- At the Emergent Literacy stage, you are also teaching children about letter formation: handwriting. During this block, you can reinforce the importance of careful letter formation in communication: "Watch how I write the letter *t;* I start here, just above this line, and move the chalk down to the base line. Then I cross the *t* here. Notice that the letter is not slanted and that I left just a tiny bit of space after the *a*—not as much as between words."

Be careful not to overdo verbalization as you do collaborative writing with children. Be selective, calling attention most often to skills that have most recently been taught or that you have learned need reinforcement.

Writing: Developmentally Appropriate Writing. During this block, you assign the type of writing that has recently been taught, though students may choose their own topics. For example, you might assign children to write a friendly letter following a lesson on that form, but you would not tell them to whom the letter should go or what the content should be. The extent of the writing task is adjusted to individual abilities. This may mean that one child is directed to write "one good sentence," while another is directed to "draw a picture and tell me what you want to say about it; I'll write it for you," and still another is asked, "How many pages do you think your letter will be?"

COMMENTS

If we expect children to write competently and with pleasure, we must begin in the early grades. The two instructional writing blocks in the Comprehensive Balanced Literacy Program ensure that ample time is given to writing. Children come to see writing as a normal part of every day.

Though these two blocks are designated as instructional periods, children will write during other times of the day as well, such as during the Daily Independent Writing block. They may also write in journals first thing in the morning, collaborate on writing morning messages, write reports for science or social studies, write letters to pen pals, and so forth.

For struggling readers additional instruction is needed through intervention:

Intervention. As we emphasized earlier, intervention is in addition to (not instead of) the daily literacy blocks just described. These programs may be pullout, in-class, or extended day. They may be delivered by you or by another qualified teacher. See the description of intervention programs and the sources in Chapter 6.

CONTINUOUS ASSESSMENT

Throughout this book, we have stressed the concept of continuous assessment, which means you use every moment of the day as an opportunity to learn about your children. Continuous assessment means adjusting the way you listen to and view children as you interact with them during daily activities. As children change from day to day, you can change your instruction accordingly.

Meeting Individual and Group Needs in Diverse Classrooms

You need to think about four areas when planning to meet the needs of individual children as well as your whole class: 1) the range of stages in your classroom, 2) the routines and techniques appropriate for the children at each stage, 3) materials to use during appropriate instruction, and 4) accommodating children with special needs. We dealt with each of these areas earlier in this book, often in several ways. Here we review the kinds of thinking necessary to incorporate these needs into your everyday classroom.

RANGE OF STAGES

You must accept that you *will* have a range in your classroom. As children grow in years, the range in any given classroom is apt to widen. Though we identify children by stage based on assessment, each child is unique—even within a stage. There are differences among children from the day they are born. These differences may be related to intellectual capacity (such as that measured on an intelligence test), to life experiences, to health, to home and neighborhood milieu, to interests, and more. Whatever the cause of the differences, you must acknowledge that they exist and accept them.

While you cannot be a private tutor to each child, you must do your best to meet individual needs. How you do that depends on allocating time for different modes of reading and writing and on building into your day time for one-on-one instruction for children who need it.

ROUTINES AND TECHNIQUES

All of the routines and techniques emphasized in Chapter 8 are appropriate at this stage as well:

1. Teacher read-alouds
2. Activities for oral language development
3. Shared reading
4. Shared writing
5. Language experience
6. Development of phonemic awareness

Additional routines and techniques from Chapter 6 are used at the Emergent Literacy stage, including these:

1. The literacy lesson
2. Minilessons
3. Explicit phonics/structural elements routines
4. Explicit comprehension routines
5. Modes of reading

6. Fluency

7. Discussion groups

8. Modes of writing

We already discussed some of these routines as we described the literacy blocks. Here we elaborate on several to illustrate typical ways of incorporating reading and writing into every day at this stage.

Modes of Writing. Most of your time with children at this stage will involve providing heavy support through teacher write-alouds and shared writing.

Shared Writing: Morning Message. We described two kinds of morning message in Chapter 7: teacher written and child dictated (collaborative). Here are two more.

Formula. Provide a pattern, or formula, for children to follow as they begin to compose morning messages themselves. For example, you may post the names of two children each day whose first task of the day is to compose the morning message. They may write on chart paper; perhaps each uses a different color felt-tip marker. They follow a pattern that you have provided, such as the following:

- Put month, day, and year in upper right-hand corner.
- Begin with "Today is . . ."
- Write about the weather.
- Write about something you heard on a news program.

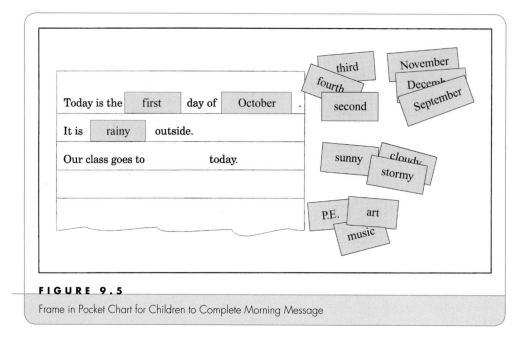

FIGURE 9.5

Frame in Pocket Chart for Children to Complete Morning Message

- Write about whatever special class is today.
- Add something personal if you want.

Frame. If children cannot yet deal independently with a formula or pattern, provide a frame for them to complete. You can photocopy frames, use a transparency, or use a pocket chart. An example is shown in Figure 9.5.

Explicit Phonics and Comprehension Routines and Minilessons. As you do literacy lessons and writing with children, you will teach explicit routines (see Chapter 6) designed to build decoding strategies and enhance the children's ability to construct meaning. Some of these lessons will be for the entire class; others may be with small groups. Most are minilessons in that they are tightly structured, focused, and quick.

Modes of Reading. Sometimes you will encourage children to use response activities after a read-aloud, a shared reading, independent reading, or developmentally appropriate reading. We know that responding to literature helps children construct meaning as well as contributes to their pleasure. The following discussion elaborates on ways to carry out some of these activities with children at this stage.

Art. Many children at this stage naturally enjoy drawing pictures to express their interests and ideas. In response to a story, they might draw their favorite part and talk about it or dictate a summary statement about it. They might also draw a character, an alternative ending, an illustration for an event that does not have a picture in the book, or something to express mood. Such visual imagery aids understanding.

Art responses might also involve clay, collage, posters, mobiles, and felt- or magnetic-backed characters and settings. The idea is to encourage children to have a personal response to a story and show that response in some way. Art responses are especially appropriate for English-language learners whose comprehension exceeds their language production.

Retelling. Retelling is part of your everyday activities related to story. The form of retelling used with expository text—summarizing—is also part of everyday instructional practice. As an individual response activity, children can retell or summarize to a partner or to you during a conference. If children have a problem with retelling, review your instructional strategies to be sure you are incorporating retelling regularly. You may need to provide a series of minilessons devoted to retelling.

Journals. Even children at the Emergent Literacy stage can keep a reading response journal. At the very least, they can record the name of the book, the author, the illustrator, and the date; these can be copied from the book and the calendar. Children can also write or draw a comment. You could begin by suggesting happy-, indifferent-, or sad-face drawings, but be sure to allow any other drawing that expresses a personal response. The children may also contribute to and refer to a word wall of possible response words and phrases from which to copy. For example, the wall might list the following:

Wonderful!	Made me sad.
Made me laugh!	Good story!
You should read it!	Good pictures.

Always tell children they may choose their own drawings or words to put in the journals if they like.

Discussion Groups. Introduce the pleasure of talking about books with a small group of friends. Whole-class discussion is not sufficient because it limits comments to only a few children, whereas a small group gives everyone an opportunity to talk. Discussion groups can fit in any of the reading blocks of the literacy program.

You will need to describe, role-play, and participate in such discussion groups until children learn to take over for themselves. By participating, we mean you will model sticking to the topic, listening to others, accepting and responding to the ideas of others, and engaging in general small-group behavior. Later you may continue to sit in from time to time, sometimes participating and guiding and sometimes observing and assessing.

Role Playing and Puppets. Before children are capable of actually writing a script and reading it (see the discussion of Readers Theater in Chapter 12), role-playing or puppets can serve as a way to respond to a story. Children assign parts and act out major events of a story. This is an informal activity, entirely carried out by the children for their own pleasure, though they may choose to show it to classmates who have not read the story. Limit the time spent on this response. Remember that children's growth in literacy is the direct result of time spent actually reading and writing.

Debate. Most debate is highly structured and follows specific guidelines. With children at the Emergent Literacy stage, this is neither possible nor desirable. Instead, introduce children to the notion of dealing with different views about an informational piece or a story. You might begin with an issue that has two clear sides to it—for example, school uniforms. Survey children and count how many are on each side. Work with each side to develop and record points to support the children's views.

SELECTION OF MATERIALS

As you gather material for use in your classroom, you may find that some decisions have already been made for you. Your school system may dictate not only the philosophy you are expected to espouse but also the materials you are expected to use. Even so, you can supplement any program with both authentic literature and decodable text for children at the Emergent Literacy stage. You will need abundant examples of both authentic literature and decodable text.

Authentic Literature. Authentic literature, as you recall, refers to any text in its original form, whether narrative, expository, or procedural. It may be used in any reading block.

For children at this stage, authentic literature that is appropriate in content is most likely found in picture books; children can enjoy these even without reading the text, or you can read them aloud. However, you may also have children who are at one of the next stages, so you need to provide books for these children to read as well.

Authentic literature will be available in your classroom in big books, literature sets (class sets), trade books, including books in other language, and anthologies that are part of a published program (sometimes referred to as *basals*). Note that some published programs include rewritten or edited versions of authentic text, and others include decodable text.

Decodable Text. Decodable text, written specifically to apply a sequence of decoding elements and high-frequency words, is particularly useful with emergent and beginning readers and writers, since it provides practice and helps children build fluency. Decodable texts are different from predictable texts in that predictable texts repeat a pattern or refrain. Decodable text is available in these forms:

* *Literature sets, either for classes or for small groups.* Several publishers offer short books, some only eight or sixteen pages long, with limited words per page and colorful illustrations. Some limit the words to those of high frequency. Some focus on a particular phonic element, such as /-ar/; such a story might be about a "farm" with a "barn," and so on. These books allow children to develop independence in decoding unfamiliar words in stories that contain many words with the same phonic element.

* *Anthologies.* Some publishers offer a series of anthologies of stories with controlled vocabulary and other decoding control.

* *Trade books.* Some trade books (that is, books not published especially for schools) stress controlled vocabulary or limited phonics elements.

COMMENTS

Make books accessible; this means putting them where children can reach them and return them easily. Some teachers keep plastic tubs of books on each group of desks or in the centers of large tables. These tubs usually contain books children may choose to use during Daily Independent Reading, though they may also contain developmentally appropriate books such as decodable texts.

You may borrow books from the school media center or the public library so that you can make them available in your classroom during a certain unit. For example, you may gather books about reptiles, stars, the ocean, or different cultures. These become part of your library temporarily. Your media specialist can help you build your library of authentic literature. At the same time, you need to keep reading new books at your library as well as reviews of new children's literature in journals and newspapers and online. For children at the Emergent Literacy stage, you'll want wonderful illustrations and content that interests your children even though they cannot yet read the words. These books can be read aloud by you, by aides or volunteers, or by older reading buddies.

Be sure there are books available that represent all the diverse ethnic and cultural backgrounds of your students as well as different family groups. Readers want books that reflect their own experiences. At the same time, such books can help students begin to learn about one another and about cultures different from their own. An excellent source for books written in English and Spanish is *Bilingual Children's Books in English and Spanish* (Dale, 2002).

STUDENTS WHO REQUIRE SPECIAL ATTENTION

In your kindergarten or first-grade class, you may have some children who need special attention. Here we look at three broad categories of such children: those with exceptional gifts; those with special physical, emotional, or intellectual needs; and those who are second-language learners.

Gifted Children. Schools may give less attention to children who can read beyond the expected stage than to those who seem at risk for falling behind. Yet the child in your kindergarten or first-grade classroom who already reads fluently also deserves appropriate instruction. Such children should still participate in the Daily Independent Reading and Writing blocks and may be very happy as part of group instruction with grade-level materials. After all, even though they read fluently, they are still only five or six years old. During the other reading blocks, they may be content to be a "group of one." Sometimes such children spend part of each day in another teacher's classroom with readers who are at the same literacy development stage. This is a fine solution only if everyone concerned, including the child, agrees.

Children with Special Physical, Emotional, or Intellectual Needs. You will need to consult specialists in your school system for ways to adjust your classroom literacy program to accommodate special physical, emotional, or intellectual needs.

The accommodations may include such items as large-print books for children with visual impairments, special microphones for those with hearing disabilities, tables that allow for wheelchairs, and communication devices for children who cannot use typical writing tools or whose speech is unintelligible. While such children may receive help outside your classroom for some of the day, they remain a part of your class.

You may find you can deal with most children who seem to be "not catching on" by giving rigorous attention to informal assessment followed by instruction that targets their needs. In other words, now is the time to deal with children who are struggling. The whole concept of Response to Intervention is that you do not wait for a serious lag to develop and then rely on special classes or teachers to try to compensate. With a sound RTI plan you will prevent many students from failing by providing them instruction that will help them learn and catch up immediately.

Whatever your assessment has revealed as behavior not yet present or not consistently present, that's where you need to focus your attention. For the whole class or a small group, this is often best done in the normal course of delivering a Comprehensive Balanced Literacy Program during the literacy lesson or during minilessons. What you emphasize in your class must make sense in terms of the particular children you teach. For example, you may need to spend more time on oral language development in one school than in another or provide more explicit instruction in helping children hear sounds and connect letters with those sounds.

Be a thoughtful user of school-dictated programs and materials. No program is an exact fit for every child. You must adjust instruction and materials to fit the particular needs of the children in your class. Your most important job is not "covering" a set of materials or a set of skills; rather, it is getting to know each child and adjusting materials and instruction to fit his or her needs.

Second-Language Learners. Many of the activities that support the acquisition of English are also appropriate for all children who are acquiring literacy. With children at the Emergent Literacy stage who are in kindergarten or first grade, much daily activity is oral, such as building vocabulary and developing phonemic awareness. Keep in mind, though, the wide variety of profiles that second-language learners may present when they come to your class: from absolutely no English to conversational English. Some may already exhibit many benchmark behaviors of the Emergent Literacy stage; some may not. Some may have begun to acquire English vocabulary while their oral speech still reflects the sounds of their first language, making phonemic awareness of English more difficult for them. In fact, some may have sounds in their first language that don't even exist in English. They face greater cognitive demands when asked to develop literacy skills at the same time they are wrestling with acquiring oral language.

Though many views exist about the best way to teach ELLs, it is dangerous to generalize about them. No single approach can meet the needs of this diverse group. Chamot and O'Malley (1994) found, after examining the research of many others, that most instructional suggestions for ELLs are the same as for any group of learners, though you may need more variety and adaptation. It will help—as it does with all children—if you can relate the materials you use to each child's cultural background and experiences. We believe you must not wait for English proficiency to develop. Just begin including the children in all activities. Your native English-speaking children will help you.

Two Classrooms at Work

To illustrate many of the suggestions made in this chapter, we give brief descriptions of the schedule and the daily activities in two classrooms: first, Mrs. Bullock's kindergarten, featured at the beginning of the chapter, and then a first-grade classroom.

Kindergarten

The kindergarten schedule varies from school to school, but it always contains literacy blocks similar to those in the preschool schedule presented for Early Emergent Literacy. Table 9.2 shows Mrs. Bullock's daily schedule for her half-day kindergarten. This is only one possible way to arrange a day.

In the following descriptions, you will see that many of the activities are similar to those in the preschool classroom presented in Chapter 8. Remember, too, that literacy learning takes place during the entire school day, even when the schedule shows another subject such as science or math.

7:45–8:00: Arrival; check-in; personal journals. Mrs. Bullock encourages her children to write in personal journals each morning as soon as they have checked in. When they swarm about her trying to tell her something, she simply puts a finger to her lips and says, "Tell me in your journal." Children often begin by rereading previous entries in

TABLE 9.2

Daily Schedule for Mrs. Bullock's Kindergarten, a Half-Day Program with Literacy Blocks

7:45–8:00	Arrival; check-in; personal journals
8:00–8:30	Reading: Application of Skills and Strategies
8:30–8:45	Daily Independent Writing
8:45–9:15	Special classes (art, music, PE)
9:15–9:30	Bathroom/snack/morning message
9:30–9:45	Daily Independent Reading
9:45–10:30	Math/science/social studies/centers
10:30–11:00	Writing: Learning to Write/Developmentally Appropriate Writing
11:00–11:30	Reading: Learning Skills and Strategies
11:30–12:00	Clean-up; story, song, finger play; dismissal

their journals. They also read the comments Mrs. Bullock has written. They are free to talk softly to a partner as they work to decode Mrs. Bullock's words.

8:00–8:30: Reading: Application of Skills and Strategies. The children gather on the rug for a literacy lesson using a big book. Say this is their second day of reading with *If You Give a Mouse a Cookie* (Numeroff, 1985, 1989). The children begin by retelling the story. Then they reread it, with many children chiming in confidently at various points as others silently follow Mrs. Bullock's pointer. They discuss how the story made them feel and talk about the techniques the author used to make them feel that way. Mrs. Bullock then begins a literacy lesson with a new book. Children make predictions based on the cover and title. Mrs. Bullock does a picture wall. These activities with the new book will continue the next day.

8:30–8:45: Daily Independent Writing. The children know that independent writing comes next. As they return to their seats, they take individual folders from the plastic tub on each table. Each child works on a writing task of his or her own choosing. Mrs. Bullock always begins the period by taking out her own writing folder to model the importance of daily writing.

After all the children are working, she holds two 5-minute individual conferences. In these conferences, she may discuss writing folders or reading logs, or she may do a brief individual assessment.

8:45–9:15: Special classes (art, music, PE). When a timer goes off, the children know they should put their writing folders away and get ready to go to whichever special class takes place that day.

9:15–9:30: Bathroom/snack/morning message. Children gather on the rug at the front of the room to go over the morning message, which has been written on chart paper.

Early in the year, Mrs. Bullock treats the morning message as a big book, moving her pointer under the words as she reads them. She guides the children to note features of written text such as upper- and lower-case letters, the date, and punctuation. She reinforces identification of letters and associated sounds and leads the children to segment sounds.

Mrs. Bullock writes the message herself at the beginning of the year. As she finds some children who are moving out of this stage and into Beginning Reading and Writing, she encourages the children to take over this task. If children are doing the morning message, they use the first block of time in the morning as other children write in personal journals.

9:30–9:45: Daily Independent Reading. To signal that the Daily Independent Reading block is beginning, Mrs. Bullock starts a tape playing some Bach *Two-Part Inventions.* The children settle down to read. At the beginning of the school year, the children did not yet know what was expected of them during this block, so Mrs. Bullock spent several days discussing, modeling, and guiding. She developed behavior guidelines with the children and created a poster that uses words and pictures to show the children what to do.

For the first couple of weeks, Mrs. Bullock chose and distributed a book to each child. She set the timer for 5 minutes. The children were to look at (read) their books until the timer rang. Then she collected the books.

When the children were comfortable with that routine, Mrs. Bullock began putting tubs of books on each table. The children selected a book when they arrived in the morning and put a marker in it with their name. They were thus able to begin reading promptly when the Bach music began. Eventually, the children were taught to choose a book from any shelf, put a marker in it, and put it at their places for Daily Independent Reading time. Some children began to choose two books.

Gradually, Mrs. Bullock extended the time until, by the end of the year, the children read independently for 15 minutes. Mrs. Bullock allows children to talk softly with a friend during this time because she values the importance of sharing books with friends. Even when her children are able to manage their independent reading consistently, Mrs. Bullock continues to model by reading her own book during this time. Sometimes she uses part of the time for individual conferences.

9:45–10:30: Math/science/social studies/centers. Mrs. Bullock often reads aloud from a trade book as part of whatever math, science, or social studies unit she is currently doing. Children may refer to other books and also write about related topics. Sometimes this period is devoted to whole-class demonstrations, sometimes small group activities, and sometimes centers. Sometimes there is a mix of activities. It is a very flexible time in this kindergarten.

10:30–11:00: Writing: Learning to Write/Developmentally Appropriate Writing. Mrs. Bullock likes to have this literacy block immediately after content areas. Often the writing she teaches or models is related to the content just learned. She alternates days between teacher-modeled writing and developmentally appropriate writing. However, every day she presents a minilesson on the mechanics of writing, such as letter formation and punctuation. Fourth-grade writing buddies come to Mrs. Bullock's class twice a week. Each kindergartner has a buddy; the buddy may take dictation, help compose or revise a story, collaborate on a report, or share any other appropriate task.

11:00–11:30: Reading: Learning Skills and Strategies. To teach word recognition skills, Mrs. Bullock may use a familiar book, such as *If You Give a Mouse a Cookie*. For example, to teach a minilesson on phonemic awareness, she turns to a page in the book and points to the word "might" as she says it aloud slowly. Starting with that word, she helps children segment the sounds into onset and rhyme and then replace the beginning sound with another sound, such as /t/ to make the word "tight." She does this with several words. Some children can perform the task with ease. Others struggle. Still, they all participate. Mrs. Bullock notes which children may need additional small-group lessons and which seem to segment sounds with little or no difficulty.

Mrs. Bullock also works with small groups of three to five children during this period, meeting each group two to three times a week. The groups are flexible, changing as needs change.

11:30–12:00: Clean-up; story, song, finger play; dismissal. Just before cleaning up, each child tells one thing he or she learned that day. During clean-up, the children often sing a familiar song or recite nursery rhymes. Then Mrs. Bullock may teach them a new song or finger play. Finally, because Mrs. Bullock wants the children to leave with wonderful language in their ears, the children settle down for a read-aloud story before going home.

COMMENTS

There is no "right" way to schedule a kindergarten day. We have suggested only one of many arrangements. In fact, Mrs. Bullock may change this schedule when she feels it isn't working. The important thing to remember is that for literacy to develop, time must be built into the everyday schedule for children to read and write, both independently and with the guidance of a teacher. Only rarely does literacy develop without a teacher. Simply exposing children to good literature is not enough. Children need to be taught.

First Grade

The first-grade schedule shown in Table 9.3 is a sample; again, schedules vary widely. Whole school days may be only about 2 hours longer than half days and include time for lunch and perhaps additional breaks.

As you can see from the table, all literacy blocks are present, but more of the additional time is allocated to daily math, spelling, and handwriting lessons. Teachers use such schedules flexibly, extending some periods and cutting short others to accommodate the interests of the children, special events or holiday celebrations, special units of study in science or social studies, or sometimes because both teachers and students feel like a change.

We comment briefly about some of the periods that differ from those in kindergarten.

9:30–10:15: Spelling; explicit minilessons for groups; centers. Part of this time is spent with the mandated basal spelling program. The teacher relates the elements in the prescribed lessons to phonemic segments, letter-sound associations, and elements of word structure that the children are learning during other parts of the day.

After spelling, small groups of children who have shown a need are given minilessons of explicit instruction in phonics or comprehension. The other children work at centers that may be tied to reading, writing, or other content areas. The children rotate through the centers according to a schedule.

10:30–10:45: Read-aloud. The book read aloud during this time may relate to a content area unit.

10:45–11:30: Reading: Application of Skills and Strategies; minilessons. The teacher does guided reading with one group as others use a different mode, such as reading with a partner or alone. Groups are flexible. The children struggling the

TABLE 9.3

Sample Daily Schedule for a First-Grade Class with Literacy Blocks

8:15–8:30	Arrival; check-in; personal journals
8:30–8:45	Daily Independent Writing
8:45–9:30	Reading: Learning Skills and Strategies
9:30–10:15	Spelling; explicit minilessons for groups; centers
10:15–10:30	Break; snack; morning message
10:30–10:45	Read-aloud
10:45–11:30	Reading: Application of Skills and Strategies; minilessons
11:30–12:00	Lunch
12:00–12:15	Handwriting
12:15–12:30	Daily Independent Reading
12:30–1:05	Special classes (alternating music, art, PE)
1:05–1:30	Math
1:30–1:45	Recess and/or read-aloud
1:45–2:15	Science/social studies (units alternate)
2:15–2:40	Writing: Learning to Write/Developmentally Appropriate Writing
2:40–3:00	Clean-up; story, song, finger play; dismissal

most may meet with the teacher every day, while others may meet with the teacher three times a week.

1:05–1:30: Math. The words for math concepts are learned as sight words, though the teacher reinforces those that fit phonic elements the children have learned. Some time is spent practicing recognition of number words, arithmetic operation words, and direction words necessary for independent practice of math skills.

1:45–2:15: Science/social studies (units alternate). As with math, some important concept words are taught as sight words. Others are used to reinforce children's growing decoding ability.

Science and social studies units are of varying length. They are planned by grade-level teams, and materials for teaching each unit rotate among the classrooms on a prearranged schedule. The "packaged" materials include reading material with big books and trade books, though each teacher often uses his or her own favorite materials as supplements. These materials are also the basis for lessons about text structure as well as such comprehension skills as compare and contrast, fact versus opinion, and main idea and supporting details. During this time, the teacher may also incorporate lessons on searching the Internet for related information as well as on using the computer for projects related to the unit.

> Though we show separate blocks for math, science and social studies, and literacy, in some first grades the entire day is integrated, making such divisions misleading. For example, a class doing a unit on endangered species may relate almost every part of the day to the overarching themes of that unit, tying reading, writing, math, and even spelling to the topic of study.

Summary

- Children usually reach Emergent Literacy during kindergarten or first grade, though some reach it earlier and some later.
- Assessment of the benchmark behaviors continues to be mostly informal, and it takes place continuously; that is, teachers focus their observation on certain behaviors while carrying on routine classroom activities.
- When a child has not yet reached a benchmark, instructional strategies are planned to foster continued literacy growth.
- In kindergarten and first grade, the classroom needs a wide variety of materials for reading and writing, including many examples of both authentic literature and decodable text.
- The physical arrangement should allow comfortable spaces for individual work, small groups, and whole-class activities.
- The schedule for each day should reflect the seven blocks of the Comprehensive Balanced Literacy Program described in Chapter 6: two blocks for Daily Independent Reading and Daily Independent Writing, four blocks for instruction (Reading: Learning Skills and Strategies, Reading: Application of Skills and Strategies, Writing: Learning to Write, and Writing: Developmentally Appropriate Writing), and one block for additional support (Intervention) for those children who may need it.
- Literacy blocks are used flexibly within each classroom, and the amount of time devoted to each depends partly on the continuous assessment the teacher does.
- Schedules vary widely from school to school. While some schools allot separate times for separate subjects, many integrate the curriculum so that virtually all activities relate to a particular topic or unit of study.
- Teachers of kindergarten or first grade must typically meet the needs of a range of literacy stages.
- In addition to the instructional routines used at the Early Emergent Literacy stage, several other routines and techniques become especially useful, including the literacy lesson, minilessons, explicit phonics/structural elements routines, ex-

plicit comprehension routines, modes of reading, discussion groups, and modes of writing.

- Teachers should also be prepared to adapt their instruction to meet the needs of children who are gifted; those who have special physical, emotional, or intellectual conditions; and those for whom English is a second language. Such children may benefit from adaptive equipment or additional professional support from special teachers or classrooms,

- We believe that all children can be well served by the assessment-based teaching that you will do in the regular classroom.

 Please visit the premium website for *Literacy Assessment,* Fourth Edition to access the TeachSource Video Cases, chapter web links, For Additional Reading, tutorial quizzes, glossary flashcards, online checklists, downloads, and much more! Go to www.cengage.com/login to register your access code.

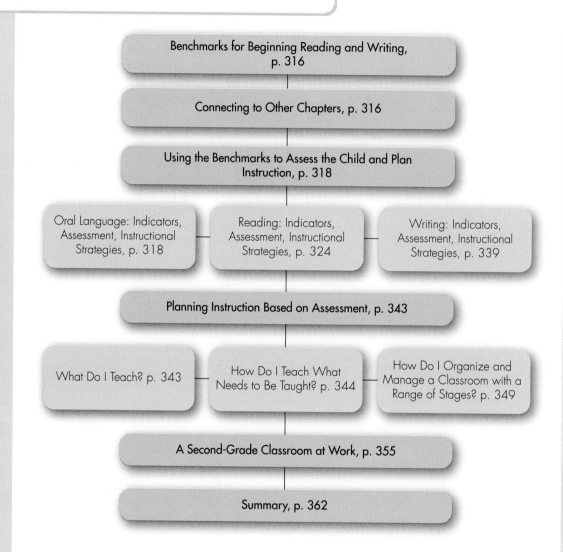

10

Beginning Reading and Writing

NEW TERMS

- encoding
- scope and sequence

Today we are visiting two assessment-based literacy teachers in the Livingston School: Mr. Pulaski, who teaches first grade, and Ms. Farrieas, who teaches second grade. Each teacher has twenty-one students. Mr. Pulaski has three second-language learners: two Spanish-speaking students and one student who speaks Hmong. Ms. Farrieas has four Spanish-speaking students.

In Mr. Pulaski's room, we see him teaching the consonants m and t and the short vowel a to a group of ten students, including the second-language learners. He is using an explicit phonics routine (see Chapter 6). At the conclusion of his lesson, he distributes copies of a little book that contains text requiring the use of the phonics skills he has just taught. He tells the children to use what they have learned in today's lesson and the other skills they know to read the text silently to find out what problem the children in the story are having.

As the children read silently, Mr. Pulaski moves from child to child, asking each one to softly read aloud two pages from the text. He listens to the second-language learners first to be sure they are gaining the ability to do sequential beginning decoding in English. He makes notes about each student's performance in decoding the words in the text. With the second-language learners, he is aware that their pronunciation may still not match standard English; what he checks is that they are developing basic decoding skills.

While Mr. Pulaski teaches this group, the remaining eleven students are working at learning stations or centers, completing a written task related to sorting words by a spelling pattern. They must also do an activity requiring them to complete a chart about two characters from a trade book they have read, such as *Cowgirl Kate and Cocoa* (Silverman, 2005).

Next door in Ms. Farrieas's class, we see similar types of activities. One group is silently reading the book *Eek! There's a Mouse in the House* (Yee, 1992). As the children finish, they write responses in their journals. Another group, including the four Spanish-speaking students, is working with a bilingual teaching assistant who is following up on the lesson Ms. Farrieas taught yesterday. The assistant is helping the students locate words in a big book that consist of two or three sounds. As they find the words, the assistant says them slowly and the children repeat them.

Then they write the words under columns headed "Two Sounds" and "Three Sounds." The final group is doing guided reading (see Chapter 6) with Ms. Farriea, who is noting their reading behaviors on a checklist.

As you looked at these classrooms, did you notice how the children are becoming readers and writers? For example, Mr. Pulaski teaches some phonics skills that students immediately apply in a book that they read silently. At the same time, the other children in his class are working at learning centers and completing a task related to a trade book they have read. Notice that Mr. Pulaski was quick to check that the second-language learners had sufficient oral language skills to handle the assigned reading task. Although we did not see it today, Mr. Pulaski's second-language learners receive daily English-language development lessons, which include literacy-based activities in which the students listen to others read books in person or recorded.

The excitement of the Beginning Reading and Writing stage is apparent in Ms. Farrieas's room as well. Some children are responding to what they have read, while others are applying strategies and skills they are learning through guided reading. It is also evident that some children in Ms. Farrieas's room are still close to the Emergent Literacy stage. These are the students who are working on phonemic awareness with the teaching assistant.

Benchmarks for Beginning Reading and Writing

The benchmarks for the Beginning Reading and Writing stage are typical of children ages six to eight in first and second grades. Read through the following benchmarks for this stage before proceeding with the remainder of the chapter.

Connecting to Other Chapters

For most children, the Beginning Reading and Writing stage usually occurs during first and second grade. The higher the grade, however, the greater the range you are likely to encounter in your classroom. The first- and second-grade classroom is likely to have children at two or three different stages of development, and perhaps more. Think about each stage discussed so far, and compare your thoughts to the following points:

- *Early Emergent Literacy.* By first or second grade, nearly all children who have been given appropriate instruction should be beyond the Early Emergent stage of literacy development. If you discover children who are still functioning at this stage, you need to use the ideas presented in Chapter 8. Further, you should consult with your schoollearning specialists to determine whether these children need special support in addition to the classroom program.

- *Emergent Literacy.* Some children in first grade are still likely to be functioning at the Emergent Literacy stage. These children need the type of instructional support suggested in Chapter 9 plus the support discussed in this chapter. By grade 2, most children will be well beyond this stage; if some are not, besides

ORAL LANGUAGE

- ☑ The student exhibits behaviors from Emergent Literacy to a greater degree.
- ☑ The student's use of standard English continues to develop.
- ☑ The student's vocabulary is growing.
- ☑ The student's facility with language is growing.
- ☑ The student continues to show pleasure in words.

READING

- ☑ The student continues to show growth in many of the behaviors from Emergent Literacy.
- ☑ The student knows letters and many sight words.
- ☑ The student uses phonics and structural elements to determine the pronunciations of words.
- ☑ The student uses context to determine word meaning and build vocabulary.
- ☑ The student is beginning to use critical comprehension strategies such as visualizing, predicting, identifying important information, self-questioning, monitoring, summarizing, synthesizing, and evaluating.
- ☑ The student exhibits fluency and comprehension of a variety of materials.
- ☑ The student is confident about reading ability.
- ☑ The student begins to explore using research tools and skills.

WRITING

- ☑ The student exhibits continued growth in many of the Emergent Literacy behaviors.
- ☑ The student exhibits a variety of general writing behaviors.
- ☑ The student is growing in the use of the mechanics and conventions of writing.
- ☑ The student uses the writing process.

referring to the ideas presented in Chapter 9, you should consult with school's learning specialists to determine whether the children need additional support beyond the regular classroom program.

- *Beginning Reading and Writing.* This stage, discussed in this chapter, is where most children in first and second grade are likely to be functioning. Some first graders and many second graders are likely to be well into this stage of development as the school year begins.

- *Almost Fluent Reading and Writing.* For most children, this stage begins toward the end of second grade or at the beginning of third grade and is likely to continue through the fourth grade or beyond. It is possible, however, to have some children in first and second grade who are already functioning at this stage. For these children, you should refer to the ideas presented in Chapter 11. A first or second grader who has reached this stage also needs many opportunities to participate in reading and writing activities with peers who are functioning at other stages of development.

- *Fluent Reading and Writing.* This stage typically begins around the fourth or fifth grade. However, you may have a first or second grader who is at the fluent stage. The ideas suggested in Chapter 12 would be appropriate in this case.

Meeting the needs of an increasingly wider range of stages requires that you use a variety of small-group and individual activities throughout your program. This chapter will frequently refer to the instructional routines presented in Chapter 6, which will help you create the appropriate mix of activities.

Using the Benchmarks to Assess the Child and Plan Instruction

In this section, we show you how to assess students' oral language, reading, and writing at the Beginning Reading and Writing stage. The assessment takes place primarily through instructional activities, although some specific informal and formal procedures are suggested. As an assessment-based literacy teacher, you will continually adjust instruction on the basis of what you determine about each student's performance in relationship to the benchmarks.

Oral Language: Indicators, Assessment, Instructional Strategies

At the Beginning Reading and Writing stage, children's oral language continues to expand. As before, it serves as the foundation for reading and writing. We present five major areas in this stage:

- Continued development of Emergent Literacy behaviors
- Continued development of standard English
- Growing vocabulary
- Growing language facility
- Pleasure in words

A class checklist for all of these behaviors appears in Figure 10.2 at the end of this section. Assessment of all these oral language benchmarks is based on observation and the use of checklists.

> ☑ **The student exhibits behaviors from Emergent Literacy to a greater degree.**

Think back to the Emergent Literacy stage. What behaviors were identified for the oral language benchmarks? Most children will continue to show these behaviors, but to a greater degree. For example, children will keep developing their abilities to retain oral directions and to use new words they learn from stories.

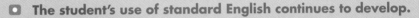

◘ The student's use of standard English continues to develop.

- If speaker of nonstandard English is learning to switch between two languages
- Self-corrects while speaking

Assessment. As students talk, note that some are using standard English while others are using nonstandard English. Second-language learners are likely to be using their native language and making attempts to use English. As children learn standard English, they often continue to use nonstandard English as well. Note which students are learning to switch between standard and nonstandard forms according to the situation. Mastery of standard English is not a prerequisite to proficient reading; however, it is important for all students to acquire standard English because it is the language of formal writing and of the books they will read.

At this stage, a child's oral language often directly influences his or her use of phonics. For example, a child who drops endings in speaking will often drop endings in reading. This is not a reading problem; it is a language difference. For second-language learners, this influence is even more significant. Until students develop good use of oral English, their progress in learning phonics and other decoding skills is likely to move more slowly (Freeman & Freeman, 2001).

As children develop more facility with standard English, they will often correct themselves while speaking. Support efforts to switch to "school language." Don't allow nonstandard usage to become an embarrassment.

Instructional Strategies. The best way to help children's use of standard English grow is to provide many good models and opportunities to interact with these models. Offer many opportunities for children to listen, discuss, and respond: read-alouds, daily sharing times, role plays with other students or use of puppets, class visitors who use standard English, and so forth.

◘ The student's vocabulary is growing.

- Is using increased vocabulary
- Will ask for meaning of unknown words in class

Assessment. Note that students' vocabulary increases over time. Be aware of which students ask for word meanings, thus showing an interest in words. Some primary teachers take a sample of a child's oral language by recording the child oral description of a picture or photograph. Several months later, the process is repeated using the same picture, and growth in the child's vocabulary is usually obvious. This is also a good way to show parents evidence that their child's vocabulary is increasing.

Instructional Strategies. Increasing oral vocabulary does not require direct instruction. Rather, it requires many opportunities for students to listen, respond, talk, and interact with others. Use activities such as the following to expand oral language:

- Have a daily sharing time during which students, you, and other adults talk about something of interest.
- Keep and discuss a bulletin board with labeled pictures that are updated periodically.
- Have a "word of the day" displayed on the chalkboard or bulletin board. The word is discussed and used in a variety of sentences and can be provided by you or your students. Focus on general vocabulary as well as technical vocabulary related to particular topics or areas of study.
- Read aloud and discuss books that contain rich vocabulary.

▣ The student's facility with language is growing.

- Listens to classmates and can paraphrase what others have said
- Is interested in collaborative work with classmates
- Can participate in a discussion
- Can plan and ask oral questions

Assessment. As other students are talking or reading aloud, note which students pay attention and can respond by stating what they heard in their own words. As children begin to collaborate with peers on projects and participate in discussion about what they have read, note those who are comfortable with this process and those who need extra encouragement or guidance. Which students ask good questions during lessons, following read-alouds, or following presentations by special guests or fellow students? Are the questions logical? Do they focus on pertinent points?

When working with second-language learners, keep in mind that they can participate in group discussions (Martinez-Roldan & Lopez-Robertson, 1999/2000), though their willingness to do so may depend somewhat on their use of oral English. These students may feel more comfortable working with just one other student at first.

Instructional Strategies. Students should have many opportunities to listen to others read aloud or present an oral report. Model paraphrasing and then encourage your students to restate what they heard in their own words. Also model the process of asking good questions that focus on important aspects of a topic. Teach children how to ask a variety of questions related to who, what, when, where, and why.

You should also model paraphrasing during group or whole-class discussions before adding your own comments. Gradually reduce the frequency of your restatements until children are comfortable paraphrasing each other's ideas without your intervention. Encourage children to speak directly to each other during discussions.

Teach your children to follow the guidelines for discussion groups presented in Chapter 6. Discuss and evaluate how things are going. With your students, generate guidelines related to behavior as well as focused discussion.

Second-language learners may be grouped together from time to time to hold a discussion in their first language. The student from that group who has the best command of English can then report the group's ideas to the class. This procedure is especially successful when there is also an adult who speaks the student's language.

> **◘ The student's facility with language is growing. (continued)**
>
> - Will plan and present an oral report

Assessment. As students make oral presentations, look for such signs as the following:

- Has a logical order
- Sticks to the topic
- Uses complete thoughts or ideas
- Includes a beginning, middle, and end

Instructional Strategies. Model the process of good oral reporting. Stress the importance of the role of the presenter and the role of the audience. Use guidelines such as those behaviors just suggested to show students how to plan and give an oral report. Plan an oral report as a class, and have different students give parts of it. After the report, discuss ways to improve it. Develop a chart of guidelines, generated by the students themselves, about how to give a good oral report (Figure 10.1).

> **◘ The student continues to show pleasure in words.**
>
> - Makes jokes related to plays on words
> - Shows interest in the history of words
> - Enjoys nonsense and silly poems
> - Enjoys making own dictionary

Assessment. This part of Beginning Reading and Writing is really fun for teachers and children. Note children who show an interest in words through behaviors like the ones listed under the benchmark. Add any other such behaviors that are appropriate for your classroom. Keep in mind, though, that second-language learners often lack the language and cultural background to understand certain jokes, word plays, or figurative language. When you notice that second-language learners start to get jokes, it is a sure sign of English acquisition.

Our Guidelines For A
GOOD
Oral Report

- Have a clear topic.

- Stick to your topic.

- Have a beginning, middle, and end.

- Speak clearly.

- Be natural.

FIGURE 10.1

Sample Student-Generated Guidelines for Oral Reports

Instructional Strategies. Do as many things as possible to interest children in words. Some of the following strategies should be very helpful:

- Have children keep personal Joke Books.
- Share your own "word of the day." Make a big deal out of it. Reward those who can use the word during the day.

For ideas, refer to Bear, Invernizzi, Templeton, and Johnston (2004) in "For Additional Reading" on the premium website for this text.

- Use a bulletin board to display information about word histories and origins.
- Share lots of nonsense poems. Encourage children to recite them. Use such poets as Jack Prelutsky, Judith Viorst, and Shel Silverstein.
- Have children make individual word banks or dictionaries to collect their own special words.

Figure 10.2 presents a class checklist for all the oral language benchmarks.

Oral Language Checklist: Beginning Reading and Writing Stage

Teacher_____   Date_____   Grade_____

Students

+ = behavior present
- = behavior absent
✓ = somewhat present

Benchmark

Emergent Literacy Behaviors

Use of Standard English
Switches between standard and nonstandard English
Self-corrects

Vocabulary
Increased vocabulary
Asks for meanings of unknown words

Facility with Language
Listens and paraphrases
Collaborates with classmates
Participates in discussion
Plans and asks oral questions
Plans and presents oral report

Pleasure in Words
Makes jokes related to plays on words
Shows interest in word history
Enjoys nonsense and silly poems
Makes own dictionary

FIGURE 10.2

Sample Class Checklist for Beginning Reading and Writing: Oral Language Benchmarks and Behaviors

Reading: Indicators, Assessment, Instructional Strategies

You can do much of your reading assessment informally during instruction, while sometimes using more formal things to assess students' application of reading strategies and skills or assessing for intervention purposes.

These are the main areas of Beginning Reading behaviors:

- Continued development from the previous stage
- Knowledge of letters and sight words
- Use of phonics and structural elements
- Use of context to determine meaning and build vocabulary
- Use of comprehension strategies
- Increased fluency
- Confidence in reading
- Use of research tools

A sample class checklist for reading benchmarks appears in Figure 10.8 at the end of this section.

> **◘ The student continues to show growth in many of the behaviors from Emergent Literacy.**

Students will continue to show growth in many of the behaviors from the two previous stages. It is not necessary—or defensible—to wait until a student shows development in *all* aspects of earlier stages to begin instruction that will foster growth of the behaviors in the Beginning Reading and Writing stage.

> **◘ The student knows letters and many sight words.**
>
> • Recognizes and can name all letters in random order

Assessment. Children at this stage can name all the letters of the alphabet, both upper and lower case. You can assess this knowledge informally:

- During class writing activities, note which children use the letter names to refer to letters as they write.
- When children wait in line to leave the room and/or any time you have a few extra minutes, ask individuals to name letters in the room as you point to them.

At this stage of literacy development, you may assess letter-name knowledge directly by using a set of 3″ × 5″ index cards printed with upper- and lower-case letters. Mix up the cards, and ask each child to name the letters at random. Record your results on a sheet like the one in Figure 10.3.

Name _____Jean R._____ 10-10

Upper Case	Match	Lower Case
___ A		___ a
___ B		___ b
___ C		___ c
___ D		___ d
___ E		___ e
___ F		___ f
___ G		___ g
___ H		___ h
___ I		___ i
___ J		___ j
___ K		___ k
___ L		___ l
___ M		___ m
___ N		___ n
___ O		___ o
___ P		(___ p)
(___ Q)	(___)	(___ q)
___ R		___ r
___ S		___ s
___ T		___ t
___ U		___ u
___ V		___ v
___ W		___ w
(___ X)		___ x
___ Y		___ y
___ Z		___ z

Observations:

___ Says all upper- and lower-case letters by name

___ Matches all upper- and lower-case letters

✓ Needs help with:

_____Q and X (upper-case). p and q (lower-case)_____

_____matching upper and lower q_____

FIGURE 10.3

Sample Letter-Name Sheet

Instructional Strategies. If children do not know the letter names, use the following strategies to help them gain this knowledge:

1. After determining the letters children do not know, provide direct instruction on several of the unknown letters at one time.

   a. Show the letter on a card. Include the name and picture of an object to help children remember the letter name.

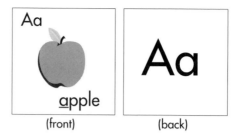

(front)   (back)

b. Say the letter and name the object.

c. Have children repeat the name.

d. Follow this procedure with several other letters.

e. Shuffle the cards with only the letters showing. Have children name the letter. If they have difficulty, turn the letter to the picture side to help children link the name of the picture with the letter name. Repeat as often as needed.

2. Play games that require children to match upper- and lower-case letters and name them.

3. Read aloud many alphabet books. Share the illustrations and discuss the letter names. Have children join in reading aloud the books.

4. During write-aloud and shared writing, have children name letters of the alphabet as they write. Do the same as they observe you write.

5. If you are using a published reading, spelling, or handwriting program, use the index of the teacher's manual to locate activities that teach the letter names.

Children who are having serious problems learning the names of letters may need several months to develop this knowledge as you continue with other reading skills and strategies. If this is the case, use ideas suggested in Chapters 8 and 9, and continue to provide short periods of instruction and practice with the alphabet each day until children's knowledge of it is automatic. Lack of alphabet knowledge, however, should not stop you from teaching other skills and strategies of Beginning Reading.

❏ The student knows letters and many sight words. (continued)

- Recognizes and can name many words at sight

Assessment. Children at the Beginning Reading and Writing stage are starting to build an extensive sight vocabulary. This vocabulary will consist of words important to them, high-frequency words, and other words they are able to decode independently and automatically (including the Dolch words, discussed in Chapter 4 and listed in the Resource File at the end of this book). In addition to assessing a child's sight-vocabulary knowledge, you are assessing fluency.

The best way to assess a child's sight vocabulary and fluency is to periodically sample oral reading of the connected text being used for instruction. You should assess students' sight-vocabulary knowledge by taking an oral reading sample or running record (see Chapter 3) every two or three weeks until you are confident a child has a large stock of sight words. Save the sheets you used for coding the children's oral reading and compare them over time to note the number of words children read instantly by sight. These oral reading samples will also provide information on other skills and strategies, such as the phonics skills discussed in the next section.

Instructional Strategies. To help children increase their sight vocabulary, you should do four primary things:

1. Systematically teach decoding skills so that children become independent in figuring out words they do not know when they are reading. This ultimately leads to an increase in sight vocabulary.

2. Before students read a text, use the decodable words routine and phonetically unpredictable words routine suggested in Chapter 6 to introduce high-frequency vocabulary or words students are unable to decode. (In the next section, we will discuss systematic decoding.)

3. Provide daily opportunities for students to read and reread (both orally and silently) books in which they know all the words. Occasionally, time students' reading. Have students keep a graph or other type of record of their reading times. (See the section "Oral Reading Fluency and Word Recognition Strategies" in Chapter 3.)

4. Provide daily reading practice with books at students' instructional reading level—that is, books they can read capably with guidance and instruction—or with slightly more difficult books. This will give them the opportunity to use the skills and strategies they are learning (Snow, Burns, & Griffin, 1998). This activity can form a part of the Reading: Learning Skills and Strategies block or the Reading: Application of Skills and Strategies block of the Comprehensive Balanced Literacy Program.

Daily practice reading in books appropriate to the student's reading level, or slightly harder, can be provided in several ways. Use books that have been leveled as described in Chapter 6. If your school is using a published program, that program probably has sets of leveled books to use for guided reading. If your school does not use a published program, you can obtain sets of leveled books from such publishers as Houghton Mifflin Harcourt Company, Rigby Educational Publications, the Wright Group, or Richard C. Owen Company.

To provide additional practice, place sets of books in tubs or baskets in your room. Each tub or basket can be color-coded to correspond to the level of the book, and you can also place a colored dot on the back of each book to signify its level:

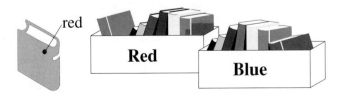

Post a chart in the reading center or reading area to help children determine the order of moving from one color-coded set of books to another. Children can also have

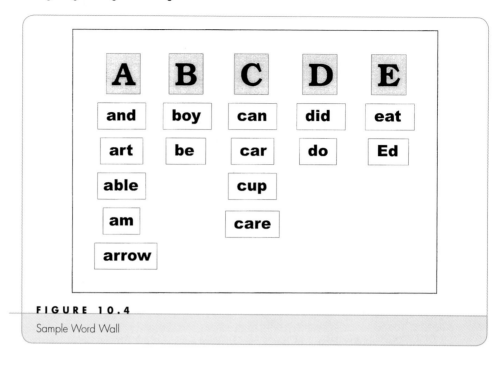

FIGURE 10.4

Sample Word Wall

individual lists of book titles to check off as they read. Most often, students should read the books silently. From time to time, students may read cooperatively to add interest and fun to fluency practice.

For a detailed discussion of word walls, see Cooper & Kiger (2009) and Cunningham (2000), listed in "For Additional Reading" at the premium website for this text.

Another good way to reinforce learning of sight vocabulary is through the word wall, an idea we introduced in Chapter 8. As high-frequency words and other words are introduced, place them on the wall under the letter with which they begin, as shown in Figure 10.4. Students should be encouraged to use the word wall to identify words needed for writing. Each day words on the wall should be reviewed with a short activity, such as "Who can read the words listed under *D?*" Words should remain on the wall until most students have mastered them. Mastered words are removed to make room for new words.

> **The student uses phonics and structural elements to determine the pronunciations of words.**
>
> • Chooses appropriate strategies and skills to identify unfamiliar words

For a detailed discussion on phonics and structural analysis, see Cooper (2006) listed in "For Additional Reading" at the premium website for this text.

Assessment. Within the categories of phonics and structural analysis, there are many subskills that students must learn.

The best way to assess the use of phonics, structural analysis, and other strategies to figure out words is to listen to a child's oral reading. Take a running record and then examine the miscue patterns. The running record is a natural part of routine activities, which keeps assessment where it belongs—as a part of instruction.

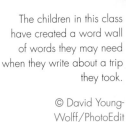

The children in this class have created a word wall of words they may need when they write about a trip they took.

© David Young-Wolff/PhotoEdit

If you note in a running record that a student has difficulty using certain phonics skills or structural elements, you might turn to specific skill tests for these items. (See Chapter 4 for a discussion of such tests.) If you are using a published program, it will include specific skill tests. Because these tests often assess the skills in isolation, rather than in the context of real reading or writing, we believe it is better to use samples of students' oral reading.

Analyzing how students spell words is another way to tell which phonics and structural analysis skills students are using. Use caution in drawing conclusions, because writing is an **encoding** process in which students go from sounds to letters, whereas reading is a decoding process in which students go from letters to sounds.

It is possible for students to use certain skills in one process and be unable to use them in the other; when making a determination about a student's use of certain skills, look at both a reading and a writing sample. By comparing the two, you can determine where to place emphasis in instruction. For example, if you see that a student uses digraphs and inflectional endings in decoding words but does not use them in spelling words as she or he writes, you know that in teaching these elements you need to emphasize the connection between reading and spelling.

Instructional Strategies. Three of the instructional routines presented in Chapter 6 will be most useful in helping students develop the use of phonics and structural skills: the literacy lesson, minilessons, and the explicit phonics/structural elements routine.

If you are using a published program, it will include a **scope and sequence** of strategies and skills that your students are expected to learn. Or your district may have a curriculum guide listing the skills that your students need in order to achieve the standards or benchmarks for beginning readers. You should use that sequence of skills to help you determine what to teach and what adjustments to make based on your own determination of your students' needs. As you teach the needed phonic and structural skills, provide decodable books for practice and application, and use the guided reading strategy described in Chapter 6. Periodically take a running record using these books to determine how students are applying the skills and strategies they have been taught.

For students who need help in learning to use strategies for sounding out words, teach them a plan like the one shown in the poster in Figure 10.5. This plan helps students sound out words by looking first for word parts they know (structural elements). If that doesn't lead them to the word, they then try looking at the letter-sound associations (phonics). Following each step, they will read or reread, checking whether the word they have sounded out makes sense. Finally, if these steps don't work, students can ask someone for help or use a dictionary. Even students at the Beginning Reading and Writing stage use simple dictionaries. The goal of all decoding instruction is to help students independently apply phonics and structural analysis, along with other skills, to figure out unknown words.

> **▣ The student uses context to determine word meaning and build vocabulary.**

Assessment. The middle box in Figure 10.5 indicates the role of context as part of the strategy for sounding out words. Context is an even more important skill in determining word meaning and building vocabulary. Students use context to verify the word they have sounded out by determining whether it fits the meaning of the sentence or paragraph. If the word is in the child's oral vocabulary, and he or she has pronounced the word orally or silently, the context helps to verify the meaning. If the word is not in the child's oral vocabulary, the context may help the child predict the type of word that the unknown word must be (thing, descriptive word, and so forth) or predict the word's general meaning (fruit, form of transportation, and so on).

You can assess students' use of context to determine the meanings of words through oral reading and follow-up discussion, and also by taking a running record. Here are some examples:

- A student who miscalls a word in oral reading but corrects it after reading to the end of a sentence shows use of context to verify accurate decoding. In the following example, the student originally read "apple" as "ape," but then self-corrected the miscue after realizing that "ape" did not have the appropriate meaning for the context.

  sc
  ape
  The big red ~~apple~~ was delicious.

- A student who substitutes a word that means the same or nearly the same thing as a given word shows the use of context. In fact, if a student does this often, it may indicate an over-dependence on context, which can lead to inaccurate reading. In the following example, the student has used the context to determine the meaning for "mountain":

  hill
  The boy climbed to the top of the ~~mountain~~.

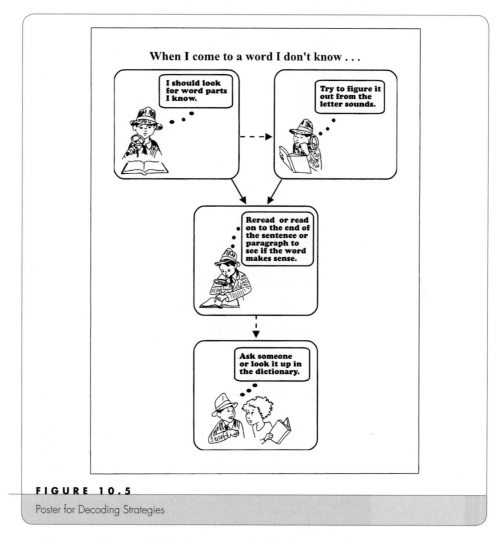

FIGURE 10.5

Poster for Decoding Strategies

- In a follow-up discussion, you can ask the child to explain how he or she figured out the meaning of a particular word, and the answer will often reveal the use of context. For example, after reading silently or aloud,

  "The big red apple was delicious. It was very sweet and juicy,"

  you might ask the child how he or she could figure out the meaning of "delicious." The child might say, "I could tell it was a word that meant the apple tasted good by the words 'sweet' and 'juicy.'"

Instructional Strategies. A good way to teach the use of context to determine word meaning is to use the cloze procedure with big books or chart stories written by the teacher.

  1. Choose a text that children can decode, and place a self-adhesive note over key words that are easily determined by using the context.
  2. Have a student read the text aloud, asking children to supply the covered words.

3. List all possibilities given by the students; then discuss which ones make sense in the text. The goal is not to get the exact word but to get one whose meaning fits the text.

4. Finally, uncover each word and talk about how the letter-sound associations would be used to determine the exact word and how the context would help to verify the meaning.

Another good way to develop students' abilities to use context is through read-alouds. After reading aloud, go back and discuss the meanings of selected words and how the context would help to determine the meaning. Model your thinking by explaining to students how you would figure out word meaning using context.

Context is especially important for second-language students who are still developing standard English. Since phonics may be difficult for these students, they should be particularly encouraged to use context cues as well as their own background knowledge to comprehend texts.

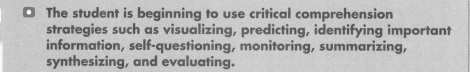

◘ The student is beginning to use critical comprehension strategies such as visualizing, predicting, identifying important information, self-questioning, monitoring, summarizing, synthesizing, and evaluating.

Assessment. Research shows that the strategies included in this behavior are critical for helping readers across all stages to become effective constructors of meaning. At the Beginning Reading and Writing stage, children are beginning to use all of these strategies.

The best form of assessment for these strategies is observation of students' reading during reading lessons. Look for such behaviors as these:

- Can visualize
- Makes logical predictions based on text information and own knowledge
- Begins to see that predictions change as more information is acquired
- Begins to ask questions based on logic and own knowledge
- Can answer own questions and those of others after reading
- Begins to know when something read does not make sense (monitoring)
- Rereads, looks at illustrations, or asks for help when something does not make sense (monitoring)
- Can summarize stories with key elements: setting, characters, problem, events related to problem, and outcome related to problem
- Can summarize informational texts by giving the main ideas with a few details
- Can synthesize
- Begins to evaluate by noting likes and dislikes for text

Instructional Strategies. To help students develop their abilities to use these critical comprehension strategies, you will need to model frequently and provide many opportunities to use the strategies with increasingly difficult text. The literacy lesson,

For a detailed discussion of strategies, see Cooper (2006), listed in "For Additional Reading" on the premium website for this text.

minilesson, and explicit comprehension routine are the instructional routines most pertinent here (see Chapter 6).

> **▣ The student exhibits fluency and comprehension of a variety of materials.**
>
> - Can read and retell familiar stories
> - Reads own writing

Assessment. As we said in the previous chapter, once students begin to read you need to assess fluency on a regular basis. You may begin by having children read aloud from a text that they are able to read and noting whether they are reading smoothly and accurately. As their fluency increases, you may assess with new text. Table 9.1 in Chapter 9 gives criteria for end-of-year fluency, which includes rate and accuracy. We consider fluency a component of comprehension in that speed and accuracy without understanding isn't reading, so ask students to tell you about what they have read and note their ability to read with expression.

Many children come into the Beginning Reading and Writing stage having been read to a great deal. They have heard many wonderful stories, such as *The Three Bears* (Galdone, 1972), *The Three Little Pigs* (Marshall, 1989), *Brown Bear, Brown Bear, What Do You See?* (Martin, 1967), and *This is the House That Jack Built* (Taback, 2002), to name just a few. A sign of children's beginning ability to construct meaning is that they often begin to read these stories and retell them on their own. Because some of these stories are predictable texts, with repeated patterns that children can recognize, children often memorize them. This is a natural part of the beginning reading process and helps children see themselves as readers.

Many children at this stage will read these familiar stories aloud, but some will move toward silent reading. Children often think that silent reading is softer oral reading; they may mumble to themselves or subvocalize. This is quite natural at this stage.

The assessment for this behavior is primarily observational. You will observe children sitting with favorite storybooks, often reading to a stuffed animal or a real friend. You can often hear children retelling the story after they have read it. You can check for decoding and construction of meaning by using the retelling and running record procedures described in Chapter 3. Keep in mind, however, that when children are reading favorite stories that have been read aloud to them, they may not be able to decode every word correctly because they are relying partly on what they have memorized or on picture clues.

Children also begin to read their own writing at this stage. You will observe children reading something they have written to a friend, to a stuffed animal, or to the group. As children progress through this stage, they will share more and more of what they have written. Even when the children "read" an elaborate story, however, you may see very few scribbles, letters, or words on their papers.

Instructional Strategies. Help students build fluency by encouraging rereading of familiar stories. The more students read books they know and like, the more secure they will feel in their ability to apply skills independently. Encourage them to apply skills and strategies to reading text, and model fluent reading by reading aloud to your students.

Wide reading also builds fluency. Stimulate interest in reading by providing a wide range of materials in your classroom and by introducing students to the use of school and public libraries. Also encourage groups of children to talk about what they are reading.

If children are unable to read and retell favorite stories, this may indicate they have not been read to outside of school. These children need a strong oral language program with lots of time for stories to be read aloud, retold, and discussed. Second-language learners will also need a strong oral language program.

For children who seem to lack interest in reading their own writing to others, you should use the write-aloud and shared-writing routines presented in Chapter 6. The read-alouds plus write-aloud and shared writing will give children who need this background a strong foundation.

> ◻ **The student exhibits fluency and comprehension of a variety of materials. (continued)**
>
> • Attempts to read and retell unfamiliar texts (narrative and expository)

Assessment. To assess students' increasing ability to read unfamiliar text, use the retelling procedure presented in Chapter 3. You may do this informally as a part of everyday instruction or at specific times in your instructional program when you take a retelling for each student. Actually, it is best to use both procedures. We suggest that every two or three weeks you combine retelling and the running record using the same text. First, have the child read the text silently and retell it to you. Then have the child read the same text orally. With two samples of behavior using the same text, you can determine if the child is having problems with comprehension, decoding, or both. This helps you focus your instruction.

When you do these assessments, always note the approximate grade-level designation for the text. Save the record sheets (often known as *protocols*) for each assessment, and compare them over time to determine the child's progress.

Instructional Strategies. Ongoing assessment of students' ability to read increasingly difficult texts is critical in determining what instruction will help that student continue to grow. Study the information for two students in Figures 10.6 and 10.7. How would you make decisions about these students? Here is the analysis we would suggest:

• Becky Smith (Figure 10.6) is having difficulty with the primer-level text; it is too difficult for her, so an easier text is needed. She also seems to need direct instruction with vowel patterns. Therefore, we would use the explicit phonics/structural elements routine and provide a lot of reading with decodable texts using the vowel patterns taught. We would also continue work with story elements through listening activities until we were sure she was overcoming any decoding problems.

• Roger Bickel (Figure 10.7) is decoding and comprehending accurately at the primer level. We would continue instruction with new skills and strategies and gradually increase the difficulty of his text. Since Roger is exhibiting no problems

Name: Becky Smith

Date: 10-1

Text Level: Preprimer

Type of Text: narrative

Retelling: 75%
 (Gave setting, problem, some events, part of outcome)

Running Record: 95%
 (Good self-corrections, missed two hf words — saw & was; no other patterns)

Date: 10-18

Text Level: Primer

Type of Text: narrative

Retelling: 40%
 (Only able to give characters & setting)

Running Record: 70%
 (Had problems with words using long vowel patterns oa, ai, ea)

FIGURE 10.6

Retelling and Running-Record Data for Becky Smith

Name: Roger Bickel

Date: 10-1

Text Level: Preprimer

Type of Text: narrative

Retelling: 100%
 (good complete retelling)

Running Record: 98%
 (no pattern of miscues)

Date: 10-19

Text Level: Primer

Type of Text: expository

Retelling: 100%
 (good use of strategies — Summarizing & Monitoring)

Running Record: 100%
 (no problems)

FIGURE 10.7

Retelling and Running-Record Data for Roger Bickel

with decoding, he may be approaching independence and be ready to move into more authentic literature rather than decodable text.

As you can see from these two examples, the instructional strategies you select must be based on the students' strengths and needs. Only through ongoing assessment can you make this determination.

> ☑ **The student exhibits fluency and comprehension of a variety of materials. (continued)**
>
> - Self-corrects when reading

Assessment. Self-correcting means that during oral reading students correct miscues they have made, often because they are aware that what they said does not make sense. This behavior is a part of the monitoring strategy discussed earlier. Self-corrections clearly indicate that a student is constructing meaning while reading. You assess this behavior using oral reading or a running record. You assume that when children self-correct in oral reading, they also self-correct in silent reading.

Instructional Strategies. Self-correction is best taught through teacher modeling and discussion. Talk to students about the importance of rereading and self-correcting and periodically model the process yourself.

> *Today as I was reading the story to myself, I read a sentence that said, "Harry was a house." That didn't make sense to me because houses don't usually have names. I reread the sentence to myself and looked more carefully at the last word. It had orse on the end. It had to be horse—Harry was a horse. Now it made sense.*

If students don't self-correct because they lack the necessary understanding of language or background knowledge about the text topic, you need to teach the needed skills or concepts. If students are so focused on decoding that they forget about meaning, provide material with fewer decoding challenges.

Second-language learners are especially likely to focus on decoding at the expense of meaning; therefore, you should encourage them to use background knowledge and context cues to check comprehension.

> ☑ **The student is confident about reading ability.**
>
> - Is willing to take risks
> - Chooses to read during free time
> - Sees self as a reader
> - Likes to read to others

Assessment. Observation of children in a variety of reading situations will give you many opportunities to determine which students exhibit these behaviors. Some teachers like to make up their own checklists to guide their observations. Here are some signs that we suggest you look for:

RISK TAKING

- Tries harder texts
- Attempts to sound out a word even when unsure

- Volunteers to read aloud
- Is not afraid of reading

FREE-TIME READING

- Picks up books or magazines as soon as other work is completed
- Wants longer independent reading times; often groans when it is time to stop
- When given time to play, often reads

SEEING SELF AS READER

- Attempts to read familiar stories that have been read aloud
- Says, "I can read."

READING TO OTHERS

- Volunteers to read aloud to class or group during instruction
- Is often seen reading aloud a book to a friend

You may also want to use a process interview, or reading interview, in which you attempt to learn how a student thinks about reading by asking a series of questions about such things as how they choose a book, how they remember what they read; and how they figure out words they don't know. For more about this procedure see *Literacy: Helping Students Construct Meaning, 7th edition* (Cooper & Kiger, 2009).

Instructional Strategies. The development of these behaviors in students comes through the general classroom atmosphere and the overall approach to your Comprehensive Balanced Literacy Program. You must create an exciting, print-rich environment that supports and promotes reading and writing. At the same time, you must express an attitude that encourages children to take risks, to see reading as important, to read during free time, and to read to others.

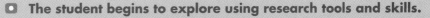

◻ The student begins to explore using research tools and skills.

- Uses glossary, table of contents, dictionary or picture dictionary, beginning encyclopedias, CD-ROMs, the Internet, and the library

Assessment. Students at the Beginning Reading and Writing stage will have had minimal introduction to the use of research tools and skills. They may have limited knowledge of such tools as the table of contents, glossary, and library sources. Some students may be familiar with CD-ROMs and Internet sources. The best way to assess students' knowledge of these tools is by observing how they use them in the classroom.

Instructional Strategies. To introduce research tools and skills to students, we suggest you use minilessons. If more time is needed for the initial instruction, expand the amount of time devoted to the lesson.

The most effective way to teach research tools and skills also involves using short projects related to selections students are reading, themes or topics of study, or science, social studies, or other subject areas. Systematically identify the specific tools and skills you want to teach, and develop projects around them.

Figure 10.8 presents a sample class checklist for all of the reading benchmarks at the Beginning Reading and Writing stage.

Reading Checklist:
Beginning Reading and Writing Stage

Teacher_____ Date_____ Grade_____

Students

+ = consistently present
- = not present
✓ = somewhat present; recheck

Benchmark

Emergent Literacy Behaviors

Letters and Sight Words
Names letters in random order
Recognizes many sight words

Phonics and Structural Elements
Chooses strategies for sounding words

Context and Vocabulary

Comprehension Strategies

Fluency and Variety
Reads and retells familiar stories
Reads own writing
Attempts unfamiliar texts (narrative and expository)
Self-corrects

Confidence in Ability
Takes risks
Reads in free time
Sees self as reader
Reads to others

Research Tools and Skills

FIGURE 10.8

Sample Class Checklist for Beginning Reading and Writing: Reading Benchmarks and Behaviors

Writing: Indicators, Assessment, Instructional Strategies

Most writing assessment is done informally through observation of instructional activities and through group and individual conferences with students. There are four main areas of writing in this stage:

- Continued development of Emergent Literacy behaviors
- Use of general writing behaviors
- Growing use of mechanics and conventions of writing
- Use of the writing process

These aspects of writing grow together, not sequentially, as students develop literacy. A sample class checklist for the writing benchmarks appears in Figure 10.10 at the end of this section.

> **☑ The student exhibits continued growth in many of the Emergent Literacy behaviors.**

In writing, just as in oral language and reading, children should show continued development in the benchmarks from the preceding stage. Watch for further growth in the writing behaviors described in Chapter 9: for example, use of a journal, sharing of writing with others, and ability to report in writing on personal events and feelings.

> **☑ The student exhibits a variety of general writing behaviors.**
>
> - Enjoys writing
> - Is confident about own writing
> - Communicates with others spontaneously
> - Attempts to read others' writing
> - Writes in a variety of formats for different purposes, such as journals, learning logs, notes, lists, stories, poems, reports, and labels

Assessment. These behaviors are best assessed through observation as students write during instruction and independently. Collect samples of students' writing over time as a basis for measuring progress and for sharing that progress with the family. You may choose to scan writing samples and store them electronically. A checklist (see Figure 10.9) is one way to keep track of which students demonstrate these behaviors. You will probably assess the quality of writing through the use of rubrics; rubrics and anchor papers are provided in many published reading and language arts programs.

Instructional Strategies. Two factors contribute most to children's pleasure in writing and their willingness to write for a variety of purposes and in a variety of forms: instruction and time to write. You will provide instruction through the various modes of writing. You begin by demonstrating a form with a write-aloud and gradually guide

General Writing Behaviors Checklist: Beginning Reading and Writing Stage

Teacher_____   Date_____ Grade_____

Y = yes
N = no
S = somewhat

Students

Behaviors										
Enjoys writing										
Is confident about own writing										
Communicates with others spontaneously										
Reads others' writing										
Formats:										
– Journals										
– Logs										
– Notes										
– Lists										
– Stories										
– Poems										
– Reports										
– Labels										
– Other (_____)										

FIGURE 10.9

General Writing Behaviors Checklist

children to acquire proficiency in that form, releasing responsibility until they are able to write independently. With the blocks of the Comprehensive Balanced Literacy Program, your children will learn how to write and have time to grow in their ability. A special writing center or area signals that you value writing as a choice of activities. The Author's Chair allows children to share what they have written.

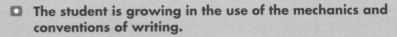

◘ The student is growing in the use of the mechanics and conventions of writing.

- Forms letters conventionally (mostly)
- Shows increased use of phonemic awareness, along with increased visual memory and spelling sense
- Invents spelling using knowledge of sound/symbol relationships when conventional spelling not known
- Is beginning to learn spelling patterns that reflect phonics knowledge
- Edits and proofreads spelling and conventions if writing is to be published
- Recognizes nonstandard usage and grammar in own writing and edits/proofreads
- Uses word processing

Assessment. Assessment of all of these behaviors comes primarily through analysis and evaluation of students' writing. When students begin formal spelling instruction (about two or three months into grade 1 in most schools), spelling tests serve as an additional assessment.

By this stage of development, phonemic awareness is more firmly connected to writing and spelling. Therefore, looking at students' use of spelling patterns provides additional information about their phonemic awareness.

Note which children already know how to use the computer for games and for a variety of Internet resources. Note whether they also know something about keyboarding.

For more on the teaching of phonemic awareness, spelling, and grammar, see Cooper & Kiger (2009) in "For Additional Reading" on the premium website for this text.

Instructional Strategies. The explicit phonics/structural elements routine (see Chapter 6) incorporates phonemic awareness development, reading instruction, and spelling instruction in relation to each letter-sound association pattern. Continue to help children make letter-sound associations in both reading and spelling.

If you have the resources, teach your children keyboarding, word processing, and other computer skills to use in their writing.

◘ The student uses the writing process.

- Participates in and understands the purpose of all steps of the writing process
- Uses the writing process collaboratively and independently
- Listens to or reads the writing of others and makes positive comments related to story parts or text structure

Assessment. Note which students are becoming more adept at using all steps of the writing process alone and in collaboration with others. Observe which students are able to read and give suggestions for improving the writing of peers. Assessment of these behaviors occurs through observation as students write, have peer conferences, and share their writing with others.

For more on the writing process, see "For Additional Reading" at the premium website for this text.

Instructional Strategies. The Comprehensive Balanced Literacy Program has two blocks of writing instruction: Learning to Write and Developmentally Appropriate Writing. Consistently providing these blocks using the modes of writing routine affords you many opportunities to model the steps of the writing process: selecting the topic, drafting, revising, proofreading, and publishing.

Figure 10.10 presents a class checklist for the writing benchmarks at the Beginning Reading and Writing stage.

Writing Checklist:
Beginning Reading and Writing Stage

Teacher _____   Date _____   Grade _____

Students

+ = consistently present
− = not present
✓ = sometimes/needs instruction

Benchmark

Emergent Literacy Behaviors

General Writing Behaviors
Enjoys writing
Is confident about writing
Communicates spontaneously
Reads others' writing
Writes in a variety of formats

Mechanics and Conventions of Writing
Forms letters conventionally
Shows increased phonemic awareness
Uses invented spelling and edits
Learning spelling patterns
Edits and proofreads
Recognizes nonstandard usage and edits own writing
Uses word processing

Writing Process
Participates in writing process
Writes collaboratively and independently
Reacts to others' writing

FIGURE 10.10

Sample Class Checklist for Beginning Reading and Writing: Writing Benchmarks and Behaviors

Planning Instruction Based on Assessment

Now that we have looked at the benchmarks for the Beginning Reading and Writing stage, we need to think about how to plan instruction based on each student's stage of development. This section is organized around three important questions:

What do I teach or emphasize for students?

How do I teach what needs to be taught?

How do I organize and manage a classroom with a range of stages and needs?

What Do I Teach?

Through systematic, ongoing assessment using the benchmarks as guidelines, you are able to tell where students are in their development and determine what needs to be taught and emphasized within their instructional program. Most students in a typical first- or second-grade classroom will be functioning at the Beginning Reading and Writing stage. However, within this classroom you will have a range of stages.

MEETING THE NEEDS OF DIVERSE LEARNERS

Remember that as you go up the grades, the range of stages within each grade increases. Meeting the needs of students at different stages within one classroom entails the use of whole-class, small-group, and independent activities.

You may also have students for whom English is a second language. English-language learners (ELL students) at the Beginning Reading and Writing stage follow the same basic patterns and stages of development as other learners (Gibbons, 1993). However, as a part of your assessment of these children's needs, you must ask two questions:

- Do my ELL students know how to read in their native language?
- Are my ELL students proficient in English? (See Chapter 3.)

These two questions will guide you toward the type of instruction that is best for these students (Snow, Burns, & Griffin, 1998).

- If students already read in their first language, try to determine if any elements of that language are transferable to reading in English. For example, if the student can read in Spanish, many English words may be understandable because they share a cognate, or root. On the other hand, virtually no vocabulary or grammar will be transferable from an Asian language such as Chinese. Reading in any language, however, requires comprehension skills; you can help students see how to apply these thinking skills to their new language.

- If beginning ELL readers and writers are speaking only their native language, they should be taught to read in that language and then make the transition to English. However, this may not be possible for all languages, given the enormous number of languages in some communities.

- The next choice is to start ELL students with a strong oral English program before they are taught to read (Snow, Burns, & Griffin, 1998). Then their oral language will continue to develop as they learn to read in English. Oral language development should include many experiences with book language through read-alouds and taped readings.

- In the regular classroom, ELL students should take part in the oral language lessons, read-alouds, and shared reading. They will, however, still need a separate time to begin learning to read in English.

- Starting ELL students with oral English first means they may not reach the benchmarks of the Beginning Reading and Writing stage at the same rate as other students. However, having the oral language activities take place at the same time as learning to read in English minimizes the delay these students will face in learning to read. Once they start to read in English, their rate of growth will increase.

For suggestions for ELL students at the Beginning Reading and Writing stage, see Freeman and Freeman (2001) in "For Additional Reading" at the premium website for this text.

MAKING DECISIONS USING ONGOING ASSESSMENT

As you start each school year, begin by looking at records from previous teachers, keeping in mind that this is only an indication of where the student was functioning at the end of the previous school year and does not account for any growth (or decline) over the summer.

Some teachers think this may bias their judgment before they get to know a child, but it can help you avoid wasting time in unnecessary testing. Therefore, we recommend that you use the previous records to help you determine how much initial assessment you will need.

Then, use the tools and procedures suggested in the first portion of this chapter and in other places throughout this book to determine each student's stage of development and needs. You can summarize the information you gain using *some* of the checklists and forms presented in this text. If all teachers in your school operate using the same basic stages of literacy development, this task will not be an overwhelming one.

As you provide instruction and literacy learning opportunities, keep your assessment ongoing. Refer to the benchmarks for each stage as guidelines to help you determine how each child is progressing. This procedure will help you answer the question "What do I teach?" and plan your instruction accordingly.

How Do I Teach What Needs to Be Taught?

Once you have made your initial decisions about each student's stage of development and what needs to be taught, you must decide how you will teach and support your students. This process involves thinking about three principal matters: 1) selecting materials for instruction appropriate for each child, 2) continuing the Comprehensive Balanced Literacy Program, and 3) choosing instructional routines appropriate for each child. This section focuses on each of these points in turn.

SELECTING MATERIALS FOR INSTRUCTION

Published Series. Most likely you will be teaching in a school that uses a published reading/language arts series, which usually provides literature in an anthology. You should familiarize yourself with *all* of the materials in the series and make sure you understand the purpose of each type of text, such as the anthology and the teacher's manual.

Make certain you also have appropriate decodable texts and trade book literature. If you don't, talk with your principal or supervisor about what you need and why you need it.

Recall that beginning reading has two big jobs: decoding and comprehension. At this stage of development, the bigger of these two jobs is still decoding. Therefore, children must have many opportunities to read decodable texts in which they can apply the strategies and skills they are learning.

Decodable texts. As we mentioned in Chapter 6, decodable texts may be created (written by someone using a list of given words or letter-sound patterns) or may be authentic trade books selected because they offer many opportunities to use certain skills. In either case, decodable texts are usually single-story books, though some publishers issue them in anthologies or as big books. The form they come in is unimportant. The main point is that you will need lots of them; children read them very quickly because their ability to decode is growing so rapidly.

Authentic texts. You will also need plenty of authentic narrative and expository trade books; these offer richer language because they have not been limited to certain decoding elements. Trade book literature may come in single-title books, big books, or anthologies. You'll use these books to provide reading practice and rich language development beyond the decodable texts.

Trade books should be sequenced from simple to complex. A good way to organize all the books needed for instruction other than the anthologies is to create a room in the school where the books are organized by level. See Chapter 6 for criteria for doing this.

Classroom library. In addition to the decodable texts and trade book literature, you'll need a classroom library for independent, self-selected reading. We recommend a rotating collection that stays in your room for six to eight weeks and is then replaced by another. These collections can come from the school's central library or a public library, or they can be rotated among several classrooms. By having rotating classroom collections rather than static ones, you always have fresh, new titles for children to read. These collections should include magazines and newspapers that show environmental print appropriate for the beginning reader and writer.

Books to read aloud. You also need many trade books for reading aloud to the class. These can be even richer and more challenging to help students expand their oral vocabularies and overall general listening abilities. They are chosen for the children's interest, as well as for being conceptually appropriate, even though they may be beyond the students' decoding abilities.

CONTINUING THE COMPREHENSIVE BALANCED LITERACY PROGRAM

In Chapter 6, we described the Comprehensive Balanced Literacy Program. But what does this look like in a first- or second-grade classroom in which most students are at the Beginning Reading and Writing stage and some are at other stages? Remember that six blocks should occur every day for all students: Daily Independent Reading, Daily Independent Writing, Reading: Learning Skills and Strategies, Reading: Application of Skills and Strategies, Writing: Learning to Write, and Writing: Developmentally Appropriate Writing. For those students needing additional support, the Intervention block is also provided. Let's examine these blocks one by one.

Daily Independent Reading. By the time students reach the Beginning Reading and Writing stage, the habit of independent reading should be somewhat established. You should allot 5 to 15 minutes per day for this activity. At the beginning of grade 1 and even grade 2, you will still need to build up independent reading time by starting with 5 minutes and gradually increasing the time until you reach 15 minutes.

You should read to yourself during part of this time to model reading. However, you should also move through the class coaching and monitoring students' reading. From time to time, have short conferences; for example, listen to individuals read orally to check their decoding and the appropriateness of the text. Ask children to re-tell what they have read. You might use a log sheet like the one shown in Figure 10.11 to keep track of observations as part of your ongoing assessment.

Independent Reading and Writing Log Sheet

Name	Reading	Writing
Mark A.	10–10 Enjoying book on frogs. 10–19 Book too difficult. Suggested he select a different one.	
Lisa C.		
Andy D.		10–1 Drew picture in log. Did not write about it but could tell about it. Encouraged him to write one or two words about his drawing.

FIGURE 10.11

Independent Reading and Writing Log Sheet

Ideas for Independent Writing

I might write a:

- story
- letter
- poem
- list
- riddle
- joke

FIGURE 10.12

Chart for Independent Writing Ideas

Daily Independent Writing. This block requires 10 to 15 minutes per day of actual writing time, not counting the time spent getting out materials and so forth. The goal is to give children writing practice and help them establish the habit of writing for their own purposes. At the Beginning Reading and Writing stage, some children will be drawing and labeling while others may be writing full sentences.

Children at all stages often need help with ideas for independent writing. A good way to help students make selections is to post a class chart for independent writing ideas (see Figure 10.12). The chart suggests types of writing, not specific topics. You can keep adding ideas as the year progresses.

For children who need help making a decision, first offer two ideas to pick from, such as a pet or a family member. Gradually increase the number of suggestions to three or more until children are selecting their own topics. You want them to choose their own topics as soon as possible because doing so leads to better writing.

Model the process yourself by writing during some of this time. Share your writing with the children often. Use part of your time to coach, monitor, and conference with children as they write. A form like the one in Figure 10.11 can help you keep a record of your observations.

In addition to the suggestions just offered, many of the ideas given in Chapter 9 for Daily Independent Reading and Writing may be used for children at this stage.

Reading: Learning Skills and Strategies. During this block, you provide systematic, explicit instruction in decoding and comprehension. Students read decodable texts that gradually increase in difficulty as you teach decoding skills. As students become independent in decoding, more attention is paid to comprehension skills.

Exactly what you teach is determined by two factors: (1) students' needs from previous stages that you have identified through ongoing assessment and (2) strategies and skills that are reflected in the benchmarks for the Beginning Reading and Writing stage. If you are using a published series, the scope and sequence of skills will help guide you.

This block is not the only one in which students will learn decoding skills. During the next block described, students also develop some abilities to decode through listening to texts, shared reading, and guided reading.

Reading: Application of Skills and Strategies. In this block, students apply what they have been learning while doing shared and eventually guided reading in instructionally appropriate materials. You also provide richer text by reading aloud.

Writing: Learning to Write. In this block, you model how to write in various forms as well as how to use the process of writing. Further development of spelling and phonemic awareness takes place. Through many shared writing experiences, students learn to write, compose their own writing, spell, and use standard grammar.

Writing: Developmentally Appropriate Writing. As soon as students learn to do one type of writing in the Learning to Write block, they have the opportunity to perform the same type of writing on their own, but selecting their own topic. For example, if you model how to write a sentence about a picture or drawing in the Learning to Write block, children can draw their own pictures and write about them during the Developmentally Appropriate Writing block. Some children may still be labeling, while others are writing full sentences.

Intervention. For those students who appear to be having difficulty learning to read, you must add a component of intervention. You will be able to identify those students who need intervention quickly through your ongoing assessment. At the first- and second-grade levels, intervention usually can be handled in a small, flexible group within the classroom. This instruction should be delivered by a certified teacher, not a paraprofessional or volunteer.

CHOOSING INSTRUCTIONAL ROUTINES

Many of the instructional suggestions given in Chapter 9 for students at the Emergent Literacy stage are also useful for students at the Beginning Reading and Writing stage.

By this stage, you will be making full use of all the instructional routines presented in Chapter 6. Many of them can be used in several blocks; you select which routines meet your instructional goals and the needs of your students. For example, discussion groups could be used in all six of the core blocks, each time serving a different purpose:

- In the Daily Independent Reading and Daily Independent Writing blocks, discussion groups are used for students to share what they are reading independently or what they are writing on their own.

- In the Reading: Learning Skills and Strategies block, discussions are used following the reading of a simple decodable text as a way to bring out the understandings students have developed.

- In the Reading: Application of Skills and Strategies block, discussions are used following listening, shared reading, or guided reading activities to focus on strategies or enjoyment of what was read.

- In the two instructional writing blocks, discussions allow students to talk about elements of the writing process as well as to share their writing, perhaps using the Author's Chair.

A later section of this chapter, "A Second-Grade Classroom at Work," will give some examples of how different routines are used.

Now that we have examined what to teach and how to teach it, we turn to how to organize and manage a classroom with a range of stages and needs.

How Do I Organize and Manage a Classroom with a Range of Stages?

The daily blocked plan is the basic structure we suggest you use for organizing your classroom. Before you can develop a daily blocked plan, however, you especially need to consider four areas: 1) your children's attention spans and interests; 2) how to use whole-class, small-group, and independent activities; 3) how to develop routines to manage a classroom using a variety of types of groups; and 4) how to use learning centers.

ATTENTION SPANS AND INTERESTS

The attention span of first and second graders varies, so keep this in mind when planning instruction. As the year progresses, attention spans typically will increase. During the first few days of school, note and record who sticks to a task until completion, who stops before a task is done, and who requires lots of your attention to get a task finished.

Directly related to attention span are students' interests. If students are doing tasks that interest them, their attention spans are likely to be longer. Knowing something about each child's interests becomes even more important in planning instruction.

This kind of information will help you organize groups and plan instructional activities. It will help you decide how long activities should last, the types of activities you need, and how many activities you need for a given amount of time. For example, students with short attention spans require shorter, more interactive activities to keep them focused.

HOW TO USE WHOLE-CLASS, SMALL-GROUP, AND INDEPENDENT ACTIVITIES

Three types of activities will help you meet the range of needs you have in your classroom: whole-class, small-group, and individual activities.

With *whole-class activities,* as the name implies, everyone in the class does the same task. Sometimes these are independent; at other times they are teacher directed or coached. For example, a shared writing lesson focusing on how to write a letter or note might be done with the whole class.

Small-group activities bring together two or more students who have the same needs to focus on a particular activity or to give them more individual attention. For example, you might conduct the shared reading of a big book with a group of six to nine students who need to expand their vocabulary and language; the small-group situation allows you to observe each student's progress more closely.

Individual activities are used when each student needs to work alone on a task or when only one student has the need for particular instruction. For example, you may have one student who needs more help with the comprehension strategy of predicting. You may decide to meet with this student alone and use the explicit comprehension routine to show him or her how to make predictions.

Using different types of groups with varied activities helps you meet the range of stages and needs in your class. You can also meet that range of needs by using what Cunningham and Allington (2006) call *multileveled activities* during whole-class instruction. In Chapter 9 we used an example of multileveled prompts based on the big book *If You Give a Mouse a Cookie* (Numeroff, 1985, 1989), describing how you might ask different students different questions about the book. That is an illustration of a multileveled activity, because the questions are based on each student's particular stage of development.

HOW TO DEVELOP CLASSROOM MANAGEMENT ROUTINES USING VARIOUS TYPES OF GROUPS

Managing the first- and second-grade classroom (or any other classroom) requires that students learn some routines. Think of it as teaching a brief social studies unit on helping children learn to work together in the classroom. There are five important steps for developing student routines: (1) develop class guidelines, (2) appoint monitors, (3) identify independent activities, (4) role-play working in groups, and (5) evaluate with students. Let's look at how to carry these out.

1. Develop Class Guidelines. Having guidelines for students to use while working in the classroom is important, especially when you have several groups doing different things, and you are meeting with one group. At the beginning of the school year, talk with your class about the need for everyone to know how to act while you are working with another student or a group. Ask students for their suggestions. Give one or two examples of what guidelines might include. During the discussion, elicit or suggest such things as the following:

- Do your own work.
- If you need to talk with someone, use a soft voice.
- Go to a class monitor for help if the teacher is busy.
- When your work is done, do a special activity from the Activity Box.
- Try to solve your own problems first.

As children give suggestions and you add your own, write them where everyone can see. Make sure you keep the ideas reasonable. Don't include such absolutes as "Never interrupt the teacher working with a group;" after all, an emergency might arise that requires a student to interrupt the teacher. When you have the guidelines assembled, you can post them on a chart like the one in Figure 10.13.

Our Class Guidelines

1. Do your own work.

2. If the teacher is busy, go to a monitor.

3. Use soft voices.

4. Get an Activity Box pack when your work is done.

5. Solve your own problems.

FIGURE 10.13

Sample Class Guidelines Chart

2. Appoint Monitors. While you are working with a group, other children may need help. Appoint monitors who can answer simple questions about an assignment, where to find materials, and so forth. You may have special monitors for different subjects, such as reading, spelling, or math, or you may have general monitors. One teacher we know gives the monitors special badges to wear so that the other children will know who they are. Monitors may be changed daily or weekly so that every child has an opportunity to be a monitor.

3. Identify Independent Activities. You'll need to establish activities that students may do after completing their assigned work. Such activities help keep children busy and prevent problems; they ensure that students never have idle waiting time. Independent or partner activities work best. Make available a limited set of activities, and change them frequently. These are a few possible types of activities:

- Self-checking folder games or activities
- Independent reading of books

Children are working at the science center. They are recording their observations.

© David Young-Wolff/ PhotoEdit

- Assessment tasks for particular strategies or skills (you will check them later)
- Math practice, such as counting pictures and doing simple addition or subtraction
- Independent writing for the student's own purposes or for a special project
- Listening center activities
- Map activities
- Learning centers (see the next section)
- Computer activities

The important thing about all of these activities is that they should be meaningful and constructive. They should always provide problem-solving experiences, practice or reinforcement, or extension of basic learning.

4. Role-Play Working in Groups. Once you have your class guidelines, monitors, and independent activities, you need to take a "dry run." Role-play the class doing an assignment while you are working with a group. First, talk the class through the way this will work. Next, walk through the procedures with no one doing work. Finally, carry out your plans. Keep times short and tasks simple.

5. Evaluate with Students. After your first full trial of your routine, discuss with students how things went. Refer to the class guidelines: Did they work? Do some need to be added? Do some need to be deleted? During the first few weeks of school, evaluate regularly. Don't get discouraged. It takes first and second graders a few weeks to establish these routines. As children become comfortable with your pattern of working, the evaluation step can be done less frequently.

We have used these types of guidelines to develop management routines in our own classrooms. We have seen thousands of successful teachers use them. They work!

HOW TO USE LEARNING CENTERS

As you saw in Chapter 8, learning centers, sometimes called *learning stations,* are places in a classroom where students perform tasks that have specified objectives. Effective learning centers have several common characteristics:

- *Manipulative activities.* Students often do matching and sorting types of activities involving hands-on manipulation. Sometimes writing is involved.
- *Specific focus.* Each learning center has a specific focus: for instance, to practice using vocabulary from a recently completed story.
- *Provision of all needed materials.* Everything students need to do the job is provided: pencils, paper, cards, crayons, computers, tape recorders, and so forth.
- *Self-checking system.* Usually some system allows students to check their own work. This may be a simple answer key or some other type of coding system. Figure 10.14 shows an example of self-checking cards for a vocabulary activity. After pairing a word on one card with its definition on another, the student can check the match by looking to see if the images on the backs of the cards fit together to form a whole picture.
- *Specified place to put completed work.* Students know exactly where to put their completed work. This may be a file box, a shoebox, or a storage tray on your desk.

Front
(Match word and definition)

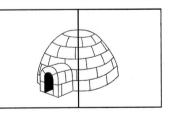
Back
(Check by seeing if picture pieces go together. The picture does not always have to relate to the word.)

FIGURE 10.14

Self-Checking Cards for a Vocabulary Game

• *Recordkeeping system.* A system is provided to help the student and you know whether all the activities of a particular center have been completed. This might be a simple card like the one shown in Figure 10.15. If it is laminated, students can mark on it with an erasable marker and use it over and over. These cards can be stored in the center area so that you can easily see how each student is doing.

Notice in Figure 10.15 that Larry Brown wrote the name for center 2, but he apparently didn't do the activity. Maybe he couldn't get to it because the center was occupied. Maybe the activity was too difficult or he didn't understand it. You would

Name Larry Brown

☐ **My Center Record** ☐

Center Number	Name	Date Completed
1	Word Match	9-4
2	Sounds I Hear	
3	Fun Facts	9-6
4	Color ~~Capers~~ Capers	9-6
5	Story Stop	9-7
6		
7		
8		

FIGURE 10.15

Learning Center Record Card for Students

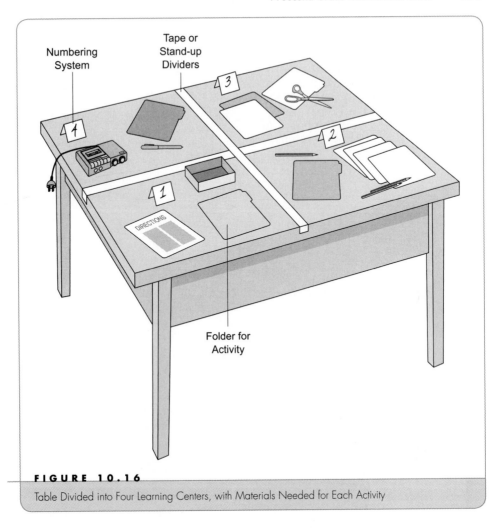

Numbering
System

Tape or
Stand-up
Dividers

DIRECTIONS

Folder for
Activity

FIGURE 10.16

Table Divided into Four Learning Centers, with Materials Needed for Each Activity

want to check on this. The record card and any completed worksheets become a part of your ongoing assessment.

If space is limited, you may have to be inventive. Figure 10.16 shows how you can create a set of four learning centers using a table. Some teachers just push together several extra desks to create learning centers. Still others construct learning centers in file folders. Students pick up the center and take it to their desk or work area.

A Second-Grade Classroom at Work

Now let's look at how all of the concepts discussed in this chapter work in a second grade classroom that contains native English speakers, second-language learners, and inclusion students. Mr. Russo's class has twenty-two children at various stages of literacy development, and he meets their needs with the Comprehensive Balanced Literacy Program. Table 10.1 presents his full-day schedule.

TABLE 10.1

Daily Schedule for Mr. Russo's Second Grade

8:15	Arrival (children sign in each day)
8:25	Morning message
8:45	Literacy block
	• Reading
	• Writing/handwriting
	• Spelling
	• Oral language
	• Daily Independent Reading
	• Daily Independent Writing
12:00	Lunch and recess
12:30	Math
1:00	Special classes (art, music, PE) three days per week. On the two days with no special classes, second-language learners and children who need intervention go to the appropriate teachers; other students have project/activity time or teacher conferences.
1:40	Science/social studies/health (alternating units; some children go to intervention teachers during this time, and second-language students go to English-language development lessons)
2:20	Activity time
2:40	Read-aloud
2:50	Preparation for dismissal
2:55	Dismissal

Four students in Mr. Russo's class who need Tier II reading intervention are pulled out at 1:00 on two days and at 1:40 on two additional days. This allows these students to get intervention without missing the classroom literacy block or the art, music, or PE classes; they miss some, but not all, periods of science, social studies, and health.

There are also four students who are second-language learners. They speak Spanish and can read some materials in their native language. They are at the early production level (see Chapter 3) in their oral language; this means that they listen attentively, speak a few words of English, but most often use key words. They go to a language specialist for English-language development lessons at the same times other students go to intervention.

In the following section, we will present a detailed look at Mr. Russo's literacy block on one sample day. Study the plan carefully, read the discussion that follows it, and complete the questions at the end of the plan.

Mr. Russo's Literacy Block Schedule (twenty-two second graders)

TIME

8:45 to noon daily (includes morning break)

ARRANGEMENTS FOR INDEPENDENT WORK

Five learning centers: one for writing, one for vocabulary, one for spelling practice, and two for phonics practice.

8:45 READING: APPLICATION OF SKILLS AND STRATEGIES

Activities

- Reread the big book *The Lady with the Alligator Purse* (Westcott, 1988).
- Discussion

Routines

- Modes of reading routine (shared reading)
- Discussion groups

COMMENTS

This previously read book provides application of letter-sound associations and high-frequency words taught earlier. The activity also serves as a warm-up for the day. Since shared reading is a group-type choral reading, the four second-language learners can successfully participate. After the shared reading, the class divides into four small groups to discuss the book.

9:00 DAILY INDEPENDENT READING

Activities

- Conferences with Jeff, Leisa, Elaina, and Martha

COMMENTS

During this time, students are practicing reading. Conferences help Mr. Russo check for decoding and other skill applications to self-selected books. Elaina, one of the second-language learners, is reading a Spanish book. Mr. Russo discusses the book with her in Spanish.

9:10 READING: LEARNING SKILLS AND STRATEGIES

Activities

- Teach digraphs *sh, ch, th*
- Practice and apply digraphs
- Read *Charlie's Shoes*

Routines

- Explicit phonics/structural elements routine
- Decodable words routine
- Modes of reading routine (observational guided reading)
- Phonetically unpredictable words routine

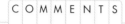

COMMENTS

Mr. Russo is continuing to teach the decoding skills students need. Meeting with three small groups, he uses the above four routines. While he meets with one group, the other children go to an assigned learning center. Because the four second-language learners are not yet ready for this skill, they go to one of the learning centers that has a taped story; they follow along in a picture book while listening to the story and then respond to it with a short writing (in English or in their first language) or with labeled pictures.

10:10 DAILY INDEPENDENT WRITING

Activity

- Children add to their journals.

COMMENTS

Mr. Russo moves from child to child to check how they are spelling using the letter-sound associations taught so far this year. He also notes how their overall writing is developing. He encourages the second-language learners to draw and to write in both Spanish and English. The inclusion students also participate in this activity.

10:20 WRITING: LEARNING TO WRITE

Activity

- Write a group story.
- Review spelling words with *sh, ch, th:* "chair," "show," "think," "much," "shop."

Routine

- Modes of writing routine (shared writing)

Mr. Russo is connecting the explicit phonics instruction with spelling. The children help him write a group story. He works the spelling words into the story. The second-language learners have a list of five other words that they have identified with Mr. Russo from their English-language development class that they will use for spelling.

10:40 MORNING BREAK

10:55 READING: LEARNING SKILLS AND STRATEGIES

Activities

- Practice spelling words with digraphs *sh, ch, th*.
- Add spelling words to word wall.
- Review words on word wall.

Routines

- Making words (a routine in which students build words using letter cards; see Cooper, 2006)
- Word wall

Mr. Russo returns to this block to provide more individual and small-group practice and connections for students. All students participate in these activities.

11:15 WRITING: DEVELOPMENTALLY APPROPRIATE WRITING

Activities

- Children write own stories.
- Use of words from word wall is encouraged.

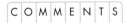

This is a follow-up to the teacher modeling through shared writing done earlier in the day. Mr. Russo moves from student to student to provide coaching. He is looking for application of skills previously taught and evidence of students' writing progress.

11:30 READING: APPLICATION OF SKILLS AND STRATEGIES

Activities

- Children write own stories.
- Use of words from word wall is encouraged.

This is a follow-up to the teacher modeling through shared writing done earlier in the day. Mr. Russo moves from student to student to provide coaching. He is looking for application of skills previously taught and evidence of students' writing progress.

11:30 READING: APPLICATION OF SKILLS AND STRATEGIES

Activities

- Read aloud *The 500 Hats of Bartholomew Cubbins* (Seuss, 1938) to introduce the concept of identifying important information using a story map.
- Partners practice reading (each pair of students selects any book already read).

Routines

- Modes of reading routine (read-aloud)
- Modes of reading routine (cooperative reading)

Mr. Russo uses listening in preparation for teaching reading comprehension.

Children select any books they have read today or on another day. They read with a partner. Mr. Russo moves from pair to pair to note fluency and application of skills.

11:50 CLOSING THE LITERACY BLOCK

Activities

- Discuss what was learned today. Make a list on the board.

C O M M E N T S

Mr. Russo concludes his literacy schedule for the day by having children talk about what they have learned. For example, children might say, "I learned a new word" or "I learned to read better." This helps to keep children focused and helps them see the value of their day.

12:00 END OF LITERACY BLOCK/LUNCH/RECESS

A DISCUSSION OF MR. RUSSO'S LITERACY BLOCK PLAN

Let's look at how instruction for children at the Beginning Reading and Writing stage differs from instruction in earlier stages. We can do this by looking at each time block during the day.

8:45: Reading: Application of Skills and Strategies. Mr. Russo uses shared reading as might be done with children at an earlier stage. Children at this stage, however, are likely to join in the reading sooner than children at an earlier stage might.

Although he has children at several different stages in his class, Mr. Russo can use shared reading in the same book by using different questions and prompts and calling different students' attention to different skills or elements of the text.

9:00: Daily Independent Reading. Children at the Beginning Reading and Writing stage will begin to read increasingly more difficult texts. However, some children at this stage like reading simpler texts until they feel more secure in reading. This helps them develop fluency.

9:10: Reading: Learning Skills and Strategies. The instruction being provided in digraphs was selected on the basis of students' strengths and needs. This is a review for some children and a skill need for others. While Mr. Russo teaches one group, children who have other needs work at learning centers on tasks more appropriate for them. The second-language learners work at a learning center using oral language tapes.

10:10: Daily Independent Writing. Children at the Beginning Reading and Writing stage are writing more than in earlier stages. Even though the class includes children at various stages, Mr. Russo can meet the needs of all the children by working with individuals as they write their own pieces.

10:20: Writing: Learning to Write. During this time, Mr. Russo models writing. He connects phonics, spelling, and writing by using shared writing. He is combining what children have learned about phonics, and he is showing them how to write using what they have learned.

10:40: Morning Break. This is a restroom and stretch break.

10:55: Reading: Learning Skills and Strategies. Since his class contains a range of stages, Mr. Russo provides more time for practice for those who have just received instruction in the skill of digraphs. This gives him time to work with other students with different needs.

11:15: Writing: Developmentally Appropriate Writing. The children at the Beginning Reading and Writing stage are ready to write their own stories based, in part, on the modeling that Mr. Russo did during shared writing. This block gives him time to work with the children who are ready to write full stories as well as those who need more teacher modeling.

11:30: Reading: Application of Skills and Strategies. Mr. Russo is modeling the use of an important comprehension strategy at the listening level. Children practice fluency reading and receive coaching.

11:50: Closing the Literacy Block. Mr. Russo and the children discuss what they have done for the day and what individuals think they have learned.

Notice that Mr. Russo was meeting the needs of a range of stages and students' abilities as well as using the concept of ongoing assessment.

Summary

- At the Beginning Reading and Writing stage, students take on more and more of the characteristics of readers and writers.

- Benchmarks at this stage are usually achieved by most students in first or second grade.

- Most procedures for assessing the benchmarks for this stage are informal and can be carried out as a part of assessment-based literacy instruction.

- Students at this stage expand their use of standard English and grow in their facility to use language.

- Students continue to show pleasure in knowing more words and in word play.

- In reading, students acquire additional word recognition skills and strategies.

- Students learn to construct meaning more readily by using key strategies such as visualizing, predicting, identifying important information, self-questioning, monitoring, summarizing, synthesizing, and evaluating.

- Students begin to use and explore research tools and skills.

- Students exhibit a variety of general writing behaviors, showing increased interest and enjoyment of writing, reading others' writing, and writing on their own using a variety of formats for many purposes.

- Within any classroom, there will be students at various stages of literacy development. Some will be second-language learners, and others may be students who have a variety of disabilities. Instruction in the classroom for all students should be adjusted to their needs, interests, and attention spans.

- The Comprehensive Balanced Literacy Program described in Chapter 6 and all the instructional routines detailed in that chapter are appropriate for this stage in a mixture of whole-class, small-group, and individual activities.

- To organize and manage your classroom, you will need to develop class guidelines, appoint monitors, identify independent activities, role-play working in groups, and evaluate your routines with your students.

- Effective use of learning centers also becomes particularly important at this stage.

 Please visit the premium website for *Literacy Assessment*, Fourth Edition to access the TeachSource Video Cases, chapter web links, For Additional Reading, tutorial quizzes, glossary flashcards, online checklists, downloads, and much more! Go to www.cengage.com/login to register your access code.

Standards Focus (See inside back cover)

IRA Standards for Reading Professionals: 1, 2, 3, 4

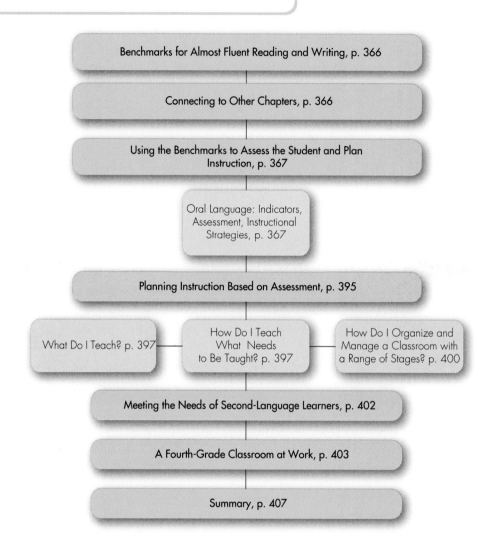

11 Almost Fluent Reading and Writing

NEW TERMS

- domains of writing
- multisyllabic
- reciprocal teaching

Mrs. Benson, a fifth-grade teacher at Redwood Elementary School, has invited us to visit her classroom today. She has twenty-eight students, thirteen boys and fifteen girls. One boy is Vietnamese, and three girls are Colombian. All of the second-language learners have made the transition from their first language and now do all of their reading, as well as their work in other subjects, in English.

One group of students at a round table is discussing a selection they just finished reading in their anthology. One boy is directing the discussion by referring to four ideas Mrs. Benson has listed on the board. As students take turns adding to the discussion, they all write in their journals.

In another part of the room, Mrs. Benson is teaching a group of students a lesson on summarizing. She is modeling how she would write a summary. As she writes, she shares with the students why she wrote what she did in her summary. Afterward, Mrs. Benson and the students develop a chart of guidelines for a good summary. She directs students to return to their desks to write a summary of the article on sea mammals they have just read, using the guidelines from the chart to help them.

Mrs. Benson now moves to her desk, where she makes notes on several students. Then she calls for another group to meet at the table. She tells the students they are going to work on ways to decode unfamiliar long words and infer the words' meanings from the text.

In terms of their reading and writing, were you able to see a difference between the students in Mrs. Benson's room and those you met in earlier classrooms? In this class, notice that students were taking a leadership role in the discussion, even though they were focusing on points the teacher had listed on the board. Notice, too, the range of students' needs: to one group Mrs. Benson was teaching the strategy of summarizing, while with other students she continued to give some instruction in decoding.

All of the behaviors we observed in Mrs. Benson's classroom are typical of students in the Almost Fluent Reading and Writing stage. Even though Mrs. Benson has students who are at other stages of development, most of them are at this Almost Fluent stage.

Benchmarks for Almost Fluent Reading and Writing

Benchmarks for the Almost Fluent Reading and Writing stage are typical of children ages seven to nine, from the end of second grade through fourth or fifth grade. In these higher grades, we find an increasing range of stages of literacy development. Even at fourth grade, a teacher may have one student who is still at the Beginning Reading and Writing stage and one who can read adult material with understanding. The challenge becomes greater as the range increases.

Connecting to Other Chapters

As you read about the Almost Fluent Reading and Writing stage, you may want to refer to other chapters for ideas about assessment and instruction to meet varying needs. Many students will begin the school year functioning at the Beginning Reading and Writing stage and become more fluent readers and writers by the end

B
E
N
C
H
M
A
R
K
S

ORAL LANGUAGE

- The student exhibits continued growth in many behaviors from Beginning Reading and Writing.
- The student's use of standard English continues to develop.
- The student's facility with language is growing.
- The student's oral and listening vocabulary reflects increased growth and pleasure in language.

READING

- The student exhibits continued growth in behaviors from Beginning Reading and Writing.
- The student shows increasing fluency and appropriate use of all word recognition strategies.
- The student's comprehension, or construction of meaning, is growing.
- The student reads for a variety of purposes.
- The student is learning research skills.

WRITING

- The student exhibits continued growth in behaviors from Beginning Reading and Writing.
- The student writes for a variety of purposes.
- The student shows growth in the mechanics and conventions of writing.
- The student shows pleasure and confidence in writing.
- The student connects reading and writing.

of the year. Therefore, it becomes increasingly important to know the assessment procedures and instructional strategies used at all the stages of development. Others may already be fluent.

Using the Benchmarks to Assess the Student and Plan Instruction

Assessment of each benchmark for the Almost Fluent Reading and Writing stage can be done informally during instruction as well as through more structured informal procedures and some formal procedures. In this section, we first discuss ways to assess each benchmark and then provide some suggestions for instruction for those students who need it.

Oral Language: Indicators, Assessment, Instructional Strategies

Oral language becomes increasingly important as students progress through the Almost Fluent Reading and Writing stage. Students have many more opportunities, as well as a greater need, to listen critically and speak clearly. There are four main areas of oral language behaviors for the Almost Fluent Reading and Writing stage:

- Continued growth in Beginning Reading and Writing behaviors
- Use of standard English
- Growing facility with language
- Increased vocabulary and pleasure in using language

A sample oral language class checklist appears at the end of this section in Figure 11.3.

> ☑ **The student exhibits continued growth in many behaviors from Beginning Reading and Writing.**

Children in the Almost Fluent Reading and Writing stage will continue to develop in the behaviors characteristic of the Beginning Reading and Writing stage. For example, they will ask about the meanings of words they don't know, and they will show an increasing ability to paraphrase what others say.

> ☑ **The student's use of standard English continues to develop.**
> - Is aware of own problem areas
> - Accepts diverse usage or varieties of English from others without criticism

Assessment. Students must begin to assess their own speaking and listening abilities and become aware of any problem areas. This can be encouraged by providing students with a checklist for their own use of language, such as the one in Figure 11.1,

ORAL LANGUAGE
SELF-EVALUATION

Name_____ Date _____

Think about your use of listening and speaking. Check the areas where you feel you have strength.

LISTENING

_____ I pay attention as others speak.

_____ I ask appropriate questions.

_____ I listen to responses to questions.

SPEAKING

_____ I speak clearly and distinctly.

_____ I use appropriate words.

_____ I choose language that fits the audience.

_____ My subjects and verbs agree when I speak.

_____ I use articles and prepositions appropriately.

Strengths	Areas Where I Need to Improve

(Use the back if needed)

FIGURE 11.1

Student Self-Evaluation Checklist for Oral Language

which they can complete periodically. By comparing completed checklists several times during the year, you can note changes in perceptions.

Listen to and watch students interact with others in the classroom, on the playground, or in the lunchroom. Do you hear students make fun of the way(s) someone speaks? Do you hear students correcting others in a demeaning manner?

Instructional Strategies. By talking about and modeling the process of self-evaluation in speaking and listening, you can help students develop this ability in themselves. You want them to see how important it is to be aware of one's own problem areas. A checklist like the one in Figure 11.1 offers a good basis for discussion with your students.

- Be sure they realize that most people have areas of language use that need improvement. For instance, we often speak one way in a more formal situation and another way in a less formal situation, and making the shift is not always easy.

- When you are working with English-language learners (ELL students), keep in mind that they may have a more difficult time evaluating their use of English than native speakers do. For example, it takes a long time for ELL students to master the use of prepositions and noun-verb agreement. Therefore, a bit more teacher guidance may be required when asking ELL students to do self-evaluation.

- Create an atmosphere in your classroom that promotes and accepts diversity. You do this mainly by example. You let your students see that you yourself are accepting of diversity in language. Be sure everyone in the class realizes that, although the second-language students are just learning English, they speak their first language very well. If problems arise among your students, have open and honest discussions about how people express themselves differently depending on their background. At the same time, all students should realize that there is a standard form of English that is considered most appropriate for school, and the goal for all is to use this form comfortably.

- In addition, during your language lessons, discuss how different people talk differently. Have students look for examples from television and other media of people talking with variations of the same language.

> ◻ **The student's facility with language is growing.**
>
> - Collaborates with classmates in speaking and listening situations
> - Participates in discussion without adult supervision
> - Can listen to and then question or respond to (use an idea expressed by) a speaker
> - Speaks in front of a group using written notes but no script

Assessment. These behaviors are best assessed by observing students in a variety of speaking and listening situations. As you observe, ask yourself the following questions and make notes about students' behaviors:

1. Does the student pay attention when classmates are talking?

2. Does the student participate in discussions with other students in a polite and cooperative manner?

3. Does the student participate in discussions with other students in your absence?

4. While listening to classmates, does the student raise relevant questions?

5. Is the student able to give a talk in front of a group using only notes?

Figure 11.2 shows a form for recording your answers to these observational questions.

LANGUAGE FACILITY RECORD SHEET

Name_____ Date_____

	Yes	No	Comments
1. Pays attention while others talk.			
2. Participates in discussion politely and cooperatively.			
3. Participates in discussion without teacher present.			
4. Raises questions when listening to others.			
5. Gives talk in front of group using only notes.			
6. Uses a variety of words.			
7. Uses same words over and over.			
8. Adds new words to usage.			

FIGURE 11.2

Form for Recording Observations of a Student's Facility in Use of Oral Language

Instructional Strategies. Many of the suggestions given in Chapter 10 for increasing facility with language are also useful at this stage. Wide reading plays an increasingly important role in expanding students' oral language. Make sure you include the Daily Independent Reading block in your Comprehensive Balanced Literacy Program.

To develop their ability to give a talk or report using notes alone, teach students how to create an outline and write key words on cards. Then provide many opportunities for them to practice giving talks. Also continue to focus on listening.

> ☑ **The student's oral and listening vocabulary reflects increased growth and pleasure in language.**
>
> - Uses new vocabulary
> - Appreciates symbolic language such as metaphor
> - Enjoys listening to and telling riddles and jokes
> - Begins to appreciate shades of meaning, connotation, precise word choice, and the evocative power of certain words
> - Recognizes and begins to use persuasive techniques

Assessment. Pay attention to whether children are using a variety of words when expressing themselves. Do they use the same words over and over? Are they trying out new words first encountered in reading or listening experiences?

Observing students in a variety of listening and speaking situations is the best way to assess other behaviors. To see what persuasive techniques your students use, for example, note how they conduct themselves during discussions. See Figure 11.2.

Instructional Strategies

- Continue to make students aware of new words. For instance, have students listen for new words they hear others use; then post these words on a bulletin board and discuss them.
- Students' pleasure in the use of language begins with the rich literature they are reading and listening to.
- From time to time, discuss the shades of meaning represented by certain words in a story or note a particular technique an author has used to sway the reader. Encourage students to use these elements in their own oral language.
- With the shared-writing method, you can also model the use of these elements in writing.
- You may use the minilesson routine to teach lessons on metaphor, similes, connotation, and various persuasive techniques.
- But above all else, have fun with language yourself. Share jokes and riddles with your students and encourage them to do the same with the class.
- Serve as a good language model by using and talking about exciting or interesting words and different ways to express oneself.

Figure 11.3 presents a class checklist for all the oral language benchmarks at the Almost Fluent Reading and Writing stage.

Reading: Indicators, Assessment, Instructional Strategies

Oral Language Checklist:
Almost Fluent Reading and Writing Stage

Teacher_____ Date_____ Grade_____

Students

+ = behavior present
- = behavior absent
✓ = somewhat present

Benchmark										
Beginning Reading and Writing Behaviors										
Use of Standard English										
Is aware of own problems										
Accepts diverse usage										
Growing Facility with Language										
Collaborates in speaking and listening										
Participates in discussion without adult										
Listens to and questions speakers										
Speaks with notes										
Oral and Listening Vocabulary/Pleasure in Use										
Uses new vocabulary										
Appreciates symbolic language										
Listens to and tells jokes/riddles										
Appreciates shades of meaning										
Recognizes and uses persuasive techniques										

FIGURE 11.3

Sample Class Checklist for Almost Fluent Reading and Writing Stage: Oral Language Benchmarks and Behaviors

There are five main areas of reading behaviors for the Almost Fluent Reading and Writing stage:

- Continued growth in Beginning Reading and Writing behaviors
- Increased fluency and word recognition
- Growing comprehension (construction of meaning)
- Reading for a variety of purposes
- Use of research skills

A sample class checklist appears in Figure 11.9.

> ### ▣ The student exhibits continued growth in behaviors from Beginning Reading and Writing.

As with oral language, you should notice that your students at the Almost Fluent stage show continued development of various reading behaviors from the preceding stage: for instance, the ability to read and retell both familiar and unfamiliar texts, sense of self as a reader, and growth in the number of words recognized at sight.

> ### ▣ The student shows increasing fluency and appropriate use of all word recognition strategies.
>
> - Uses structure, phonics, and syntax (language structure) to determine word pronunciation
> - Uses context to determine word meaning
> - Selects appropriate skills and strategies to sound out unknown words
> - Reads orally with 90 percent accuracy in grade-level materials
> - Self-corrects
> - Takes risks

Assessment. You will be able to tell what skills students are using to pronounce words by studying their oral reading behaviors and analyzing their miscues. Look for a pattern of miscues (at least two or three examples) before you draw conclusions. Table 11.1 presents examples of behaviors that would indicate a student has achieved the various benchmark components. All of these behaviors are observable during a student's oral reading.

Beginning readers depend heavily on letter-sound associations and sequential decoding. As they become more fluent, readers use context to determine what type of word fits in a slot and then use structure and phonics to determine the pronunciation of unknown words. They also use context to determine word meaning.

Sometimes it is hard to pinpoint the exact problem students are having because they are using so many different skills and strategies at once. If you encounter this situation, you might check a student's decoding abilities by giving him or her a list of pseudo-words (made-up words, sometimes referred to as nonsense words) to read.

TABLE 11.1

Oral Reading Behaviors Showing Benchmark Accomplishment for Word Recognition

BENCHMARK BEHAVIOR	ORAL READING BEHAVIORS
Phonics and/or structural analysis	• Pronounces most words correctly • Miscues show student pronounces phonic/structural elements correctly; for example: *debat* ~~debate~~ (knows beginning consonants or syllable *de*; does not know the v̄c̸e̸ generalization; reader should self-correct) *ûnselish* ~~unselfish~~ (knows prefix *un* and suffix *ish*; does not focus on middles of words; reader should self-correct) • Slowly analyzes word in oral reading but blends together in reading: *pre-his-tor-ic*; finally says *prehistoric*
Syntax	*The snake moved across the grass in a sinewy, slithering motion.* (Can't pronounce *sinewy* but knows it must be a word that describes how the snake moves because of its position in the sentence)
Context	*The rhea displayed beautiful feathers.* (Is unable to pronounce *rhea*, but comments, "It's some kind of pretty bird")

Selects appropriate skills and strategies to sound out unknown word	• Breaks an unknown word into parts and finally blends it together in oral reading:
	  Says: dĕv-ə-stāte
	  Blends: *devastate*
	
	(Shows good use of chunking and application of vowel generalizations)
	
	• Skips an unknown word and reads to end of sentence to get a sense of the type of word that belongs in the slot. Then goes back and tries to analyze the word:
	  Larry and Ted were having a <u>heated</u> talk.
	  (Skipped *heated;* then sounded it out: héat-əd – *heated*)

Oral reading 90 percent accurate	• Reads orally 90 percent or more of the words correctly • Reads with fluency

Self-corrects	• Miscues in oral reading and then corrects:
	  galloping sc
	  The dinosaur was ~~gobbling~~ up everything in sight.
	
	This correction might result from reexamination of the letters, but more likely from meaning because *galloping* doesn't make sense.

Takes risks	• Does not stop when oral reading and comes to an unknown word; tries to analyze the word even if not totally correct: for *lubricate,* says *lub rick at*

For example, if you suspect a problem with vowel sounds, have students read aloud some pseudo-words containing common vowel patterns to see if they are pronouncing the words according to the generalizations they should be following:

zeat (zē̆ạt)   lakint (lăk ĭnt or lā kĭnt)
rapple (răpp əl)   darump (dar ŭmp or dā rŭmp)

There is disagreement among literacy specialists about using pseudo-words with students. We have sometimes found them useful to better pinpoint a student's specific decoding problems at the more advanced levels of reading. However, you should be cautious about reading too much into the way students pronounce nonsense words because they may try to make them "real." Also, be aware that second-language learners and students struggling with language are often confused by pseudo-words.

Instructional Strategies. If students are having problems with decoding at this stage, first try to identify their specific needs. Then use the instructional routines suggested in Chapter 6 to meet those needs.

Some students who are entering and moving through the Almost Fluent Reading and Writing stage know the various decoding elements but do not apply them when they encounter longer words. We suggest that you teach students the following steps to guide them as they attempt to decode a longer word:

1. Look for chunks or parts of words you recognize. These chunks might include prefixes, suffixes, base words, or root words (*not* little words within big words). Try to orally say or silently think the word. Then use context to verify the word's meaning.

2. If you are unable to recognize the word by using the chunks, look to the letter-sound associations. Again, say the word orally or silently in your head; then use context to check or verify meaning.

3. If neither word chunks nor letter-sound associations lead to the pronunciation, ask someone or go to the dictionary.

Figure 10.5 presented a poster to remind students about this decoding strategy. Its simple steps give the reader a system for thinking about an unknown word. Teach and model it using longer, **multisyllabic** words followed by many opportunities to practice and apply the strategy in reading experiences. Table 11.2 shows a sample lesson. Use your ongoing assessment of students' reading to determine the amount of reteaching, practice, and application your students need.

Another approach to teaching students to decode longer words is the *Making More Big Words* system developed by Cunningham and Hall (2001), listed in "For Additional Reading" on the premium website for this book. This is an interactive system in which students manipulate chunks of words to build and decode longer words.

☐ **The student shows increasing fluency and appropriate use of all word recognition strategies. (continued)**

● Uses a dictionary both for pronunciation and for meaning

TABLE 11.2

Model for Lessons in Decoding Longer Words

Objective	Teach students a systematic strategy for decoding longer words and applying known phonics and structural elements.
Materials	• Transparency or poster showing the strategy (see Figure 10.5) • List of multisyllabic words in sentences
Procedures	

Teach	1. Tell students that the purpose of this lesson is to teach them how to approach a longer unknown word when they encounter it in reading.
	
	2. Display the poster. Ask students to read each step aloud. Discuss and explain the meaning of the step.
	
	3. Present a multisyllabic word underlined in the context of a sentence:
	
	    The students in the science class were studying the <u>muscular</u> structure of the human body.
	
	4. Model how you would approach the word by saying:
	
	    When I came to this word in my reading (point to *muscular*), I didn't know it. I started thinking about the steps of our strategy. I looked for chunks I knew. I knew *mus*•(/mŭs/) and I knew *ar*•(/är/). I thought of three chunks mus•cul•ar. I couldn't quite say the word. I looked at *cul* and thought about the letter-sound associations. I knew the /c/ and /l/ sounds. I also knew that the vowel in the middle of a chunk is usually short. I said /mŭs/•/cŭl/•/är/. I read the sentence aloud, and it didn't sound like any word I knew. Then I put the /l/ with the /är/. The vowel (*u*) at the end of a chunk is usually long. I said *mŭs*•*cū*•*lar*. I had heard *muscular*. I read the sentence, and it made sense. I knew the students in this class were studying the muscles of the body.
	
	5. Repeat modeling with several examples as needed.

Practice	Provide students several sentences containing multisyllabic words. Have pairs of students select any multisyllabic word and tell how they would use the strategy to approach the word.
Apply	Give students a piece of text (narrative or expository) you believe is *slightly* more difficult than their usual reading material. Direct them to read the text silently, looking for places where they could use the strategy for determining an unknown word. After reading, ask different students to name a word they have found and explain how they used the strategy.

Assessment. This word recognition ability involves a variety of skills, including the following:

- Uses alphabetical order to the second and third letter
- Uses the elements and symbols in a dictionary, such as the entry word, the phonetic respelling of a word, the definition, the pronunciation guide, various symbols (n = noun; v = verb), and so forth

- Locates entries rapidly
- Selects the appropriate definition

Two primary ways to assess students' ability to use the dictionary are (1) to give specific tasks for students to do in relation to each skill just mentioned and (2) to observe their behaviors as they actually use the dictionary on their own during daily literacy activities or complete tasks or answer questions that you give them. If you are using a published program for reading/language arts, use some of the suggestions given in the teacher's manual for this purpose. The checklist presented in Figure 11.4 should help you keep track of students' progress in learning to use the dictionary.

Instructional Strategies. The dictionary can become a valuable tool in helping students pronounce unknown words and determine their meanings. Most students will come into this stage with some familiarity with the dictionary. As early as the Emergent Literacy or the Beginning Reading and Writing stage, students learn to use a picture dictionary or make their own simple dictionaries. By the Almost Fluent stage, students should receive more formal instruction in the use of the dictionary. They should be introduced to all elements of the dictionary and show increased use of the dictionary on their own.

Once students have been taught the basics of using the dictionary, the best way for them to master its use is through many authentic opportunities involving actual reading or writing. Avoid giving students long lists of words to look up; students usually write the first or shortest definition. They gain nothing from this kind of activity. Rather, encourage dictionary use for authentic reasons, such as to look up the meaning or the pronunciation of an unknown word or to verify spelling.

Be cautious, however, about thoughtlessly telling students to use the dictionary to find the spelling of an unknown word. Unless they have some idea about how a word is spelled, the dictionary is of limited value for spelling. Therefore, you need to teach students to hypothesize probable spelling as a starting point.

> ### ◘ The student's comprehension, or construction of meaning, is growing.
>
> - Enjoys listening to selections that may be beyond his or her reading ability

Assessment. Listening to stories and informational texts beyond their actual reading level continues to be a good way for students to expand their oral language and vocabulary, which in turn expands their foundation for constructing meaning. You assess this behavior through observation.

Instructional Strategies. Continue to read aloud to students for enjoyment on a regular basis. Include various types of texts in your reading, and provide opportunities for discussion and reaction to what you have read. Do not turn enjoyable listening experiences into tests or formal lessons by requiring students to write or do other activities following the listening experience.

Some students may find more pleasure in listening to tapes or CDs if they have a choice of what to listen to.

DICTIONARY CHECKLIST

Name_____   Date_____

	Uses Appropriately	Needs Improvement	Comments
LOCATING WORDS			
Locates words by first, second, third, fourth letter			
Uses guide words			
Finds words whose exact spellings are unknown			
PRONUNCIATION (uses)			
Parts of dictionary entry			
Abbreviations in entry			
Pronunciation guide			
Phonetic respelling			
Diacritical marks			
Accent marks			
Alternate pronunciations			
WORD MEANING AND USAGE			
Understands abbreviations			
Recognizes different definitions given			
Selects appropriate definition			
Relates derived forms to base word			
Understands etymologies			

FIGURE 11.4

Checklist for Assessing Student's Use of the Dictionary

Good contemporary literature captures a reader's interest.

© Susan Van Etten/ PhotoEdit

> **◙ The student's comprehension, or construction of meaning, is growing. (continued)**
>
> - Reads independently
> - Enjoys reading a variety of genres
> - Chooses to read outside of school
> - Prefers to read silently

Assessment. These behaviors are best assessed through observation. By the time students reach the Almost Fluent Reading and Writing stage, they should be reading a great deal more on their own both in and out of school. The form in Figure 11.5 is a good way for students themselves to keep track of these behaviors. Students' reading should be silent except when they are reading aloud to share information, prove points, or entertain others.

Instructional Strategies. These behaviors require no direct instruction, but students must have ample opportunities to do independent, self-selected reading during the day. If you have students who don't seem to enjoy independent reading, consider the following:

- Does the student have books that interest him or her? Independent reading can also be done in magazines and newspapers. You might need to use an interest inventory (see Chapter 2) to get a better picture of the student's interests.

- Are the books the student is trying to read too difficult? Talk with the student about selecting books that he or she can read. Show the whole class how to

Independent Reading Record

Name _____

		In-School		Out-of-School	
		Date	Minutes	Date	Minutes
Title _____					
Author _____					
Type of Book _____					
Started _____ Completed _____					
Comments: _____					
_____					
_____					
Title _____					

FIGURE 11.5

Independent Reading Form for Students to Use

select a book by reading a page silently and looking for unknown words. If there are five or more unknown words on a page, the student may want to select a different book.

• Is the student interested only in one type of book or series of books? This is not really a problem; the important thing is that the student is reading. However, you might want to make other reading materials available on related topics. Also, be sure to introduce a variety of books when you read aloud to students.

If you have students at the Almost Fluent Reading and Writing stage who are still reading aloud to themselves, look at their overall reading behavior. Is there a problem with decoding or comprehension? Are the students having difficulty remembering what they read? If so, does the problem occur with all types of text or just with certain types? Are the texts too difficult? Examining all of these factors will help you determine how to encourage students to read silently.

□ **The student's comprehension, or construction of meaning, is growing. (continued)**

• Continues to grow in the use of comprehension strategies: visualizing, predicting, identifying important information, self-questioning, monitoring, summarizing, synthesizing, and evaluating

Assessment. You can assess students' use of strategies for constructing meaning in two ways: through an informal reading inventory (see Chapter 4) and through listening to daily text reading. In Chapter 10, we discussed a variety of behaviors to look for. Those same procedures should be used for students at this stage of development. You'll notice that students are becoming more sophisticated in their use of the strategies. For example, as students use the evaluation strategy, they will judge a greater range of things, such as an author's qualifications to write on the topic and how clearly ideas were presented and supported.

Instructional Strategies. Think back to Mrs. Benson, and how she modeled summarizing. This is the kind of procedure that should be used for students at this stage. The strategies remain the same as at earlier stages, but the materials the students read become more difficult. In addition, for students who have reached the Almost Fluent Reading and Writing stage, we suggest that you use the research-based strategy called *reciprocal teaching* (Palincsar & Brown, 1984, 1986; Oczkus, 2003; Rosenshine & Meister, 1994).

Reciprocal teaching is an interactive process; teacher and students take turns modeling four strategies after reading a meaningful chunk of text silently. The four strategies are *predict, question, summarize,* and *clarify.* This process was developed to help struggling readers in upper elementary and middle schools accelerate their reading growth and learn to construct meaning more effectively. It is one of the cornerstone strategies in the proven intervention program Project SUCCESS and its published program *Soar to Success* (Cooper, Boschken, McWilliams, & Pistochini, 2000). An additional benefit of reciprocal teaching is improved ability to decode words (Rosenshine & Meister, 1994). Reciprocal teaching is not difficult to use, but it does take practice on the part of both teacher and students. Table 11.3 presents the steps.

TABLE 11.3

Model for Using Reciprocal Teaching

---

1. Make a poster for the four strategies like the one shown in Figure 11.6.

2. Introduce the four strategies to students using a *very easy, short* piece of text (not more than two pages). Present the poster and explain each strategy. Model one strategy at a time for students, each time having them model right after you model. Remember, your goal is just to introduce the strategies. After your introductory lesson (40–60 minutes total), use the process on a daily basis with students.

3. Select a narrative or expository text for your group of students to read.

4. Divide the text into meaningful sections or chunks. In the beginning, use fairly short sections or chunks (3–5 pages each).

5. Introduce the text by activating prior knowledge and building background.

(Continued)

TABLE 11.3

Model for Using Reciprocal Teaching *(Continued)*

6. Have students *predict* or pose *questions* for the first chunk of text.

7. Remind students to use the four strategies as they *silently* read the chunk of text.

8. After the silent reading, have students verify their predictions or answer the questions posed. As students answer, have them locate places in the text to support their answers and read them aloud.

9. Model a *summary* for the chunk of text read. Then call on different students to give a model. In the beginning, students' models will be very similar to yours.

10. Next, model either *clarify* or *question*. For example, to model use of the question strategy, you might say, "One question I had while reading this text was ..." In the beginning stages of this process, model using a literal question. Over time, use inferential and critical questions. A student should then answer the question posed in your model. Always follow your models by having students themselves model.

11. Conclude the reading of the first chunk by having students talk about what they think they now know and *predict* what they think they will learn next or what will happen next.

12. Continue by reading the next chunk, or wait until the next day to read it. (If continued on a different day, spend some time reviewing the previous day's lesson.)

13. After students complete each day's reading, have them talk about the strategies they used and how the strategies helped them in their reading.

Points to Remember

• Continue to make your models more sophisticated over time.

• When students have difficulty with a strategy, provide another model and then have another student present a model.

• Gradually increase the difficulty of the books over time.

• Students should do more and more modeling as you withdraw support and become more of an observer and coach. Eventually, you provide modeling only when needed.

▢ The student reads for a variety of purposes.

• Appreciates levels of meaning in stories
• Has a growing interest in authors, illustrators, and genres
• Is aware of own purpose(s) for reading

Assessment. By the Almost Fluent Reading and Writing stage, students begin to realize that stories have multiple levels of meaning. For example, students should already know that any story has the basic elements of character, setting, plot, and so forth.

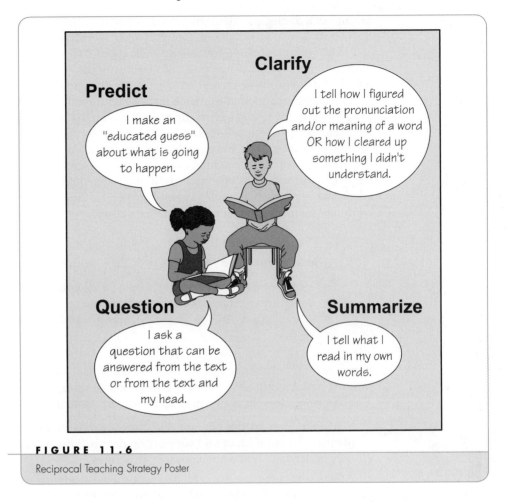

FIGURE 11.6

Reciprocal Teaching Strategy Poster

However, they also begin to know that stories have a theme, a lesson, or a moral. At the beginning of this stage, many students will recognize the basic elements but will need instructional support in becoming aware of additional levels of meaning. By observing students' responses as they write and talk about what they have read, you can easily tell whether they are able to get multiple levels of meaning from stories.

The best way to ascertain whether students are becoming aware of different authors, illustrators, and genres is to observe their independent, self-selected reading. The form presented earlier in this chapter (Figure 11.5) can be useful in making this assessment.

Awareness of one's purpose for reading is important because knowing the purpose for reading influences the way a person approaches the reading task and the rate at which she or he reads. Assess this by asking students their purpose for reading when they are reading for pleasure or reading science, social studies, and so forth. Note the differences in how they respond. Sometimes even good readers are vague about their purpose for reading, but they really do have one. For example, a student might say, "I thought this book about turtles had neat photographs, and I don't know much about turtles, so I decided to read it to find out more information."

Instructional Strategies. Help students develop these behaviors using routines such as the literacy lesson or discussion groups, which were described in Chapter 6.

When you read aloud to students, talk about different authors, illustrators, and genres. Share your favorites, and talk about why you like them. Use classroom bulletin boards to promote various authors, illustrators, and genres.

When you read aloud to the class, talk about reading and listening for pleasure as opposed to other types of reading and listening that may require more care, such as listening to directions. Make the connection to reading. Before students begin reading, talk about their purpose. Help them formulate a purpose and write it down before they read. After reading, ask students to return to their purpose and evaluate whether it was accomplished. Help them to articulate how their reading varies according to their purpose; for example, when reading technical material such as a computer manual, one reads much more carefully.

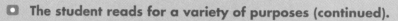

◻ The student reads for a variety of purposes (continued).

- Is beginning to understand text structure in expository text
- Uses a variety of print sources for information
- Is learning to synthesize information from more than one source

Assessment. Assessment of these behaviors takes place most often when students are working with expository texts in science, social studies, and other curricular areas. The following ideas should be helpful in your assessment:

- When students read a content text (science, health, and so forth), have them identify the main ideas and supporting details. This will let you know whether they understand text with expository structures.

- Assign a report on a topic related to a theme students are studying. Ask each student to create a bibliography, and note the sources they use. By this stage, students should be using a variety of sources, such as books, magazines, the Internet, newspaper articles, CD-ROMs, and encyclopedias.

- As students write reports, note whether they can actually pull together ideas from various sources and synthesize those ideas. Do they create their own synthesis of the ideas they have encountered, or do they just copy from a particular book or present ideas from each source separately?

Instructional Strategies. You can use the following instructional strategies to develop students' understanding and use of expository text material:

- Use the reciprocal teaching strategy suggested earlier. It will help students develop an understanding of expository text structures by focusing them on summarizing the main ideas and important details.

- Combine the use of the minilesson and the explicit comprehension routines to teach students a lesson on main ideas and supporting details, showing how these are used in different types of texts, such as science and social studies.

- Teach students to write a report using the shared-writing mode. As you work with them on a shared group report, use minilessons to teach students how to use encyclopedias, magazine articles, CD-ROM sources, and so forth. Make class posters recording the procedures and guidelines for using multiple sources and writing reports (see Figure 11.7 for an example of such a poster). This procedure will teach students to use multiple sources as well as synthesize information.

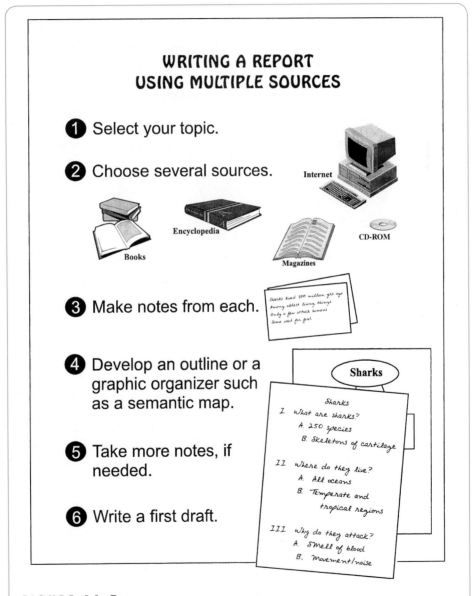

FIGURE 11.7

Poster Showing How to Write a Report Using Multiple Sources

> ☐ **The student is learning research skills.**
>
> • Uses card catalog or computer search engine
> • Is learning to narrow search in print and online sources
> • Operates a computer, including keyboarding

Assessment. The best time to assess student learning of research skills is during their involvement with projects and reports. For example, a project on local history may require using a card catalog or its computer equivalent. As students make plans for a project or report, note whether they are able to define a topic they can reasonably cover. For example, if the broad subject is mountains, note whether students can choose a particular aspect related to mountains and focus their search. One project might limit the topic to the impact of mountains on the explorations of Lewis and Clark.

Students' computer skills will vary widely. Some will have been using computers since early childhood. Others may have had little or no prior experience. You should note everything from the ability to turn the computer on, open and close applications, and shut down to the ability to access sites on the Internet and use CD-ROMs.

Instructional Strategies. Use the minilesson routine to teach students how to use the card catalog or whatever means your school uses for searching. Incorporate in your lessons the following topics:

• Alphabetical arrangement of cards (or entries) by author, subject, or title

• The fact that all entries contain the same information

• How to read each type of entry

• How to narrow the subject

• How to evaluate whether a book is worth pursuing

As you teach the use of the catalog, provide many opportunities for students to use this skill.

As you determine which students do or do not have which research skills, plan to incorporate instruction into the overall process of teaching students to carry out projects and write reports. These skills are best learned as needed.

You may find that students can teach each other computer skills just as effectively as you can. They can also teach each other research skills. Students engaged in group projects have various skills. The best person to teach something is often the one who just learned it.

> ☐ **The student is learning research skills. (continued)**
>
> • Is learning to read graphic materials such as graphs, charts, tables, timelines, and maps
> • Uses a dictionary, thesaurus, encyclopedia, and other references in print on CD-ROM or online

Assessment. Two processes are related to using graphic materials: reading them and making them. These processes should be taught together. Students' use of graphs is best assessed as they carry out projects or activities that require graphs. You may also choose to give students a sample of graphic material, such as that shown in Figure 11.8, and ask questions. Similarly, you can give students data and ask them to construct a graph, chart, table, or other visual representation.

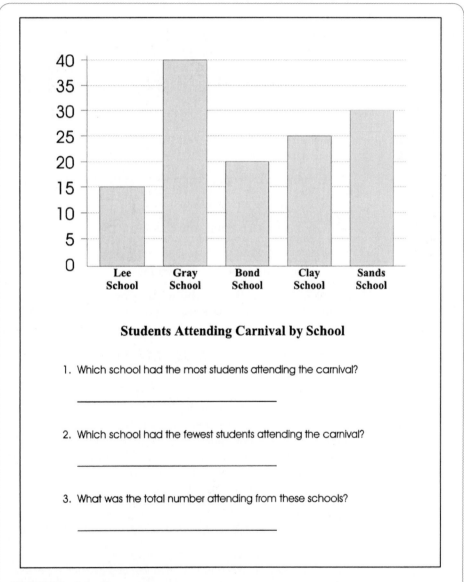

Students Attending Carnival by School

1. Which school had the most students attending the carnival?

   _____

2. Which school had the fewest students attending the carnival?

   _____

3. What was the total number attending from these schools?

   _____

FIGURE 11.8

Sample Sheet for Assessing Ability to Read a Graph

Get suggestions for assessment techniques from Miller (2001) in "For Additional Reading" on the premium website for this text.

The use of reference materials is best assessed as students are using them in the course of carrying out a project or activity.

Instructional Strategies. Use the minilesson routine to teach students to read each type of graphic material. Connect this teaching to report writing, as discussed earlier. When you teach students to read graphic materials, also teach them to construct their own. Encourage students to use some of these graphics in their reports.

Use the minilesson routine to teach lessons showing students how to use reference sources. Again, remember to connect these lessons to your lessons on report writing.

Figure 11.9 presents a sample class checklist for all of the reading benchmarks at the Almost Fluent Reading and Writing stage.

◘ Writing: Indicators, Assessment, Instructional Strategies

The writing benchmarks for the Almost Fluent Reading and Writing stage are divided into five categories:

- Continued growth in behaviors from the previous stage
- Writing for a variety of purposes
- Use of mechanics and conventions
- Pleasure in writing
- Connection of reading and writing

A class checklist for the writing benchmarks for this stage is presented in Figure 11.14 at the end of this section.

◘ The student exhibits continued growth in behaviors from Beginning Reading and Writing.

Keep in mind that students just moving into the Almost Fluent Reading and Writing stage may still exhibit many behaviors from the previous stage. These behaviors should show continued improvement. Even if some students are having difficulty in one or two areas, it is not necessary to drop back totally to the earlier stage in your assessment or instruction. Rather, provide strong support for students' individual needs as they move toward fluency.

◘ The student writes for a variety of purposes.

- Is aware of the power of the written word
- Can identify a topic and theme and develop a paper to fit a given rubric
- Can plan and put together a report
- Writes stories with all the literary elements present

Reading Checklist:
Almost Fluent Reading and Writing Stage

Teacher_____　**Date**_____　**Grade**_____

Students

+ = consistently present
- = not present
✓ = somewhat present; recheck

Benchmark

Benchmark								
Beginning Reading and Writing Behaviors								
Fluency and Word Recognition Strategies								
Uses Structure								
Uses Phonics								
Uses Syntax								
Uses Context								
Selects Appropriate Strategies								
Reads Orally at 90% Accuracy								
Self-corrects								
Takes Risks								
Uses Dictionary								
Comprehension/Construction of Meaning								
Enjoys Listening								
Reads Independently								
Enjoys Reading a Variety of Genres								
Reads Outside of School								
Reads Silently								
Continues to Grow in Use of:								
- Visualizing								
- Predicting								
- Identifying Important Information								
- Self-questioning								
- Monitoring								
- Summarizing								
- Synthesizing								
- Evaluating								
Variety of Purposes								
Appreciates Levels of Meaning								
Has Growing Interest in Authors, Illustrators, Genres								
Is Aware of Own Purpose								
Begins to Understand Expository Text Structure								
Uses Variety of Sources								
Synthesizes Information								
Research Skills								
Uses Card Catalog/Computer								
Narrows Search								
Operates Computer								
Reads:								
- Graphs								
- Charts								
- Tables								
- Timelines								
- Maps								
Uses:								
- Dictionary								
- Thesaurus								
- Encyclopedia								
- CD-ROMs								
- Internet								

FIGURE 11.9

Sample Class Checklist for Almost Fluent Reading and Writing: Reading Benchmarks and Behaviors

Criteria for Evaluating a Personal Narrative

- The story is about a personal experience and is told in the first person.
- The story has a beginning, a middle, and an end.
- The beginning gets the reader's attention.
- Details, including dialogue when appropriate, are used to help the story come to life.

Sample Scoring Rubric

1	2	3	4
The paper does not tell about a personal experience; or, if it does, there is no or little narrative structure.	The story is sketchy. There may be gaps in sequence that cause confusion. Details and dialogue are insufficient.	The story has a beginning, middle, and end. Details and dialogue are included but could be enhanced. Significant usage, mechanics, or spelling errors may keep the story from rating a 4.	The story has a strong narrative structure, including a good beginning, with realistic and well-distributed details and dialogue. It has a minimum of usage, mechanics, and spelling errors.

FIGURE 11.10

Criteria for Writing a Personal Narrative and Sample Scoring Rubric

Assessment. The first of these behaviors, awareness of the power of words, may be evident when you observe students using writing to move people to action or to change opinions. It is also evident as students share personal writing that affects classmates (or you) emotionally.

To assess the other three behaviors, have students write pieces and then evaluate them through the use of rubrics. Figures 11.10 and 11.11 present two appropriate rubrics, one for a personal narrative and the other for a research report. You should also become familiar with the Six Trait Analytical Assessment model for writing because it is used in many schools.

For other suggestions, see Cooper (2006), listed in "For Additional Reading" on the premium website for this text.

Instructional Strategies. Instruction provided for students should entail using all the modes of writing, from write-aloud to independent writing. Using the modes of writing routine, as outlined in Chapter 6, gives you the basic support you need to teach your students to become better writers.

The student shows growth in the mechanics and conventions of writing.

- Uses spelling patterns to attempt to spell words
- Uses increasingly conventional spelling, demonstrating increased visual memory and spelling sense
- Uses increasingly appropriate grammar and punctuation in writing
- Uses word processing tools to check spelling, to format, to revise, and to edit

Criteria for Evaluating Research Reports

- The report presents factual information about a topic.
- The report includes topic sentences that present main ideas.
- Relevant details support the main ideas.
- An introduction presents the topic and leads into the report.
- A conclusion sums up and closes the report.

Sample Scoring Rubric

1	2	3	4
The paper is not a report, or it meets the criteria only minimally. The report lacks focus and structure.	The report topic is clear. The facts included support the topic, but they need to be better organized into paragraphs with clear topic sentences. The introduction and conclusion are missing or weak.	The report is focused and organized, with an introduction and a conclusion. Topic sentences are supported by relevant details. The report might rate a 4 except for significant usage, mechanics, or spelling errors.	The report meets all the criteria. It is well organized, well developed, and clear. The introduction and conclusion open and close the report appropriately. There are few errors.

FIGURE 11.11

Criteria for Writing a Research Report and Sample Scoring Rubric

Assessment. These behaviors are quite closely related, and you can best assess them by analyzing students' writing samples. In the last section, we suggested the use of rubrics to assess students' level of writing. Here we suggest you do a further analysis by looking at students' spelling patterns and use of grammar and punctuation.

For spelling analysis, you can make a list of student spelling errors from a piece of authentic writing. A form like the one shown in Figure 11.12 is helpful.

For a more detailed discussion of spelling analysis, see Bear, Invernizzi, Templeton, and Johnston (2004), listed in "For Additional Reading" on the premium website for this text.

List the correct spelling and then the student's spelling, and look for patterns of errors (three or more mistakes of the same type would constitute a pattern). You can categorize the patterns of errors using the simple system presented in Table 11.4. The patterns will help you determine each student's instructional needs.

TABLE 11.4

Categories for Analyzing Patterns of Spelling Errors

BEGINNINGS	MIDDLES	ENDS
Consonants	Single vowels	Inflectional endings
Blends	Vowel patterns	
Digraphs	Double consonants	Plurals
Prefixes		Suffixes
Vowels	Digraphs	

SPELLING ANALYSIS GRID

Name _____ Grade _____ Date _____

Writing Sample _____

Correct Spelling	Student Spelling	Possible Problem

Patterns of Errors:

FIGURE 11.12

Spelling Analysis Grid

For grammar and punctuation, we suggest you use a checklist for each student similar to the one in Figure 11.13. From this analysis, you can determine where students need more instruction.

Assessment of each student's use of word processing will depend on available technology.

GRAMMAR, PUNCTUATION, AND USAGE ANALYSIS

Name_____ Grade_____ Date_____

	Uses Appropriately	Needs Instruction	Comments
CAPITALIZATION			
Beginning of sentence			
Proper nouns			
Titles of books, magazines, etc.			
PUNCTUATION			
End punctuation (period, question mark, exclamation point)			
Quotation marks			
Commas			
GRAMMAR/USAGE			
Run-on sentences			
Sentence fragments			
Noun/verb agreement			
Paragraphing			

FIGURE 11.13

Grammar and Punctuation Analysis Checklist

Instructional Strategies. Instructional routines helpful at this stage include the modes of writing and minilessons. You can use these to provide instruction that targets each particular need you have discovered.

> ### ☑ The student shows pleasure and confidence in writing.
>
> - Sees self as a writer
> - Chooses to write in free time and at home
> - Seeks suggestions for revision during peer and teacher conferences
> - Enjoys sharing writing with peers by reading aloud or by publishing in print or on disk
> - Enjoys and supports the writing of classmates, offering constructive comments when asked

Assessment. Assessment of these behaviors takes place through observation. As students participate in various writing experiences and lessons, observe whether these behaviors are apparent. For example, do students talk with peers about their writing and give and seek suggestions? Do students write during free time? Do they show that they are interested in writing and enjoy hearing and reading what others have written?

Instructional Strategies. The primary way to ensure that students achieve this benchmark is to provide a classroom atmosphere that promotes and supports writing. This includes having a literacy program that provides time for Daily Independent Writing, Learning to Write, and Developmentally Appropriate Writing. Share some of your own writing from time to time, and encourage students to do the same. Ask students for suggestions about ways you could improve your writing.

Daily Independent Writing is one of the most effective ways to promote students' pleasure in writing. Take some part of this time each day to have students share their writing with the class or with a partner. You can use the Author's Chair for this purpose.

Provide many suggestions for students to use in sharing and publishing their writing. These can include reading aloud, posting on a bulletin board, or producing a book.

> ### ☑ The student connects reading and writing.
>
> - Uses elements of narrative writing, such as form, theme, literary techniques, style, idioms, and colorful language in own writing
> - Uses various text structures to organize information in expository writing

Assessment. Observation and analysis of students' writing are the best way to determine whether students are making a connection between their reading and writing. For example, in their own writing, do students use text structures found in materials they have read? Do they use language from authors they have read, thus making their own writing more colorful and exciting? For example, after reading a fairy tale, do they begin stories with "Once upon a time ..."? If you have just read aloud a narrative told in the first person, are students trying that voice in their own writing? When writing a report, do they organize information logically by sequence, cause and effect, or some other familiar text structure?

Instructional Strategies. One of the most effective ways to help students make connections between reading and writing is to directly connect them in your teaching. This means that instead of teaching reading and writing as separate subjects, you integrate language arts, systematically blending reading, writing, spelling, and grammar.

For more on teaching writing, see Cooper (2006), listed in "For Additional Reading" listed on the premium website for this text.

When students are reading a persuasive piece, for example, you teach them how to write using persuasion. You help students note the features in the piece that make it persuasive, and then you use the write-aloud and shared-writing modes to model how to write persuasively, drawing parallels from the reading. Finally, you move to developmentally appropriate writing in which students write persuasive pieces on topics of their own choice.

> **◻ The student connects reading and writing. (continued)**
>
>   ● Appreciates poetry forms and attempts to write them

Assessment. Observation of students' daily independent writing is a good way to assess this behavior. Do students write poetry? Do they enjoy listening to poetry?

Instructional Strategies. The first step in getting students to appreciate and enjoy poetry is to read it aloud to them on a regular basis. Begin with poetry that is fun and has lots of rhyme and rhythm. Read such authors as Shel Silverstein and Jack Prelutsky. You might also share poetry from around the world, such as *Come to the Great World: Poems from Around the Globe* (Cooling, 2004). Follow poetry read-alouds by writing poetry together as a group. Students should then be encouraged to write their own poetry and share it in many ways, such as through read-alouds, booklets, and bulletin boards. In our classrooms, we always kept a class anthology of poetry to which students added from time to time.

Figure 11.14 presents a sample class checklist for the writing benchmarks of the Almost Fluent Reading and Writing stage. Now let's look at how we use all of the benchmarks presented in this chapter to plan instruction.

Planning Instruction Based on Assessment

Recall that in Chapter 10 we posed three questions you should consider in planning instruction based on each student's assessed stage of development. Those same questions should guide your decision making for students at the Almost

**Writing Checklist:
Almost Fluent Reading and Writing Stage**

Teacher_____ Date_____ Grade_____

Student Names

+ = consistently present
- = not present
✓ = sometimes present/needs instruction

Benchmark

Beginning Reading and Writing Behaviors

Variety of Purposes for Writing
Is aware of power of writing
Writes paper to topic/theme/rubric
Writes reports
Writes stories

Mechanics and Conventions of Writing
Uses spelling patterns
Uses increasingly conventional spelling
Uses increasingly appropriate grammar
Uses increasingly appropriate punctuation
Uses word processing tools

Pleasure in Writing
Sees self as writer
Writes in free time
Seeks suggestions for revision
Enjoys sharing
Supports classmates

Connects Reading and Writing
Uses/learning about narrative writing
Uses/learning about expository writing
Appreciates and writes poetry

FIGURE 11.14

Sample Class Checklist for Almost Fluent Reading and Writing Stage: Writing Benchmarks and Behaviors

Fluent Reading and Writing stage:

What do I teach or emphasize for students?

How do I teach what needs to be taught?

How do I organize and manage a classroom with a range of stages and needs?

In this section, we look at some possible answers to these questions in relation to the Almost Fluent Reading and Writing stage.

What Do I Teach?

By using some of the assessment techniques we have suggested, you can determine each student's strengths and needs and pinpoint what you need to teach. Even more than at younger ages, however, you will find that your students represent an increasing range of literacy stages. For that reason, it becomes especially important to use ongoing assessment based on the benchmarks from several stages. Beyond your initial assessment at the beginning of the school year, you must continuously assess students' growth by using some of the suggestions given in the benchmark discussions in this chapter as well as in Chapters 8, 9, and 10.

For most students, the Almost Fluent Reading and Writing stage occurs somewhere between third and fifth grade. For some, it may start as early as the end of second grade (or even earlier for a very few). Thus, in grades 3 through 5, the majority of students will be at the Almost Fluent Reading and Writing stage. Typically, though, students will range from the Beginning Reading and Writing stage through the Fluent Reading and Writing stage. Few students in these grades are still at the Early Emergent or Emergent Literacy stage, and those who are must be given very specialized attention in your classroom and supported by a learning specialist in your school.

Meeting the needs of this range of stages requires consistent use of flexible grouping, along with many instructional activities that allow students at different stages to participate successfully. You will find many uses for the multileveled types of activities described in Chapters 9 and 10.

How Do I Teach What Needs to Be Taught?

In deciding how to teach what needs to be taught, you need to consider the same three basic areas discussed in Chapter 10: selecting materials for instruction appropriate for each student, continuing the Comprehensive Balanced Literacy Program, and choosing instructional routines appropriate for each student. Let's look at how these areas apply to the Almost Fluent Reading and Writing stage.

SELECTING MATERIALS FOR INSTRUCTION

Published series. Since your school is likely to be using a published reading/language arts series, much of your instructional material will come from this resource. The anthologies provide core trade book literature, and your series will probably include a range of paperback books as well.

The materials in your reading/language arts series will already be organized by level of difficulty. However, in some cases you may find you do not agree with the publisher's leveling. In such a case, use the criteria for leveling we discussed in Chapter 6 to guide your decisions about text difficulty (see Table 6.10; also see Chapter 4 for a discussion of readability formulas).

Trade books. In addition to the published series, you will need sets of trade books. Because of the range of stages you will probably have in your classroom, your instructional materials should include a wide spectrum of trade books, organized by level of difficulty. Each set should consist of five to nine copies of each title. The most efficient and useful way to organize these trade books is for all the teachers in the upper grades to work together to establish a central materials resource center where the books are stored for easy access.

Many schools have a reading specialist who works out of this center and helps teachers select materials and determine appropriate instructional strategies. In schools that do not have such a center, the upper-grade teachers work together to organize and manage one.

We cannot stress enough the importance of every school having some way to provide a range of trade book literature for teachers to use for instruction. Without this resource, the teacher's hands are virtually tied in trying to meet the reading and writing needs of students functioning at a range of stages.

Books in other languages. To meet the needs of second-language learners and to expose English speakers to other languages, some books in other languages are needed. By this stage, second-language learners who have been in school several years have made or are making the transition to English. However, you may get older students from other countries who do not speak English and have not been in school until now. Books in their language are critical. Where available, books recorded in English and in other languages are also helpful.

Library. In addition to sets of trade book literature, you will need the resources of a library (either a school library or a nearby public library) to support independent reading and to help you find books for reading aloud to students.

Decodable texts. Finally, you will need some decodable texts for students functioning at earlier stages who are still developing independence in decoding. Usually these texts are needed for at least some students in grade 3 and perhaps beyond.

THE COMPREHENSIVE BALANCED LITERACY PROGRAM

As you will recall, the Comprehensive Balanced Literacy Program contains six blocks for all students: Daily Independent Reading, Daily Independent Writing, Reading: Learning Skills and Strategies, Reading: Application of Skills and Strategies, Writing: Learning to Write, and Writing: Developmentally Appropriate Writing. For those students needing additional support, there is a block of intervention as well. Let's examine each of these blocks in relation to the Almost Fluent Reading and Writing stage.

Daily Independent Reading. Research strongly supports the importance of the Daily Independent Reading block as a part of a student's continued literacy growth (Snow, Burns, & Griffin, 1998). You should allow 15 to 20 minutes per day for this block. Students at this stage should be doing much more independent reading in school as well as at home. Yet the following problems may arise even at this stage:

1. *Selecting books that are too difficult.* Some students always want to read books that are beyond their abilities. Usually this is brought on by peer pressure and the student's belief that it will please you, the teacher. One of the best ways to handle this situation is to share books you are reading. Select a book that would appear to be "too easy" for you. Talk about how you really enjoyed the book even though you thought it was easy. Also, discuss with students how to select books. Focus on making an initial selection based on interests. Then show students how to test a book by reading the first paragraph or two to determine whether it will be hard to read. Model this process as often as needed to help students select their materials for independent reading more effectively.

2. *Changing books frequently during independent reading.* Teachers frequently ask us, "How do you deal with a student who wants to change books every 2 or 3 minutes?"

Students should select their reading material (books, newspapers, magazines, and so forth) prior to the independent reading time. Encourage students to stick to what they have selected. However, if a student has selected a book or other material that is too hard or that he or she does not like, alternate choices should be at hand. You yourself don't continue books that you can't read or don't like.

3. *Not wanting to stop reading.* What a great problem to face! However, some students really do want only to read and don't want to stop when the time is up. Provide some extra time during the day for independent reading for these students, and be sure that they are free to check books out to take home to read.

4. *Not wanting to read.* Some students at the Almost Fluent Reading and Writing stage may have a negative attitude about reading. They *can* read, but they don't *want* to. This is a tough situation to deal with, and there are no simple answers. One way to approach this problem is to be supportive and to talk about times when you yourself may not have liked to read. Reading aloud to students is another good way to motivate them to read. Try to capitalize on students' interests. Provide books on tape or CD. Encourage them to read comics, magazines, pages on the Internet, books on CD-ROM, and other types of materials. Provide some special materials for each such student. Try to find out why a particular student doesn't like to read. However, you must keep in mind that not everyone is an avid reader.

Daily Independent Writing. Allow at least 15 to 20 minutes per day for this block. It should involve whatever kind of writing students select; *it is not assigned writing.* The purpose of this block is to help students build power in writing and to practice their writing. During some of this time, you should write to serve as a model. However, you should devote much of your time to conferencing with students and monitoring what they are doing. Even though the writing students do during this time will not be evaluated, this is a good time for you to note how students are writing and applying the various techniques and skills you have been developing through instruction.

Reading: Learning Skills and Strategies. During this block, all students work with the same text. This text may be a selection from the anthology of your published reading/ language arts series, or it may be a trade book that you want everyone to experience.

Even though everyone works with the same book, not everyone does the same things with it. You use small groups to provide different types of instruction and activities designed to meet the assessed needs of individual students.

Reading: Application of Skills and Strategies. In this block, all students read books that are appropriate to their reading level and receive needed instruction with these books. This block provides an opportunity for students to apply strategies and skills taught in the Learning Skills and Strategies block.

By the time students reach the Almost Fluent Reading and Writing stage, their books are too long to read in one day. Therefore, the Learning Skills and Strategies block and the Application of Skills and Strategies block do not take place on the same day. Most teachers spend two or three days with the Learning Skills and Strategies block and the remaining days of the week with the Application of Skills and Strategies block. Some teachers alternate, having one block each week.

Writing: Learning to Write. Showing students how to write continues to be important at this stage. During this block, you model various types of writing for students, focusing more on voice and style than you would at earlier stages. Also, you teach students the elements of spelling and grammar needed to help them continue to grow into more effective writers.

By this stage, students will be able to understand various types or domains of writing. The **domains of writing** are usually described as sensory/descriptive, imaginative/narrative, practical/informative, and analytical/expository. Select the domain to be modeled for the class on the basis of students' assessed needs.

Writing: Developmentally Appropriate Writing. In this block, all students write, focusing on the domain of writing you have modeled. The topic of the writing is the student's choice. During this block, students apply what they have learned about the particular domain of writing and the strategies and skills of grammar and spelling. The writing done during this block can be evaluated (as opposed to the writing done in the Daily Independent Writing block).

These six blocks make up the Comprehensive Balanced Literacy Program for all students. For students experiencing difficulty in learning to read, an additional block of Intervention is provided. See Chapter 6 for a detailed discussion of intervention methods.

CHOOSING INSTRUCTIONAL ROUTINES

The basic instructional routines presented in Chapter 6 continue to be used with students at this stage, with adjustments for the types of materials being used and the sophistication of the routines and skills being taught.

We have addressed two of the important instructional questions—"What do I teach?" and "How do I teach what needs to be taught?" Now let's turn our attention to the final question.

How Do I Organize and Manage a Classroom with a Range of Stages?

Knowing how to organize and manage your classroom in grades 3 to 5 becomes increasingly important because you have students functioning at so many stages. In Chapter 10, we discussed the answer to this question in detail in relation to the Comprehensive Balanced Literacy Program. The same principles apply for organizing and managing your classroom when most students are at the Almost Fluent Reading and Writing stage. The following discussion builds on what we said in that chapter.

KNOW YOUR STUDENTS

Throughout this text, we have discussed the importance of getting to know your students and using ongoing assessment to keep track of where they are in developing their literacy skills. You must, however, go further than this; you need to determine which students have independent work habits and which need continual guidance and support. Use the first few days of school to note how students work. Make a list of the names of students who can work well independently and those who cannot. Having this information will help you manage your class more effectively.

USE FLEXIBLE GROUPS AND ACTIVITIES

There is no effective way to teach a class of twenty to thirty students in grades 3, 4, or 5 without using flexible groups and individual activities. Flexible groups usually range from five to nine students who are grouped together or who choose to work together for a particular need or task. They remain together until the need is met or the task completed, and then the grouping is dropped.

There are many reasons to form flexible groups in grades 3, 4, and 5, including the following:

- To teach a lesson to students at a stage of development different from that of most others in the class
- To discuss a core book or selection
- To teach a strategy or skill minilesson
- To have small groups reading the same developmentally appropriate book
- To conduct group conferences
- To allow several students to discuss the same type of book

At times, each student will be doing a different activity. The trick to successful classroom organization and management is to use the appropriate balance of small, flexible groups and individual activities to meet the range of needs. Many teachers in grades 3 to 5 mistakenly try to teach everything to the whole class as one large group. Even when the entire class reads the same book, small groups are necessary to meet individual needs.

DEVELOP CLASSROOM ROUTINES

In order for you to work with small, flexible groups and with individuals, your students need to know the classroom routines and follow them. In the upper grades, students work more independently. However, we have found that it is still important to take time at the beginning of the school year to develop the routines you want students to follow in your classroom.

These students discuss a book without teacher guidance.

© Monkey Business Images, 2009/Used under license from Shutterstock.com

In Chapter 10, we discussed five steps for developing classroom routines. These same steps can also be applied here: (1) develop class guidelines, (2) appoint monitors, (3) identify independent activities, (4) role-play, working in groups, and (5) evaluate with students. Developing a system of routines is critical to organizing and managing your classroom.

Meeting the Needs of Second-Language Learners

Classrooms throughout the United States represent a cross section of our society. They include children who represent many cultures and many countries of origin. Some of these students come to school speaking English; others do not. Some start school at age five or six; others don't come to this country until they are much older, still speaking their native language. Although most students in grades 3, 4, and 5 are at the Almost Fluent Reading and Writing stage, some may be unable to speak English proficiently.

If your ELL students started school in kindergarten, they have probably made the transition to English by now or are very close. For students still acquiring English, the following procedures may help ease their acquisition of the language:

- *Buddies.* Provide a "learning buddy" for each ELL student to serve as a model in the use of English. If a buddy is bilingual, he or she can also provide short previews before reading in the ELL student's native language or in English. Even for ELL students who have made the transition to English, a learning buddy is a good way to expand their English.

- *Peer translators.* During small-group discussions, English-language learners may be able to understand more than they can say. Pair such a learner with one who can interpret his or her comments for the group. This will allow students to share more of the complex thoughts they may be able to state only in their native language.

- *Tapes or CDs, software,* CD-ROMs, and videos. These materials also provide good models of English and can help students expand their vocabularies. Most published reading/language arts series provide tapes of anthology selections as well as software technology that can support ELL students in improving their use of English.

Provide books that are in the students' first language and also give an English version on the same page or facing page.

- *Volunteers.* Invite volunteers from the cultures of the ELL students to bring both the language and the culture into the classroom. These types of experiences are excellent for helping make your classroom truly multicultural as well as multilingual.

For other suggestions for teaching ELL students, see Young and Hadaway (2006), listed in "For Additional Reading" on the premium website for this text.

- *Minilessons.* Conduct minilessons as needed on figures of speech and phrases in English that have a meaning other than the literal one. This is very helpful to ELL students and any others who need support in improving their English. Teaching students the meanings of such idioms as "big as an ox," "turned green with envy," and "grew as big as a house" helps them develop a more authentic understanding of the English language. These lessons should not be taught in isolation but in relation to texts students are reading.

A Fourth-Grade Classroom at Work

Now let's see how an upper elementary class, in which most students are at the Almost Fluent Reading and Writing stage, functions. We will focus on Ms. Boyd's fourth-grade class. Table 11.5 lists her full-day schedule. Notice that her literacy block is shorter than the one for the second-grade classroom you saw in Chapter 10. Ms. Boyd has 2 hours per day for literacy instruction, including time for independent reading and writing.

Ms. Boyd has twenty-four students, thirteen girls and eleven boys. Two students are functioning at the end of the Beginning Reading and Writing stage, nineteen at the Almost Fluent Reading and Writing stage, and three at the Fluent Reading and Writing stage. One student at the Beginning Reading and Writing stage is an English-language learner from Puerto Rico who is making the transition to English. Four other students at the Almost Fluent Reading and Writing stage are also from Puerto Rico but have made a complete transition to English.

In the following section, we will present a detailed look at Ms. Boyd's literacy block. As you read Ms. Boyd's plan, notice how Ms. Boyd fits in all of the blocks of the Comprehensive Balanced Literacy Program, how she uses flexible groups to meet

TABLE 11.5

Daily Schedule for Ms. Boyd's Fourth Grade

8:15	Arrival
8:25	Daily news
8:40	Literacy block
	• Reading
	• Writing (including spelling and grammar)
	• Daily Independent Reading
	• Daily Independent Writing
10:40	Morning break
10:50	Math
11:45	Lunch and recess
12:20	Science/health (alternating units; students who need intervention go at this time; second-language learners go to English Language Development lessons)
1:00	Special classes (art, music, PE, computers) for four days each week; the fifth day is used as an activity period in the room.
1:45	Afternoon break
1:55	Social studies
2:50	Prepare to dismiss
3:00	Dismissal

individual needs, what instructional routines she uses, and where you think Ms. Boyd is conducting ongoing assessment.

Ms. Boyd's Literacy Block Schedule (24 fourth graders)

TIME

8:40–10:40 daily

ARRANGEMENTS FOR INDEPENDENT WORK

Four learning centers: two for comprehension, one for writing, one for decoding longer words.

8:40 DAILY INDEPENDENT READING

Activities
- Independent reading
- Lesson on decoding longer words (small group)

Routine
- Minilesson
- Fluency

> While some students read independently, Ms. Boyd pulls out a small group of other students who need instruction in decoding longer words and another group to work on fluency. Students in this group will read independently at another time.

9:00 READING: LEARNING SKILLS AND STRATEGIES/APPLICATION OF SKILLS AND STRATEGIES

Activities
- Introduce *Koya Delaney and the Good Girl Blues* (Greenfield, 1992).
- Read first chapter in *Koya Delaney* (twelve students read independently; six students read cooperatively; six students read with teacher).

Routines
- Literacy lesson
- Modes of reading routine
- Learning centers for those who finish early

> Although everyone is introduced to the same book, using different modes of reading helps meet individual needs.

9:30

Activity
- Discuss Koya Delaney.

Routine
- Discussion groups

The discussions focus on the portion of the book that has just been read.

9:40 WRITING: LEARNING TO WRITE/DEVELOPMENTALLY APPROPRIATE WRITING

Activities
- Students write story of own choosing.
- Teacher-student conferences are held during writing.

Routine
- Modes of writing routine

Students practice writing their own story. Meanwhile, Ms. Boyd assesses students' writing for strengths and needs.

10:10

Activity
- Conduct spelling lesson (words with suffixes *-ness* and *-tion*).

Routine
- Minilesson

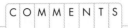

Ms. Boyd does direct teaching of spelling elements.

10:25 DAILY INDEPENDENT WRITING

Activities
- Engage in independent writing.
- Give a grammar lesson (run-on sentences) for ten students.

Routine
- Minilesson

Grammar is taught as an outgrowth of assessed writing needs and Ms. Boyd's knowledge of new skills that have not yet been taught.

10:40 MORNING BREAK

A DISCUSSION OF MS. BOYD'S LITERACY BLOCK PLAN

You now have a sense of Ms. Boyd's literacy block schedule. You probably have many questions as to why she did what she did. We will try to anticipate your questions by discussing each block.

8:40: Daily Independent Reading. Ms. Boyd starts off her literacy block with Daily Independent Reading. This choice provides her with a management tool: she can pull out a small, flexible group for teaching the skill of decoding longer words. The students who receive this instruction were identified over the past several days. She varies the type of strategy or skill taught according to the students' needs. Ms. Boyd is very careful not to pull out the same students two days in a row.

Students who miss the scheduled Daily Independent Reading get a chance to do it at other times during the day. No one ever is denied Daily Independent Reading. This pattern of instruction allows Ms. Boyd to meet a wide range of needs and stages in her classroom. Remember, too, that this block makes it possible for *all* students to read developmentally appropriate books every day.

9:00: Reading: Learning Skills and Strategies/Application of Skills and Strategies. Each day Ms. Boyd does one or the other of these two blocks. (Note: in the lower grades, especially kindergarten and grade 1, both of these blocks are usually done on the same day.) Typically Ms. Boyd works three to five days on a core book, depending on its length. First, she introduces the book; then, to meet students' individual needs, she uses small groups and has the first chapter read in different ways by different groups. This is what we see her doing with *Koya Delaney.* The subsequent discussion then allows all students to discuss and share this common book.

9:40: Writing: Learning to Write/Developmentally Appropriate Writing. Today, Ms. Boyd is doing Developmentally Appropriate Writing because for the past two days she has been doing Learning to Write—using shared and guided writing of a story. Now students are writing their own story on a topic of their choice. She usually does not try to do both types of writing on the same day.

This block also provides the time to directly teach spelling. On some days, Ms. Boyd teaches a grammar lesson if most students need it.

10:25: Daily Independent Writing. During this block, Ms. Boyd may pull out a small group for a short period of time, as she does today in teaching a grammar lesson to a group of ten students. On many days, she does not teach a grammar lesson but uses the time instead to conference with individuals or small groups.

Notice that Ms. Boyd worked in all parts of the Comprehensive Balanced Literacy Program.

Summary

- Students at the Almost Fluent Reading and Writing stage continue to exhibit growth in literacy development from prior stages.

- Assessment of students' individual behaviors continues to be primarily informal.

- The increasing range of stages within a classroom makes it even more important for teachers to plan an assessment-based, comprehensive literacy program, using small groups and multileveled activities to address the needs of all students.

- Oral language becomes increasingly important as students expand their use of standard English and become more aware of their own areas of need. They note and accept diversity in the use of language in themselves and in others. They use more vocabulary and participate in discussions, responding with questions or comments as they listen to others. At this stage, students are developing a deeper appreciation for and the ability to use all aspects of language.

- In reading, students are using all the word recognition strategies and selecting the ones appropriate for sounding out an unknown word. Dictionary use for both pronunciation and meaning is growing.

- Students' abilities to comprehend, or construct meaning, is improving.

- Students read independently from a variety of genres, both in and out of school.

- Students grow in their ability to use strategies such as predicting, identifying important information, visualizing, self-questioning, monitoring, summarizing, synthesizing, and evaluating.

- Students are learning to understand different text structures and to conduct research using a variety of sources, which requires them to synthesize and organize information in many ways.

- Students continue to develop their ability to write for a variety of purposes. They make connections between reading and writing, seeing how their own writing can incorporate techniques learned from what they have read.

- Students' use of the mechanics and conventions of writing continues to grow.

- Second-language learners at this stage have generally made or are in the process of making the transition to English. However, there may be some ELL who are performing at a much earlier stage of development. For these students, learning buddies, volunteers, minilessons, and a variety of tapes and other resources can help ease the transition.

- Ms. Boyd's classroom showed how a fourth-grade teacher working predominantly with students at the Almost Fluent Reading and Writing stage can pull all of these ideas together to meet the needs of a range of stages within the classroom. Using flexible, small groups is a key ingredient.

Please visit the premium website for *Literacy Assessment*, Fourth Edition to access the TeachSource Video Cases, chapter web links, For Additional Reading, tutorial quizzes, glossary flashcards, online checklists, downloads, and much more! Go to www.cengage.com/login to register your access code.

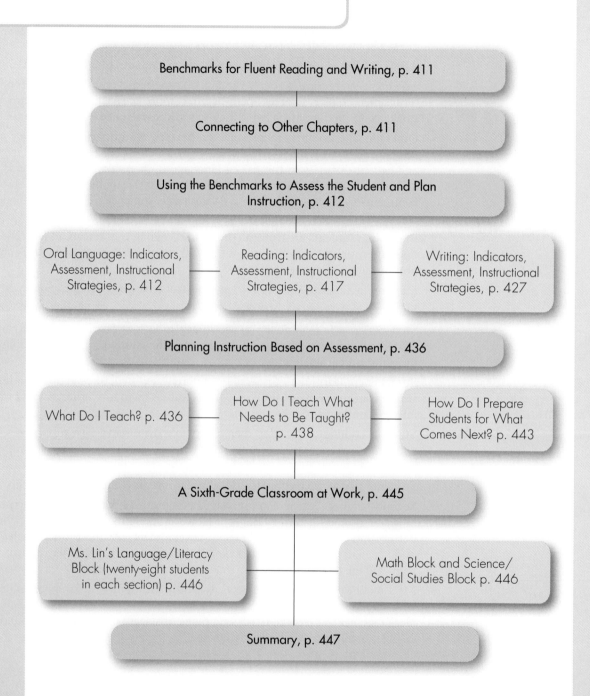

12   Fluent Reading and Writing

We will look in on Mrs. Collins's fifth-grade language arts class in just a moment. But first, a word about how this fifth grade is organized. At this school, the fifth grade is departmentalized to help students make the transition into middle school the following year. The fifth-grade teachers work as a team of three. Students have a homeroom teacher with whom they do routine activities. The homeroom groups are heterogeneous: that is, each group has students performing at more than one literacy stage, as well as students representing several first languages and various exceptionalities.

The homeroom groups rotate among the three teachers for major curriculum areas. Mr. Herbert teaches the social studies and science units. Ms. Street teaches the math units. Mrs. Collins teaches the language arts classes.

The three-teacher team plans units for the entire year so as to integrate learning whenever possible. (Often the physical education, music, and art teachers also integrate their activities with the curriculum.) Each knows what is occurring in the other classes and helps students make connections. For example, when students are preparing a final project for a science unit, Mrs. Collins collaborates with Mr. Herbert to plan lessons focused on research and report writing.

Today we begin by visiting Mrs. Collins during her morning literature block. She is reading aloud from *The Lion, the Witch, and the Wardrobe,* by C. S. Lewis (1950/1994). Most of her students could certainly read this independently (and, in fact, many already have), but it is a book rich with potential for discussion, so she plans to read a chapter a day and then have students discuss whatever they have found interesting—words, plot development, author's craft, character traits. Mrs. Collins has already shared some information about C. S. Lewis's life. Today, after the first chapter, Mrs. Collins asks the students to discuss the pictures they have made in their minds about the house, the wardrobe, and the faun. Then they spend some time talking about why an author might choose to tell a story that was pure fantasy. Mrs. Collins seems to be leading the class to the notion of the theme of the novel.

Students then take out their writing folders and begin to work independently on reports for science class. They are choosing topics to research further and write about. Some may use computer programs to create multimedia presentations. Some may choose expository writing. Some may choose design/art/graphic presentations with supporting text. Some may make oral presentations. Mrs. Collins moves among the students, helping each think through what to report on and possible ways to approach the task. The students will do the actual research for the report while they are with Mr. Herbert in science class.

Next, Mrs. Collins has the students examine a piece of writing displayed on a transparency. It is part of one student's science report from a prior year, and the name has been obliterated. The class reads the piece, and a general discussion follows about how it might be revised to make a stronger statement and make the ideas clearer to the reader. Then pairs of students work on actually revising the piece. Following this, the students work on revising their own writing; then each person shares with his or her partner, who offers feedback. The students are clearly comfortable giving and accepting comments about revision.

Finally, the class breaks into literature discussion groups. Each group has been reading a different genre. One group has read biographies. Another has read nonfiction about the *Titanic*. Each group functions well without teacher direction, sharing ideas, clearly following the posted guidelines for that group. Mrs. Collins participates in each group briefly and her comments spur more divergent and deeper thinking than might have occurred without her.

Next, we follow the students to Mr. Herbert's science class, where he will supervise their research for their reports. Each student has brought the science writing folder from Mrs. Collins's room. Mr. Herbert explains the various methods of research available: Internet, encyclopedias and other references in the classroom, the school library, and so forth. Then each student is asked to choose one of these sources to pursue first. Mr. Herbert lets students work in pairs so that they can help each other.

After school, we sit in as the three fifth-grade teachers have one of their regular grade-level meetings. Mr. Herbert is generally pleased with the students' ability to choose a narrow enough topic to research and report on. He asks Mrs. Collins to work with him to develop some minilessons focused on evaluating the validity of sources, especially on the Internet. For the next few days, Mrs. Collins and Mr. Herbert will work together to develop lessons on planning a research report format, outlining, taking notes, attributing sources, writing rough drafts, revising, editing, and generating a final product.

Ms. Street, who teaches mathematics, is beginning a unit on ratio, and she asks that both Mrs. Collins and Mr. Herbert stay alert to examples of ratio in literature and science. They agree that both the music and art teachers will be able to contribute many examples of the importance and role of ratio in those fields.

The fifth-grade students in this class are mostly at the Fluent Reading and Writing stage. They are able to do many things independently, but they still need strong teaching and guidance to help them develop critical thinking skills and apply such thinking to various curriculum areas.

Attaining this stage does not mean students have finished growing in literacy. On the contrary, they are at a perfect age to grow in leaps and bounds with good teaching. They are capable decoders and fluent readers; they understand how fiction and nonfiction are organized; they understand the writing process and the many purposes for writing. They are reading wonderful literature independently. They are ready to examine the author's craft, read critically, weigh opinions, recognize persuasion, and write purposefully as well as for personal pleasure.

This chapter examines the benchmarks and behaviors of the Fluent Reading and Writing stage, as well as instructional strategies you can use to keep students progressing in their literacy development.

Benchmarks for Fluent Reading and Writing

The benchmarks for the Fluent Reading and Writing stage are typical of students in grades 4 or 5 and up, ages nine or ten and above. Yet even those who are not yet at this stage may function fairly well in other academic areas and understand the concepts of various content areas.

Connecting to Other Chapters

As you read and think about the benchmarks in this chapter, you will see references to prior stages of literacy development as well as ideas, concepts, tools, techniques, and routines introduced in Chapters 1 through 6. Many students at the Fluent Reading and Writing stage continue to exhibit some of the behaviors from prior stages, while

BENCHMARKS

ORAL LANGUAGE

- The student exhibits continued growth in behaviors from previous stages.
- The student's vocabulary and facility with language are growing.
- The student uses oral language for a variety of purposes.
- The student continues to enjoy language.

READING

- The student continues to display many of the behaviors from the Almost Fluent Reading and Writing stage.
- The student seldom seeks or needs assistance with word recognition.
- The student uses a wide variety of comprehension strategies to construct meaning.
- The student enjoys reading.
- The student is refining research skills begun at the previous stage.

WRITING

- Prior writing behaviors strengthen and deepen.
- The student writes for a variety of purposes and reasons.
- The student is growing in the mechanics of writing.
- The student is using the writing process.
- The student sees self as a competent writer.
- The student connects reading and writing.

other literacy behaviors are firmly rooted, automatic, and no longer developing. For students in grade 4 or higher who may not yet be fluent readers and writers, teachers should use the information and suggestions from previous chapters, both for assessment and for instruction.

Remember, even a child showing all the behaviors of the Fluent stage will need strong teaching to continue to grow. At this stage, every behavior can be enhanced, extended, and carried further. Literacy growth continues for a lifetime.

Using the Benchmarks to Assess the Student and Plan Instruction

In this section, we show you how to assess reading, writing, and oral language to determine whether students are at the Fluent stage. Because your instruction is assessment based, you will make frequent instructional adjustments as you detect a need.

Oral Language: Indicators, Assessment, Instructional Strategies

Assessment of most oral language benchmarks will occur during normal classroom activities. You will rely almost entirely on observation and checklists. Particular projects that involve oral presentations may sometimes require rubrics and checklists specific to those presentations only.

We discuss four major benchmarks for oral language:

- Continued growth in prior behaviors
- Increased vocabulary and facility with language
- Use of language for a variety of purposes
- Enjoyment of language

Near the end of this section you will find a sample class checklist for Fluent oral language benchmarks and behaviors (Figure 12.1).

> ☐ **The student exhibits continued growth in behaviors from previous stages.**

At the Fluent stage, the oral language benchmarks from earlier continue to develop. For instance, fluent readers and writers are increasingly aware of their own problem areas. They can accept and enjoy diverse usage, and they use language with more ease and pleasure. In fact, many of the Almost Fluent behaviors are never mastered; rather, they continue to grow and develop over one's lifetime.

> ☐ **The student's vocabulary and facility with language are growing.**
>
> - Shows increasing vocabulary in oral language
> - Shifts from formal to informal usage to suit occasion
> - Listens to oral presentations with understanding

Assessment. Students encounter many new words as they read and listen to more and more adult texts. Observe that some of these words are finding their way into students' everyday usage.

Note that students are switching usage when situations change and making increasing effort to use standard English within the classroom. If a student who clearly *can* use standard English isn't doing so, try to determine whether it is a lack of sensitivity to the situation or a minor act of defiance. Second-language learners may prefer to speak in their first language, especially in informal situations, but will show an awareness of when it is appropriate to use English.

Oral reports are common at this stage. Following such reports, you will want to lead a discussion or ask students to write about what they heard. If listeners were not able to grasp the main ideas of an oral report, your next step is to figure out why, with the help of the students. Failure to understand might be the result of inadequate listening, but it might also stem from a poorly prepared or poorly presented report.

Instructional Strategies

- Make a point of discussing words during literature discussions, guided reading, and read-aloud sessions.

- Be sure to include derivation and word history, along with subtleties of denotation and connotation. For example, share the origin of such words as "kindergarten," the term Friedrich Froebel coined from the German words *kinder* (children) and *garten* (garden) to describe what he believed to be the kind of place children need before beginning school—a place to play and grow, a "garden of children."

- Share how some words have shifted in connotation over time. For example, the word "square" once denoted something true, upright, and honest. Later, the connotation in some contexts became pejorative, so that a square was someone who was not "cool."

- Provide resources to support students' growing interest in word histories, the history of language, idioms, and foreign language words and phrases commonly used in English. Students who are familiar with another language may particularly enjoy researching the history of words that have entered English from the other language.

- Students whose first language isn't English find figurative language, especially idiomatic language, particularly difficult. Some books of sayings may be helpful: *There's a Frog in My Throat* (Leedy & Street, 2003), *Super Silly Sayings That Are Over Your Head: A Children's Illustrated Book of Idioms* (Snodgrass, 2007), *Scholastic Dictionary of Idioms, Revised* (Terban, 2006), *Monkey Business: Fun with Idioms* (Hambleton, Turhan, & Tullet, 2007), and *In a Pickle: And Other Funny Idioms* (Terban & Maestro, 2007). Be alert to idioms in reading materials as well as in oral language, and provide explanations or discuss the meanings. You may want to begin a class collection of idioms in a notebook or on a poster.

- If you find that a student is unable to use standard English comfortably, you will need to do some direct instruction. If the student can use standard English comfortably but doesn't seem to realize when and where it is required, or why, discussions and modeling are in order. Students might role-play various situations, such as how they might tell a friend about a ball game if they were visiting at that friend's home or on the playground. Then have them role-play how they might talk if they were in the classroom, at church, or in a group of adults.

- Talk about the language children hear around them and on television. The fact that they hear famous, respected people using nonstandard English in public does not give them license to do the same at school.

- Remember that second-language students may retain some accent for many years, perhaps for a lifetime. This is especially true if they have begun speaking English at a relatively late age. With such students, you should focus on syntax and vocabulary rather than on pronunciation, which is difficult to change.

- If students have difficulty understanding oral reports, analyze the activity with students from both the presenter's point of view and the listeners' point of view. Collaborate with students to draw up guidelines related to what makes an oral presentation understandable as well as what the listener must contribute in order to understand the material. From this collaboration, you and your students can decide what they need to learn. For example, you may present lessons on ways to enhance oral presentations using a program such as PowerPoint.

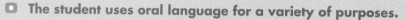

◻ The student uses oral language for a variety of purposes.

- Discusses literature with pleasure and understanding
- Enjoys role playing and Readers Theater
- May enjoy debate or speech competition

Assessment. As with other oral language indicators, these are best observed during regular classroom activities. Note which students participate fully when discussing literature, as well as which students participate willingly during role-playing or Readers Theater.

Some fluent readers and writers may never be comfortable with the public nature of debate or speechmaking. Some teachers require all students to participate in speech competitions; perhaps they believe this allows children to discover abilities or interests hitherto unknown. You will need to decide for each student how far to push him or her into speaking in front of an audience.

Instructional Strategies. Normal activities are probably sufficient to bring out each of these behaviors in your students. Perhaps most important are encouragement and opportunity. Encourage all students to express themselves orally and accept such expression with pleasure.

When discussing literature, solicit comments from every participant. Be sure to model acceptance of all ideas. Students should feel free to express personal opinions in discussion without fear of ridicule or argument. Your comments should support the understanding that discussion is an occasion for expanding thinking, not for finding right answers.

Readers Theater (a story is rewritten as a play to be read aloud) requires direct instruction and supervision until students are comfortable with it. Teach your students how to turn a story into drama. You may do this collaboratively until students are comfortable taking over the task entirely.

Find more information about Readers Theater in the web links on the premium website for this text.

Debate has formal rules of procedure that you may or may not decide to teach to your students, depending on their level of maturity. Even if you do not teach them formal debating, you and they may develop guidelines for presenting both sides of an issue. If your school participates in speech competitions, the sponsoring organization undoubtedly has guidelines that must be followed. You can help your students prepare and rehearse their presentations.

□ **The student continues to enjoy language.**

- Is sensitive to body language and tone of others and self
- Appreciates the importance of speech in interpreting the written word; for example, news reports, actors, comedians

Assessment. At this stage, students will be acquiring an extra layer of awareness to add to their enjoyment of language. Observe them to judge their sensitivity to subtleties of oral language such as body language and tone. By fourth or fifth grade, children have been aware of some such elements for years; you have heard them say, "He looked at me funny!" "She's mad at me!" "Don't talk to me in that tone of voice!" Because body language and tone convey many things to one's audience, it is important that students become aware of their own body language and tone when they speak and be sensitive to others' use of the same indicators.

Observe your students and enjoy with them the skill involved in using one's voice to enhance and lend additional meaning to the written word. Call attention to such oral interpretation when appropriate.

Instructional Strategies. You can help your students become more aware of both body language and tone of voice.

- Along with them, you might watch some television or film with no sound and try to use the characters' body language and facial expressions to decide how they are feeling.
- Or you can have students role-play a situation wordlessly; the art of mime is built partly on the ability to convey feelings and ideas without words.
- Similarly, as you watch television or movies, you can make your students aware that acting requires the use not only of body language but also of tone and inflection to convey meaning beyond the actual words.

Body language, facial expression, and vocal inflection may be culture specific. Students new to the United States may find the nonverbal communication they encounter quite different from what they grew up with. You can help them learn this kind of communication in U.S. culture. You can also encourage them to investigate similarities and differences between their first culture and the prevailing culture in which they now live. All students will benefit from raised awareness of cultural differences as long as you are careful not to suggest that one way is better than another.

You can help students become sensitive to the way different oral interpretations elicit diverse reactions. For example, one of the authors used the book *Love You*

Forever (Munsch, 1986) to illustrate how interpretation can influence response to text. The book was read to one group of undergraduates in a sweet and gentle tone of voice; the listeners were moved, some almost to tears. Then the same book was read to another group in a slightly sarcastic tone; that group laughed and hooted at almost every page. Of course, we then discussed what had occurred with both groups.

Figure 12.1 presents a sample class checklist for the entire set of oral language benchmarks and behaviors.

Oral Language Checklist: Fluent Reading and Writing Stage

Teacher _____ Date _____ Grade _____

Students

+ = consistently present
− = not present
✓ = somewhat present; recheck; insufficient evidence

Benchmark									
Continued Growth in Previous Behaviors									
Vocabulary and Language Facility									
Shows increasing vocabulary									
Shifts from formal to informal usage									
Listens to presentations with understanding									
Variety of Purposes									
Discusses literature									
Enjoys role playing/Readers Theater									
Enjoys debate/speech competition									
Enjoyment									
Is sensitive to body language and tone									
Appreciates speech interpretation									

Instructional Plans:

_____

_____

_____

_____

_____

FIGURE 12.1

Sample Class Checklist for Fluent Reading and Writing: Oral Language Benchmarks and Behaviors

Reading: Indicators, Assessment, Instructional Strategies

Fluent reading behaviors fall into five main areas:

- Continued growth from the previous stage
- Increased competence in word recognition
- Use of various strategies for comprehension, or construction of meaning
- Enjoyment of reading
- Refinement of research skills

A sample class checklist for Fluent reading benchmarks appears in Figure 12.2.

> **The student continues to display many of the behaviors from the Almost Fluent Reading and Writing stage.**

Growth from the Almost Fluent stage to the Fluent stage may be fluid and seamless. Most behaviors from the previous stage have been refined. These students are now using reading abilities skillfully and automatically.

> **The student seldom seeks or needs assistance with word recognition.**

Assessment. Students at this stage deal with print independently most of the time, and we do not break out discrete skills or behavioral indicators in this category at this stage.

You will have no trouble tracking which children display this benchmark. Actually, it is the *lack* of the behavior you need to note. Note which children are continuing to request help with word recognition; then try to determine why they are asking for help.

- It might be that their word recognition skills are still at an earlier stage, even though their overall reading is strong.
- Frequent requests for assistance might simply indicate a lack of confidence; that is, if you nudged the student to apply decoding skills, he or she would be able to say the word.
- You may also find that some students need assistance but do not recognize their own need. You will note this when students have read an assignment without requesting help, but further activities, such as a discussion, a report, or a quiz, reveal that they have misread one or more significant words. This calls for individual consultation with each student to try to get at the root of the problem. Is it too hasty reading? Is it failure to keep in mind that what is read must make sense, and if it doesn't, a word may have been misread? Is it fear of asking for help? Is it lack of ability in using a word recognition skill you thought everyone in the class knew, such as suffixes, context, or a rare grapheme/phoneme relationship? Is it lack of background knowledge or concepts?

Asking yourself such questions can help you decide what to do. Do you need to reteach a skill? Do you need to boost self-confidence? Do you need to devise a way for the student to become more aware of misreading caused by haste or lack of focus?

Instructional Strategies. If your observation reveals that a student (or group of students) is not using a word recognition skill competently or appropriately, you need to plan minilessons to address that need. These lessons will likely involve reteaching; that is, the word element or the strategy will have been taught in an earlier grade and will probably seem familiar to the students.

- For example, students will have received lessons about using the structure of words to help figure out both the probable pronunciation and the probable meaning. Your task now is to reteach the skill and provide grade-appropriate practice opportunities. As students work independently and in small groups, you can coach them to use the skill.

- For those students who seem to know the skill but don't use it, you may need to build self-confidence, helping them see that they have all the skills they need to deal with unfamiliar words.

- The most difficult word recognition problem at this stage may involve students who don't seem to know when they have misread a word. Actually, this may or may not be a word recognition difficulty. Some students may have wonderful word recognition skills but remain oblivious to the need for text to make sense. These students can read right through an incorrect word without being bothered at all. The focus for them, then, is not necessarily on slowing down and "reading more carefully." Rather, the emphasis is on helping them maintain focus on meaning as they read.

- Remind students to have a purpose in mind as they read, a question to answer, a fact to search for, a clue to detect. Remind them, too, that when a sentence doesn't seem to make sense, it might mean they have misread a word and should take another look.

- Discuss with students how lack of background knowledge can inhibit word recognition, and encourage them to ask for help when they feel ill prepared to read a particular passage. Share instances in your own reading when you have misread something and realized it only because what you were reading didn't make sense. With this focus on meaning, students will catch miscues and self-correct or at least look again; they will also learn when they need help because they are insufficiently prepared to deal with the conceptual load of a text.

> ☐ **The student uses a wide variety of comprehension strategies to construct meaning.**
>
> - Grasps differences among genres
> - Perceives text structure
> - Appreciates levels of meaning in a story
> - Varies reading according to purpose for reading

Assessment. Students at this stage are able to read, learn from, and enjoy a wide variety of materials. They are not learning new reading strategies and skills so much as learning to apply known skills and strategies to a wide range of materials and for a variety of purposes.

Keep in mind that reading is never "mastered." Any reader, no matter how fluent, will struggle if he or she has insufficient background information to understand the text or is trying to grasp new concepts and deal with unfamiliar vocabulary, symbolic language, allusion, and so forth.

- Note during class and small group discussions which students can both talk about the distinguishing characteristics of various genres and recognize them while reading.

- As your class reads and responds to nonfiction, note which students demonstrate awareness of text structure. You can detect this through discussion or examination of written responses. For example, after reading a book about reptiles that has one chapter about each of several reptiles, students may recognize this structure as only one way the author might have chosen to present the material. They also should be able to discuss other ways the same information might have been organized: a chapter on each of several topics (habitat, feeding, appearance, reproduction), a chapter on reptiles found in each of several parts of the world, a comparison of one kind of reptile to another, or a sequential presentation showing the evolution of reptiles since the beginning of recorded history. Students should also be able to discuss advantages and disadvantages of various kinds of text structure.

- As students read and respond to a story, observe which individuals read beyond the plot and are able to deal with theme, character development, conflict, and subplot. Such readers won't just say that *Charlotte's Web*, by E. B. White (1952), is a story about a pig and the spider that saves his life. They will recognize the underlying themes of friendship, life cycles, self-esteem, and death.

- Also notice whether your students vary their reading approach according to the purpose they have in mind. For example, a student who is beginning a novel may open to the first page and just begin, but even with novels there should be variation in pace. The minithriller, for example, demands little thought and can be read quickly; a more substantial novel, such as *Hatchet* (Paulsen, 1987), though equally thrilling, requires more careful and thoughtful reading.

- With nonfiction, you should see an even more pronounced difference in approach. For example, when a student is beginning a book about deserts, note whether he or she surveys the book; looks at the table of contents; leafs through to examine charts, maps, and tables; and notices whether there are a glossary and an index. In other words, before beginning an informational book, the student should get acquainted with it, not just open to page 1 and begin.

Instructional Strategies

Genres. If some students seem unfamiliar with various genres, you may need to teach minilessons about the characteristics of each genre. Such lessons might be largely deductive, because by now all the children will have read almost every genre. You should be able to elicit from them the distinguishing characteristics. Then, as you continue to use a wide variety of books in your class, make genre part of your introduction and your follow-up discussion. For example, as your students read *Roll of Thunder, Hear My Cry* (Taylor, 1976), review with them the characteristics of historical fiction, touching on historical accuracy, setting, appropriate language, characterization, plot and theme, and illustrations.

Text structure. You may have students who are not yet familiar with various kinds of text structure, or do not recognize them as they read. Some of the most familiar organizational patterns used in informational writing are description, collection, cause and effect, problem and solution, and comparison. See Table 12.1 for examples of each pattern.

TABLE 12.1

Examples of Expository Text Structures

EXPOSITORY STRUCTURE	EXAMPLE
Description	The tiger is the master of the Indian jungle. It stalks its prey in deadly silence. For half an hour or more, he carefully watches and then slowly, placing one foot softly in front of the other, closes in.
Collection	As master of the Indian jungle, the male tiger plays a number of roles. First, he is the hunter of prey who stalks in deadly silence. He is the beauty of the jungle, an expert at doing nothing in order to rest to be ready for his hunt. Finally, the lord of the jungle is the active seeker of mates, who begins his mating with a nuzzle but ends with a roar.
Causation, or cause and effect	We observed the tiger from our vehicle as it stalked the herd of deer. As a result of the slight noise from our running camera, the tiger turned and knew we were there. This didn't stop it from returning to its intended prey. Slowly and carefully it moved forward, not making a sound. The deer were initially unaware of its presence, but because of the shifting winds, they caught the tiger's scent. This was enough to scare them away.
Response, problem solution, question-answer, or remark-reply	One problem to be resolved in tiger watching is transportation. How is it possible for observers to get close enough to a tiger without scaring it away or being attacked? Nature has helped solve this problem by making the tiger and the elephant friends. It is possible for an elephant carrying several people to get very near a tiger without even being noticed. If it wasn't for this natural friendship, tiger watching would be virtually impossible.
Comparison	The great tiger displays terrific power. With one steady lunge, it can destroy its prey, seemingly without any effort at all. Unlike other predators, the tiger basks in the sun after an attack in order to prepare for its next kill. The power and actions of the tiger resemble those of no other animal in the Indian jungle.

If your students have had little instruction about text structure, you will need to plan a series of lessons devoted to each kind of structure and include many chances for students to examine informational writing. Follow the guidelines for any good teaching: explain, show examples, analyze familiar text, and analyze unfamiliar text. You may want to have students apply what they have learned in their own writing. For example, students may have read an article about the fires in Yellowstone Park organized in a cause-and-effect pattern. Then, when students are preparing to write a report of their own on some topic, you can help them recall this pattern and decide whether it is appropriate for what they are writing.

Reading deeper. Your students, no matter how fluent, may typically read superficially; that is, they may read only for facts or for plot rather than digging for deeper meaning. It may be tempting, since they have few word recognition problems, just to leave them to read on their own and discuss their reading with their peers. This is probably a mistake. You are the more experienced reader. You are aware of the depth of meaning one can derive from literature. It is up to you to help make the deeper levels of meaning apparent to children by guiding discussions, asking open-ended questions, and probing. With your prompting, students can read beyond the story line of a book such as *Charlotte's Web* to the bigger issues of life, death, balance of nature, and friendship, not to mention the impact and power of words. Students can compare pieces of literature on the same theme, different books from the same author, similar plot lines in different genres, different viewpoints, and much more.

Varying reading according to purpose. Students can also be nudged to vary their reading according to their purposes for reading: "Why are you going to read the encyclopedia?" you might ask. "What are you looking for? If you are looking for only certain pieces of information, you might scan. If you are trying to decide if the entry will tell you what you want, you might skim to get a general idea." Give them the same kind of guidance with fiction and poetry: "If you are beginning a novel that will be the focus of a discussion, you'll want to read thoughtfully. If you are reading a mystery for pleasure, you can read as quickly as you like. If you are reading poetry, you might read it aloud to yourself to savor the language." Students who are unable to vary their reading even when prompted may need more direct instruction and modeling.

> ◘ **The student uses a wide variety of comprehension strategies to construct meaning. (continued)**
>
> • Effectively uses strategies: visualizing, predicting, identifying important information, self-questioning, monitoring, summarizing, synthesizing, and evaluating
> • Can verbalize process used to construct meaning; that is, is aware of own thinking (metacognition)

Assessment. These strategies and abilities have been emphasized for students since they first began to read—or even earlier, as they listened to stories. The fluent reader uses them all, though he or she may no longer be aware of doing so on a conscious level. Whenever you guide prereading, reading, and postreading activities, you have an opportunity to check that students are using basic strategies that aid in constructing meaning.

Predicting. Before beginning a new book (or proceeding in an ongoing book), ask for predictions to check whether students are combining what they already know about the book with their own experience to make logical predictions. Then check to see whether they are adjusting predictions as they read on the basis of new evidence.

Particularly with informational reading, check that students are preparing for reading by asking questions focused on what they expect or hope to learn from their reading. As they read, some questions should be answered, while new ones should arise.

Monitoring one's reading. Fluent readers monitor their own reading; that is, they keep asking themselves such questions as "Am I getting it?" "Do I understand what I'm reading?" "Is it making sense to me?" "Am I finding answers to my questions?" "Do I understand why that character did what he did?" Not only do fluent readers monitor their reading, but they also take action if the answer is *no*. They reread, ask for help, or choose another book.

Summarizing. Summarizing during reading, which involves identifying important information, helps the reader monitor his or her reading. Fluent readers can do so overtly if asked. From time to time, interrupt a student who is reading independently and ask him or her to summarize what has been read so far.

Evaluating. Fluent readers also evaluate what they read. This means they don't simply take in the words and ideas; they connect their own experiences and prior reading to what they read and evaluate it. Ask students to form opinions about what they read and to support those opinions with what they have read elsewhere or with personal experience.

Verbalizing. Finally, fluent readers are able to verbalize what they do and how they do it. One way to assess whether a reader is using the strategies we have discussed is to ask the reader to describe what he or she did while reading. Remember, though, that children can sometimes verbalize the acceptable behavior while not actually performing that behavior in real reading situations.

This area of assessment can be tricky, and what you think is evidence may be misleading. For example, if you call attention to a strategy by directly asking a child to demonstrate it to you, you haven't really learned what you want to know. Fluent readers use the strategies all the time, even when no one is asking them to do so.

Instructional Strategies. Instruction in these strategies at this stage is mostly a matter of guiding students before, during, and after reading, calling for the use of the strategies whenever appropriate. If you have some students who are particularly deficient in any strategy, explicit reteaching will be appropriate. Remember that students at this stage have had all these strategies taught to them before. However, they may not have been ready to learn them when they were taught. So reteaching is appropriate. However, helping students make these strategies their own requires monitoring actual reading activities closely to nudge, remind, and elicit strategy use.

Strategies for constructing meaning are not like phonics skills. A reader can master the sound/symbol relationships of letters and know them forever. Constructing meaning is a new challenge each time new and "harder" material is confronted. No one ever" comprehension.

> ☑ **The student uses a wide variety of comprehension strategies to construct meaning. (continued)**
>
> ● Is learning study strategies such as taking notes
> ● Uses graphic material to construct meaning

Assessment. Students in the upper elementary grades and in middle school need to use study strategies, especially when reading in content areas such as social studies or science. You will want to familiarize yourself with the scope and sequence of such skills in your school system to determine if these strategies have been taught prior to the grade you are teaching. Probably this will include such skills as outlining, using graphic organizers such as Venn diagrams or webs, notetaking, skimming and scanning, using an index, using library resources, and interpreting charts and tables.

At the beginning of the school year with a class of mostly Fluent Reading and Writing students, you might informally assess the use of such strategies by setting tasks. For example, assign a piece of reading in a content area and ask students to "take notes" in whatever manner they generally use. Ask students to outline a chapter of an informational book. Distribute text that can be written on, such as a weekly newspaper, and ask students to underline or highlight the information they think is important.

In small groups or one on one, ask students how they approach an assignment to read a chapter in a social studies text on their own. Through such discussion, you will determine whether they preview the text before beginning to read, whether they ask themselves questions based on subtitles, and whether they preread summaries and end-of-chapter questions. Ask students whether they look at graphic material before reading, during reading, or not at all. If they do look at graphic material, ask what they are thinking as they do.

Don't be surprised if you find students who are not yet adept at using study strategies such as these. Even though the strategies may have been taught previously, students may not have been ready or able to use them independently. Count on having to teach or reteach these strategies.

Instructional Strategies. Direct teaching followed by immediate and frequent practice and application is probably the best way to ensure that your students learn study strategies. As an example, we present the following steps for a lesson on notetaking:

1. Present a transparency of informational text.
2. Explain the purpose for notetaking.
3. Model taking notes.
4. Have students collaborate with a partner to take notes on another passage.
5. Debrief with discussion.

6. Have students practice taking notes independently.

7. Debrief students by examining their notes and talking about what they did.

8. Assign notetaking during assigned reading in content areas.

9. Provide for continuing practice in learning centers.

Don't present more than one study strategy at a time. Wait until that strategy seems firm before presenting another one. Make sure the point of learning the strategy isn't lost; that is, students must see the strategy not as an end in itself but as a way to help them do assigned reading more efficiently and with better understanding.

After assigning independent reading, talk with students about strategies they might use to help them grasp and retain the important information. Gradually release students to their own decision making about study strategies. Discussion after reading can help students think about why a strategy was (or was not) helpful and what they might do differently for the next assignment. Your goal, of course, is to have students use strategies independently, without being reminded, and carry that ability into future years of learning.

COMMENTS

One final caution study strategies are idiosyncratic; that is, your own favorite method of taking notes may not be the choice of all your students. Just because it has stood you in good stead all these years doesn't mean you should force it on your class. For example, you may prefer to take notes in a linear fashion, rather like an outline. Some students may prefer to organize their ideas in a web. Others may like making tiny checks in the margin next to important ideas (or placing gummed notes on the pages) as they read and then returning to those places to make notes. However, having too many choices is confusing, so you probably should concentrate on teaching thoroughly one or two methods and help students choose the one that works best for them. If some students still are not successful using one of these strategies, you may need to present other methods.

Test-taking strategies, sometimes considered part of study skills, were discussed in Chapter 5.

☑ **The student enjoys reading.**

- Recommends books to others
- Is exploring young adult and adult fiction and nonfiction
- Sees self as a competent reader
- Sets goals and self-evaluates
- Is aware of own purposes for reading

Assessment. Most students at the Fluent stage probably enjoy reading. Occasionally, however, someone may read competently but without pleasure. People who enjoy reading like to tell others about what they are reading. Such readers also begin to stretch beyond what they have been reading, looking for new challenges and new themes and topics. You'll be able to note which children are exhibiting these behaviors.

Fluent readers are confident. They tackle unfamiliar text willingly and are not afraid of challenges. They seek wider and wider reading experiences because they know they can deal with them. They know what they want to read and why they have chosen a particular text to read. For example, one student may be reading a biography of John Glenn because she wants to be an astronaut, another could be reading every book by Katherine Paterson, another may be reading a mystery recommended by a friend, and yet another may be reading a book about ancient Greece because he is fascinated by Greek history and mythology.

These students also know whether they have read successfully. They know they understand what they read. They know when something is too challenging and can make another choice without losing self-confidence. You will be able to note which children exhibit these behaviors by observing during the Daily Independent Reading block as well as at other times and by examining records the students keep of independent reading done in school and at home.

Instructional Strategies. When you note that a student does *not* exhibit the behaviors that indicate enjoyment of reading, try to determine why. For example, if a student is not confident, first identify the student's level of reading for yourself. If the student is not reading fluently in grade-level materials, adjust your instruction and the materials you use so that she or he will feel successful. If the student *can* read fluently in grade-level materials but lacks confidence, your task is related more to psychological and emotional support than to instructional support.

You can do some things to encourage pleasure in reading, of course. You can encourage and provide time for students to share their reading with each other. You can share what you are reading with your students. You can suggest specific, more challenging books to individual students on the basis of their interests. You can continue to introduce authors and genres by reading aloud to the class. You can help students as they choose what to read by asking questions:

What kind of book are you looking for? A mystery? A scary book?

How could you find such a book in the library?

Do you need more information for a science project? Where might you look?

How will you decide if a book you find will meet your purposes?

Do not neglect reading aloud to your fluent readers. This is the door to new authors, new genres, new ideas, and new visions. Hearing wonderful books read aloud is still a most potent contributor to pleasure in reading.

> ◘ **The student is refining research skills begun at the previous stage.**
>
> - Can plan a research project
> - Knows how to locate print and electronic information
> - Takes notes in a variety of ways; attributes sources
> - Synthesizes information into a final product

Assessment. Before students have reached the Fluent Reading and Writing stage, they likely have already been taught some aspects of research. They have "looked things up." They have prepared and presented reports of various kinds.

You may decide early in the school year to assign a small research project and, without directions of any kind, simply observe closely as students begin to work. You will soon know which students are comfortable with research skills and which need further instruction.

Even if you know there has been considerable prior instruction, summer vacation has intervened, or perhaps students were not at the literacy stage that allowed them to absorb such instruction. For example, if some students were still struggling with fluency, they might have had a difficult time reading various information sources even though they were competent at locating them.

Students with Internet access at home may be more adept than others at using the computer as a resource. Related but different skills are needed for locating information using a search engine and using an index to a book. Beyond locating information, students need to be taught how to evaluate information for its validity and for its appropriateness for a particular purpose. They need to learn ways to take notes about information they find and how to credit the source of that information. Finally, they need to be able to synthesize information from several sources into one cohesive whole.

You can assess your students' familiarity with and ability to use research skills as you help them prepare for their first project calling for research. Through discussion you can get a general idea of the class's readiness to do research, though there may be wide variation among individuals. On the basis of the initial activities, note which students are able to verbalize how to plan a research project and which do not participate in a discussion about planning.

See more with the TeachSource Video Case, "Teaching Technology Skills: An Elementary School Lesson on PowerPoint."

Instructional Strategies. Though some students may already be skilled, chances are you should plan specific lessons for your whole class in each area of research. These will serve as a refresher for skilled researchers as well as an introduction for students with no prior instruction.

Two students collaborate on a research project using a computer.

© Michael Newman/ PhotoEdit

If you use a published reading or literacy program, it probably has a research or study skills component. You should examine your program for such lessons and decide, on the basis of what you are learning about your particular students, which lessons to teach the whole class, which to teach only to small groups, and which to omit altogether. You may decide that your students lack prerequisite skills for some of the lessons in your published program. Your job is to make the lessons fit the students. We suggest that you spend considerable time presenting detailed and thorough lessons related to research skills and provide many opportunities for students to apply these skills in authentic assignments related to content areas.

You may also do on-the-spot instruction with individuals. For example, if Joel is struggling to locate information in an encyclopedia, your best instructional choice may be to give him a quick lesson right then. Model and think aloud how you would approach the task. Let's say Joel is doing a report about African animals and is reading the entire entry on Africa. You can show him how to scan for pertinent information and thus narrow his search. If Charmine has found a site on the Internet, you can model how to decide what one should take notes on (or print out) and what is irrelevant to the project at hand. Perhaps, as Juan is writing a report, you note that he is simply reporting, in sequence, information from each of several sources. Show him how to go back to his plan, identify important ideas, and then synthesize information to support each main idea. When you notice several students with similar difficulties, you may decide to plan small-group explicit lessons.

Figure 12.2 presents a sample class checklist for all the reading benchmarks at the Fluent Reading and Writing stage.

Writing: Indicators, Assessment, Instructional Strategies

Most assessment of writing will be done by observing students as they write and by examining various writing products. These observations will guide you in making instructional decisions.

We discuss six major areas of writing at this stage:

- Strengthening and deepening of prior behaviors
- Writing for a variety of purposes and reasons
- Growing competence in mechanics
- Use of the writing process
- Seeing self as a competent writer
- Connects reading and writing

A sample class checklist (Figure 12.3) for Fluent writing benchmarks appears near the end of this section.

▢ Prior writing behaviors strengthen and deepen.

Your students should be showing evidence of prior writing instruction and experience as the year begins, and you should see their abilities continue to develop.

Reading Checklist:
Fluent Reading and Writing Stage

Teacher_____ Date_____ Grade_____

Students

+ = consistently present
- = not present
✓ = somewhat present; recheck;
    insufficient evidence

Benchmark

Behaviors from Almost Fluent Stage								
Word Recognition								
Comprehension/Construction of Meaning								
Grasps genres								
Perceives text structure								
Appreciates levels of meaning								
Varies reading according to purpose								
Uses strategies to construct meaning								
Is aware of own thinking								
Is learning study strategies								
Uses graphic material								
Enjoyment								
Recommends books to others								
Is exploring adult reading								
Sees self as competent reader								
Sets goals/self-evaluates								
Is aware of own purposes								
Research Skills								
Can plan a research project								
Knows how to locate print and electronic information								
Takes notes/attributes sources								
Synthesizes information								

Instructional Plans:
_____
_____
_____

FIGURE 12.2

Sample Class Checklist for Fluent Reading and Writing: Reading Benchmarks and Behaviors

◻ The student writes for a variety of purposes and reasons.

- Is aware of how writing can contribute to self-awareness
- Uses writing to persuade

Assessment. Children have probably been writing in personal journals since kindergarten. Gradually, students become reflective, finding that they learn about themselves as they write (and reread their writing). Look for evidence of self-examination and hypothesizing about self. For example, a student may write, "Writing about my reactions to the concert helps me think about why I like certain kinds of music."

Students have also been writing to entertain or inform for some time. Now, they are also showing their ability to write in order to persuade. They may recommend a book to others in such a way that others want to read it. They may write posters and speeches supporting their opinions about a school issue. They may express their viewpoints through letters to the editor of a school or local newspaper. You can learn whether students understand and use writing for persuasion by discussing possible courses of action related to an issue of some kind. You might ask, for example, "What can we do to let elected officials know how we feel?" Students should know they can mail letters or send e-mails.

When your students understand that they can use writing for persuasion, they should also realize that powerful writing can persuade them as well. Discussion of writing that expresses or attempts to sway opinion, including advertisements, will reveal whether students have grasped a little of the power of words.

Instructional Strategies. Even if your students seem to understand the power of persuasive writing, you will want to reinforce what they already are doing and deepen their understanding and abilities. Lessons on persuasive writing may be part of your published reading/language arts program. If so, examine the lessons carefully to determine if they are suitable for your students or if you need to expand them with further examples and exercises.

The skill of critical reading is closely linked to writing persuasively. Students must be helped to recognize persuasive writing, whether its goal is to persuade others to take action, change beliefs, vote for a candidate, or buy a product. One good way to learn to recognize such writing by others is to do such writing oneself.

◻ The student writes for a variety of purposes and reasons. (continued)

- Can write in response to a prompt to fit a given rubric

Assessment. At school, district, and state levels, writing assessment usually requires students to write in a certain way and in response to a given prompt. Although such assessments are more authentic than answering questions "about" writing, fixing wrong sentences, and identifying parts of speech, they are still a long way from the writing one does for one's own purposes. Still, these assessments are a fact of life, and this type of task is realistic in that such writing may be required of students throughout their adult lives. Many jobs, for example, require very specific writing about a given topic.

You may have some information about the previous performance of each student on this kind of task. If so, you'll be glad to have it, but at the same time you must remember that students may have lost some ability over a vacation. On the other hand, those who enjoy writing may have increased in ability during a vacation.

You may want to begin with a discussion about what students remember from prior writing assessments when they were given a topic and knew they would be evaluated on the basis of a rubric. Help them recall the writing process steps, the need for planning, and the need for showing rough drafts. Then mimic the conditions of such an assessment: assign a topic and have them write. You may want to do this twice, once for "creative" writing and once for informational writing.

Collect and read the papers and sort them roughly into those that seem to show an understanding of the task and ability to carry it out, and those that do not. The quality of the writing, of course, is key, and we will address that in the next sections. Here we are concerned only with whether students can work in this way.

Instructional Strategies. If your students are not comfortable with writing to a prompt and meeting the standards of a specific rubric, you'll need to prepare lessons to accustom them to this task. You will need to review with them the many purposes for writing. While much of writing is self-determined, personal, and free, there are times when students will be required to write what they are told to write and in the way they are told to write. They need to learn how to do this. Review or reteach the steps of the writing process, forms such as essay and story, and text structures.

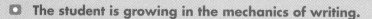

> **◘ The student is growing in the mechanics of writing.**
>
> - Edits own work
> - Can edit the work of others
> - Can independently verify spelling, grammar, and usage

Assessment. By the Fluent stage, your students should understand the importance of mechanics and be on their way to standard use of spelling, grammar, and punctuation. Although writers usually don't address the mechanics of their writing until the final step before publishing, mechanics are apt to be the first thing a reader notices. Careless mechanics can interfere with a reader's ability to grasp ideas.

Observe closely as students put the finishing touches on their writing. Note which are editing their own work. All writers need an editor, of course, so understand that it is difficult—perhaps impossible—for a writer to be completely successful in self-editing. Nevertheless, look for behavior showing that the student is going over his or her work after revision to check spelling, punctuation, and usage. Part of self-editing, of course, is recognizing that something may need correcting.

You should also note which students are able to do this editing task for others when asked. Further, which students know how to find answers to their own questions about mechanics by consulting dictionaries, usage references, spell-checking features, or a human authority?

Instructional Strategies. If students are not editing their own work or are doing it poorly, you'll want to plan specific lessons addressing this important step. You may want to teach your students a system for editing, such as first checking the spelling of each word, then the punctuation, then the grammar. Because it is almost impossible to watch for problems in all these areas in one reading, we suggest you teach students to read for one area at a time. Here are some ideas to remember:

1. **Spelling is tricky to edit**. Successful editing presumes that you will recognize a word that is misspelled and either know how to spell it correctly or know how to locate the correct spelling. Poor spellers may or may not recognize an incorrect spelling when they see one, especially in their own writing. We all tend to see what we expect to see; reading right past an incorrect spelling is common, even for good spellers. Further, relying on a spelling check in a word processing program is risky; if a word is a real word, the computer doesn't care whether it's a homonym of the correct word—hence the many mistaken uses of "their" for "there" or "they're." Catching these kinds of errors requires an eagle eye.

2. **What if your students are pretty sure the word is spelled incorrectly, but they don't know the correct spelling**? Assuming your students have detected a spelling error, what next? Here comes the usual objection to dictionaries: if I don't know how to spell it, how can I look it up? Teach your students to hypothesize about probable spelling, a process that can lead them to the correct spelling in the dictionary. Remember what we said in earlier chapters about "invented" spelling? This is what one must do when the correct spelling is unknown: one must invent a probable spelling and use that as a starting point in the dictionary.

3. **Teach your students to edit another's writing**. You'll need to teach your students how to do this without creating hard feelings or causing the author to become defensive or discouraged. The trick is to stay focused on the work; both students should have the same goal—improving the work. Model ways to point out problems, without damaging egos. For example, don't say, "You didn't use quotation marks right." Instead, say, "When I came to this paragraph, I wasn't sure who was speaking. Let's look at the paragraphing and quotation marks to be sure they are clear." Students should use the same system they use on their own work, reading carefully for each area and marking questionable items. You'll need to decide if peer editors should actually make corrections or merely indicate the problems for the author to address. Be sure all students understand that they are looking only for mechanics and perhaps for clarity during this task. They are not criticizing content in any way or suggesting revisions.

You may want to post editing guidelines in your classroom

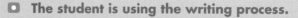

> **◻ The student is using the writing process.**
>
> - Uses all steps of the writing process independently
> - Varies prewriting techniques according to task
> - Revises own work extensively

Assessment. Fluent writers should be using all the steps of the process when appropriate: prewriting, writing the rough draft, revising, editing/proofreading, and publishing the final copy.

Observe closely as students approach a writing task for which the writing process is appropriate. Note which are able to use a prewriting technique to generate ideas and whether the technique chosen seems to produce good thinking. Continue to observe as students proceed through the steps. Note which students are using the steps independently, indicating that they have internalized the process, and which are doing thoughtful revision after producing a rough draft. This seems to us to be one of the last steps students are willing or able to do. Often they want to proceed directly to editing and proofreading or to combine revision with editing.

Instructional Strategies. We believe a writer is never through learning about the writing process, so even those who seem to use all the steps independently will benefit from continued instruction. However, the type of instruction should vary according to students' present level of skill. Therefore, you may decide to teach to small groups.

For example, those students who are using all the steps may need extra guidance in only one area, such as revision. While they may already be revising, you may decide you can teach lessons that will help them increase the effectiveness of their revision.

Other students may need additional instruction related to prewriting techniques. Still others may need reminding of how the writing process can serve them in their efforts to write for their own purposes. Until young writers see the writing process as an aid to better, more satisfying writing, they may not use it unless requested. You can help them see the process as a means to an end rather than an end in itself.

> **◻ The student is using the writing process. (continued)**
>
> - Is developing a personal writing style, or voice

Assessment. Some students may already be writing in a personal voice, whereas others still write in a lifeless series of declarative sentences such as "We went to the circus. We had fun. There were lots of animals and clowns." Examine samples of your students' writing frequently to note whether they are developing a personal writing style, remain largely imitative, or still use the stilted language of younger years.

Especially in creative writing (as opposed to informational or report writing), fluent writers will already have a voice, a way of saying things that is uniquely theirs. One student may use fresh metaphors from sports. Another may be developing a gift for poetry. Even in assigned writing that must conform to guidelines, some students will have strong individual styles.

Instructional Strategies. Developing a personal style or voice is probably the result of a supportive writing environment and continual encouragement and engagement in writing. Help young writers find their own ways to express ideas and tell stories. This means more than just completing exercises in avoiding trite similes, although that sort of exercise can help.

When you discuss good literature, help students see beyond plot. Help them note the author's craft. How did the author do what he or she did? How did the author make you feel sad or happy or scared? How did this author's way of making you feel sad differ from the approach of that other author who also made you sad? Was it the events? The choice of words? The figurative language? The images?

Ask your students, "Why do you often want to read another book by the same author? Is it because you like the way that author writes? That's the author's voice. Others may try to imitate it, but the best authors have voices so unique that no one can truly imitate them."

> ## ☐ The student sees self as a competent writer.
>
> - Sets goals and evaluates own writing

Assessment. Writers at the Fluent Reading and Writing stage are confident in their ability to fulfill writing assignments as well as to write for their own purposes. They should be aware that they can still grow a great deal in their ability, but they are not afraid to write; they accept writing tasks willingly, and they are comfortable in doing so.

The one specific indicator at this stage is the students' ability to set goals and self-evaluate as they work on various assignments involving writing. For a while, you might devise and post a checklist of some kind to help students monitor their own ability to set goals and evaluate their work. The checklist may be as simple or as elaborate as you choose. Here is a sample:

Personal Writing Goals

- Can I state my purpose for this piece of writing?
- Have I accomplished my purpose?
- Did I revise and polish my writing until I am proud of it?
- Can I state what needs improvement?
- Do I have a plan for becoming a better writer?

Bear in mind, though, that you want your students to set goals and self-evaluate independently—without prompting or checklists.

Instructional Strategies. Modeling and prodding, rather than direct instruction, will move students toward this benchmark. During conferences, and frequently in between, ask the student such questions as these:

What did you want to accomplish with this piece of writing?

Did you accomplish what you wanted to? If not, what will your goal be for the next piece of writing?

What do you want to do better? How can you learn to do it better?

Use your conferences and all your other interactions with students to provide the environment and support they need.

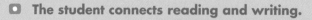

> **◘ The student connects reading and writing.**
>
> - Recognizes author's craft and uses in own writing
> - Is experimenting with writing in many forms

Assessment. Throughout this book, we have emphasized the important connection between reading and writing. We have reinforced that wide reading improves writing, just as writing improves one's ability to read. One constructs meaning when one reads and when one writes; each process involves similar ways of thinking. At this stage, we highlight two writing behaviors that may be new: recognition of the author's craft and experimentation with forms and genres.

Earlier we discussed the importance of helping students become aware of aspects of the author's craft. This serves two purposes: it enhances pleasure in reading, and it also affects the individual's own writing. We believe you should be on the lookout for evidence that students are connecting the craft they are learning to appreciate as they read with their own ability to use such techniques to improve their own writing.

Observe which students are trying different forms and genres as they write independently. You, of course, will be teaching and assigning many different kinds of writing during the Developmentally Appropriate Writing block. Here you are concerned with students' interest in trying different forms when it is their choice. Recall the reference to 6+1 Traits™ in Chapter 11 and the website related to the use of this way of looking at student writing.

Instructional Strategies. As you read with students, continue to go beyond discussion of plot, character, setting, and conflict. Address the issue of how authors did what they did and whether the students might attempt similar techniques in their own writing (Atwell, 1987). It may help to comment frequently that such wonderful writing probably did not flow out in the author's first draft but was the result of much thoughtful revision.

You need to help your fluent readers and writers grasp that good writing is not just telling what happened. If it were, we could simply tell this story: a teenage boy and girl fell in love, but their families were enemies. They figured out a way to be together by faking suicide, but it backfired and at the end they both died. Who needs William Shakespeare to write *Romeo and Juliet?* Who needs the musical *West Side Story?*

Continue to present many forms and different genres to students so that they can at least try them out. With some forms, students definitely need to acquire confidence: letters and reports, for example. Other forms or genres, such as various types of fiction and poetry, may or may not be part of every student's life, but you can nevertheless give students your support as they try different kinds of writing to see which fits them best.

Figure 12.3 presents a sample checklist for all the writing benchmarks and behaviors at the Fluent Reading and Writing stage.

Writing Checklist:
Fluent Reading and Writing Stage

Teacher_____   **Date**_____   **Grade**_____

Students

+ = consistently present
- = not present
✓ = somewhat present; recheck;
    insufficient evidence

Benchmark									
Growth in Prior Writing Behaviors									
Variety of Purposes/Reasons									
Knows writing adds to self-awareness									
Uses writing to persuade									
Can write to fit prompt/rubric									
Mechanics									
Edits own work									
Edits work of others									
Independently verifies									
Writing Process									
Uses all steps independently									
Varies prewriting techniques									
Revises own work									
Developing personal style/voice									
Sees Self as Competent									
Sets goals and evaluates									
Connects Reading and Writing									
Recognizes and uses author's craft									
Experiments with forms/genres									

Instructional Plans:

_____

_____

_____

FIGURE 12.3

Sample Class Checklist for Fluent Reading and Writing: Writing Benchmarks and Behaviors

Planning Instruction Based on Assessment

We now address three important questions: what to teach, how to teach, and how to prepare these fluent readers and writers in fifth grade and up for what awaits them in the next stage of their education.

What Do I Teach?

Though this chapter has dealt primarily with the Fluent Reading and Writing stage, you will, of course, have students in your fifth or sixth grade who are not yet at this stage. Your assessment will have made this evident. Instructional decisions are still an important part of your job. Further, you have an increased need to be sure that literacy is a part of the entire curriculum, not just language arts. In addition, you have a responsibility to help your students acquire the study skills they will need to deal with increasingly complex curriculum materials, as well as learn to manage and plan their own time to fulfill the requirements imposed by different teachers. In this section, we address the following: 1) meeting the needs of a range of stages, 2) making instructional decisions, 3) applying literacy across the curriculum, and 4) reinforcing study skills and strategies.

MEETING THE NEEDS OF A RANGE OF STAGES

Most likely, the majority of your students in fifth grade and above will be at or almost at the Fluent Reading and Writing stage; in other words, they will be consistently displaying the benchmarks discussed in this chapter and Chapter 11.

It is possible, however, that you will have someone who is still at the Beginning Reading and Writing stage, perhaps a student who has been socially promoted within your school system or transferred from another system. Such students may be given reading instruction in some kind of intervention program. Yet these students may still be with the others during social studies, science, and math. Teachers of these subjects must teach the concepts required by the curriculum even when some students cannot read the material independently. For such students, several instructional strategies and materials discussed in earlier chapters are appropriate: providing audio versions of content textbooks, providing study buddies, varying the questioning to permit all students to participate in a discussion, and providing alternative, simpler materials that cover the same content.

MAKING INSTRUCTIONAL DECISIONS

At the beginning of the school year, you will need to assess the literacy stage of each of your students. You can use the suggested procedures, tools, and techniques from this and earlier chapters. You may also decide to administer an informal reading inventory to each student during the first two or three weeks of school (see Chapter 4).

Once you have an idea of each student's literacy stage, you will proceed with teaching your curriculum, continuing to use every teaching activity as an opportunity to gather information. When a lesson doesn't turn out the way you planned, evaluate what you did to determine what adjustments you need to make in future lessons to accommodate your students' needs.

An important part of your instructional decision-making relates to the range of stages in your class. You may have chosen to teach upper grades because you prefer dealing with content areas rather than basic skills. Nevertheless, *all* teachers need to be prepared to teach every student in the class, regardless of stage. This may require a great deal of small-group or individual instruction.

Second-Language Learners. Some students may be fluent in another language but not yet fluent in English, and some may not yet be fluent either in the first language or in English. Such students need programs designed to help them acquire English, and they may need an intervention program as well. It is risky to generalize. An individual plan must be drawn up for each student, and it should be based on whatever combination of needs is present.

Meanwhile, you, as the classroom teacher, will need to make adjustments to accommodate students who are not yet fluent in English. Even those who appear to be fluent in English may still wrestle with idiomatic and figurative language. Many teacher manuals now provide suggestions with virtually every lesson for addressing difficult terms and concepts for ESL students. Students may benefit from having a reading partner, and they may also benefit from literature discussion groups that support their efforts to express ideas.

Give your second-language learners as many opportunities to speak as you can and as they are willing to take, but resist forcing students who may be shy or embarrassed by their lack of fluency.

Continue to focus on the various cultures represented in your class, whether or not they include other-language speakers. Sometimes you may be able to tie literacy activities to social studies units. Such units may include costumes and foods from

More teaching suggestions are listed in "For Additional Reading" at the premium website for this text.

The teacher is helping her students learn about cultures other than their own.

© Michael Newman/PhotoEdit

various cultures, along with study of history and geography. Your job will be to learn what you can of the cultures represented in your particular class and then use the many ideas found in teacher manuals to make your students feel comfortable and valued, as well as to enlighten other students about our diverse society.

LITERACY ACROSS THE CURRICULUM

Fluent readers and writers are presumed to be ready to apply their abilities to curriculum areas such as science, social studies, and math. This presumption may be somewhat misplaced; that is, the literacy demands of these content areas may differ from those of the materials in a reading/language arts program.

Each content area has its own vocabulary, and the organization of each content area textbook is unique. Information may be incremental; for example, dealing with a chapter in a science book may depend on prior knowledge to a far greater extent than reading a new novel. The type of prior knowledge may also differ: prior knowledge that supports reading fiction is likely personal experience; prior knowledge that supports content-area reading is often specific to that particular content area. You must teach your students how to read each particular text along with teaching the content itself.

STUDY SKILLS AND STRATEGIES

The term *study skills* is sometimes used to refer to a group of abilities, such as dealing with a wide variety of text organization, using learning strategies such as K-W-L, taking notes, summarizing, outlining, using references, preparing for tests and using test-taking strategies, managing time, and juggling multiple assignments from several teachers. Some of these skills have been introduced to students earlier. If you teach fifth to eighth grade, your careful reteaching (and introduction of new skills) may be students' last chance to receive thorough instruction. Teachers in later grades may expect students to know these strategies already and feel no need to provide further instruction.

You need to reinforce what students already know, provide practice, and reteach or introduce skills and strategies students clearly are not yet using competently. While the content of science, social studies, and math is vital to the education of your students, teaching them *how* to learn such things now and for the future is equally valuable.

Certain study skills are appropriate for studying material online. Students can be taught to use color, copy and paste, note-making, and outlining features on computers to keep track of and organize ideas they find online or on CD-ROMs. These skills will also help students prepare written and oral projects.

How Do I Teach What Needs to Be Taught?

In answer to the question of how you will teach, there are three main areas to consider: selecting materials, maintaining a Comprehensive Balanced Literacy Program, and choosing instructional routines that best support student learning.

SELECTING MATERIALS

At every stage of literacy, your job is to provide materials that suit the interests and abilities of your students. Now that students are fluent in reading and writing, you may find you have broader choices, but you must still pay attention to this area.

Published program. If you are using a published reading/language arts program, anthologies are probably provided that contain a wide selection of fiction and nonfiction. They are designed to help students sample many genres, many nonfiction text structures, and a wide range of topics, cultures, and experiences. Such anthologies are wonderful for just this purpose; students can sample a little bit of the vast published literature. These tastes will, one hopes, lead students to read widely beyond the prescribed program. You will want to stay abreast of new books published for readers of this age, but also continue to read the older, beloved classics. Many of your readers will be sampling young adult and adult literature.

Books at lower reading levels. For students who are not yet at the Fluent Reading and Writing stage, you will need books appropriate to their reading level. These may be from the adopted published program or from sets of trade books.

Access to information about trade books. Students should be encouraged to browse in libraries and in card catalogs, whether real or virtual, and to look at displays of new books in bookstores to get ideas of books they might want to buy or check out of a library. They can be introduced to the many publications in print and online where new books are reviewed. For example, at online sources like Amazon, your students can learn about new books as well as post their own reviews. Many authors maintain their own websites where students can read about their lives, their craft, and their publications.

Books to read aloud to students. For all students, you will want to continue to choose books to read aloud. We have never found anyone of any age who does not enjoy listening to someone read aloud a good book. Reading aloud stimulates students to read more for themselves. It opens doors to other cultures and times. It expands vocabulary. It provides fodder for intense discussion. It allows you to share the beauty of language.

MAINTAINING THE COMPREHENSIVE BALANCED LITERACY PROGRAM

The model of the Comprehensive Balanced Literacy Program (introduced in Chapter 6) continues to be vital in your classroom of mostly fluent readers and writers. The same six core blocks are necessary for all students, along with individual Intervention for those students who need it. While all the blocks will still be part of your program, the times allotted for each may be different at this stage.

Daily Independent Reading. By this stage, students are comfortable with independent reading and are able to do so for extended periods. You may decide to allot as much as 30 minutes to this activity, at least on some days. Students may need a refresher and a rehearsal early in the school year to remind them about selecting material and behaving appropriately during independent reading.

As with earlier stages, you may choose to read during this time, modeling the value of reading in your life. You may also use the time, if needed, for individual conferences, sampling oral reading, doing special assessments, checking reading logs, and touching base with students about their interests.

Daily Independent Writing. Students are now more comfortable generating ideas and can write for more extended periods of time. Encourage English-language learners (ELLs) to write in their first language if that is more comfortable; but when they do so, be sure they understand that you may ask them to summarize in English from time to time.

You may use this time for your own writing. You may also use some of it for individual conferences with students—monitoring, coaching, aiding with revisions, and so forth. Because of time restrictions, it may not be possible to have students write independently during the literacy block every day. Many teachers provide opportunities for this at other times during the day, such as during the period when students are arriving in the morning. Teachers also encourage students to make personal writing a part of their everyday lives outside of school.

Reading: Learning Skills and Strategies/Application of Skills and Strategies. During the Learning Skills and Strategies block, you continue to provide instruction to help students solidify and extend their skills. During the Application of Skills and Strategies block, you provide the materials and time for students to apply these skills while reading books at their own level.

It may be tempting to think that because your students are at the Fluent stage, they no longer need direct instruction. This is a mistake. As we have said repeatedly, none of us is ever as proficient a reader as we might be. Everyone continues to benefit from a wise teacher who helps us interact with text at different levels and for different purposes.

The scope and sequence of skills in your published reading/language arts series will guide you to teach study skills; story elements; author's craft; text organization or structure; etymologies; literary techniques such as hyperbole, allusion, irony, and metaphor; and much more. Because fluent readers are comfortable with decoding and basic comprehension, you can focus on leading them to read critically; for example, they may learn to consider the source, question validity, detect bias, and compare and contrast various viewpoints. You will deal with these "skills" during the Reading: Learning Skills and Strategies block and provide material for immediate application during the Reading: Application of Skills and Strategies block. You want students to become accustomed to applying these skills and ways of thinking even when not directed to do so.

Writing: Learning to Write/Developmentally Appropriate Writing. As with reading, no one is ever through needing good instruction about writing. You will continue to teach spelling, grammar, and mechanics through direct instruction. In addition, you will continue to model various forms of writing, lead students in collaborative and cooperative writing, teach and reteach the steps of the writing process, and provide a block of time during which students apply what you have taught.

Increasingly, the types of writing students are doing will connect to various curricular areas. They will be writing informational reports for social studies and science; they will write letters regarding issues and when in need of information; they will compose commentary to post on the Internet; they may correspond with students in other countries. You will also continue to encourage and support personal writing, such as entries in journals, as well as what is often called creative writing—stories and poems.

You will use both reading and writing blocks for teaching students how to plan and do research for various written reports. This involves not only the critical reading skills that lead to wise identification of sources, but also specific instruction about taking notes, carefully recording information about sources, paraphrasing, using direct quotations, synthesizing information from several sources, planning the presentation of information, and revising the plan as new information is learned.

Students in your classroom who are at the Almost Fluent stage can probably be taught in the classroom through careful assessment and small-group and individual instruction. Others may be lagging further in their literacy development and need the additional Intervention block.

INSTRUCTIONAL ROUTINES FOR DEPTH AND BREADTH

Chapter 6 presented an overview of instructional routines that support a Comprehensive Balanced Literacy Program and that have been appropriate throughout the developmental literacy stages. Many still serve the needs of students, though you will find your emphasis shifting.

By this stage, you will no longer need the routines for phonics, high-frequency words, or decodable words. You will, however, still teach lessons related to the structure of words as well as etymology.

Virtually every routine related to comprehension still belongs in your classroom, as comprehension is never mastered. As one continues to read more and more challenging material, the demands on the reader increase. Now these demands are seldom related to answering such questions as "What happened?" and "To whom?" Rather, fluent readers wrestle with such concepts as theme, conflict, allusion, literary techniques, connotation, bias, and layers of meaning. Perhaps an occasional student becomes a deep reader and thinker without any help, but most students need guidance to help them appreciate what reading has to offer.

To that end, here are some routines that should still have a place in your classroom at the Fluent Reading and Writing stage.

Minilessons Routine. The minilesson is useful no matter what stage you teach, and it will continue to include the five parts described in Chapter 6: (1) introduction, (2) teacher modeling, (3) student modeling and guided practice, (4) summarizing and reflecting, and (5) follow-up. This format is suitable for specific skills, strategies, concepts, or processes, whether in literacy or in any content area.

Explicit Comprehension Routine. Recall that this routine involves three main steps: concept, listening, and reading. Thus, if you were preparing a lesson focused on the literary element "conflict," your initial plan might look like the one that follows. Completing the three steps may take several days.

1. *Concept.* Use a familiar story to introduce the concept of conflict. For example, recall the fairy tale "Little Red Riding Hood." Have students identify the problem and then the source of the problem (another character: the wolf). Have students recall other stories they all know, identify the conflict, and decide whether it is between characters, within a character, between a character and nature, or between a character and society. Here are some examples of the latter types:

    Conflict within a character: In *Ira Sleeps Over* (Waber, 1972), Ira must decide whether to take his favorite teddy bear with him when he goes to spend the night with a friend.

Conflict between a character and nature: In *Hatchet* (Paulsen, 1987), the main character struggles throughout the book to survive in the wilderness.

Conflict between a character and society: In *Number the Stars* (Lowry, 1989), the conflict relates to Nazi soldiers marching into the characters' hometown, Copenhagen.

2. *Listening.* Read aloud some short stories, and guide students to identify the major problem and what kind of conflict that problem represents. Discuss how the author reveals the conflict.

3. *Reading.* Assign short pieces for students to read for the express purpose of identifying the conflict. Any piece of fiction will be appropriate, since without conflict there is no story.

This model for explicit comprehension routines will suit whatever area of literature you choose to focus on.

Modes of Reading Routine. Recall the modes of reading: teacher read-aloud, shared reading, guided reading, cooperative/collaborative reading, and independent reading. Each of these modes still has a place in a classroom of fluent readers, though they will not look the same in fifth grade and above as they did in first grade.

Read-aloud. You should still read aloud to students to share wonderful literature, introduce an author or a book that students will then read independently, read material that may be conceptually difficult so that ideas can be discussed as students listen, and share unfamiliar authors' work.

Shared reading. At the earliest literacy stages, shared reading meant first reading to students and then along with students, from big books and classroom sets of little books. At the Fluent stage, you might still read to students as they follow along when studying poetry. Poetry should be read aloud, and you may want to project or provide a blown-up copy of a poem so that all eyes are focused on the text as students hear a good reader (you) read it aloud.

Guided reading. Guided reading is often appropriate as students read content-area material such as social studies or science textbooks. You may find that the teacher's manuals that accompany your content textbooks provide detailed ideas for guiding the reading of each chapter. We caution you again that such reading should be silent for the most part. That is, you introduce concepts, present vocabulary, preview the chapter, construct a K-W-L chart, or do whatever is appropriate before students begin to read, but then they should read the first (predetermined by you) chunk of the text silently. After this silent reading, you guide discussion about what they read, going back to the text to clarify thinking if necessary. Then you discuss and set purposes for students' reading of the next chunk—and so on through the day's reading. Some students may be able to read the entire text independent of guidance, but better learning of content will occur (as well as increased skill in reading informational text) if you guide a significant portion of the reading.

Cooperative-collaborative reading. Partners may find it helps both of them to read content material together if you are not conducting a whole-class guided reading. Students at this stage also enjoy partnering with younger readers. English-language learners, who may find silent reading difficult, may benefit from reading with another student who speaks the same primary language or with a congenial native English speaker. If ELL students do read alone, their silent reading may involve subvocalization (reading aloud to themselves).

Independent reading. Students at this stage will read most self-chosen material independently, and independent reading should continue to play a big part in your day.

Modes of Writing Routine. You may find you still use all the modes of writing suggested in Chapter 6. Students will continue to need the modeling you provide in a quasi write-aloud, during which you plan and make a rough draft. They will also continue to benefit from shared whole-class writing, guided writing as they begin to work on a writing project, collaboration with peers, and independent writing.

All writers, even the most prolific and skillful, benefit from the help and guidance of others at some points during the writing process. Like reading, writing is never mastered, and one is never finished learning about it.

Discussion Groups Routine. Discussion allows readers to share their thoughts about what they have read. By this stage, students are probably adept at holding and managing discussion groups without much guidance or supervision. At the beginning of the school year, you will assess this ability and step in if needed. Follow whichever steps from Chapter 6 your students need.

At this stage, you may introduce some more sophisticated aspects to literature discussions. For example, you may encourage students to read various books by one author and focus a discussion on the author's themes and craft. You might suggest that students read several books dealing with the same theme or genre. Students may research in the library or on the Internet to find critical commentary about some of the books and authors they are reading and bring that information to the discussion. When a book has a film version, students may enjoy comparing the book with the film, considering the unique challenges of telling a story in each art form.

Reserve some time in your schedule for students to give brief "book chats" about books they have discovered. Great readers have always relied on friends for ideas about what book to read next.

How Do I Prepare Students for What Comes Next?

If you teach students in fifth grade or above, you are probably trying to prepare them for whatever kinds of school experience they might face next. In this section, we address two areas directly related to literacy and to thriving in that new setting: independent learning and change in curriculum and schedule.

HELPING STUDENTS BECOME INDEPENDENT LEARNERS

As your students move into the higher grades, they may be monitored less closely by their teachers. They will be expected to manage their assignments for themselves. They will be expected to know how to read content-area textbooks, how to study for tests on that content, and how to prepare reports and other kinds of projects stemming from various subject areas. Teachers at those higher levels may believe students should already be using the study techniques we discussed earlier; they may not think they should teach such techniques to those who don't already know them.

As the school year progresses, you may want to move your students into situations that are more and more like what lies ahead for them, while at the same time continuing to provide the support they need right now. Such a balance can be tricky, but the payoff is significant.

Some teachers like to suggest ways for students to keep track of assignments in each curricular area, along with blocking out study times so that no area is short-changed. Even if you teach all subjects, you can help students take charge of this kind of personal time management, just as though they were answerable to several teachers.

For example, let's say your students are doing a long-term project, due on May 1. You can help them learn to lay out a timeline of tasks, perhaps working backward from the end date:

I need to start writing/inputting the final copy by April 30. So revising and editing must be done between April 15 and April 30. That means I need to have two peers and my teacher read it and suggest revisions before April 15. That may take a week. I need at least two weeks to write the first draft, so I have to start writing by the last week in March. I need at least two weeks to research my topic; start that by March 8.

PREPARING FOR CHANGE IN CURRICULUM AND SCHEDULE

For students who have been in self-contained classrooms, a big change will occur when they have different teachers for each subject and have to move from one room to the next. Of course, if your elementary school has departmentalized the subjects, students will already be familiar with this procedure, but even so the change will be significant. Teachers at higher grades may not work as closely with each other to be sure that assignments are reasonably distributed among the subjects. These teachers may also not work to link content areas across the curriculum.

Students may or may not be with the same group of peers in all classes. They may or may not be given ample time to ask questions, get individual help during class, and work collaboratively. No matter what your school system does to ease the transition, moving to the next level of schooling isn't easy.

To this end, if you teach the last grade before students move to a different school, gradually change your method of interacting with students as the year progresses. By the end of the school year, your students should be well on their way to managing their own workloads, planning their time, keeping track of assignments, and being responsible for their own learning.

Find out what awaits your English-language learners in terms of bilingual or ESL classes or other special support, and inform students and their families of the services available to them for the next year. Reassure them that your school system will continue to help them become fluent readers and writers of English.

In the next section, we will describe the schedule of a typical sixth-grade group of students as they move from classroom to classroom for different subject areas.

A Sixth-Grade Classroom at Work

Once again we use the Comprehensive Balanced Literacy Program as a framework for looking at one departmentalized sixth grade (see Table 12.2). If there were students in need of intervention in this class, they would be pulled out on alternate days from the time slot devoted to music, art, physical education, and conferences.

Please bear in mind as you read that this is a hypothetical class. Many variations of scheduling exist across the country. Here we suggest generic ideas related to supporting continued literacy development for fluent readers and writers regardless of scheduling details.

TABLE 12.2

Daily Schedule for Ms. Lin's Homeroom*

8:00	Ms. Lin's homeroom students report to her classroom. Schoolwide announcements are broadcast on closed-circuit television. Details related to homework, upcoming field trips, library books, and so forth are dealt with.
8:30	Language/literacy block
	• Independent reading
	• Direct instruction in mechanics, spelling, grammar
	• Reading: Learning Skills and Strategies/Application of Skills and Strategies
	• Writing process/report writing
	• Independent writing
10:00	Ms. Lin's students leave for math class. Another sixth-grade class enters for its block of language/literacy.
11:30	Sixth graders' lunch
12:00	Sixth-grade special classes (music, art, physical education); intervention classes; conferences; study time
1:00	Ms. Lin's third language/literacy block
2:30	Homeroom class back with Ms. Lin; minilesson on scheduling, planning, and homework
2:50	Read-aloud to students
3:15	Dismissal

*Similar schedules exist for the other two sixth-grade teachers: Mr. Martin, who teaches math blocks, and Mr. Santiago, who teaches social studies and science.

As you read the schedule and plans, note how this schedule differs from the samples we presented earlier. Notice which parts of the block are independent of the rest of the curriculum, which are integrated, and how the integration is done. Note the use of whole-class, small-group, and independent activities. Note opportunities for ongoing assessment. Think about how the information presented in this section would be the same (or different) if the sixth grade was self-contained.

Ms. Lin's Language/Literacy Block (twenty-eight students in each section)

Each of Ms. Lin's language/literacy blocks is 90 minutes and meets daily. During this time, Ms. Lin makes sure her students spend the appropriate amount of time on each of the Comprehensive Balanced Literacy Program blocks. However, she may not have every student in each block every day.

For example, her week might be arranged as follows:

8:30–9:00	M-W-F	Independent reading/individual conferences
	Tu-Th	Independent reading/small-group instruction
9:00–9:30		Reading: Learning Skills and Strategies/Application of Skills and Strategies (alternate days)
9:30–10:00	M-Th	Learning to Write/Developmentally Appropriate Writing: instruction in mechanics, spelling, and grammar (alternate days)
	F	Independent writing

Each time segment varies only in degree of difficulty from those at the previous stage. Note that reading aloud to students is not part of the literacy block presented here. It occurs instead at the end of each homeroom teacher's schedule.

If the literacy block was longer, Ms. Lin might arrange the time differently. For example, she might have time for students to do independent writing every day. Instead, she encourages independent writing when students first come into their homerooms in the morning. She might also have time for both guided reading and literature groups for every student every day. She might use part of the block to teach literacy skills for specific application to content areas. In the arrangement suggested here, she consults with the content-area teachers and assists them in planning their own literacy lessons in their fields.

Math Block and Science/Social Studies Block

Mr. Martin's math block and Mr. Santiago's alternating science/social studies blocks also meet daily for 90 minutes. Each teacher devotes time during his block to teaching literacy skills and strategies specific to the content area. Ms. Lin has met with both content teachers to help them identify what needs to be taught and to help them plan instruction and gather or prepare materials. Lessons are designed to conform to school standards as well as to meet individual and group needs. Some schools may have a staff resource teacher who helps teachers with this sort of planning.

Mr. Martin uses the math text as his guide for math instruction because it matches local standards closely. Within each unit in that book, he has identified literacy skills that are necessary if students are to benefit from math instruction. These include but are not limited to:

- reading and writing cardinal, ordinal, fraction, and decimal numbers.
- reading and writing specific math terms.
- reading and interpreting charts and tables.
- reading and interpreting picture, circle, line, and bar graphs.
- reading, interpreting, and writing symbols and notations used in math.
- reading, interpreting, and constructing diagrams such as Venn diagrams.
- reading, interpreting, and constructing timelines.
- reading and interpreting narrative problems with relevant and irrelevant information.

Mr. Santiago has examined the curriculum standards for his subject areas, science and social studies, as well as the instructional manuals accompanying his textbooks. While content-area textbooks are changing all the time in terms of format, organization, style, and use of graphic materials, Mr. Santiago's students need some generic literacy skills to read and write competently in his specific content areas. Some of these connect to math instruction as well as to literacy instruction. They include but are not limited to:

- reading and writing terminology and concept words specific to each topic.
- reading and writing special notation of various kinds, such as for temperature, elevation, and density.
- reading and interpreting various kinds of maps, including symbols and legends.
- reading and interpreting charts, tables, graphs, diagrams, timelines, captions, and any other graphics found in the reading material.
- taking notes and outlining from reading material (both the textbook and multiple other reading sources) as well as listening and viewing material.
- using text structure to aid in understanding text.
- searching through print sources and the Internet for information.

As you have seen, even when various content areas are taught by different teachers, a great deal of overlap occurs. Literacy skills are needed for most curricular areas. It behooves each content-area teacher to work closely with literacy teachers to be sure students are making the necessary connections. Notice in the plans that all parts of the Comprehensive Balanced Literacy Program were included.

Summary

- The benchmarks and sample indicators for the Fluent Reading and Writing stage help you identify readers and writers who have moved to a level of competence in literacy that will support continued growth.
- Fluent readers and writers continue to refine skills, read more widely, explore writing in various forms, and explore literature and subject matter in more depth.

- Even with students' fluency, teachers still need to promote the development of their students through appropriate assessment and instruction.

- In planning instruction you will face three major questions: what to teach, how to teach, and how to prepare students for what lies ahead.

- Decisions related to what to teach involve meeting the needs of the inevitable range of stages and making instructional decisions to serve all your students.

- At this stage, you need to think about teaching literacy across the curriculum and teaching study skills and strategies.

- How to teach what needs to be taught involves selecting appropriate materials, maintaining a balanced literacy program as outlined in earlier chapters, and using appropriate instructional routines.

- Instructional routines are the same as those used with students in earlier stages, though the manner of teaching them and the materials used will change according to the students' literacy level.

- Students in upper elementary grades, or in middle school, may soon be facing new school experiences. Because significant changes in curriculum and school structure may lie ahead, students must also be informed and prepared for such changes.

- A critical part of teaching fluent readers is helping them become independent learners who are able to take responsibility for managing their own time.

- English-language learners and their families need to know what kinds of services will be available at the next level of schooling.

- Though the Fluent Reading and Writing stage is the final stage in literacy development presented in this book, by no means have students finished developing. In fact, no one we know has ever finished developing as a reader or writer. We are all still learning.

 Please visit the premium website for *Literacy Assessment*, Fourth Edition to access the TeachSource Video Cases, chapter web links, For Additional Reading, tutorial quizzes, glossary flashcards, online checklists, downloads, and much more! Go to www.cengage.com/login to register your access code.

This section gives directions for accessing and using the premium website for this book. It also contains the benchmarks and sample behaviors (indicators) for all five stages of literacy development. These are followed by the graph and directions for using the Fry Readability Formula and several word lists.

Using the *Literacy Assessment*, Fourth Edition, Premium Website

At the website for this text, you can access the TeachSource Video Cases, 4-6 minute video modules presenting actual classroom scenarios, supported by viewing questions, teacher interviews, artifacts, and bonus videos. Other resources include links to websites related to the content in each chapter, references in For Further Reading, and useful study aids and resource materials to help you with this course and in your teaching career. Practical resources include electronic versions of the assessment forms and checklists that appear throughout the text in an easy-to-reuse format. To access the premium website, log on at www.cengage.com/login using the access code that came with your new text, or purchase access at www.iChapters.com.

B
E
N
C
H
M
A
R
K
S

In the field of education, benchmarks refer to certain stages of achievement or development. The achievement of a benchmark is determined by observing the presence or absence of one or more behaviors. Literacy mostly develops through the stages we have presented in this book, though that development varies from child to child in terms of rate. Children often have, in effect, one foot in each of two stages.

Following are the stages we presented in Chapters 8 through 12, along with behaviors to help you determine whether a child has achieved a benchmark. In the chapters, we gave suggestions for assessing and recording these behaviors as well as suggestions for planning instruction based on this assessment.

Separating oral language, reading, and writing is almost impossible because they work together and, in part, develop together. For purposes of discussion, however, it is necessary to present the language systems separately. The overlap is apparent.

While benchmarks guide instruction for all students, English-language learners may develop differently from native speakers. Getting at the true competence of diverse learners may require special methods. We have addressed these differences throughout our discussion of assessing benchmarks.

Early Emergent Literacy

Oral Language

The child shows through both receptive (listening) and productive (speaking) behaviors that language development is occurring.

The child shows pleasure in stories, poems, and informational texts.

- Attends to read-alouds
- Attends to CD-ROMs and to programs on television and will predict future events during commercials
- Can retell stories in sequence or tell what a story or an expository text is "about"
- Uses book language when retelling a story or informational text
- Likes to make up stories
- Tells a story or gives information to go with a picture

☑ **The child shows growing facility with the functions (uses) of language.**

- Retains oral directions to do more than one thing; usually can tell the directions back
- Makes verbal requests or gives verbal orders that others understand
- Asks questions for information and for permission
- Converses with peers and adults
- Reports orally on events in his or her life

☑ **The child enjoys word play.**

- Likes to play word games
- Pretends or role-plays using appropriate language
- Repeats and uses (sometimes inappropriately) new words

☑ **The child shows increasing knowledge of grammar and other language conventions.**

- Tells you a sentence doesn't make sense or sound right if incorrect syntax or incorrect facts are presented
- Is generalizing about such language oddities as irregular plurals and verb forms
- May be able to identify what is or is not a complete sentence, though cannot tell why

Reading and Book Knowledge

☑ **The child has acquired many concepts about print.**

- Understands concepts about books and print
- Knows that labels name products or tell something about them
- Knows the purpose of some print
- Likes playing with movable and/or magnetic letters
- Asks questions about print and about own writing, scribbling, or drawing

☑ **The child is familiar with various genres.**

- Knows several/many nursery rhymes
- Knows several/many traditional stories such as fairy tales

☑ **The child begins to construct meaning.**

- Predicts what will happen next or what word or phrase comes next during a read-aloud
- Makes up stories to go with pictures

- Can retell a story he or she has heard
- Can play games such as "what if ...?"

☐ **The child enjoys literature and language.**

- Enjoys listening to stories read aloud
- Wants favorite stories read over and over
- Looks at books independently
- Pretends to read
- Enjoys playing with sounds and words

Writing and the Uses of Writing

☐ **The child knows the purpose of writing.**

- Understands that the marks on a paper mean something
- Wants to write messages, letters, greeting cards, and shopping lists

☐ **The child tries to communicate in writing.**

- Uses paper and pencil (marker, crayon, chalk, typewriter, computer) to attempt to write
- Arranges movable letters, writes string of letterlike shapes, or hits random strings of letters on a keyboard and then asks, "What did I say?"

☐ **The child connects reading and writing.**

- Wants to label own pictures
- Understands that stories are made up by a person who thought of the story and then wrote it down, and that he or she can do this also
- Can spin out a story to go with attempts at writing and with drawings

Emergent Literacy

Oral Language

☐ **The student exhibits behaviors of Early Emergent Literacy to a greater degree.**

☐ **The student uses standard sentence construction and grammar.**

- Is recognizing use of nonstandard language in self and others
- Is developing a sense that school/book language is perhaps different from home or neighborhood language

◻ The student's facility with oral language is growing.

- Makes self understood by peers and adults
- Follows "rules" for conversation and discussion
- Paraphrases what others have said
- Participates in sharing
- Retains oral directions
- Can ask questions for clarification

◻ The student's oral language reflects literature to which he or she is exposed.

- Uses new words from stories
- Uses "book language" when appropriate; that is, storytelling narrative is clearly different from conversation or simply relating an event
- Enjoys "making a play" of a favorite story

◻ The student shows pleasure in language.

- Enjoys jokes related to words, such as puns
- Enjoys tongue twisters
- Enjoys hearing humorous books related to idioms
- Is proud of learning new words
- Tries out new words and asks what words mean

Reading

◻ The student exhibits behaviors of the Early Emergent Literacy stage to a greater degree.

◻ The student has acquired most or all of the concepts about print.

- Handles book in correct position; knows where to begin reading and in what direction to read
- Can point to a word, two words, a letter, two letters
- Knows that print should match the voice of the reader
- Knows about such book parts as title, author, and illustrator

◻ The student is using print in everyday life.

- Can locate a specific book, record, CD, audiotape, and so forth
- Recognizes some environmental print, such as brand names and fast-food restaurant signs

☑ **The student is learning decoding skills: letters and words.**

- Recognizes and can name most letters
- Can match many upper- and lower-case letters
- Recognizes and can name some words
- Recognizes own name in print and perhaps other names

☑ **The student shows evidence of phonemic awareness and the alphabetic principle.**

☑ **The student is beginning to use phonics; knows many letter-sound associations, both consonants and vowels.**

☑ **The student is beginning to use other decoding strategies to begin to build fluency: sight words, context, graphics, and word structure.**

☑ **The student is constructing meaning.**
- Can retell a story page by page
- Can summarize
- Participates in small-group and whole-class discussions about books and stories
- Talks about books with others
- Responds to books in writing
- Begins to see self as a reader

Writing

☑ **The student exhibits continued growth in many of the Early Emergent Literacy behaviors.**

☑ **The student knows and writes his or her name and some letters and uses some other writing conventions.**

- Can write own name (perhaps first name only), with all or most of the letters present, though not necessarily formed correctly
- Can name most letters in random presentation
- Forms letterlike shapes and some correct letters
- Uses some punctuation

☑ **The student is using phonemic awareness in writing.**

☑ **The student is using sound/symbol association in writing.**

- Can give a letter sound or say a word that begins with the letter sound

☑ **The student is using writing for own purposes.**

- Can keep a journal that may combine drawing and writing

- Shows interest in practicing writing, often through copying favorite stories from books
- Shares writing with others
- Attempts to read others' writing

◨ **The student is becoming familiar with the writing process.**

- Uses the steps of the process appropriately with guidance
- Understands that the author of what is read has also gone through a process of some kind

◨ **The student is constructing meaning in writing.**

- Responds to reading
- Composes both narrative and expository pieces
- Expresses and reports on personal events and feelings

Beginning Reading and Writing

Oral Language

◨ **The student exhibits behaviors from Emergent Literacy to a greater degree.**

◨ **The student's use of standard English continues to develop.**

- If speaker of nonstandard English, is learning to switch between two languages
- Self-corrects while speaking

◨ **The student's vocabulary is growing.**

- Is using increased vocabulary
- Will ask for meaning of unknown words in class

◨ **The student's facility with language is growing.**

- Listens to classmates and can paraphrase what others have said
- Is interested in collaborative work with classmates
- Can participate in a discussion
- Can plan and ask oral questions
- Will plan and present an oral report

◨ **student continues to show pleasure in words.**

- Makes jokes related to plays on words
- Shows interest in the history of words
- Enjoys nonsense and silly poems
- Enjoys making own dictionary

Reading

☑ **The student continues to show growth in many of the behaviors from Emergent Literacy.**

☑ **The student knows letters and many sight words.**

- Recognizes and can name all letters in random order
- Recognizes and can name many words at sight

☑ **The student uses phonics and structural elements to determine the pronunciations of words.**

- Chooses appropriate strategies and skills to identify unfamiliar words

☑ **The student uses context to determine word meaning and build vocabulary.**

☑ **The student is beginning to use critical comprehension strategies such as visualizing, predicting, identifying important information, self-questioning, monitoring, summarizing, synthesizing, and evaluating.**

☑ **The student exhibits fluency and comprehension of a variety of materials.**

- Can read and retell familiar stories
- Reads own writing
- Attempts to read and retell unfamiliar texts (narrative and expository)
- Self-corrects when reading

☑ **The student is confident about reading ability.**

- Is willing to take risks
- Chooses to read during free time
- Sees self as a reader
- Likes to read to others

☑ **The student begins to explore using research tools and skills.**

- Uses glossary, table of contents, dictionary or picture dictionary, beginning encyclopedias, CD-ROMs, the Internet, and the library

Writing

☑ **The student exhibits continued growth in many of the Emergent Literacy behaviors.**

☑ **The student exhibits a variety of general writing behaviors.**

- Enjoys writing
- Is confident about own writing
- Communicates with others spontaneously
- Attempts to read others' writing
- Writes in a variety of formats for different purposes, such as journals, learning logs, notes, lists, stories, poems, reports, and labels

☑ **The student is growing in the use of the mechanics and conventions of writing.**

- Forms letters conventionally (mostly)
- Shows increased use of phonemic awareness, along with increased visual memory and spelling sense
- Invents spelling using knowledge of sound/symbol relationships when conventional spelling not known
- Is beginning to learn spelling patterns that reflect phonics knowledge
- Edits and proofreads spelling and conventions if writing is to be published
- Recognizes nonstandard usage and grammar in own writing and edits/proofreads
- Uses word processing

☑ **The student uses the writing process.**

- Participates in and understands the purpose of all steps of the writing process
- Uses the writing process collaboratively and independently
- Listens to or reads the writing of others and makes positive comments related to story parts or text structure

Almost Fluent Reading and Writing

Oral Language

☑ **The student exhibits continued growth in many behaviors from Beginning Reading and Writing.**

☑ **The student's use of standard English continues to develop.**

- Is aware of own problem areas
- Accepts diverse usage or varieties of English from others without criticism

☑ **The student's facility with language is growing.**

- Collaborates with classmates in speaking and listening situations
- Participates in discussion without adult supervision
- Can listen to and then question or respond to (use an idea expressed by) a speaker
- Speaks in front of a group using written notes but no script

☑ **The student's oral and listening vocabulary reflects increased growth and pleasure in language.**

- Uses new vocabulary
- Appreciates symbolic language such as metaphor
- Enjoys listening to and telling riddles and jokes
- Begins to appreciate shades of meaning, connotation, precise word choice, and the evocative power of certain words
- Recognizes and begins to use persuasive techniques

Reading

☑ **The student exhibits continued growth in behaviors from Beginning Reading and Writing.**

☑ **The student shows increasing fluency and appropriate use of all word recognition strategies.**

- Uses structure, phonics, and syntax (language structure) to determine word pronunciation
- Uses context to determine word meaning
- Selects appropriate skills and strategies to sound out unknown words
- Reads orally with 90 percent accuracy in grade-level materials
- Self-corrects
- Takes risks
- Uses a dictionary both for pronunciation and for meaning

☑ **The student's comprehension, or construction of meaning, is growing.**

- Enjoys listening to selections that may be beyond his or her reading ability
- Reads independently
- Enjoys reading a variety of genres
- Chooses to read outside of school
- Prefers to read silently
- Continues to grow in the use of comprehension strategies: visualizing, predicting, identifying important information, self-questioning, monitoring, summarizing, synthesizing, and evaluating

- **The student reads for a variety of purposes.**

  - Appreciates levels of meaning in stories
  - Has a growing interest in authors, illustrators, and genres
  - Is aware of own purposes(s) for reading
  - Is beginning to understand text structure in expository text
  - Uses a variety of print sources for information
  - Is learning to synthesize information from more than one source

- **The student is learning research skills.**

  - Uses card catalog or computer search engine
  - Is learning to narrow search in print and online sources
  - Operates a computer, including keyboarding
  - Is learning to read graphic materials such as graphs, charts, tables, timelines, and maps
  - Uses dictionary, thesaurus, encyclopedia, and other references in print, on CD-ROM, or online

Writing

- **The student exhibits continued growth in behaviors from Beginning Reading and Writing.**

- **The student writes for a variety of purposes.**

  - Is aware of the power of the written word
  - Can identify a topic and theme and develop a paper to fit a given rubric
  - Can plan and put together a report
  - Writes stories with all the literary elements present

- **The student shows growth in the mechanics and conventions of writing.**

  - Uses spelling patterns to attempt to spell words
  - Uses increasingly conventional spelling, demonstrating increased visual memory and spelling sense
  - Uses increasingly appropriate grammar and punctuation in writing
  - Uses word processing tools to check spelling, to format, to revise, and to edit

- **The student shows pleasure and confidence in writing.**

  - Sees self as a writer
  - Chooses to write in free time and at home
  - Seeks suggestions for revision during peer and teacher conferences

- Enjoys sharing writing with peers by reading aloud or by publishing in print or on disk
- Enjoys and supports the writing of classmates, offering constructive comments when asked

☑ **The student connects reading and writing.**

- Uses elements of narrative writing, such as form, theme, literary techniques, style, idioms, and colorful language, in own writing
- Uses various text structures to organize information in expository writing
- Appreciates poetry forms and attempts to write them

Fluent Reading and Writing

Oral Language

☑ **The student exhibits continued growth in behaviors from previous stages.**

☑ **The student's vocabulary and facility with language are growing.**

- Shows increasing vocabulary in oral language
- Shifts from formal to informal usage to suit occasion
- Listens to oral presentations with understanding

☑ **The student uses oral language for a variety of purposes.**

- Discusses literature with pleasure and understanding
- Enjoys role playing and Readers Theater
- May enjoy debate or speech competition

☑ **The student continues to enjoy language.**

- Is sensitive to body language and tone of others and self
- Appreciates the importance of speech in interpreting the written word; for example, news reports, actors, comedians

Reading

☑ **The student continues to display many of the behaviors from the Almost Fluent Reading and Writing stage.**

☑ **The student seldom seeks or needs assistance with word recognition.**

☐ **The student uses a wide variety of comprehension strategies to construct meaning.**

- Grasps differences among genres
- Perceives text structure
- Appreciates levels of meaning in a story
- Varies reading according to purpose for reading
- Effectively uses strategies: visualizing, predicting, identifying important information, self-questioning, monitoring, summarizing, synthesizing, and evaluating
- Can verbalize process used to construct meaning; that is, is aware of own thinking (metacognition)
- Is learning study strategies such as taking notes
- Uses graphic material to construct meaning

☐ **The student enjoys reading.**

- Recommends books to others
- Is exploring young adult and adult fiction and nonfiction
- Sees self as a competent reader
- Sets goals and self-evaluates
- Is aware of own purposes for reading

☐ **The student is refining research skills begun at the previous stage.**

- Can plan a research project
- Knows how to locate print and electronic information
- Takes notes in a variety of ways; attributes sources
- Synthesizes information into a final product

Writing

☐ **Prior writing behaviors strengthen and deepen.**

☐ **The student writes for a variety of purposes and reasons.**

- Is aware of how writing can contribute to self-awareness
- Uses writing to persuade
- Can write in response to a prompt to fit a given rubric

☐ **The student is growing in the mechanics of writing.**

- Edits own work
- Can edit the work of others
- Can independently verify spelling, grammar, and usage

☑ **The student is using the writing process.**

- Uses all steps of the writing process independently
- Varies prewriting techniques according to task
- Revises own work extensively
- Is developing a personal writing style, or voice

☑ **The student sees self as a competent writer.**

- Sets goals and evaluates own writing

☑ **The student connects reading and writing.**

- Recognizes author's craft and uses in own writing
- Is experimenting with writing in many forms

Fry Readability Formula

Fry Readability Formula (Chapter 4)

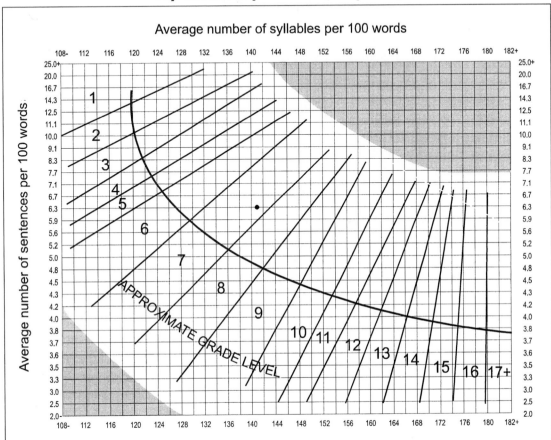

Instructions:

1. Select three 100-word selections from the beginning, middle, and end of the text. Don't count proper nouns.
2. Count the number of sentences in each selection. Estimate to the nearest tenth of a sentence.
3. Average the sentence count.
4. Count the number of syllables in each selection.
5. Average the syllable count.
6. Plot the two scores on the graph to get the grade level.

From "A Readability Formula That Saves Time" by Edward Fry (1968), *Journal of Reading, 11*, pp. 513–516, 578. International Reading Association. Reprinted by permission.

Word Lists

The Fry Instant Word List: 300 High-Frequency Words (Chapter 4)

The Fry Instant Word List

The Instant Words: First Hundred

First 25 Group 1a	Second 25 Group 1b	Third 25 Group 1c	Fourth 25 Group 1d
the	or	will	number
of	one	up	no
and	had	other	way
a	by	about	could
to	word	out	people
in	but	many	my
is	not	then	than
you	what	them	first
that	all	these	water
it	were	so	been
he	we	some	call
was	when	her	who
for	your	would	oil
on	can	make	now
are	said	like	find
as	there	him	long
with	use	into	down
his	an	time	day
they	each	has	did
I	which	look	get
at	she	two	come
be	do	more	made
this	how	write	may
have	their	go	part
from	if	see	over

Common suffixes: *s, ing, ed*

The Instant Words: Second Hundred

First 25 Group 2a	Second 25 Group 2b	Third 25 Group 2c	Fourth 25 Group 2d
new	great	put	kind
sound	where	end	hand
take	help	does	picture
only	through	another	again
little	much	well	change
work	before	large	off
know	line	must	play
place	right	big	spell
year	too	even	air
live	mean	such	away
me	old	because	animal
back	any	turn	house
give	same	here	point
most	tell	why	page
very	boy	ask	letter
after	follow	went	mother
thing	came	men	answer
our	want	read	found
just	show	need	study
name	also	land	still
good	around	different	learn
sentence	form	home	should
man	three	us	America
think	small	move	world
say	set	try	high

Common suffixes: *s, ing, ed, er, ly, est*

The Instant Words: Third Hundred

First 25 Group 3a	Second 25 Group 3b	Third 25 Group 3c	Fourth 25 Group 3d
every	left	until	idea
near	don't	children	enough
add	few	side	eat
food	while	feet	face
between	along	car	watch
own	might	mile	far
below	close	night	Indian
country	something	walk	real
plant	seem	white	almost
last	next	sea	let
school	hard	began	above
father	open	grow	girl
keep	example	took	sometimes
tree	begin	river	mountain
never	life	four	cut
start	always	carry	young
city	those	state	talk
earth	both	once	soon
eye	paper	book	list
light	together	hear	song
thought	got	stop	leave
head	group	without	family
under	often	second	body
story	run	late	music
saw	important	miss	color

Common suffixes: *s, ing, ed, er, ly, est*

Word list from Fry, Edward B. (1980, December). "The New Instant Word List," *The Reading Teacher, 34*(3), 284–289. Reprinted with permission of Edward B. Fry and the International Reading Association. All rights reserved.

227 Core Words Derived from 400 Storybooks for Beginning Readers (Chapter 4).

The numeral to the right of each word indicates the number of times it occurred in the storybooks surveyed.

word	count	word	count	word	count	word	count
the	1334	good	90	think	47	next	28
and	985	this	90	new	46	only	28
a	831	don't	89	know	46	am	27
I	757	little	89	help	46	began	27
to	746	if	87	grand	46	head	27
said	688	just	87	boy	46	keep	27
you	638	baby	86	take	45	teacher	27
he	488	way	85	eat	44	sure	27
it	345	there	83	body	43	says	27
in	311	every	83	school	43	ride	27
was	294	went	82	house	42	pet	27
she	250	father	80	morning	42	hurry	26
for	235	had	79	yes	41	hand	26
that	232	see	79	after	41	hard	26
is	230	dog	78	never	41	push	26
his	226	home	77	or	40	our	26
but	224	down	76	self	40	their	26
they	218	got	73	try	40	watch	26
my	214	would	73	has	38	because	25
of	204	time	71	always	38	door	25
on	192	love	70	over	38	us	25
me	187	walk	70	again	37	should	25
all	179	came	69	side	37	room	25
be	176	were	68	thank	37	pull	25
go	171	ask	67	why	37	great	24
can	162	back	67	who	36	gave	24
with	158	now	66	saw	36	does	24
one	157	friend	65	mom	35	car	24
her	156	cry	64	kid	35	ball	24
what	152	oh	64	give	35	sat	24
we	151	Mr.	63	around	34	stay	24
him	144	bed	63	by	34	each	23
no	143	an	62	Mrs.	34	ever	23
so	141	very	62	off	33	until	23
out	140	where	60	sister	33	shout	23
up	137	play	59	find	32	mama	22
are	133	let	59	fun	32	use	22
will	127	long	58	more	32	turn	22
look	126	here	58	while	32	thought	22
some	123	how	57	tell	32	papa	22
day	123	make	57	sleep	32	lot	21
at	122	big	56	made	31	blue	21
have	121	from	55	first	31	bath	21
your	121	put	55	say	31	mean	21
mother	119	read	55	took	31	sit	21
come	118	them	55	dad	30	together	21
not	115	as	54	found	30	best	20
like	112	Miss	53	lady	30	brother	20
then	108	any	52	soon	30	feel	20
get	103	right	52	ran	30	floor	20
when	101	nice	50	dear	29	wait	20
thing	100	other	50	man	29	tomorrow	20
do	99	well	48	better	29	surprise	20
too	91	old	48	through	29	shop	20
want	91	night	48	stop	29	run	20
did	91	may	48	still	29	own	20
could	90	about	47	fast	28		

Eeds, Maryann. (1985, January). "Bookwords: Using a Beginning Word List of High Frequency Words from Children's Literature K-3," *The Reading Teacher, 38(4),* 418–423. Reprinted with permission of the International Reading Association.

Dolch Basic Sight Vocabulary (Chapter 4)

a	don't	if	over	they
about	down	in	own	think
after	draw	into	pick	this
again	drink	is	play	those
all	eat	it	please	three
always	eight	its	pretty	to
am	every	jump	pull	today
an	fall	just	put	together
and	far	keep	ran	too
any	fast	kind	read	try
are	find	know	red	two
around	first	laugh	ride	under
as	five	let	right	up
ask	fly	light	round	upon
at	for	like	run	us
ate	found	little	said	use
away	four	live	saw	very
be	from	long	say	walk
because	full	look	see	want
been	funny	made	seven	warm
before	gave	make	shall	was
best	get	many	she	wash
better	give	may	show	we
big	go	me	sing	well
black	goes	much	sit	went
blue	going	must	six	were
both	good	my	sleep	what
bring	got	myself	small	when
brown	green	never	so	where
but	grow	new	some	which
buy	had	no	soon	white
call	has	not	start	who
came	have	now	stop	why
can	he	of	take	will
carry	help	off	tell	wish
clean	her	old	ten	with
cold	here	on	thank	work
come	him	once	that	would
could	his	one	the	write
cut	hold	only	their	yellow
did	hot	open	them	yes
do	how	or	then	you
does	hurt	our	there	your
done	I	out	these	

Dolch, E. W. (1936). "Basic Sight Vocabulary." *Elementary School Journal, 26,* 456–560. Reprinted by permission of The University of Chicago Press.

accountability The need to show that money allocated to educational purposes is having desired results.

adequate yearly progress The expected amount of growth a student should make in reading during one school year. A term used in various government-supported educational programs. Currently defined for each state by its state education agency.

aesthetic listening Listening for pleasure. The term *aesthetic* in this sense can also apply to reading.

age-equivalent score A score based on the average age of the people in the standardization population who earned that score; also called *age norm*.

Almost Fluent Reading and Writing (stage) The fourth stage of literacy development, during which the student becomes more sophisticated in all aspects of literacy.

alphabetic principle The assumption that each speech sound has a corresponding graphic representation.

anchor papers Samples of writing that illustrate the levels of acceptability in terms of a given rubric.

anecdote A brief note you make about something you have observed in a particular child; part of the observing process. Sometimes called *anecdotal records*.

anthology A collection of texts bound in one volume.

apply (application) To use a skill, strategy, or process in an authentic literacy situation.

assessment The process of collecting data about a student's performance.

assessment-based literacy classroom A classroom in which instructional decisions about literacy are based on each student's performance in relation to stages of literacy development.

attention-deficit disorder (ADD) A developmental disorder involving one or more of the basic cognitive processes relating to orienting, focusing, or maintaining attention (Harris & Hodges, 1995).

attention-deficit-hyperactivity disorder (ADHD) Difficulty in concentrating and staying on a task, accompanied by hyperactivity (Lerner & Kline, 2006).

attitude/self-concept check An instrument designed to reveal students' attitudes toward themselves as learners and toward school and learning.

authentic assessment Using actual literacy tasks for the purpose of determining student performance, as opposed to relying solely on typical kinds of tests.

authentic literature Text that has not been altered or edited; presented as originally written.

Author's Chair A special chair in which students sit while reading aloud their writing to others.

Beginning Reading and Writing (stage) The third stage of literacy development, during which the student actually starts to read and write.

bell curve A bell-shaped graph that represents the probability of distribution of large numbers of scores or results on a given measure; also called *normal curve* or *normal frequency curve*.

benchmarks Behaviors exhibited by students at a certain stage of development.

checklist An instrument that allows a teacher to check whether behaviors or abilities are present, sometimes present, or not present in an individual child or a group or a class. May be teacher-made to meet a particular purpose.

coaching In teaching, the process of helping teachers internalize a set of instructional strategies through observation and feedback.

Comprehensive Balanced Literacy Program A plan for literacy instruction that incorporates essential blocks for effective learning.

conference Usually a meeting between a teacher and a student to discuss some aspect of the student's work. Conferences can also be held between two students or between a teacher and a student's family members.

connected text Two or more words that convey meaning. Can be narrative or expository.

construct validity The degree to which a test assesses the theoretical characteristic it is said to measure.

content validity The degree to which the content of a test reflects the content it is intended to measure; sometimes also called *curriculum* or *instructional validity.*

context The words surrounding a given word; they may constitute a phrase, a sentence, a paragraph, or the entire text. Attention to context sometimes helps a reader figure out an unfamiliar word.

conventional stage The last stage of spelling development, in which a child spells most words correctly, is aware of when a word is spelled incorrectly, and knows how to locate words not known.

cooperative/collaborative reading Mode of reading in which students read with a partner.

cooperative/collaborative writing Mode of writing in which students write with partners to develop a single piece of writing.

core books Books experienced by all students in a class.

criterion validity The degree to which a given test predicts future performance; or the degree to which the test correlates with a different test that is supposed to measure the same factors.

criterion-referenced test A test that measures what a person is able to do in terms of what the test maker decides should be tested; compare *norm-referenced test.*

critical listening Listening in order to make judgments. The term *critical* also applies in the same sense to reading.

decodable text A text that has been identified or created as one that allows application of previously taught phonic skills.

decoding The process of translating written language into verbal speech. Decoding is one part of reading.

developmentally appropriate books Books that are at the students' instructional reading level.

developmentally appropriate writing Writing in which the teacher assigns a type or mode of writing appropriate to students' abilities, but individual students are allowed to select their own topics; a block in the Comprehensive Balanced Literacy Program described in this book.

diagnostic test A test designed to reveal the strengths as well as weaknesses of an individual. Such tests often include suggestions for analyzing strengths and weaknesses in order to plan appropriate instruction.

directionality The understanding that print goes from left to right and from top to bottom on the page; one of the key concepts about print.

discussion group (discussion circle) A small group of students (usually three to five) who get together to talk about a piece of text they have read. For instructional purposes, the teacher may give them some prompts.

domains of writing Particular types of writing; usually discussed as sensory/descriptive, imaginative/narrative, practical/informative, and analytical/expository.

Early Emergent Literacy (stage) The very beginnings of literacy development, in which the foundations are laid for future learning.

efferent listening Listening in order to learn, as from informational text. The term *efferent* can also apply to reading.

Emergent Literacy (stage) The second stage of literacy development, during which children become more interested in literacy.

encoding Changing spoken language into written symbols. Encoding is the process associated with spelling.

English-language learners (ELLs) Students who are acquiring English as a second language.

environmental print Print and other graphic symbols that are found in one's everyday life, such as street signs, products, advertisements, and names of stores.

evaluation Judging assessment data about a student on the basis of a set of criteria or guidelines.

explicit teaching Teacher modeling of a specific skill, strategy, or process.

expository text Text written to inform or explain something; often called *informational writing* in K–8 programs.

extended-day program A program in which instruction beyond the core program is made available to a small group before or after school hours.

fluency In reading, the ability to read words of connected text aloud smoothly and without significant word recognition problems. A fluency record is taken by keeping track of words read correctly and those not read correctly. See also *running record*.

Fluent Reading and Writing (stage) The fifth stage of literacy development, during which the student uses all aspects of literacy. This stage continues to develop throughout one's life.

formative Pertaining to ongoing assessment for the purpose of judging progress toward a goal; often used in the phrase *formative assessment* or *formative evaluation*. Compare *summative*.

frustration reading level The level of material that is too difficult for a reader, even with good instructional support.

full inclusion The policy of placing and instructing all children, including all categories of disability and levels of severity, in their neighborhood schools and in the general education classroom (Lerner & Kline, 2006).

functions of language Term used by Halliday (1975) to describe seven ways one uses oral and written language: instrumental, regulatory, interactional, personal, imaginative, heuristic, and informative.

gifted and talented Demonstrating sufficient talents or abilities to warrant special programs. *Gifted* often refers to students with high intellectual or cognitive ability; *talented,* to outstanding ability in a particular area, such as one of the arts.

grade level Can refer to the student's position in the educational program, the student's achievement, the level of educational materials, or the level of performance on a test.

grade-equivalent score Score on a standardized test typical of the norming group at a certain grade. The score is given as year and month: for instance, 3.5 means third grade, fifth month.

gradient of difficulty Refers to where a book falls in terms of difficulty; see also *leveling text*.

graphic organizer A visual way to show how a text is organized; see also *story map*.

graphics Nonprint information and special arrangement or presentation of print material. Includes illustrations, photographs, charts, tables, maps, sidebars, special typefaces, different type sizes, arrows, and colors.

graphophonic cues Cues that arise from the relationship between the orthology (written symbol) and the phonology (sound) of letters.

group-administered tests Tests designed to be administered to groups; often standardized.

guided reading A process in which the teacher guides students through the reading of a text. Guided reading may be *observational* (teacher observes students' use of strategies and skills in reading a complete text) or *interactive* (teacher guides students in reading a text in meaningful chunks).

guided writing Mode of writing in which students work on individual writing tasks while the teacher models, coaches, and prompts.

holistic scoring In writing, assigning one score based on a combination of several factors, including both content and mechanics; may use anchor papers for samples of levels of performance.

inclusion programs Programs that place students with special needs or disabilities in the regular classroom program for instruction. See also *full inclusion*.

independent reading A time when students self-select materials they want to read. The model for the Comprehensive Balanced Literacy Program described in this book features a block of Daily Independent Reading.

independent reading level The level of material that a reader can read, with few word recognition problems and good comprehension, without instructional support.

independent writing A time when students select what they want to write. The model for the Comprehensive Balanced Literacy Program described in this book features a block of Daily Independent Writing.

individually administered tests Tests designed to be administered to one person at a time; may be standardized; usually require a trained examiner.

informal reading inventory (IRI) A series of graded passages designed to measure a reader's overall ability, as well as strengths and needs in word recognition and comprehension.

inservice Occurring during a teacher's employment; often used to describe staff development programs; see *staff development*.

instructional reading level The level of material that a reader can read with instructional support.

instructional routine A pattern of teaching that always includes specified steps; a pattern used over and over.

interactive writing A process in which students help the teacher write a piece by taking the pen, chalk, or marker and trying to spell specific words.

interest inventory An instrument designed to reveal a student's interests in school subjects, topics, outside activities, and so forth. Such inventories can be paper and pencil or oral.

interest level (IL) Information sometimes provided by a publisher to suggest the grade or age level(s) of readers who would find a particular book or story of interest.

inter-rater reliability A scoring system's ability to produce the same score for a given piece of work no matter who does the scoring.

intervention Instruction designed to prevent or halt problems such instruction is in addition to regular classroom instruction. In the Comprehensive Balanced Literacy Program, an additional support block provided for students who are experiencing difficulty in learning to read or who have special learning needs; see also *reading intervention program*.

K-W-L A strategy for guiding the reading of nonfiction. The letters stand for What I Know, What I Want to Learn, and What I Learned.

language experience A method of teaching that involves recording (writing down) a child's language and using that text as reading material for the child.

language-rich environment A setting, at school or at home, in which oral language and written language are pervasive, allowing a child's language and literacy to flourish.

learning center A specific space (table, desk, or cubicle) within a classroom where individual students go to perform a particular task related to learning.

learning disabilities Difficulties in the acquisition and use of speaking, listening, reading, writing, or mathematics.

learning log A student's record of learning activities and understanding of concepts.

leveling text Placing texts in order of difficulty.

listening level The highest grade level of material that can be understood when the material is read aloud to the student.

literacy development Learning to speak, listen, read, write, and view. Thinking is an integral part of all of these processes.

literacy lesson A lesson that follows an instructional framework for using a piece of text for reading and writing; includes Introducing, Reading and Responding, and Extending.

local norms The range of test scores of a restricted or defined population, used to compare scores to that population rather than to the national population on which many tests are normed.

metacognition Knowledge and control of one's own thinking and learning. In reading, metacognition relates to the reader's being aware of when reading makes sense and adjusting his or her reading when comprehension fails.

minilesson A short, teacher-directed, planned lesson focused specifically on a skill, strategy, or process.

miscue A mismatch between the word on the page and the word a reader says. The term implies that a reader's misreading may result from paying attention to inappropriate cues.

modeling The process of demonstrating or showing students how to use a strategy, skill, or process. Think-alouds are often involved.

modes of reading Different ways in which a text may be read, moving from teacher directed to independent.

modes of writing Ways in which students may write, moving from writing with heavy teacher support to independent writing.

monitoring (progress monitoring) The process of looking at each student's performance in daily learning experiences and tests, noting how he/she is progressing in relation to what has been taught and what the student is expected to learn.

morning message A written activity many teachers use to begin the day. The message may be written by the teacher or by students. It may be collaborative. It can serve to remind students of a schedule, inform them about events, or share news. It is sometimes also used to reinforce reading and writing skills.

morphology The study of the meaningful parts of words, such as bases, roots, compounds, inflections, and affixes.

multisyllabic Having two or more syllables.

narrative (text) In K–8 education, usually a story, whether true or fictional (as contrasted with *expository text*).

networking Connecting and communicating with other professionals in your field.

nonstandard English Usage that deviates from standard English in some way.

normal curve equivalent (NCE) score A score based on a normal curve and ranging from 0 to 99, with the points on the scale defined so that there is an equal number of raw-score points between each pair of scores.

normal distribution The probable way (graphically represented by a bell curve) in which a very large number of values (such as scores on a test) will distribute from lowest to highest, with most falling in the middle; also called *normal frequency distribution*.

norming population The group of individuals used to establish the norms for a particular test; often composed of many subgroups.

norm-referenced test A test that allows comparison of individual scores to those of the group (the norming population) on which the test was standardized.

observing An assessment tool that involves close watching of student behavior—while the student is engaged in a particular activity or task—to make inferences about the student's literacy.

onset The consonant sound that precedes the vowel in a syllable. For example, in the word "cat," /c/ is the onset; see also *rime*.

parallel talking Activity in which children (usually very young children) take turns talking but do not actually have a conversation that involves an exchange of ideas.

percentile rank A score that allows comparison of an individual performance to that of the norming population.

performance assessment Assessment of learning based on the student's performance of certain tasks. These may be either regular activities or tasks specially assigned for the express purpose of assessment.

phonemes The smallest units of sound in speech; for example, the word "cat" has three phonemes.

phonemic awareness Awareness of the sounds (phonemes) that make up words.

phonetic stage Pertaining to speech sounds; in spelling development, the stage when children develop phonemic awareness (also called the *phonemic stage*).

phonetically unpredictable words Words that do not conform to phonics generalizations or that students do not yet have sufficient phonics knowledge to decode.

phonics Using one's knowledge of the relationship between the letters and the sounds the letters represent to aid in figuring out the pronunciation of a word.

picture walk Talking through a story or book by looking at and talking about the pictures; see also *text walk*.

portfolio A collection of an individual student's work designed to show evidence of performance and growth.

practice To try out, in a directed situation, a skill, strategy, or process that has been taught.

precommunicative stage In spelling development, the stage when children do writing that is not meaningful to anyone else; they may use letters or marks that resemble letters.

predictable text A text with some type of repeated pattern that allows the reader to anticipate what is likely to follow on subsequent pages.

print-rich environment An environment, at home or school, in which print is evident in books, magazines, signs, and labels. Such an environment stimulates and supports literacy.

productive language Language an individual generates by speaking or writing.

pullout program A program in which students who need special assistance leave their regular classroom to receive instruction beyond the core program.

raw score The number of items correct on a given test.

readability (readability level) Ease or difficulty of a piece of text. May be based on a formula or on a combination of variables within the reader, the text, and the environment.

readability formula A numeric formula for estimating text difficulty.

read-aloud See *teacher read-aloud*.

reading intervention program Instruction designed to prevent or stop reading failure; given in addition to the core classroom program.

reading levels The three levels—independent, instructional, and frustration—identified using an informal reading inventory. The term is also used to indicate the grade levels appropriate for written material.

receptive language Language an individual receives through listening or reading.

reciprocal teaching An instructional strategy in which teacher and students take turns modeling four strategies—predict, question, summarize, and clarify—after silent reading of a chunk of text.

reliability The degree to which a test's results are consistent from one time to another and from one set of conditions to another.

Response to Intervention A multi-tiered approach to the early identification and support of students with learning and behavior needs.

retelling Restating in one's own words the essential parts of a story or expository text. Can be used as a measure of comprehension and of knowledge of story elements.

rime The vowel and any following consonants in a syllable. For example, in the word "school," /ool/ is the rime, while /sk/ is the onset; see also *onset*.

risk-taking Students' willingness to make an effort, try new things, and express opinions. A classroom in which students feel free to behave in this way may be referred to as a "risk-free environment."

routine See *instructional routine*.

rubric A standard by which to measure a piece of work. In education, a rubric generally includes specific guidelines and criteria for assessing students' performance.

running record A record of the accuracy of a child's oral reading. As used by Clay (1985), it involves a particular way of listening and coding.

scaffolding The process of providing strong teacher support at the beginning of new learnings and gradually taking it away to allow the student to achieve independence.

scope and sequence A listing of strategies and skills that are developed in programs and/or that individuals are expected to learn. These are most often organized by grade level.

second-language learner One who is learning a language other than his or her native language.

self-correction Recognizing a miscue and spontaneously correcting it.

self-reflection Thinking about oneself in terms of learning. The term is sometimes used interchangeably with *self-assessment* and *self-evaluation*, which refer to making a judgment about one's own work and drawing conclusions about one's ability.

semantic Pertaining to the meanings of words, phrases, sentences, or longer texts.

semiphonetic stage In spelling development, the stage when children have grasped the alphabetic principle but may not yet represent every sound with a letter or letters.

shared reading A mode of reading in which the teacher reads aloud while students look at the text and follow along and join in when they are able.

shared writing A mode of writing in which the teacher and students work together to compose a piece of writing. When the students do the actual writing, it is sometimes called *interactive writing*.

sight word A word that is recognized instantly without the need to apply word recognition strategies. *Basic* *sight words* are those considered to be of such high frequency that every reader must learn them.

significant miscues Miscallings or misreadings of words that significantly change the meaning. In calculating fluency, often only significant miscues are counted as wrong. See also *miscue.*

staff development Educational and training programs offered by a school district for its teachers and other professional staff members.

standard A degree or level of performance that is expected for students at a certain time.

standard error of measurement (SEM) A measure of how much one can trust an individual score. For example, a standard error of measurement of 6 means that an earned score of XX probably really is XX, give or take 6.

standard score A score that indicates how far an individual is from the average score (mean) on a test in terms of the standard deviation.

standardized tests Tests whose value depends on their being given in specific ways, following specific procedures; tests that have been normed.

stanine score A standard score, ranging from 1 to 9, based on the norming population. A stanine of 5 represents average performance.

story map A graphic organizer that visually shows the elements of a story.

summarizing Retelling the story elements in narrative text or the main points in expository text.

summative Pertaining to a final assessment used to assign a grade. The term generally appears in the phrase *summary assessment* or *summative evaluation.*

syntactic Pertaining to the grammatical construction of language.

syntax The grammatical construction of language; the rules by which words and other elements are combined to form sentences; word order.

teach To present a skill or strategy to students; precedes practice and application.

teacher-modeled writing A procedure in which the teacher shows students how to do a particular type of writing and shares his or her thinking about the process.

teacher read-aloud Session during which someone reads aloud to children.

text walk Talking students through a segment of text before they read it so that they will know what is coming in the text. Sometimes called a *picture walk* at the primary levels and a *guided preview* at the intermediate levels.

think-aloud The process of verbalizing to model or demonstrate one's thinking process.

transitional stage In spelling development, the stage when children spell all the sounds in a word, are beginning to learn spelling generalizations, and are applying knowledge of morphology.

validity The degree to which a test measures what it says it measures; see also *construct validity, content validity,* and *criterion validity.*

voice-to-print match The ability to look at print as someone reads aloud and point to a word as it is heard.

word bank A personal file of words a student has learned or is interested in learning.

word structure The way words are formed. Understanding word structure means knowing the parts of a word that carry meaning—including prefixes, suffixes, inflected endings, base words, and roots—as well as compound words and contraction

word wall A space, usually on the wall of a classroom, where words are posted in alphabetical categories as they are taught to students. Word walls may focus on high-frequency words, phonic or structural elements, or new vocabulary by categories.

work sample Evidence of a child's actual classroom work. Can be a paper, report, project, model, or any product that shows what kind of work a child has done.

zone of proximal development A term used by Vygotsky (1978) to describe the distance between a child's actual level of learning and his or her potential level of learning. Simply stated, the difference between what a child can do alone and what a child can do with help.

Ackerman, K. (1988). *Song and Dance Man.* New York: Scholastic.

Bang, M. (1987). *The Paper Crane.* New York: Mulberry Books.

Barbot, D. (1990). *A Bicycle for Rosaura.* Brooklyn, NY: Kane/Miller.

Baum, L. F. (1900/1990). *The Wonderful Wizard of Oz.* Chicago/New York: Geo. M. Hill.

Blume, J. (1974). *Blubber.* New York: Bradbury.

Cooling, W. (2004). *Come to the Great World: Poems from Around the Globe.* Illus. S. Moxley. New York: Holiday House.

Cox, J. A. (1980). *Put Your Foot in Your Mouth and Other Silly Sayings.* New York: Random House.

Galdone, P. (1972). *The Three Bears.* New York: Clarion.

Gibbons, G. (1994). *Emergency.* New York: Holiday House.

Greenfield, E. (1992). *Koya Delaney and the Good Girl Blues.* New York: Scholastic.

Grifalconi, A. & Pinkney, J.(2007) *Ain't Nobody a Stranger to Me.* New York: Hyperion Books.

Gwynne, F. (1988). *The King Who Rained.* New York: Simon & Schuster.

Hambleton, L., Sedat, T. & Tullet, H. (2007) *Monkey Business: Fun with Idioms.* Chicago: Milet Publishing.

Kirk, D. (2007). *Library Mouse.* New York: Abrams Books for Young Readers.

Leedy, L., & Street, P. (2003). *There's a Frog in My Throat.* New York: Holiday House.

Lewis, C. S. (1950/1994). *The Lion, the Witch, and the Wardrobe.* New York: HarperCollins.

Loewen, N. (2007). *Homonym or a Homophone?* Mankato, MN: Picture Window Books.

Lowell, S. (1992). *The Three Little Javelinas.* New York: Scholastic.

Lowry, L. (1979). *Anastasia Krupnik.* Boston: Houghton Mifflin.

———. (1989). *Number the Stars.* Boston: Houghton Mifflin.

Marshall, J. (1989). *The Three Little Pigs.* New York: Dial Books for Young Readers.

Martin, B., Jr. (1967). *Brown Bear, Brown Bear.* New York: Henry Holt.

McNamara, M. & Karas, G. B. (2007). *How Many Seeds in a Pumpkin?* New York: Schwartz & Wade.

Munsch, R. (1986). *Love You Forever.* Willowdale, Ontario, Canada: Firefly Books.

Nevin, A., & Nevin, D. (1977). *From the Horse's Mouth.* Englewood Cliffs, NJ: Prentice-Hall.

Numeroff, L. F. (1985/1989). *If You Give a Mouse a Cookie.* New York: Scholastic Big Books.

Parish, P. (1963/1981). *Amelia Bedelia.* New York: Harper & Row/Avon Camelot.

Paulsen, G. (1987). *Hatchet.* New York: Macmillan, Bradbury.

Rawls, W. (1961/1974). *Where the Red Fern Grows.* New York: Scholastic.

Say, A. (1988). *A River Dream.* Boston: Houghton Mifflin.

Seuss, D. (1938). *The 500 Hats of Bartholomew Cubbins.* New York: Vanguard.

(2005). *Cowgirl Kate and Cocoa.* Illus. B. Lewin. San Diego, CA: Harcourt Children's Books.

Snodgrass, C. S. (2004). *A Children's Illustrated Book of Idioms.* Higganum, CT: Starfish Specialty Press.

Stine, R. L. (1993). *Piano Lessons Can Be Murder.* New York: Scholastic.

Taylor, M. (1976). *Roll of Thunder, Hear My Cry.* New York: Dial.

Terban, M. (2006). *Scholastic Dictionary of Idioms.* New York: Scholastic.

Terban, M. & Maestro, G. (2007). *Eight Ate.* London: Sandpiper Books.

Terban, M. & Maestro, G. (2007). *In a Pickle and Other Funny Idioms.* London: Sandpiper Books.

Vogt, G. (1989). *Predicting Earthquakes.* New York: Watts.

Waber, B. (1972). *Ira Sleeps Over.* Boston: Houghton Mifflin.

Westcott, N. B. (1988). *The Lady with the Alligator Purse.* Boston: Little, Brown.

White, E. B. (1952). *Charlotte's Web.* New York: HarperCollins.

Yee, W. H. (1992). *Eek! There's a Mouse in the House.* Boston: Houghton Mifflin.

References

Adams, M. J. (1990). *Beginning to Read: Thinking and Learning about Print.* Cambridge, MA: MIT Press.

Afflerbach, P. (2007). U*nderstanding and Using Reading Assessment K-12.* Newark, DE: International Reading Association.

Allen, R. V. (1976). *Language Experiences in Communication.* Boston: Houghton Mifflin.

Allington, R. L. (2009). *What Really Matters in Response to Intervention: Research-based Designs.* Boston: Allyn & Bacon.

Allington, R. L., & Walmsley, S. A. (Eds.). (2008). *No Quick Fix: Rethinking Literacy Programs in America's Elementary Schools, The RTI Edition.* New York: Teachers College Press.

Anderson, R. C., Hiebert, E. H., Scott, J. A., & Wilkinson, I. A. G. (1985). *Becoming a Nation of Readers: The Report of the Commission on Reading.* Washington, D.C.: National Institute of Education.

Armbruster, B. B., & Osborn, J. (2001). *Put Reading First: The Research Building Blocks for Teaching Children to Read (K–3).* Ann Arbor: Center for the Improvement of Early Reading Achievement, University of Michigan. Distributed by National Institute for Literacy Health, National Institute of Child Health and Human Development, and the U.S. Department of Education.

Atwell, N. (1987). *In the Middle: Writing, Reading, and Learning with Adolescents.* Portsmouth, NH: Boynton/Cook, Heinemann.

Bear, D., Invernizzi, M., Templeton, S., & Johnson, F. (2004). *Words their Way: Word Study for Phonics, Spelling, and Vocabulary Development* (3rd ed.). Englewood Cliffs, NJ: Prentice-Hall.

Beaver, J. (2002). *Developmental Reading Assessment, Revised Edition.* Parsipanny, NJ: Celebration Press/Pearson Learning Group.

Beaver, J. M., & Carter, M. A. (2003). *Developmental Reading Assessment, Grades 4–8.* Parsippany, NJ: Celebration Press/Pearson Learning Group.

Betts, E. A. (1946/1957). *Foundations of Reading Instruction.* New York: American Book.

———. (1949). "Adjusting Instruction to Individual Needs." In N. B. Henry (Ed.), *Reading in the Elementary School (Forty-eighth Yearbook of the National Society for the Study of Education)* (Part II, pp. 266–280). Chicago: University of Chicago Press.

Brown, A. L. (1980). "Metacognitive Development and Reading." In R. J. Spiro, B. C. Bruce, & W. F. Brewer (Eds.), *Theoretical Issues in Reading Comprehension* (pp. 453–481). Hillsdale, NJ: Lawrence Erlbaum.

Calkins, L. M. (1994). *The Art of Teaching Writing, Revised Edition.* Portsmouth, NH: Heinemann.

Chall, J. S. (1967). *Learning to Read: The Great Debate.* New York: McGraw-Hill.

Chamot, A. U., & O'Malley, J. M. (1994). "Instructional Approaches and Teaching Procedures." In K. Spangenberg-Urbschat & R. Pritchard (Eds.), *Kids Come in all Languages: Reading Instruction for ESL Students* (pp. 82–107). Newark, DE: International Reading Association.

Chard, D. J., & Osborne, J. (1999). "Phonics and Word Recognition Instruction in Early Reading Programs: Guidelines for Accessibility." *Learning Disabilities Research and Practice, 14*(2), 107–117.

Clay, M. M. (1985). *The Early Detection of Reading Difficulties, Third Edition.* Auckland, New Zealand: Heinemann Education.

———. (1991). *Becoming Literate: The Construction of Inner Control.* Portsmouth, NH: Heinemann.

———. (2000). *Running Records for Classroom Teachers.* Portsmouth, NH: Heinemann.

Cohen, J. H. & Wiener, R. B. (2002). *Literacy Portfolios, Second Edition.* Upper Saddle River, NJ: Prentice Hall.

Collier, V. (1992). "A Synthesis of Studies Examining Long-term Language Minority Student Data on Academic Achievement. *Bilingual Research Journal, 16*(1&2), 187–212.

Cooper, J. D. (1986). *Improving Reading Comprehension.* Boston: Houghton Mifflin.

Cooper, J. D., Boschken, I., McWilliams, J., & Pistochini, L. (1998). *Soar to Success: The Intermediate Intervention Program, Levels 3–6.* Boston: Houghton Mifflin.

———. (2000). "A Study of the Effectiveness of An Intervention Program Designed to Accelerate Reading for Struggling Readers in the Upper Grades." In T. Shanahan & F. V. Rodriguez-Brown (Eds.), *National Reading Conference Yearbook 49* (pp. 477–486). Chicago: National Reading Conference.

Cooper, J. D., Chard, D. J., & Kiger, N. D. (2006). *The Struggling Reader: Interventions that Work.* New York: Scholastic.

Cooper, J. D. & Kiger, N. D. (2009). *Literacy: Helping Students Construct Meaning, Seventh Edition.* Boston: Houghton Mifflin.

Cooper, J. D., Warncke, E., Shipman, D., & Ramstad, P. A. (1979). *The What and How of Reading Instruction.* Columbus, OH: Merrill.

Cummins, J. (1996). *Negotiating Identities: Education for Empowerment in a Diverse Society.* Ontario, CA: California Association of Bilingual Education.

Cunningham, P. M., & Allington, R. (2006). *Classrooms that Work: They Can All Read and Write, Fourth Edition.* New York: HarperCollins.

Cunningham, P. M. & Hall, D. P. (2001) *Making More Big Words.* Torrance, CA Frank Schaffer.

Dale, D. C. (2002). *Bilingual Children's Books in English and Spanish.* Jefferson, NC: McFarland.

Delpit, L. D. (1986). "Skills and Other Dilemmas of a Progressive Black Educator." *Harvard Educational Review, 56*(4), 379–385.

Dolch, E. W. (1942). *Basic Sight Word Test.* Champaign, IL: Garrard.

Dorr, R. (2006). "Something Old is New Again: Revisiting Language Experience." *The Reading Teacher, 60,* 138–146.

Durkin, D. (1966). *Children Who Read Early.* New York: Teachers College Press.

Ehri, L., et al. (2001). "Systematic Phonics Instruction Helps Students Learn to Read: Evidence from the National Reading Panel's Meta-analysis." *Review of Educational Research, 71*(3), 393–447.

Ehri, L. S., & Sweet, J. (1991). "Fingerpoint-reading of Memorized Text: What Enables Beginners to Process the Print." *Reading Research Quarterly, 24,* 442–462.

Flood, J., Jensen, J. M., Lapp, D., & Squire, J. R. (Eds.). (1991). *Handbook of Research on Teaching the English Language Arts.* New York: Macmillan.

Fountas, I. C., & Pinnell, G. S. (1996). *Guided Reading: Good First Teaching for All Children.* Portsmouth, NH: Heinemann.

Fountas, I. C. & Pinnell, G. S. (2001) *Guiding Readers and Writers: Grades 3–6.* Portsmouith, NH: Heinemann.

Fuchs, D., Fuchs, L. S., & Vaughn, S., Editors, (2008). *Response to Intervention: A Framework for Reading Educators.* Newark, DE: International Reading Association.

Freeman, D., & Freeman, Y. (2001). "The California Reading Initiative: A Formula for Failure for Bilingual Students?" *Language Arts, 76*(3), 241–248.

Freppon, P., & Dahl, K. L. (1998). "Theory and Research into Practice: Balanced Instruction: Insights and Considerations." *Reading Research Quarterly, 33*(2), 240–251.

Fry, E. B. (1968). "A Readability Formula that Saves Time." *Journal of Reading, 11,* 513–516.

———. (1980). "The New Instant Word List." *The Reading Teacher, 34,* 284–289.

Fry, E. B., Kress, J. E., Fountoukidis, D. L., & Polk, J. K. (1993). *The Reading Teacher's Book of Lists* (3rd ed.). Englewood Cliffs, NJ: Prentice-Hall.

Garcia, G. E. (1994). "Assessing the Literacy Development of Second-language Students: A Focus on Authentic Assessment." In K. Spangenberg-Urbschat & R. Pritchard (Eds.), *Kids Come in all Languages: Reading Instruction for SL students* (pp. 180–205). Newark, DE: International Reading Association.

Gentry, J. R. (1987). Spel . . . Is a Four Letter Word. Portsmouth, NH: Heinemann.

Gentry, J. R., & Gillett, J. W. (1992). *Teaching Kids to Spell.* Portsmouth, NH: Heinemann.

Gibbons, P. E. (1993). *Learning to Learn in a Second Language.* Portsmouth, NH: Heinemann.

Glazer, S. M. (1998). *Assessment is Instruction: Reading, Writing, Spelling, and Phonics for All Learners.* Norwood, MA: Christopher-Gordon.

Good. R. H., & Kaminski, R. A. (2002). *Dynamic Indicators of Basic Early Literacy Skills, Sixth Edition.* Eugene, OR: Institute for the Development of Educational Achievement.

Goodman, Y. D., Watson, D. J., & Burke, C. L. (2005). *Reading Miscue Inventory, Second Edition.* Katonah, NY: Richard C. Owen.

Goodman, Y. M., Watson, D. J., & Burke, C. (1987). *Reading Miscue Inventory: Alternative Procedures.* Katonah, NY: Richard C. Owen.

Hall, D. P., Prevatte, C., & Cunningham, P. M. (1992). *Eliminating Ability Grouping and Failure in the Primary Grades.* Paper presented at the National Reading Conference, San Antonio, TX.

Halliday, M. (1975). *Learning How to Hear.* London: Edward Arnold.

Hancock, J. (Ed.). (1999). *The Explicit Teaching of Reading.* Newark, DE: International Reading Association.

Harris, A. J., & Jacobson, M. D. (1982). *Basic Reading Vocabularies.* New York: Macmillan.

Harris, T. L., & Hodges, R. E. (Eds.). (1995). *The Literacy Dictionary.* Newark, DE: International Reading Association.

Hasbrouck, J. E., & Tindal, G. (1992). "Curriculum-based Oral Reading Fluency Norms for Students in Grades 2 through 5." *Teaching Exceptional Children* (Spring), 41–44.

Hasbrouck, J., & Tindal, G. A. (2006). "Oral Reading Fluency Norms: A Valuable Assessment Tool for Reading Teachers." *The Reading Teacher, 7,* 636–644.

Henderson, E. (1990). *Teaching Spelling, Second Edition.* Boston: Houghton Mifflin.

Hiebert, E. H., Colt, J. M., Catto, S. L., & Gury, E. C. (1992). "Reading and Writing of First Grade Students in a Restructured Chapter 1 Program." *American Educational Research Journal, 29*(3), 545–572.

Hiebert, E. H., Pearson, P. D., Taylor, B. M., Richardson, V., & Paris, S. G. (1998). *Every Child a Reader.* Ann Arbor, MI: Center for the Improvement of Early Reading Achievement.

Hillerich, R. L. (1977). "Let's Teach Spelling— Not Phonetic Misspelling." *Language Arts, 54,* 301–307.

Holdaway, D. (1979). *The Foundations of Literacy.* Sydney: Ashton Scholastic, distributed by Heinemann, Portsmouth, NH. http://www.rtinetwork.org/Learn/What/ar/WhatIsRTI

International Reading Association, (2009). "IRA Commission on RTI: Working Draft of Guiding Principles, *Reading Today,* 26, No. 4, 1, 4–6.

International Reading Association (December 2008/January, 2009). *Reading Today,* Vol, 26, No. 3, p. 8.

International Reading Association. (2004). *Standards for Reading Professionals—Revised 2003.* Newark, DE: International Reading Association.

International Reading Association/National Council of Teachers of English. (1984). *Joint Statement of Readability.* Newark, DE/Urbana, IL: International Reading Association.

Jimerson, S. R., & Kaufman, A. M. (2003). "Reading, Writing, and Retention: A Primer on Grade Retention Research." *The Reading Teacher, 56*(7), 622–635.

Johns, J. L. (2005). *Basic Reading Inventory,* Ninth Edition. Dubuque, IA: Kendall/Hunt.

Johnson, D. D. (1971). "The Dolch List Reexamined." *The Reading Teacher, 24,* 455–456.

Jones, C. (1997, September 24). "Educators Challenged by Diversity's Demands." *USA Today,* pp. 1–2.

Juel, C. (1988). "Learning to Read and Write: Longitudinal Study of 54 Children from First through Fourth Grades." *Journal of Educational Psychology, 80,* 437–447.

Klare, G. R. (1988). "The Formative Years." In B. L. Zakaluk & S. J. Samuels (Eds.), *Readability: Its Past, Present, and Future* (pp. 14–34). Newark, DE: International Reading Association.

———. (1995). "Readability." In T. L. Harris & R. E. Hodges (Eds.), *The Literacy Dictionary* (p. 204). Newark, DE: International Reading Association.

Krashen, S. (1982). *Principles and Practice in Second Language Acquisition.* New York: Pergamon Press.

———. (1993). *The Power of Reading.* Englewood, CO: Libraries Unlimited.

Krashen, S., & Terrell, T. (1983). *The Natural Approach: Language Acquisition in the Classroom.* Hayward, CA: Alemany Press.

Lerner, J., & Kline, F. (2006). *Learning Disabilities and Related Disorders: Characteristics and Teaching Strategies, Tenth Edition.* Boston: Houghton Mifflin.

Learning First Alliance. (1998, June). *Every Child Reading: An Action Plan of the Learning First Alliance.* Washington, D.C.: Author.

Martinez-Roldan, C. M., & Lopez-Robertson, J. M. (1999/2000). "Initiating Literature Circles in a First-grade Bilingual Classroom." *The Reading Teacher, 53*(4), 270–281.

McKenna, M. C., & Walpole, S. (2005). "How Well Does Assessment Inform our Reading Instruction?" *The Reading Teacher, 59*(1), 84–86.

McLaughlin, M., & Allen, M. B. (2002). *Guided Comprehension: A Teaching Model for Grades 3–8.* Newark, DE: International Reading Association.

McTighe, J., & O'Connor, K. (2005). "Seven Practices for Effective Learning." *Educational Leadership, 63*(3), 10–17.

Menyuk, P. (1988). *Language Development: Knowledge and Use.* Boston: Scott, Foresman.

Mesmer, E. M. & Mesmer, H. A. E. (2008). "Response to Intervention (RTI): What Teachers of Reading Need to Know." *The Reading Teacher, 62*(4), pp. 280–290.

Morrow, L. M. (1989). "Using Story Retelling to Develop Comprehension." In K. D. Muth (Ed.), *Children's Comprehension of Text: Research into Practice* (pp. 37–58). Newark, DE: International Reading Association.

Mulligan, J. (1974). "Using Language Experience with Potential High School Dropouts." *Journal of Reading, 18,* 206–211.

Mullis, I. V. S., Campbell, J. R., & Farstrup, A. (1993, September). *NAEP, 1992: Reading Report Card for the Nation and States.* Washington, D.C.: U.S. Department of Education.

Murphy, M. (2000). Stopping short of effective staff development. *Results.* www.nsdc.org/library/results/11–00murp.html

NAEP. (1995). *NAEP 1994 reading: A First Look—Findings from the National Assessment of Educational Progress* (Rev. ed.). Washington, D.C.: U.S. Government Printing Office.

National Center for Technology Innovation, (2008). Reading First Impact Study Released by IES, Washington, D.C.: National Center for Technology Innovation.

National PTA. (1998). *National Standards for Parent/family Involvement Programs.* Chicago: Author.

National Reading Panel. (2000). *Report of the National Reading Panel—Teaching Children to Read: An Evidence-based Assessment of the Scientific Research Literature on Reading and its Implications for Reading Instruction.* Washington, D.C.: National Institute of Child Health and Human Development.

Oczkus, L. D. (2003). *Reciprocal Teaching at Work.* Newark, DE: International Reading Association.

Ogle, D. M. (1989). "The Know, Want to Know, Learn Strategy." In K. D. Muth (Ed.), *Children's Comprehension of Text* (pp. 215–223). Newark, DE: International Reading Association.

Opitz, M. F. & Harding-DeKam, J. L. (2007, March). "Understanding and Teaching English-Language Learners," *The Reading Teacher*, 60(6), 590–593.

Palincsar, A. S., & Brown, A. L. (1984). "Reciprocal Teaching of Comprehension-fostering and Comprehension-monitoring Activities." *Cognition and Instruction, 1*(2), 117–175.

———. (1986). "Interactive Teaching to Promote Independent Learning from Text." *The Reading Teacher, 39*(8), 771–777.

Pearson, P. D. (1985). "Changing the Face of Reading Comprehension Instruction." *The Reading Teacher, 38*, 724–738.

Pehrsson, R. S., & Robinson, H. A. (1985). *The Semantic Organizer Approach to Writing and Reading Instruction.* Rockville, MD: Aspen Systems.

Peterson, B. (1991). "Selecting Books for Beginning Readers." In D. E. DeFord, C. A. Lyons, & G. S. Pinnell (Eds.), *Bridges to Literacy* (pp. 119–147). Portsmouth, NH: Heinemann.

Pikulski, J. J., & Chard, D. J. (2003). *Fluency: The Bridge from Decoding to Reading Comprehension.* Boston: Houghton Mifflin.

Pikulski, J. J. (1994). "Preventing Reading Failure: A Review of Five Effective Programs." *The Reading Teacher, 48*(1), 30–39.

Pinnell, G. S., Fried, M. D., & Estice, R. M. (1990). "Reading Recovery: Learning How to Make a Difference." *The Reading Teacher, 43*, 282–295.

Pinnell, G. S. & Fountas, I. C.(2007). *The Continuum of Literacy Learning Grades K–8: Behaviors and Understandings to Notice, Teach, and Support.* Portsmouth, NH: Heinemann.

Pressley, M. (1998). *Reading Instruction that Works: The Case for Balanced Teaching.* New York: The Guilford Press.

Reading Today, (2009). "IRA Commission on RTI: Working Draft of Guiding Principles," *Reading Today*, 26, No. 4, 1, 4 -6.

Resnick, L. B. & Snow, C. E. (2009). *Speaking and Listening for Preschool Through Third Grade, Revised Edition.* Newark, DE: International Reading Association.

Rhodes, L. K. (Ed.). (1993). *Literacy Assessment: A Handbook of Instruments.* Portsmouth, NH: Heinemann

Rhodes, L. K., & Shanklin, N. (1990). "Miscue Analysis in the Classroom." *The Reading Teacher, 44*, 252–254.

Roe, B. D., & Burns, P. C. (2007). *Informal Reading Inventory: Preprimer to Twelfth Grade.* (Seventh Edition, Revised by B. D. Roe). Boston: Houghton Mifflin.

Rosenshine, B. V., & Meister, C. (1994). "Reciprocal Teaching: A Review of Research." *Review of Educational Research, 64*(4), 479–530.

Rubin, R., & Carlan, V. G. (2005). "Using Writing to Understand Bilingual Children's Literacy Development." *The Reading Teacher, 58*(8), 728–739.

Rupley, W. H., Wilson, V. L., & Nichols, W. D. (1998). "Exploration of the Developmental Components Contributing to Elementary School Children's Reading Comprehension." *Scientific Studies in Reading, 2*(2), 143–158.

Salvia, J., & Ysseldyke, J. (2007). *Assessment, Tenth Edition.* Boston: Houghton Mifflin.

Sharp, S. J. (1990). "Using Content Subject Matter with LEA in Middle School." *Journal of Reading, 33*, 108–112.

Slavin, R. E., Madden, N. A., Dolan, L. J., Wasik, B. A., Ross, S., Smith, L., & Dianda, M. (1996). "Success for All: A Summary of Research." *Journal of Education for Students Placed at Risk, 1*(1), 41–76.

Snow, C. E., Burns, M. S., & Griffin, P. (Eds.). (1998). *Preventing Reading Difficulties in Young Children.* Washington, D.C.: National Academy Press.

Spache, G. (1953). "A new Readability Formula for Primary-grade Reading Materials." *Elementary School Journal, 53*, 410–413.

Stauffer, R. G. (1969). *Teaching Reading as a Thinking Process.* New York: Harper & Row.

Swanson, H. L., with Hoskyn, M., & Lee, C. (1999). *Interventions for Students with Learning Disabilities: A Meta-analysis of Treatment Outcomes.* New York: The Guilford Press.

Taylor, B. M. (2008) "Tier I: Effective Classroom Reading Instruction in the Elementary Grades" in *Response to Intervention: A Framework for Reading Educators*, Fuchs, D. , Fuchs, L. S., & Vaughn, S., Eds. Newark, DE: International Reading Association, pages 5–25.

Taylor, B. M., Frye, B. J., Short, R., & Shearer, B. (1992). "Classroom Teachers Prevent Reading Failure Among Low-achieving First-grade Students." *The Reading Teacher, 45,* 592–597.

U. S Department of Education (2006). Individuals with Disabilities Act (IDEA), Public Law 108–446.

Vygotsky, L. S. (1978). *Mind in Society.* Cambridge, MA: Harvard University Press.

Young, T. A., & Hadaway, N. L. (2006). *Supporting the Literacy Development of English Learners.* Newark, DE: International Reading Association.

Yopp, H. K. (1995). "A Test for Assessing Phonemic Awareness in Young Children." *The Reading Teacher, 49,* 20–22.

Note: Numbers followed by an n denote a note reference.

Note: numbers in *Italic* indicate tables, figures, or notes.